Bruce Grit

Bruce Grit

The Black Nationalist Writings of John Edward Bruce

William Seraile

THE UNIVERSITY OF TENNESSEE PRESS
Knoxville

Copyright © 2003 by THE UNIVERSITY OF TENNESSEE PRESS / Knoxville.
All Rights Reserved.
Cloth: 1st printing, 2003.
Paper: 1st printing, 2011.

LIBRARY OF CONGRESS CATALOGING-IN-PUBLICATION DATA
Seraile, William, 1941–
Bruce Grit: the Black nationalist writings of John Edward Bruce /
William Seraile.— 1st ed.
    p. cm.
Includes bibliographical references (p.) and index.
ISBN 10: 1-57233-897-0
ISBN 13: 978-1-57233-897-5

1. Bruce, John Edward—Political and social views.
2. Bruce, John Edward—Archives.
3. African American intellectuals—Biography.
4. African American intellectuals—Archives.
5. Black nationalism—History.
6. Black nationalism—History—Sources.
7. African Americans—History.
8. African Americans—History—Sources.
9. Pan-Africanism—History.
10. Pan-Africanism—History—Sources.
 I. Title.

E185.97.B895 A6 2003
973'.0496073—dc21   2002011045

Contents

Preface vii

Acknowledgments xiii

1. Youth and Early Writings, 1856–1883 1

2. National Politics, 1884–1900 20

3. National Politics, 1900–1923 64

4. From Civil Rights to Pan-Africanism, 1890–1920 100

5. Bruce's Racial Ideology, 1883–1919 122

6. African Emigration and Economic Investment, 1889–1919 152

7. The Garvey Movement, 1918–1922 163

8. The Final Years, 1922–1924 182

Epilogue 201

Notes 205

Bibliography 241

Index 249

Illustrations

Following Page 99

John Edward Bruce, circa 1922

Marcus Garvey, Christmas 1919

Alex Crummell, circa 1890s

Marcus Garvey handcuffed to U.S. marshal, 1925

Mourners at John Edward Bruce's grave, 1924

Arthur Alphonso Schomburg, 1900s

Preface

I first came across the John Edward Bruce Collection more than thirty years ago while doing general research in the Schomburg Center for Research in Black Culture in the New York Public Library. Compiled in 1942, the Bruce Collection was then the largest manuscript holding in the center. Bruce was a prolific writer who corresponded with the nation's leading elected officials ranging from local politicians to presidents of the United States. His friendships extended around the world as he corresponded for years with individuals in Africa, Europe, and the Caribbean (some of whom he never met in person).

Bruce (1856–1924) witnessed the dying days of American slavery, the turbulent days of Reconstruction, the rise of Jim Crowism, lynching, the development of American imperialism in the Caribbean and Asia, and the spread of racism to the North as southern blacks moved to urban areas to escape the rising tide of prejudice. Bruce shared his birth year with Booker T. Washington, a man he once admired and defended with his writings. But like others, Bruce soon became alienated by Washington's accommodationist ideology and joined the anti-Tuskegee forces. Bruce's final years were spent in defense of Marcus Garvey and the Universal Negro Improvement Association, which he joined in 1919. These and other events were chronicled by him in correspondence, letters to the editor, newspaper and magazine contributions, pamphlets, and books. Bruce wrote for at least one hundred newspapers in the United States and elsewhere under various noms de plume, including "Rising Sun," "Obscurity," and "Caleb Quotem," but he was best known as "Bruce Grit."

Bruce was also a publisher and an editor. He founded the *Weekly Argus* in Washington, D.C., in 1879, followed by the *Sunday Item* the following year in the same city, and in 1884 he founded *Washington Grit*. He edited the *Republican* in Norfolk, Virginia, in 1882; became an assistant editor of the *Commonwealth* in Baltimore in 1884; and was an associate editor of *Howard's American Magazine* from 1896 to 1901. In 1908 he founded the *Weekly Standard* in Yonkers, New York. Despite his prolific writing, it is impossible to document all of his thoughts on the leading personalities and issues of his day. Unfortunately, Bruce wrote for many publications whose records were long ago discarded.[1]

There are no full-length biographies of John Edward Bruce because little is known about his private life except for a few intimate letters to his wife, Florence, and to his mentors Edward W. Blyden, James S. Clarkson, Alexander Crummell, and Arthur A. Schomburg. Most of his innermost thoughts were never recorded or have been destroyed. Bruce's diaries are not extant except for a few jottings in the early 1900s when he resided in Yonkers. Peter H. Gilbert wrote an undergraduate honors paper on Bruce, and his publication of *The Selected Writings of John Edward Bruce* in 1971 helped present Bruce to a wider audience. Ralph L. Crowder has written articles on Bruce during the past twenty years.[2]

Much of the Bruce Collection (outside of correspondence) consists of drafts of speeches or articles. Often without dates or titles, his writings represent a gold mine of information for researchers of African American history and politics. Bruce's extant newspaper writings, which appeared in the *Gazette* (Cleveland), the *Colored American* (Washington, D.C.,) the *Negro World* (New York), and other newspapers, are available on microfilm. His correspondence is scattered throughout the papers of Booker T. Washington, John P. Green, George A. Myers, Arthur A. Schomburg, and Marcus Garvey. Bruce was well aware that writers possessed journalistic power to encourage people to seek change, but he also understood that newspaper publishers and writers needed to recognize the "spirit and temper of [their] patrons," while the reading public had to recognize the "potency and utility" of the black press. Readers soon learned to appreciate the potency of Bruce's writings, which was characterized by one admirer as "aggressive, facile, tenacious, racy and tireless." In February 1891, Charles A. Johnson of the *Chicago Appeal* described Bruce as "truthful, concise, and [one who] wields a trenchant pen. He seeks not to degrade or abuse, but unerringly strikes to the point, let it hurt whom it may." In September 1891, "Carph," the nom de plume of Ralph W. Tyler, wrote that "there is a force about Bruce's writings that sets one to thinking after reading them. There is a rapid flow of thought that connects his sentences without any perceptible break, this makes his articles attractive and interesting." Tyler insisted that Bruce was a newspaperman, not a journalist who was limited because he wrote editorials or dissected the news and opinions of others. In addition to these duties, Tyler added that a newspaperman also had to "get out and hustle for life news and shape it up to please the reader. A journalist prescribes; a newspaper man prescribes and administers." Others agreed that Bruce was one of the race's greatest writers whose articles contributed to the commercial success of many race organs.[3]

A black nationalist and later a Pan-Africanist, Bruce had a close relationship with Edward Wilmot Blyden, a native of the Danish West Indies who immigrated to Liberia; Alexander Crummell, an Episcopal priest who lived in Liberia for nearly twenty years before returning to the United States; and J. Robert Love, a journalist who resided in Jamaica. Bruce began corresponding with people of African descent in 1880 and counted among his correspondents men throughout Africa, Cuba, Central and South America, the Philippines, and the British West Indies. Along with his intimate friend Arthur Schomburg, Bruce possessed a great love for his race that was reflected in his writings. It was his interest in the history of people throughout the African diaspora that made him a champion for his people. He proudly wore the badge "race man," and in his longstanding effort to fight the battles of his race Bruce had iron in his soul. Bruce's black nationalistic fervor encompassed some of the representative types suggested by John Bracey, August Meier, and Elliot Rudwick in their seminal study, *Black Nationalism in America*.[4] A Methodist by choice, Bruce did not embrace religious nationalism, neither calling for an adoption of traditional West African religious values nor endorsing Bishop Henry M. Turner's controversial stance that "God is a Negro." There is no evidence that Bruce advocated territorial nationalism such as the movement to make parts of Oklahoma (Indian) Territory a black sanctuary. In politics, Bruce was a staunch Republican, although a critic of that party's failure to adequately protect southern black voters from mobocracy after the end of Reconstruction. Nevertheless, he saw nothing positive in the Democratic party. He did not associate himself with any of the short-lived movements to create black political parties. Bruce flirted with revolutionary nationalism when he organized the secret Loyal Order of the Sons of Africa to unite in one brotherhood the black and other colored races of the world. Revolutionary nationalism suggests violence as a means to an end. Nevertheless, Bruce primarily stressed that the battle between the races would be settled by a combination of intelligence and providential intervention. For example, in 1898 Bruce soberly warned an audience in Troy, New York, that southern terrorism needed to be met with brains because Negroes were not prepared to use the torch or dynamite in retaliation. There were, however, times when Bruce advocated retaliatory violence, which made him appear erratic; but overall he eschewed violence. Instead, he noted that God would have revenge because he made the African not to seek retaliation. Like the ancient Jew, the Negro declared Bruce was the sacrificial lamb, but his triumph over the southern beast would come when God saw fit.[5]

He stressed in his speeches and writings the necessity of black economic development. Long before he joined the Garvey movement, Bruce was involved in efforts to invest in Africa's resources. Bruce enthusiastically embraced the nineteenth-century version of cultural nationalism with its emphasis on exposing to the world the contributions of Africa to world history and civilization. He, along with Arthur Schomburg and Carter G. Woodson, were pioneer advocates of the prominence of African contributions to world history.

Bruce and Schomburg collaborated in 1911 as founders of the Negro Society for Historical Research to disseminate the history of the African race. Their ambitious endeavor to present papers and pamphlets was undermined in 1915 when Carter G. Woodson organized the Association for the Study of Negro Life and History and began in the following year publication of the scholarly *Journal of Negro History*. Bruce's intense pride in Africa's contribution to world history was revealed in the 1921 discovery of King Tutankhamen's Tomb in Egypt. This rare archaeological excavation elicited from Bruce the prediction that the world would be forced to reevaluate its assessment of Negro intelligence. Like other black cultural nationalists, Bruce proclaimed that Ethiopia taught Egypt, which disseminated knowledge to the proud Anglo Saxons by way of Greece and Rome.[6] Like his good friend Schomburg, Bruce was a bibliophile, a collector of photographs and artifacts that documented the African experience throughout the Americas. Bruce was a pioneer in urging public institutions to teach the history of African people. The existence today of Black Studies departments in colleges, universities, and other forums is in large measure a tribute to John Edward Bruce and others who labored a century ago to show the world that African people had a history that should be treasured. He would be extremely proud to know that not only in the United States but also in Europe and elsewhere universities are awarding earned doctorates in Africana Studies.

Bruce's pride in Africa's ancient glorious past was matched by his pride in the achievements of the American Negro. Influenced by Edward W. Blyden and Alexander Crummell, Bruce strongly condemned the nomenclature *colored* and *Afro-American*. The former was adopted in the 1830s by many biracial individuals who opposed the back-to-Africa proposal of the American Colonization Society. They believed that the labor of their slave ancestors entitled them to American citizenship rights, which made them "colored Americans," not Africans in exile. The term *Afro-American* was popularized in the 1890s by *New York Age* editor Timothy Thomas Fortune, but Crummell and Bruce derided it as a "milk bastard" term preferred by those of mixed-race stock who were ashamed of the African's dark complexion, broad nose, kinky hair, and full lips. To Bruce, *Negro* represented the race that built the pyramids. They were God's chosen people, he asserted. He believed the name would "stick . . . as long as God rules the universe."[7]

It was this shift in ideology that led Bruce to affiliate with the Garvey movement in 1919 despite his earlier aversion to the Jamaican's agenda. During the last few years of his life, Bruce agreed with his mentor Edward W. Blyden that the American Negro's destiny was in Africa, not America, an admission that contrasted with his earlier efforts to prove that black Americans were entitled to all the rights of American citizenship.

Bruce was essentially a private person who kept his family affairs out of public light. Little exists in his papers about his relationship with Lucy Pinkwood, who was reported in secondary accounts to have married him in the early 1880s. The Washington directory lists them as living together for only one year (1884). No marriage certificate has been located, but a child, Olive Bruce, may have been born of their relationship. While a birth certificate dated July 22, 1888, indicates that a Lucy Bruce gave birth to a female colored child, neither the baby's or the father's name is provided. Olive's 1943 death certificate, however, noted that her mother was Alice Ayers and her father was Bruce. This information was provided by Olive's daughter, Agnes Conway, now deceased. Onaway (Onnie) Millar, Bruce's granddaughter, informed me that she and her two siblings learned years after their mother's death that Lucy Pinkwood Bruce was their grandmother. She understood that Olive was raised by an abusive godmother who tended to her after a financially strapped Bruce was unable to properly care for her. Perhaps this godmother was Alice Ayers, whom the grandchildren assumed was their natural grandmother. Onnie Millar also noted that Olive, who was about seven years Florence Bruce's junior, did not get along with her stepmother and probably saw little of her father while growing up. There is no correspondence in Bruce's papers, with one exception, that even mentions he had a daughter. No correspondence between father and daughter exists (or survived) in his papers.[8]

Bruce had a reputation as a lady-killer. His cavalier approach to marriage was noted by a close friend, Thomas L. Jones, who cautioned him by letter in April 1895: "I suggest you be temperate for I know you. [Be] moral because it is the bed rock which underlies all human success; you must be truthful; quit having females rely on your promises of marriage and then desert them." If Bruce was a profligate, as suggested by Jones, he was being hypocritical. A decade earlier, he lambasted those who boasted of affairs with married women as "a disgrace to our civilization." He even urged war against them, regardless of whether they were gentlemen, clergy, deacons, or others. In mid-January 1894, Alexander Crummell wrote to Bruce to express his pleasure in being a married Episcopal priest because he believed leaders are ineffective if not touched by the "gracious influence of women." Bruce replied on January 17, 1894, that he agreed that marriage brought blessings. He promised to marry as soon as he found a woman to honor and respect. As noted by Bruce in his papers, "A worthy woman who can find? For her price is far above rubies. The heart of her husband trusteth in her, and he shall have no lack of gain. She doeth him good, and not evil, all the days of her life" (Prov. 31:10–13). Secondary accounts indicate that he married Florence Bishop, who was about nineteen (he was thirty-nine) on September 10, 1895. There are no surviving letters in Bruce's papers describing how or where they met. Florence's 1942 death certificate indicated that she had lived in New York State since 1894. The couple probably met in New York City or in Albany, where Bruce then resided (no marriage certificate could be located for either city for that date). Alexander Crummell was delighted with Bruce's marriage, even predicting that Florence would "make [him] a happy home and a more efficient public man." Bruce took joy in his marriage because he considered "a good wife . . . a thing of beauty . . . and [an] influence in the home and in the making of a husband." Like others of his generation and class who believed that a women's role was that of a homemaker, Bruce believed that a "good wife" would see that her husband had cleaned clothes, ironed ties, and polished shoes. On a loftier level, he noted that Negro wives and mothers were "the architects and builders of a race." Bruce's friend Timothy Thomas Fortune understood the importance of a supportive wife. His wife, Carrie, was not involved in his journalistic or political work. Fortune wintered alone in Florida during the 1890s and wrote to Bruce in 1897: "you are fortunate in having a wife whose judgment is sound and in whom you have absolute confidence."[9]

John Edward Bruce was pivotal in shaping the mood of black America in the late nineteenth and early twentieth centuries. Contemporaries considered Bruce militant and even radical, but at times he chose for pragmatic reasons to present conservative views alien to his reputation. While this can be attributed to his financial concerns, he, not unlike many contemporary race leaders, including W. E. B. Du Bois, did not blindly adhere to a single ideological position but rather experimented with different solutions and strategies to confront American racism. His voice challenged the bigotry that others tolerated; his pen chided not only racists and racism but also his own people who lacked racial pride by denigrating themselves with the use of skin bleachers and hair straighteners. It is hoped that this study of Bruce will provide greater exposure of his life experience, which it richly deserves.

Acknowledgments

Twenty years ago, I met Agnes Conway, a granddaughter of John Edward Bruce. She was very pleased to learn that I had come across his papers in the Schomburg Center for Research in Black Culture. As the years passed by, I consulted the Bruce papers when writing articles and books, but then I decided in 1996 to examine them carefully in order to write his biography. It was then that I learned from Joan Maynard, executive director of the Society for the Preservation of Weeksville and Bedford Stuyvesant History in Brooklyn, that Mrs. Conway had died a few years earlier. Joan then inquired if I knew Onnie, Agnes's sister. Onaway (Onnie) Millar lives in Brooklyn, a subway ride from my Harlem home. For the past several years, Onnie has shared with me her intense pride in John Edward Bruce's accomplishments. She found it remarkable that he achieved so much with only a rudimentary education. She and I both regret that her sister is not alive to see the fruits of my research and writing.

All researchers rely upon the assistance of librarians and archivists. I would like to offer my profound thanks to the staff of the Schomburg Center, where the majority of the research was conducted. The librarians at Columbia University's Butler Library were especially helpful in tracking obscure but essential papers. The staff of Yonkers Public Library in Westchester County, New York, assisted me in locating local newspapers. Robert Morris, director of the National Archives and Records Center in New York City, kindly assisted me in searching for slave census materials. I owe him a debt of gratitude.

All authors are indebted to their editors. Special gratitude is reserved for Joyce Harrison for her extreme patience and commitment to this project. The anonymous readers whose insights, criticisms, and suggestions made this book better also are highly appreciated.

I also acknowledge all of my friends who have supported me over the years with their enthusiasm for my research projects. My special thanks go to Dale Harger for retrieving copies of records from the National Archives in Washington. Again, a huge thank you to Sam Jones for his obliging patience to all my computer-related questions and for his help in eliminating computer bugs that made me frantic. Special thanks to Garnet, my daughter, who helped me improve upon my barely competent computer skills. Thanks to my wife, Janette, and our children, Aden and Garnet, for their love and support.

Finally, I wish to offer posthumous thanks to John Edward Bruce and Arthur A. Schomburg for their preservation of this remarkable collection of Bruce's correspondence, poetry, short stories, pamphlets, books, drafts of speeches, and writings. I could not have undertaken this project without the assistance of these great bibliophiles and pioneers in the preservation and dissemination of African American history. To these two giants and other pioneers in Pan-Africanism, I dedicate this book.

Youth and Early Writings, 1856-1883

The issue of human bondage plagued American politics from the inception of the United States. It dominated the 1850s, however, as a series of events that led to a dramatic rise in sectional tension. The Compromise of 1850, which led to California's admission into the Union, upset the balance between free and slave states and was followed by the 1852 publication of Harriet Beecher Stowe's *Uncle Tom's Cabin*. Both hardened passions over the slavery issue. Denying Stowe's contention that the institution was evil, supporters of "the peculiar institution" proclaimed that slavery was benign and necessary because blacks were a subhuman group that needed the tutelage of whites. The enactment of the Kansas-Nebraska Act of 1854 permitted citizens to decide if they wanted slavery in the territories. This controversial decision was a blow to the Missouri Compromise of 1820, which endeavored to keep slavery out of the territories north of the 36° 30' parallel forever. Northern reaction to the possibility of slavery extending into the territories led to the formation of the antislavery Republican Party in 1854. Tensions escalated when opposing forces fought in Kansas in 1856, an event that was a harbinger of the American Civil War five years later. The U.S. Supreme Court ruled in the Dred Scott case in 1857 that blacks were not citizens and that slaves could be taken into the territories, thus voiding the Missouri Compromise of 1820. Sectional animosity increased after Abraham Lincoln and Stephen Douglas debated the merits of slavery in the 1858 Illinois campaign for the U.S. Senate. John Brown's ill-fated assault on the federal arsenal at Harpers Ferry in 1859 led the nation to the brink of war. Southerners blamed Republican abolitionists for the attempt to arm Virginia slaves to perform what they feared would be an orgy of bloodletting. The election of Abraham Lincoln in 1860 led to seven of the fifteen slave states seceding to form the Confederate States of America. Four more of the slave states seceded after the attack on Fort Sumter.

Thousands of enslaved persons were born in the United States during the tumultuous decade before the election of Lincoln to the presidency. Under normal circumstances, they would have grown up in the anonymity shared by the four million in bondage. However, the events that rapidly accelerated the nation toward war also unleashed forces that would destroy slavery in America after more than two hundred years of holding Africans as chattel. It was an accident in historical timing, but John Edward Bruce, Timothy Thomas Fortune, and Booker T. Washington, all pivotal and influential figures in African American history, were born as slaves in 1856. Bruce and Fortune were allies throughout the late nineteenth century and joined forces to confront American racism and Republican Party indifference. They temporarily ended their relationship when they differed over Washington's leadership: Fortune defended the Tuskegee educator, whereas Bruce joined forces with individuals who were more progressive. Later, both men were affiliated with the Garvey movement. Of the three, only the astute Washington chronicled his slave experience in an autobiography, *Up from Slavery*.

Early Family History

Bruce, like Fortune and Washington, was briefly in bondage, but he wrote only a few short comments about his experiences in slavery. These were based more on family lore than on his own vivid personal recollections. Bruce was born on February 22, 1856, on a plantation in Piscataway, Maryland, to Robert and Martha Bruce (born Clark). They were owned by Maj. Thomas Harvey Griffin, who reportedly had served in the War of 1812, though no record of service has been located and perhaps the title "Major" was honorary. It is possible that the Bruces were previously the property of Thomas Bruce of Marlbrough District, Prince George's County, who owned eighteen slaves in 1850. Griffin, the owner of thirteen slaves in 1860, an increase of three from ten years previously, lived near Thomas Bruce and may have purchased one or both of young John's parents. Like countless other enslaved people, the Bruces felt the pain of separation when for unknown reasons Robert Bruce was sold in 1859. "I never knew a father's care nor do I ever remember seeing my father," Bruce wrote in 1875.[1]

John also noted the selling of other enslaved persons in an unpublished autobiographical sketch written in 1875. As he was only four years old when the transaction occurred, the "recollection" of the sales was probably told to him by his mother. In Bruce's account, a prayer meeting was interrupted by the plaintive wail of a woman who came from the field to discover that her husband had been sold to Georgia. When she heard the news, she replied, "nebber min [never mind] God's stronger den the debbil [devil] and his justice nebber fails." The prayer meeting closed with a song:

> Brethren our meetings over
> Brethren we must part
> If we never see your face again
> We'll love you in our hearts

Bruce wrote years later that this last meeting represented the forthcoming evil that could not be averted. Fifteen unfortunate souls were sold the next day. In 1919, Bruce wrote a fictional account of a slave trade based on his youthful observations.[2]

Civil War: Preserving the Union or Emancipation?

The selling of slaves, a horrific aspect of American slavery, would have probably continued for decades if circumstances had not rapidly changed after the election of Abraham Lincoln in November 1860. Although the Republican president-elect promised not to interfere with slavery in the existing states, slave owners feared that radical abolitionists would pressure the president and Congress to end the institution of human bondage. After the election, but before Lincoln's inauguration in March 1861, seven southern states seceded from the Union. The anxiety raised by the secession increased dramatically after South Carolina forces fired upon Fort Sumter in Charleston's harbor shortly after Lincoln's inauguration.

The swift call of the president for 75,000 volunteers to end the rebellion led to four other states joining the Confederate States of America. Americans would engage in a bloody war for four years that would nurture the soil with the bodies of 618,000 fallen men. Abolitionists and northern blacks welcomed the coming of war as a grand opportunity to destroy slavery. Lincoln, fearing the loss of the four border slave states if the conflict escalated into a war to end slavery, refused to sanction the abolitionists' cause. The president's conservatism perplexed the editor of the *Weekly Anglo-African,* a black New York newspaper, who inquired, "Have We a War Policy?" Former slave and abolitionist Frederick Douglass stirred readers of *Douglass' Monthly* with the message that the best way to end the war was to "LET THE SLAVES AND FREE COLORED PEOPLE BE CALLED INTO SERVICE AND FORMED INTO A LIBERATING ARMY." Douglass rightfully deemed it foolish for the Union to fight the Confederacy with one hand. He questioned, "why does the government reject the negro? Is he not a man? Can he not wield a sword, fire a gun, march and obey orders?" Fearful of losing Delaware, Maryland, Missouri, and Kentucky to the Confederacy and unsure that whites would fight a war to free the slaves,

Lincoln refused to accept black men into the army. Heavy battle losses, staunch Confederate resistance, army desertions, and fear of European intervention convinced Lincoln in 1862 that he had to make slavery an issue in the war if he wanted to preserve the Union. After the Union victory at Antietam in western Maryland in September 1862, Lincoln decided to issue the Emancipation Proclamation on January 1, 1863. As a military measure, the proclamation not only guaranteed the nation's commitment to end slavery in areas of rebellion but also sanctioned the enlistment of black men into the military.[3] Before the end of conflict in April 1865, approximately 180,000 black men would serve, with about 38,000 sacrificing their lives for the preservation of the Union and for the eradication of American slavery.

Meanwhile, the war caused uneasiness in the four border slave states. Fearing that the war would encourage slaves to run for freedom, some slaveholders tried to make the best of a grave situation. Thomas Harvey Griffin, who probably realized that his ownership was in jeopardy, gave Martha permission to hire herself out as a tavern cook, with the provision that she give half her earnings to him. Fearing a whipping from the intoxicated tavern owner, Martha left to work at Fort Washington, one mile from Piscataway, on the Merrimac River. An enterprising woman, Martha sold used clothing thrown away by Marines to build up a secondhand clothes business. This income, added to her earnings from selling pies and coffee to the enlisted men, enabled her to purchase a horse and wagon to transport her goods to the fort. The success of Martha so riled the white woman who rented her two rooms that she complained to Major Griffin that "the nigger was getting along much better than herself." Griffin suggested that she mind her own business. Still, the evil woman got partial satisfaction when she caught John and flogged him for finding a pair of Confederate epaulettes her husband had placed under the house. The war prodded many slave owners in Maryland to sell their slaves. Bruce recalled in 1875 that it sickened him during the war to see close to thirty of his childhood associates sold off without a mothers' "consolation or a parting kiss." Fearing their own sale, Martha took her children (John's brother died soon after) and marched alongside Union soldiers to Washington after the first battle of Bull Run in 1861. The runaways lived with Martha's cousin Busie Patterson while she was employed for three years as a maid in a ladies seminary. An act of Congress on April 16, 1862, emancipated slaves in the District of Columbia. Soon after, compensation was offered to loyal slaveholders in Maryland whose property was freed in the legislation. There is no evidence that Griffin petitioned for financial redress. Near the close of the war, Martha and John departed for Stratford, Connecticut, where Martha was a housekeeper while John attended an integrated school for two years. They returned to Washington in 1867 or the following year.[4]

Emancipation and Citizenship Rights

The freeing of slaves in Washington in 1862, and the subsequent emancipation of four million after the enactment of the Thirteenth Amendment in 1865, placed before the public the arduous task of integrating a large group into the mainstream of American society. Teaching illiterates to read and write became the objective of many organizations. The various Freedmen's Aid Societies, the Freedmen's Bureau, and the American Missionary Association labored to alleviate the educational, social, and economic problems of the newly emancipated slaves.

In the nation's capital, Bruce received private tutoring from a Miss Smith as well as instruction at the Free Library School. He also attended schools run by the Freedmen's Aid Society and later, the Freedmen's Bureau.[5] Neither the oppressive conditions of American slavery nor the bigotry of some whites discouraged the newly freed persons from seeking their salvation in the acquisition of knowledge. Frances Ellen Watkins noted in "Our Greatest Want," an 1859 essay, that blacks did not need money, intelligence, or talent but "soul, a higher cultivation of all our spiritual faculties." She added that people were needed to lift up slavery's "crushed humanity" into the arms of brotherhood.[6]

Many evangelical Protestants agreed with Watkins's goal of brotherhood. On February 7, 1862, the Educational Commission for Freedmen was organized. One year later it became the New England Freedmen's Aid Society, with its first school at Port Royal, South Carolina, in Union-occupied territory. Its objective was to uplift in all ways the newly emancipated slaves. The Rev. Dr. William Hague declared that the organization had the responsibility to teach the freedmen to work under contractual arrangements and to take care of all their own needs for survival. Going a step further was the Rev. Dr. E. N. Kirk, who wanted the most intelligent of the emancipated class to study the sciences and humanities. Both men understood that the Caucasian had to overlook his own "natural" superiority in assisting the former slaves or else blacks would revert to their former primitive passions and prey upon their own "life blood."[7]

This paternalism notwithstanding, the New England Freedmen's Aid Society records indicate that teachers in the District of Columbia worked under difficult conditions. Harriet Carter declared in October 1864 that she needed twenty to thirty slates for convalescents in the contraband hospital. Frances W. Perkins was pleased that students did not forget their lessons after a six-week summer recess. Emma V. Brown, a black woman who was Perkins's assistant, declared that the two had to leave Georgetown for Washington after secessionists broke up their school. She added that her shabby classroom lacked desks and did not have enough books. American Missionary Association teacher William J. Wilson wanted to make the Third Street school second to none but was in dire need of a stove, stationery, crayons, pens, slate pencils, and grammar, arithmetic and geography books.[8]

Working against the efforts of the teachers were those pessimists who believed that the former slaves faced insurmountable barriers and were perhaps better off as slaves. One observer compared the dwellings of former slaves as "not so good as good pigsties." Colorphobia made it difficult for the district's black population to receive educational funding from the government. In 1864, Congress enacted a law to set aside funding for the education of colored youth between the ages of six and seventeen. However, the city council abolished school funds and supported white children out of the general tax revenue. In April 1864, Washington blacks petitioned Congress as taxpayers, citing their willingness to field two regiments out of a population one-quarter the size of the district's white residents. Despite these obstacles, the district's black population made advances when the House of Representatives voted to strike out the word *white* from all laws qualifying male voters within the District of Columbia. The U.S. Senate passed a bill for impartial suffrage on December 12, 1866, followed by the House the next day.[9]

While some former slaves were adjusting to freedom, others had difficulty. Young John Bruce was just one of thousands who hustled to get an education and to get spare change to ward off the pain of hunger. Nevertheless, like Booker T. Washington, Bruce was determined to receive an education, formal or otherwise. Unfortunately for Bruce, the resulting chaos created by the aftermath of the war impeded his opportunities for regular instruction. He received only a rudimentary education in the school provided by the Freedmen's Aid Society. Consequently, he never had a lesson in penmanship and, despite his affiliation with newspapers as publisher, editor, and contributor, he never acquired completely the rules of punctuation. Bruce took a three-month course he never identified at Howard University in 1872. Bruce also received private instruction from Mrs. Belva A. Lockwood, who later became the first female attorney to practice before the U.S. Supreme Court. Lockwood was an advocate for women's rights and was the presidential candidate of the National Equal Rights party in 1884 and 1888.[10]

Social Contacts in Postwar Washington

Bruce grew up in a Washington that was undergoing rapid change, particularly during the war years when fortunes were easily gained and quickly lost. Recently emancipated slaves now flocked to the city, once a major slave market.

There, they lived in inadequate homes, ate coarse food, and suffered many deprivations. Some black residents, however, were not similarly deprived. Edward M. Thomas owned a private library of five to six thousand volumes, some dating from the seventeenth century. His luxurious home displayed paintings by John Chaplin and William H. Dorsey. Thomas's rare coin collection included one piece dating to 721 B.C. Approximately three thousand autographs of well-known historical figures were in Thomas's possession. Washington's black citizens were entertained and educated by stimulating debates sponsored by the Washington Lyceum under the presidency of the Rev. Benjamin T. Tanner, who would later become a prominent scholar and bishop in the African Methodist Episcopal Church.[11]

Little is known about Bruce's early youth except for tidbits of information that he divulged in later newspaper writings. Not averse to hard work, young Bruce was an enterprising youth who took many odd jobs to supplement his mother's income. Martha's employment in private homes and restaurants provided him with an opportunity to meet many famous individuals who made lasting impressions on him. It was Martha's domestic position that led Bruce to meet Charles Dickens, the great English novelist who was a guest of George Wood. Dickens was very fond of Martha's recipe for English plum pudding, and the sentient boy recalled in later years how the great writer was pleasant to all, including the dog. Bruce remembered Dickens as a raconteur and a practical joker.[12] The great black explorer and physician Martin R. Delany impressed Bruce when he was a roomer in Martha's Capitol Hill home. Bruce considered Delany "the blackest, jolliest and the most brilliant Negro I have ever seen or known."[13] Bruce recalled in 1923 that meeting Delany made the greatest impression on his young life next to the assassination of Abraham Lincoln.

Since presidential security was not as strict in the mid–nineteenth century as it is today, common citizens often saw the chief executive outside of the White House. In 1863 or 1864 Lincoln passed by young Bruce en route to the Soldiers Home, which was his summer residence. The incident evoked this reaction from the excited youth: "I thought he was about the ugliest white man I had ever seen, yet there was a kindly look on his face."[14] The next time Bruce gazed upon Lincoln's face was when the president was lying in state. Bruce claimed that he frequently saw John Wilkes Booth at Joseph Haires's café, where the young boy was employed. Booth allegedly had him deliver a sealed envelope to Mary E. Surratt at her home, 541 H Street, a safe house for Confederate spies, smugglers, and dispatch carriers. His 1922 recollection of his encounter with Booth may have simply been fabricated, or perhaps he managed to place himself into a historical situation that he had only read about. There is no evidence in the transcript of the trial of either Booth or Surratt to corroborate Bruce's account. Bruce noted that he worked the evening of the assassination in a restaurant attached to Ford's Theater. Although they were unable to leave the area due to the excitement and chaos caused by the shooting of Lincoln, Bruce claimed that he and his mother were among those permitted to view the president's body in the house opposite the theater. It is more likely that Bruce viewed the funeral cortege or saw Lincoln's body in the Capitol rotunda because the room where the dying president was taken to was too small to accommodate the grief-stricken cabinet.[15]

For a young boy, Bruce had the good fortune to come in contact with many of Washington's elite, both black and white. These contacts were made because he hustled to support the family income; his willingness to work hard at diverse chores brought him into contact with many of the city's leading figures. It was through his cousin Busie Patterson that he met Rev. Henry Highland Garnet, former slave, abolitionist, and pastor of Washington's Fifteenth Street Presbyterian Church. It was probably through Patterson, the body servant of Sen. Thomas H. Benton, that Bruce acquired the position of doorkeeper at the Mexican legation, where he had glimpses of diplomats and ambassadors. It was about 1868 when Bruce became a general utility man for Gen. F. L. Dent, Ulysses S. Grant's father-in-law. During this period, he also sold the *Daily Morning Chronicle*.[16]

While Bruce was recognized in later life for his condemnations of racists, apologists for racism, and hypocrites, this trait had appeared earlier. He joined the YMCA in 1869, but the disillusioned thirteen-year-old left two weeks after receiving his membership card. His associates decried racism but lacked the backbone to attack the practice openly. Fifty-three years later, an irate Bruce angrily recalled the hypocrisy of the cowards who sang hymns and who only privately condemned wrong.[17]

Reconstruction

Bruce was too young at the beginning of Reconstruction to take note of its impact on American politics and race relations. However, before it ended in 1877, he was fully aware of its implications for the future of African Americans. The end of the Civil War in 1865 led to the Reconstruction of the defeated Confederate States of America, first under the control of President Andrew Johnson, until Radical Republicans ushered in congressional Reconstruction in 1867. The Radical Republicans (led by Sen. Charles Sumner of Massachusetts; Thaddeus Stevens, a representative from Pennsylvania; and others) were determined to punish the leaders of the Confederacy for causing the war. The Radicals decided that President Johnson was interfering with their plans for Reconstruction and impeached him but failed by one vote to remove him from office. The Radical Republicans were intent on achieving equality between the races, but not all Republicans supported this lofty aim. As noted by historian James McPherson, conservatives in the party supported white supremacy, a fact that made it difficult for the party "to revolutionize the southern social order without first improving the status of northern Negroes." It simply became easier to deal with restoring social, political, and civil order to the defeated states than to convince northerners to grant full equality to the North's small black population.

Congress had the power to impose its will upon the South; many southerners were denied the franchise because of their high military or civilian affiliation with the former Confederacy. Emboldened by their superior numbers in Congress, in 1867 the Radicals enacted a bill that divided the defeated southern states into five military districts. Further, these states were denied membership in Congress until they revised their constitutions (with the assistance of black men) and recognized the Thirteenth and Fourteenth Amendments, which abolished slavery and granted American citizenship to the emancipated slaves. Most meaningfully, the law enfranchised 700,000 black voters in the former Confederacy. This led to black men voting and holding a wide assortment of local political offices, ranging from superintendent of state schools and justice of the peace to lieutenant governor. Black men were also elected to the House of Representatives and to the U.S. Senate.

This was indeed radical. Following the Civil War, Reconstruction offered little benefits to the North's small African American population because the Radical Republicans in Congress were more liberal than their counterparts in northern states. In 1867, when Congress provided the franchise for black men in the former Confederacy, Ohio, Pennsylvania, Connecticut, New Jersey, Delaware, Maryland, Kentucky, West Virginia, Indiana, Michigan, Illinois, Missouri, Wisconsin, and Kansas denied them the right to vote. New York's constitution required that black men own property valued at $250 or more to be eligible to exercise the franchise. Ohio strangely granted the vote to those "black" men who were 51 percent or more "white." As noted by historian C. Vann Woodward, equality was more of a revolutionary concept than freedom. Northern legislatures were reluctant to alter the status quo. Republican jurist David D. Field noted in 1866 that blacks did not "earn" the franchise merely because of their military contributions; the right to vote was "a political trust" and not "a natural right." Despite agitation on the part of blacks and their white supporters, it would take the adoption of the Fifteenth Amendment in 1870 before African Americans outside of the former Confederacy were granted the franchise on equal terms with white males.[18]

Bruce was only twenty when the disputed election of 1876 culminated in a political compromise that awarded the presidency to Republican Rutherford B. Hayes in exchange for an end to Reconstruction. Although Bruce offered no opinion in print, he certainly observed the events that radically altered the American political landscape. Like others, he displayed pride in seeing men of color act as political operatives in Congress. He undoubtedly read some of their speeches in the Washington press. The sight of prominent white Progressives fighting for the complete inclusion of African Americans into American society had a profound influence on the young man. Bruce would cultivate alliances and several close friendships with liberal whites who shared his desire to achieve full citizenship rights for African Americans. Later, both historians and bigots would argue that Reconstruction was a failure that bestowed electoral rights on an unprepared people. Worse, they would argue, incompetent and corrupt African Americans were responsible for graft and poor government. For four decades, Bruce, who never accepted this proposition, called for Americans to repeat the efforts initiated during Reconstruction and to make the nation a color-blind society.

Introduction to Journalism

The short-lived Reconstruction would have a tremendous impact on African Americans who used the period of newfound freedom to widen their horizons. It was in this era that a wider development of the black press occurred. The fear of slaveholders that black publishers would print subversive literature limited the black press before 1865 to a few northern locales. With emancipation, the black press in the South proliferated. Grateful to the Republican Party for their antislavery sentiments and advocacy for black political participation in southern Reconstruction governments, African American publishers were staunch Republicans. Bruce soon joined this group as publisher, editor, and, for fifty years, contributor of often controversial opinion pieces.

Bruce's journalistic career commenced in 1874 when the eighteen-year-old was employed by the *New York Times*'s Washington office as a messenger for L. L. Crouse, associate editor and brother of Nebraska's governor. It was in this capacity that Bruce met Sen. Charles Sumner, who lived in the Arlington Hotel Annex. Bruce would visit him every evening to obtain communications for the next day's paper. This assignment was an honor for Bruce, as Sumner was widely admired by blacks for his authorship of the 1875 Civil Rights Act prohibiting racial discrimination in public facilities. Many members of Congress stopped by Crouse's office. There, they met the loquacious Bruce, who used the opportunity to elicit useful political news. In addition to politicians, Bruce met diplomats, including the attaché of the French embassy, who expressed a great interest in the Negro. Bruce supplied him with copies of black newspapers and books by African American authors.

Bruce's writing career began in 1875 when he became a special Washington correspondent for the *Progressive American* in New York. For one whose biting political pieces would sting enemies and delight supporters, Bruce's first article, ironically, was a nonpolitical piece, "Distillation of Coal Tar," written under the nom de plume "The Rising Sun." This piece was later reprinted in Ireland's *Dublin Magazine.* According to Bruce, Frederick Douglass was so impressed with his writing style that he made him a correspondent for the *New National Era,* where Bruce wrote under the penname "Caleb Quotem."[19]

Before his death in 1924, Bruce wrote pamphlets, poetry, plays, songbooks, and essays, hundreds of opinion pieces, and several books. Inexplicably, he did not write an autobiography of note nor, except for infrequent jottings, keep a journal or diary. He did write "A Sketch of My Life" on May 1, 1875, in which he briefly described his first nineteen years. It was in this short autobiographical statement that the young man expressed the hope that his future behavior would be pleasing to God. A religious person, Bruce believed that "God ... hath shined [the light] in our favor and we hope yet to give the light of glory to God in the face of Jesus Christ."[20] This humility was a constant in Bruce's life as he struggled to be a good Christian in a land that ignored Christ's teachings that all men are brothers.

While much of Bruce's writing was direct and condemnatory, he sometimes used satire to make the piece even more biting. His first satirical essay, "Washington's Colored Society," published in 1877, described the city's three classes. The upper class, he proposed, was dominated by former slaves who had purchased their freedom. The middle class consisted of those freed by the Emancipation Proclamation or the Civil War. Finally, the poor, or lowest class, was composed of freeborn blacks who were worse off materially than the former enslaved population. The upper class, the first families of colored society, kept "a servant, two dogs, a tom cat and a rifle that saw service in 1776." They sought intermarriage with whites to "better" themselves and had illicit sexual relationships with darker-complexioned Negroes. Bruce admired the children of the "contraband" who fled to the nation's capital during the war years. They were frugal, industrious souls who did not ape whites by playing cards or speaking pseudo-French. The brunt of Bruce's criticism was reserved for the "dude" or "hog" who could not afford tailored clothes. Though he cleaned spittoons in Congress, he acted as though he influenced legislation. Bruce was contemptuous of the "blonde kin," or mixed-race, group that bragged of their white ancestry although they were bastards. He also extended his contempt to the "mahogany-colored" Yankees, who, in their self-importance, thought they knew everything about everything but were dismissed by others as "Dr. Sharpie," "Prof. Sharpie," "Captain Sharpie" or "Rev. Sharpie." This satire represented a serious concern for Bruce, who believed that it was unwise for a maligned race to set up artificial barriers among themselves. In later years, he was merciless to those who imitated white society or used their near-whiteness to escape from the Negro race.[21] Bruce's reputation for frank, informative, and well-crafted essays made it easy for him to obtain positions as a contributor or special correspondent. C. Ridgely Waller, a correspondent for *Our Boys* and the *St. Louis Tribune,* typified Bruce's admirers when he highly recommended him with unabashed praise in 1877. Such recommendations made it possible for Bruce to write for more than one hundred newspapers between 1875 and 1924.[22]

Despite Bruce's reputation for biting satire, he often wrote pensively about the relationship of human beings to God. His religious faith was shared by many others in the African American community who believed that God's will brought them to America to expose them to civilization and Christianity. Added to this controversial theory was the belief that providential determinism would settle the race question. While later generations questioned the latter view, it reflected the strong faith many nineteenth-century blacks had that God would avenge their wrongs. Others, however (including Bruce, at times), questioned the power of divine intervention. Instead, they vacillated between options for survival in America. They responded variously to the racial violence and the denial of rights with calls for moral suasion, retaliatory violence, appeals to the power of the intellect, and pleas to the Christian conscience of Caucasians. Bruce advocated all of these approaches, although he primarily put his faith in the power of the intellect and providential determinism. In 1878, an early example of Bruce's belief in divine intervention appeared in the *St. Louis Tribune:*

Dare to Do Right

When dangers surround thee and prospects grow dark
When the world and its millions would crush thee to naught
Stand up like a man and fight along bravely
Remembering always to trust in the lord
Let no failure to do so cast down your high spirit
But rather be an incentive to fight
For the greater the cross will the greater the crowns be
If you push it with vigor and dare to be right[23]

Bruce also wrote poetry. While most of his later poetry reflected his political nature, some of his earlier pieces dealt with romance and unrequited love. In 1878, an unnamed woman appealed to his amorous sentiments. The untitled poem he wrote to her expressed the pain that wishful lovers feel as they dream of that special one.

Oh, if within this heart of mine,
One ray of hope could creep
One single ray of hope divine
How peacefully I'd sleep
I'd dream of a friend far away

■ ■ ■

That friend o fair and beauteous maid.
Art thou indeed the heart hath said.

Like most men flushed with the initial glow of infatuation, Bruce later confessed, "I have learned better sense now."[24] It may have been coincidental, but in that same year Bruce informed the Washington *Sunday Republic* that news reports that he had been "cowhided" by a Miss Hardmond were blatantly false. Nevertheless, periodic gossip in the Washington press suggested that Bruce was something of a Lothario.[25]

Early Newspaper Career

Bruce published few of his poems; they were his personal and intimate feelings about family or religious sentiment. It was his political writings that made him a favorite of both readers and black editors. In 1879, William V. Turner of Raleigh's *North Carolina Republican* wrote requesting Bruce to write a weekly column about Washington politics.[26]

In addition to writing for the *Republican,* Bruce joined Charles N. Otley in early September as an associate editor for the *Weekly Argus*. Otley, then editor in chief, and Bruce decided to make the paper "Republican at all times and under all circumstances." Like the vast majority of black Americans, the pair abhorred the Democratic Party, which then stood for white supremacy and the denial of rights to Negroes. Otley and Bruce declared that the *Weekly Argus* would "be a fearless advocate of the true principles of the Republican Party, and the *moral* and intellectual advancement of the Negro American." They vowed not to attack others in public life but to judge them on how they used their qualifications to advance the race's causes. Determined to make the Republican Party a success in the 1880 presidential election, the pair received subscription pledges from many of Washington's leading citizens and Republican politicians. The *Weekly Argus* lasted for two years. After its demise, it was turned over to a stock company.[27] Starting with the presidential election of 1880, and for the next forty years, Bruce sought to aid the party of Lincoln through his political writings.

In addition to writing, Bruce also sought to entertain presidential candidate James A. Garfield. In September 1880, the partisan writer organized a quartet, the Black Republican Glee Club, to sing campaign songs in "plantation dialect." Bruce informed Garfield that the National Republican Committee refused to employ them because of lack of funds. Hoping to impress Garfield, Bruce notified him that the quartet wanted to perform for the good of the party, but they were badly in need of uniforms to look presentable. He boldly attempted to embarrass Garfield by informing him that his running mate, Chester A. Arthur, had given $20 toward purchasing uniforms that cost $168. Bruce declared that, if they received support, "we'll stand by you until the last armed Democrat expires." Two months after Garfield's presidential victory, Bruce wrote his congratulations and informed him that for the past two months he had "preached the gospel of republicanism to the children of darkness." Bruce added that the downtrodden Negro had a friend in Garfield, whose administration would be "the dawn of a new era" bringing unheard-of blessings to all citizens. Bruce hoped that his flattering praise would grant the glee club an audience at the White House, the subject of his letter to President Garfield in March 1881. There is no evidence that Bruce received permission to sing before the presidential family, but his pursuit of this objective highlighted two things about his character. First, Bruce was a hustler nonpareil who always looked for an angle to obtain funds, an interview, or a personal favor as payment for his loyalty. Secondly, as illustrated by his comments, he was not above acting obsequiously at times.[28] On several occasions Bruce would act in this manner, in contradiction to his militant image. His tendency to hustle for the sake of a paycheck placed him in messy entanglements that only caused more problems when he attempted to extricate himself.

For example, his editorial duties did not require Bruce's full-time attention or provide him with an adequate living allowance. To meet his daily expenditures, Bruce found employment as a filing clerk for the American Colonization Society. William Coppinger, secretary of the ACS, introduced Bruce to Edward W. Blyden from Liberia, who was a vice president in the ACS. Coppinger suggested that Blyden take Bruce to Africa because he had expressed interest in the continent. Bruce and Blyden became close friends and corresponded frequently until the latter's death in 1912.[29] Bruce's employment at the office of the ACS was an example of his economic pragmatism. His avowed interest in Africa at this time did not indicate a serious desire to emigrate. In fact, Bruce, not unlike other African Americans, saw his destiny in America. As someone who would constantly face financial problems, Bruce accepted money from an organization that many of his contemporaries viewed with contempt and suspicion. The vast majority of African Americans expressed hostility toward the society's efforts to assist them in returning to a land they did not consider to be their home or a place to work out their destiny. Bruce understood this, but his indifference to their concern cannot be attributed simply to youth. Bruce was hard-pressed economically. For years, he scrounged to find decent living quarters. An examination of Washington directories indicates that Bruce rarely lived at the same address for more than a year. His willingness to overlook the source in exchange for a fair income would eventually undermine his credibility. This proved true when he became allied, albeit temporarily, with Booker T. Washington. His relationship with the Tuskegee Wizard will be examined more closely later.

Bruce's color, lack of formal education, and American bigotry made it difficulty for him to find steady pay and employment in his primary love, journalism. Although Bruce occasionally submitted pieces to the white press, they rarely hired black reporters. The black press itself was erratic. Papers folded quickly due to financial difficulties brought on by limited advertisements and the unwillingness of readers to settle their arrears. Therefore, as in the case of his employment with the American Colonization Society, throughout his life Bruce sought additional funds as a porter, clerk, or messenger. Sometimes he would hold several jobs at once. Still, it was in the newspaper business that he sought his glory.

In Washington, D.C., in 1880, Bruce and S. S. Lacy published the *Sunday Item,* the nation's first black-owned Sunday newspaper. A quarrel over debts and poor communication between the two men caused hard feelings that led to the break up of the partnership and the demise of the *Sunday Item.* H. M. Shepard noted this in an 1881 letter to Bruce. Acting as a mediator, Shepard informed Bruce that Lacy believed his partner was not being aboveboard with him and, unless he could pay the debts, he needed to return to Washington and accept the consequences. (It is not clear where Bruce retreated to.) To settle the debts, Shepard advised Bruce to either close the paper or look for a clerkship and buy out Lacy's share. Bruce was also in debt to Shepard, who requested that he send the money expeditiously because he was in poor health, spitting up blood, and on the verge of mortgaging his furniture.[30]

Bruce's financial difficulties were shared. Most black publishers complained that subscribers refused to pay for their papers, or they were so delinquent that debt mounted. In October 1881, Bruce wrote "Negro Journalism," an essay that faulted readers for supporting white newspapers and ignoring their own. Bruce proclaimed that black editors had to compile their work with love and be thoroughly aware of the needs of readers. He understood that readers would remain faithful to those publishers who printed news instead of sensational or scandalous stories. In this far-ranging piece, Bruce declared that the black press should elevate the masses. Expressing an unorthodox view, anathema to most race editors, Bruce decried the ex-slave's dependency on electoral politics. The Negro was too far behind the Anglo-Saxon to waste time on politics, he asserted. Instead, Bruce argued that the race needed to acquire land, obtain an education, learn trades, and contribute to the nation's development. Bruce praised the southern black press for teaching devotion to duty and for extolling blacks to invest their dollars in legitimate businesses. He was proud of the southern black publishers and editors who encouraged their readers to have pride in seeking the knowledge that would lead them to acquire land, stores, mills, and banks. The black press, Bruce urged, had to spread the message of brotherhood. He requested that they appealed to the good conscience of whites that controlled the nation's destiny. This conservative view was shared by many who were less than two decades removed from enslavement as they sought to solve the nation's race problem. Bruce later discarded this conservative approach to race relations when he became convinced that white Americans had no interest in including blacks in a participatory democracy. Booker T. Washington shared Bruce's conservative view, which explains Bruce's initial positive response to the educator.[31]

During this developmental stage, Bruce initiated contacts in Washington that would prove highly beneficial to his journalistic interests. He knew both Chester A. Arthur and William McKinley before they became occupants of the White House. Bruce met Arthur in 1880, when the future president was chairman of the New York Republican State Committee, and he met McKinley while he was a member of the congressional campaign committee in Washington. By writing Edward McPherson with a request to find a position for Bruce, McKinley was responsible for Bruce's first political position. In this unstated capacity (probably as a messenger), Bruce was able to offer advice to national Republican leadership. Bruce credited Sen. Roscoe Conkling of New York, and Arthur, for taking his suggestion in 1881 to have Rev. Henry Highland Garnet appointed as U.S. minister to Liberia. Garnet, a former slave and abolitionist, was well known as pastor of a leading black Presbyterian church in Washington.[32]

After the demise of the *Sunday Item,* Bruce became a correspondent for the *Grand Army Journal.* Manager A. T. Bissell provided Bruce with a note, dated August 12, 1882, which acknowledged that he was employed "in the interest of the colored race . . . and will solicit subscriptions . . . for a period of not less than six months."[33] Sometime in 1882, Bruce wrote a provocative essay, "Practical Questions," for an unidentified paper. Disturbed that naturalized Americans had rights denied to African Americans, Bruce inquired, "Why is it that we as a race persist in helping the white race to ostracize us?" His analysis posited that it was poor leadership to encourage freedmen and their families to invest, not in factories, land, and business, but to place sixty million dollars in the bankrupt Freedmen's Savings and Trust Company. Without cooperation and race pride, Bruce added, blacks would not be able to compete with whites who wanted to dominate everything. Bruce urged clergymen to preach the gospel of race cooperation. For example, he suggested that black Methodists organize cooperative societies to make funds available for building houses, stores, and providing employment for clerks, bookkeepers, and cashiers instead of enriching the white community. Bruce exhorted them to be clannish "like the Jews." Wield education and wealth as weapons and combine forces, money, intelligence, talent, and labor and the race question would be solved in less than two years, he optimistically predicted. Benjamin Tucker Tanner, editor of the *Christian Recorder,* an African Methodist publication, echoed this sentiment.[34]

Bruce failed to understand that it took more than racial cooperation for black Americans to advance. As a minority, they were dependent upon a white political infrastructure to protect rights that were rapidly disappearing after the Compromise of 1877. Southern Reconstruction effectively ended when federal troops were removed, and President Rutherford B. Hayes adopted a "let alone policy" that left the freedmen helpless. By 1879, thousands left the South for Kansas and Oklahoma. This small trickle would develop into a river of migration to the north and west over the next six decades. The return to power of the Democrats in the former Confederacy quickly followed the end of Reconstruction. Their use of fraud, intimidation, and violence to terrorize blacks would be met with indifference from the business-minded Republicans who, unlike their radical predecessors, seemed to ignore the pleas for justice.

The first example that the Republican Party was deaf to the cries of African Americans occurred in 1883 when the Republican-dominated U.S. Supreme Court ruled that the 1875 Civil Rights Act was unconstitutional. This decision was a blow to all progressive Americans who had supported the prohibition against discrimination in public facilities. *New York Globe* editor Timothy Thomas Fortune wrote that the colored people felt like they were being baptized in ice water. Other editors were outraged by a decision that reflected the declining national interest in civil rights and the waning influence of black voters in the Republican Party.

On November 1, 1883, Bruce registered his protest of the decision in a lecture before the Bethesda Literary Society in Georgetown (District of Columbia). The attentive audience heard him proclaim that whites had no basis on which to claim racial superiority and could not afford to ostracize the Negro—who had proven his loyalty to the nation as a laborer and a soldier. The Court's decision provided reactionary southerners with an invitation to use oppression and terrorism against blacks, since the federal government lacked the strength to protect her weakest citizens. Five days later, Bruce wrote "Is This Our Country?" His theme—one that he would repeat for more than forty years—was that the United States was not the Negro's country socially or politically, but morally. "Our country! Oh what a mockery, what a farce! What a delusion! What a lie!" he wrote. Blacks could not claim America as their country until whites recognized the brotherhood of man and the Fatherhood of God. African Americans were tolerated in the North and despised in the South because "American Christians love God and hate the Negro," he asserted. Bruce dismissed politics as a panacea and declared that education was the key to unlock the door. He believed that knowledge led to the finance that would let one push the door wide open. Bruce's response to southern terrorism and growing northern indifference was eclectic. He had no single answer, and over the years he advocated many solutions to the southern problem. Bruce strongly believed that education provided individuals with the tools to analyze their situation and to form corrective measures. In the context of education, Bruce joined others establishing lyceums throughout the nation and debating clubs to impress upon the youth the transformative power of knowledge. They saw education as the vehicle to compete with white America, and they believed, perhaps naively, that knowledge would clear away the racial obstacles. In 1882, Bruce and Victoria Earle Matthews, who a decade later would establish the White Rose Mission, formed the Enquiring Club, a literary group for the study and discussion of racial questions. It was meant to encourage the study of Negro history as opposed to the writings of William Shakespeare, Ralph Waldo Emerson, Robert Browning, and Henry Wadsworth Longfellow. Bruce formed the club after meeting Ethiopians who resembled American blacks but whom the white press labeled Semitic. One Ethiopian remarked to Bruce, "We are all one people." This would prove to be one of Bruce's earliest encounters with Pan-Africanism, a belief in the universality of African people. This revelation came to him at a time when many African Americans disdained the African portion of their identity. Bruce also believed that ignorance of one's past left one gullible. He called upon the race to cooperate with true leaders—whom he left unnamed. Bruce based his call for race unity on the potential power of race love to overcome the problems facing black Americans. Like other black nationalists, Bruce believed that self-reliance, self-pride, and race love were, in themselves, enough to allow blacks to withstand the racism and prejudice of white Americans. This philosophy, of course, was tested over the years.[35]

While Bruce believed in the power of race love, he balanced this with an appeal to politics as an additional weapon to keep in the arsenal against bigotry. Of course, this contradicted his earlier view that blacks should eschew politics for economic development. Bruce aimed his earlier antipolitical stance more at indifferent politicians than at politics itself. He knew that radical Republican Party politics had demanded the abolition of slavery, the enlistment of black soldiers in the Civil War, and the participation of black men in southern politics. And, that it was the Republican Party that had given black men throughout the nation the right to vote in 1870, when the Fifteenth Amendment to the U.S. Constitution was adopted. The Republican Party of the early 1880s, lacking the fervor of its founders, had begun to distance itself from the mission of protecting southern blacks from racial atrocities. However, Bruce still viewed the party as morally superior to a Democratic Party that sanctioned slavery and condoned mob violence against the innocent. Bruce maintained his commitment to the Republican Party for the rest of his life.

Late in 1883, Bruce established the *Grit* as a campaign sheet to aid in the election of a Republican president in 1884. Bruce was the managing editor and W. B. Avery assumed the editor's duties.[36] The *Grit* would establish Bruce's best-known nom de plume, "Bruce Grit," bestowed upon him by Timothy Thomas Fortune, editor of the *New York Globe*. As his nickname suggested, he would use journalistic grit to agitate and irritate his opponents.

National Politics, 1884–1900

It was between 1884 and 1900 that Bruce developed a national reputation as a major writer. His investigative skills were magnificent; his writing was incisive, witty, biting, and, at times, sarcastic. These qualities endeared him to some readers but raised the ire of others. Black America faced a gradual but steady Republican abdication of responsibility for their protection in the South, and the difficulty of adjusting to life in the North when they migrated to that region. Their efforts to escape the South's segregation laws, inadequate educational opportunities, crop failures, lynch mobs, and political disfranchisement became a staple of commentary for the black press. Initially designed to be a campaign sheet, Bruce hoped to make the *Grit* a formidable race journal in the nation's capital. Its main competitors in Washington were the *People's Advocate,* edited by John W. Cromwell, and the *Bee,* the "bloody pulpit" of the irascible William Calvin Chase, who would be sued five times for libel, twice successfully. President Grover Cleveland was attracted to the paper by its name. He invited Bruce to the White House, where he entertained him in his library. Bruce informed the president that he had entered the newspaper business because he thought he could do some good for his race. Bruce told Cleveland that he had chosen "Grit" as his nom de plume because he intended to be gritty in his statements without offending anyone. Since Fortune gave Bruce his famous nickname, it is likely that Bruce appropriated ownership in later years; it was not until around 1914 that Bruce wrote of his meeting with Cleveland. The president noted that he had sympathy for the Negro race because his family had been abolitionists and involved in the Underground Railroad. About 1914, Bruce recalled that Cleveland was so pleased with his "up from slavery" accomplishments that the president donated ten dollars to the *Grit* and autographed a *Grit* subscription book.[1] (It was more likely that Cleveland gave Bruce money during the campaign, because the *Grit* was out of business when Cleveland took office in March 1885).

The inaugural edition of the *Grit* appeared on December 21, 1883. The masthead stated that "the Grit is neither for, nor against the Administration, but for the people." Bruce promised that, as associate editor, he would deal with all questions concerning his race in a manly manner. He further promised to deliver "a newsy and spicy paper" that would avoid personalizing his journalism. The *Grit,* Bruce declared, would labor on behalf of the working class, which at that time were organizing into labor unions to better their working conditions and wages. He added that the *Grit* would criticize the public acts of public servants; the "sand in our craw" would not be removed by the government's "sweet sugar." The credo of the paper would be "freedom of thought, freedom of *action,* and *freedom of expression.*" Still, Bruce understood that a paper could not survive simply on rhetorical promises. Like other black editors, Bruce warned correspondents to "write your sentences boldly; condense your news; use ink; write on one side of the paper." He urged them to keep their pieces under three sheets or they "will be sent . . . to feed the furnace." Using the humor that characterized his writing, Bruce Grit added that the paper would not take responsibility for the statements of correspondents, "as we are neither bullet or club proof."[2]

The *Grit* quickly came to the attention of the nation's black press. Timothy Thomas Fortune, who would have a fractious relationship with Bruce for forty years, gleefully wrote in the *New York Globe* that Bruce was "the ugliest colored editor" and should have named his paper "Gall." "Bruce is a jolly scribe and Grit will live," Fortune predicted. "Go to it Johnny," he added. Later, in a more serious moment, Fortune would refer to Bruce as "a rather seedy and dilapidated looking individual" who wore "baggy clothes." This aptly described Bruce's taste in clothes, but in photographs he possessed, as noted by his good friend James S. Clarkson, "Apollo like proportions" and a proud, regal bearing. The *Boston Hub* congratulated the *Grit* for securing a competent manager and urged Bruce to give the public a good deal of "Grit." The *Kansan* described Bruce as "uncompromising."[3]

Although Bruce purported to make the *Grit* an unstintingly Republican paper, he had no problem in attacking the Republicans for their declining support of black rights. The Compromise of 1877 led to the election of Rutherford B. Hayes although his Democratic opponent, Samuel Tilden, received the majority of the popular vote. The returns in several southern states were disputed. In exchange for the presidency, the Republicans agreed to end Reconstruction and to suspend federal concerns over the issues of black suffrage and civil rights. This "let alone" policy culminated in the return of white Democratic rule to the former Confederate states. Republican Party ideology shifted dramatically. Radical Republicans who had previously enacted civil rights laws were either deceased or out of office. Other politicians pragmatically decided to let the South deal with the race question, even if it meant a complete denial of African American rights. Some black politicians depended on the "patronage trough" and were unwilling to criticize the Republican Party leadership publicly. Bruce was not a member of the elite seeking a position in government. Therefore, he broke ranks with his fellow black editors who expressed blind loyalty to the party of Lincoln. Bruce believed that "when the rights or interests of the colored race are involved, we become more Negro than anything else." Bruce harshly criticized President Chester A. Arthur, who had succeeded the martyred James A. Garfield, felled by an assassin's bullet on September 19, 1881, barely seven months after his inauguration. While some black editors criticized Arthur's inaction, few agreed with William Calvin Chase, publisher and editor of the *Bee,* who openly advocated a black reign of terror as a remedy for southern atrocities.[4]

Bruce did not match Chase's militancy, but he did attribute the proliferation of southern atrocities to Arthur's lack of political leadership. Arthur, an accidental president, faced a difficult race in 1884. In early February, Bruce decried the early success of Arthur's campaign. The editor predicted that few would vote for Arthur because "the people are tired of this aesthetic white beavered and ruffle shunted administration."[5] For several months, Bruce pushed for the selection of Sen. John A. Logan. Concurring was John W. Cromwell, publisher and editor of the *People's Advocate*. Cromwell suggested that black voters heed Logan's call for the distribution of educational funds to be done by the Commissioner of Education instead of by state superintendents of education, who often deprived segregated southern schools of equal funding.[6] In mid-March, Bruce urged southern and western blacks to send to the Republican National Convention men with backbones so that the Arthur camp could not hoodwink the race. This was a reference to Arthur's effort to unite southern independent Democrats and southern Republicans to help him win both the nomination and the White House. Arthur's strategy was a bold attempt to distance himself and the party from southern black Republicans. To counter the Republican Party's growing indifference to the southern race issue, Bruce demanded that the delegates make their voices heard. Still, as a staunch Republican, he warned voters that it was better to abstain on Election Day than to vote for Democrats. He reiterated his support for Logan because he considered Arthur and James G. Blaine, a former secretary of state, too aristocratic to make suitable presidents for the common man. In May, Bruce described Blaine as an ostrich naively exposing his body to his enemy. More important, Bruce also shared the anti-Catholic views of most nineteenth-century Americans. He viewed victory by the Roman Catholic Blaine as a sure indication that the reins of government would be turned over to the Vatican.[7]

The *Grit* became the *Washington Grit* with its March 29 issue. In it, Bruce accused the Democrats of depending upon the ignorance of voters. Bruce warned that the Democrats' return to power would result in the South groping in darkness. While blacks and progressive whites shared this view, many southern whites let the fear of Negro domination control their political choices. The Democratic Party promised to keep the ex-slave in his place. Their portrayal of Reconstruction as a period of black misrule appealed to those who feared economic competition from blacks or that their daughters would be at the mercy of bestial Negro lust.[8]

Some blacks, dissatisfied with the Republicans and interested in personal gain, sought to gain favor with the Democrats. Bruce and other black Republicans were concerned that the gathering of the Colored Men's Interstate Conference, scheduled to meet in Pittsburgh in late April, would be manipulated by the Democratic Party to "disintegrate the colored vote." Although delegates heard George F. Downing, a wealthy caterer and restaurateur from Rhode Island, declare that neither the Democrats nor the Republicans served the interest of the race, the concerns of loyal black Republicans were not assuaged by the convention's denial of political connections. While Bruce admitted that the Republican Party had become neglectful of the faithful Negro, he understood that both the party and its black supporters depended upon each other for success. While Bruce considered those who would desert the Republican Party as no more than fools; he insisted that the black man had to "kick vigorously" to have the party appreciate his political importance as the leaven in the party's success. Bruce emphasized that he had criticized both Arthur and Blaine because they were not "square on the Negro question," and not because he was looking for a government position. We "do not wear anybody's collar and haven't given any of the candidates for the president a mortgage upon ourselves," he boldly declared.[9]

Bruce's outspokenness on the political question, combined with financial problems between Bruce and W. B. Avery, threatened the viability of the *Washington Grit* in 1884. On May 3, Bruce became the sole manager and proprietor. Readers were instructed not to send any money owed in arrears to Avery. Reflecting the new masthead's motto, "Hew to the Line, Let the Chips Fall Where They May," Bruce explained in the May 31 issue that when Avery came to the *Grit* from the *People's Advocate* in December 1883 it was agreed that each would pay his share of expenses. According to Bruce, Avery paid for two weeks but then failed to make any contributions for ten weeks. Bruce noted that W. M. Wright, the printer for the newspaper, could verify his account of the Avery fiasco. He added, "we never kick a dirty dog but once. This is our last kick." This promise quickly evaporated. In the July 19 issue, Bruce issued an ultimatum to Avery to speak the truth or remain silent, unless he wanted sordid personal information released that would be talked about for forty years.[10] Bruce temporarily assumed the position of publisher, relinquishing it to Col. Perry H.

Carson in the summer of 1884. George W. Stewart was added as business manager and as a reporter representing west Washington. Bruce remained as editor-in-chief and promised to increase the paper's circulation.[11]

Bruce had used the pages of the *Washington Grit* to push Logan's candidacy. However, once the Republican Party nominated James G. Blaine as their standard-bearer, Bruce succumbed to party loyalty and vowed in the June 7 issue to support Blaine. Bruce's disappointment was somewhat abated by the selection of Logan as Blaine's running mate. A week later, Bruce wrote, "Shall we bolt?" In other words, should black Republicans sit out the election or defect to the enemy's camp. His answer was clear: "To bolt, to kick, to raise a tempest, . . . to take up arms against the G.O.P.! Perish the thought!" he thundered. Bruce warned that the Democrats would seek to entice the black vote and might even nominate a black man to temporarily chair their nominating convention. "Let your watchword be Blaine Logan and victory," urged the militant editor.[12] While disappointed that Logan would not head the ticket, Bruce sent Blaine a congratulatory letter that the Republican Party's nominee graciously accepted.[13]

Despite his vow to help elect the ticket, Bruce feared that the voters would react against President Arthur's "imbecile, vacillating and cowardly administration." This remark was a reminder to the party to canvass in the South, where Republicans were beaten or killed to keep them away from the ballot box.[14] *New York Globe* editor Timothy Thomas Fortune, a nominal Republican who now regarded the party with "loathing contempt," did not share Bruce's loyalty to the Republican Party. Others agreed that the Republican Party was not the only available ship on the open sea. Bruce's reply to these critics was a swift denunciation. He called the black editor of the *Old Dominion* a "white man's nigger" for his support of the Democratic Party. Bruce branded him a "cringing, truckling, sycophantic damn fool 'nigger of the first magnitude' who believes in the superiority of the white man."[15]

Bruce felt that his harshness against black Democrats was warranted; he saw the Republicans as the party that represented the hope of his race. This belief persisted among most African Americans, despite the party's growing aloofness from its loyal black supporters. With few exceptions, most African Americans and progressive whites viewed the Democratic Party as a reactionary supporter of slavery, secession, political terrorism, and abrogation of civil rights for black Americans. Bruce understood that a Cleveland victory was possible unless black leadership convinced the rank-and-file to vote. In this context, he faulted phony race leaders interested only in fame, money, and political office. He accused them of dividing their strength into factions, cliques, and rings dominated by personality. Bruce bluntly referred to these "leaders" as leeches, since "fine talk and fat stomachs do not make leaders."

He was convinced that the Negro race produced "more political deadbeats and . . . more overrated, swell headed nobodies . . . than any other class in this country." (Bruce did not name the leaders, but he had in mind Frederick Douglass; Blanche Kelso Bruce [no relation]; and John R. Lynch, who would become the target of his barbs in a few years.)

Victory would be possible, Bruce asserted, if the Republican Party sought to swell the black vote. Providing subsidies to the black press would aid the party: "A few surplus dollars makes us feel a hundred percent more patriotic and loyal to the party than no dollars at all." Of course, Bruce was not suggesting that the black vote was available to the highest bidder; rather that it cost money to print special campaign editions in the weeklies which the cash strapped publishers could ill afford. The Republican National Committee replied that the publication committee had received many similar requests and was not obligated to honor any.[16] The failure of Republican leadership to accommodate the black press's request for campaign funds in 1884 and subsequent presidential elections would remain a point of contention until 1900.

Things heated up politically in September when Bruce denied that intelligent African Americans would switch to the Democratic Party. The editor contemptuously dismissed those who did as "wooden headed Negroes who think they are thinkers." Bruce denied that black voters were deserting in droves, but he urged loyalists to strike for concessions before Election Day because failed campaign "promises and gilded lies won't pay house rent or buy potatoes."[17]

Bruce considered himself a born Republican unlike those manufactured supporters who wanted him to sneeze because the party took snuff. He warned the Republicans that unless they continued their advocacy of political and civil rights for blacks the party would find itself without followers.[18] While much of Bruce's anger was genuine, it was largely inspired by the party's refusal to subsidize the *Washington Grit*. Bruce wanted funds to radically alter the newspaper by adding a London correspondent. In early October, he informed readers that he wanted to travel in the eastern United States to seek subsidies. He was hoping to travel to Europe, a desire he had harbored since 1865. The *Washington Grit* was only a campaign sheet that was not supposed to last beyond the election season. Bruce hoped to make it into a profit-making enterprise and, eventually, into a leading, if not *the* leading, race paper in the country.

A Democratic Victory

On election eve, Bruce confidently predicted that a Blaine victory would force the Democrats to avoid electoral politics for three thousand years. He suggested they "stand from under, something heavy is going to drop about [on] Nov. 4, 1884." Little did he realize, however, that voters would give Blaine and the Republicans a humiliating defeat.[19] The election return sealed the fate of the *Washington Grit*. Bruce's hard-hitting editorials and critique of Democratic machinations and Republican Party indifference captivated the interest of editors and electorate alike. His close contact with many of Washington's politicians provided him with valuable political information but, unfortunately lacking adequate funds, Bruce had no choice but to fold the paper after the election. Bruce was careful, however, not to have his own money invested in the *Washington Grit*. He noted in 1888 that the demise of the paper had not ruined him financially because he always sought to acquire other people's capital. This was difficult, as there were "more born journalists than ... fleas on a dog's back." [20]

Cleveland's victory, the first Democratic administration since the end of the Civil War, alarmed many blacks who feared a wholesale return to slavery. To allay this fear, prominent race leaders such as former Reconstruction Congressman Joseph H. Rainey and William Still, of Underground Railroad fame, noted that the U.S. Constitution rendered this an impossibility. Frederick Douglass, "Mr. Republican," noted that Cleveland had done some good things in New York as governor; therefore, he might do good things as president for colored people.[21]

With the shift of power to the Democrats, opportunistic blacks saw an opportunity to make inroads into Cleveland's administration as political appointees. The *Cleveland Gazette* reported on January 17, 1885, that George T. Downing's open letter to party leaders asking for appointments to government positions would do much to attract colored men to the Democratic Party. John P. Green, a black member of Ohio's legislature, dismissed Downing as a "bolter" (or independent), a "constitutional grower" who had lost his influence in the Republican Party after his mentor, Sen. Charles Sumner, had died.[22] Curiously, even with his strong aversion to Democrats, Bruce informed President Cleveland that the Sable Choristers, a musical group he managed, wanted to provide the White House with an unforgettable serenade of Negro folk music and popular musical selections. The reply cited the "pressure of official matters" as the excuse not to engage the group.[23] Was Bruce using the performance in order to gain the president's favor and perhaps obtain a low-level government appointment? There is no evidence to suggest that he was looking for anything more than a chance to earn a few extra dollars, but his effort to please a Democrat made his previous criticisms appear less sincere. It is not clear how Bruce justified in his own mind his willingness to perform for a Democratic president presumably for a fee while he criticized those who would give up their manhood to "bask in the sunlight of Democratic favor for a season." Apparently, Bruce made a distinction between entertaining a Democratic president and accepting a political appointment, which would imply agreement with the president's policies. Nonetheless, Bruce's willingness to perform before Cleveland is perplexing because he believed that no Democratic appointment could move him from his devotion to the Republican Party. This contradictory behavior was repeated in later years, earning him a reputation for being erratic. Still, his public reputation was that of a staunch Republican, which caused M. E. Dodge to write to him, "you will never find your true manhood while you blindly follow one party."[24]

A Democrat in the presidency did not lead to the restoration of slavery, as some feared; nor did the Cleveland administration engaged in race baiting. In fact, it surprised many with minor black appointments. However, Cleveland's administration failed to halt the rising tide of assaults on the rights of former slaves.

The Campaign of 1888 and a Republican Victory

During the spring and summer of 1888, Bruce and others sought to assist the Republican Party in developing strategies to regain control of the White House. During this period, Martha Bruce began to suffer from an incapacitating affliction. Bruce hoped that a Republican victory would lead to a government position and provide the wherewithal to comfort Martha. Many believed that a Republican victory would emanate from a large African American turnout, but that would be predicated on the party's clear expression of opposition to southern atrocities. In April, Massachusetts Sen. George F. Hoar suggested that a Republican victory in the November congressional and presidential elections would result in legislation to ensure free elections in the South.[25] Several months before the Republicans selected their presidential ticket, the names of potential candidates were discussed. Bruce considered Sen. John Sherman a strong candidate, but believed that his strength would weaken his chances with the party bosses.[26] Bruce canvassed the views of the Republican Party's leadership, in person or by mail, to assess their attitude toward the southern race problem. Hoar viewed the suppression of the black vote as an injury to the nation. He recommended the passage of vigorous laws in case of a Republican victory in the fall. Robert Smalls, a black congressman and Civil War hero, declared that the party was obligated to protect the rights of all citizens. Wisconsin Sen. Philatatus Sawyer called upon Negroes to divide their vote in the South, but he admitted to a lack of faith in the ability of Republicans to protect southern blacks. Sawyer suggested writing off the South. He believed that the Democrats either would prevent blacks from voting or would not count their votes. A strong response came from New Hampshire Sen. William E. Chandler, who challenged the party to enforce the U.S. Constitution, which had provided black men with the right to vote in 1870. Not only would it be cowardly to let it become a dead letter, declared Chandler, but it would also destroy the Republican Party.[27]

Bruce reported in the May 19 issue of the *New York Age* that there was increasing support among black Republicans for Gen. Russell A. Alger. Bruce endorsed the movement; he considered Alger to be a man who stood for the rights of the former slaves and the protection for American labor and industries.[28] James G. Blaine was considered again as a potential candidate, but Bruce noted that the anti-Catholic element would oppose Blaine because he had visited the Vatican. Despite Bruce's own anti-Catholic bias, he added, "here's religious intolerance for you." Bruce also wrote favorably about William McKinley's support for a protective tariff. Bruce's interest in the outcome of the impending election surpassed that of an interested newspaperman or even an aspiring officeholder. Upon accepting the position of associate editor for the *National Leader* in March 1888, Bruce informed editor Magnus L. Robinson that the race's destiny was "linked to the chariot wheel of American civilization." Failure on the part of blacks to spread the Republican Party's message would guarantee the race's insecurity.[29]

The Republicans, however, could afford to be indifferent to the dismantling of civil rights because the former slaves had no viable political alternatives. Still, the general indifference of the Republican Party to race issues angered several prominent African Americans. Timothy Thomas Fortune, editor of the *New York Age* and author of the polemical *Black and White: Land, Labor, and Politics in the South,* argued that the national policy of the Democratic Party represented the views of Thomas Jefferson and Alexander Hamilton. Fortune believed that since neither party was large enough to hold the colored voter intelligent voters should embrace the Democrats rather than pull "chestnuts out of the fire for [Republican] politicians who simulate an interest they do not feel." Despite charges that he was a race traitor, Fortune called for an organization to fight discrimination in the courts. (In 1890, Fortune organized the Afro-American League for this purpose, which Bruce joined). Surprisingly, Bruce harbored no ill feelings toward Fortune for his desertion. He believed that Fortune placed "the interests of the Negro to be above of any party." Bruce knew Fortune and applauded him for his undying love of race; otherwise, he would have seriously castigated him for his defection. This would be but one example of many where Bruce allowed a personal friendship to interfere with his race-first ideology. Other black Republicans were not as magnanimous in their judgment of defectors. After George T. Downing argued that Cleveland's reelection would foster race relations more than the election of a Republican, Henry C. Smith, editor of the *Cleveland Gazette,* wrote that neither Cleveland nor the Democrats had proved their friendship during the past three years, and that was "a *very, very,* dangerous" course. "What a sad, sad, sad spectacle is a Negro Democrat," concluded Smith.[30]

Underscoring Smith's concern was the blunt assessment of the Democratic senator from South Carolina, Wade Hampton, that Negro supremacy was a "crime against humanity, civilization and Christianity."[31] African Americans who demanded an equal opportunity to participate in the political process were not calling for black supremacy, only an opportunity to exercise their constitutional rights. Bruce hammered away at this theme. In June 1888, he emphasized that the South possessed forty-four electoral votes that were lost to the Republicans by fraud and intimidation. Bruce called upon disfranchised blacks to demand that voting protection be included in the forthcoming Republican Party platform. He added that the black vote in New York, Massachusetts, New Jersey, and Connecticut should mean more to the Republican Party than tariff protection. He argued that Republican votes in the South would remain meaningless until a courageous president punished "the miserable whining rebels . . . who . . . [shoot] Negroes and [stuff] ballot boxes." Bruce urged the Republican National Committee to include the Negro in the party's platform and politics. Bruce wrote this demand acting as the secretary of Washington's Colored Young Men's National Republican Club.[32]

The Republican convention that met in June nominated Benjamin Harrison and Levi P. Morton to run against Grover Cleveland. Neither Timothy Thomas Fortune nor Bruce was happy with the party's platform statement on the tariff. Fortune called for the abolition of taxes on tobacco and whiskey because it would take courage to commit to "free rum and free tobacco instead of free wool and free sugar." Bruce agreed, adding that since the Negro was no longer an issue in national politics, it was time for him to depend upon his own efforts for political gains because the tariff question, not racial justice, appealed to Republicans. Predicting that many blacks would divide their vote, Bruce noted that "it will be a cold day for the [Republicans] when it becomes epidemic." This statement was purely bombastic rhetoric; Bruce would have severely disapproved of a large-scale defection. His hostile reaction to former U.S. minister to Liberia J. Milton Turner's denunciation of the Republican Party was evidence of Bruce's sentiments. As proof that the Republicans were better than their opponents, Bruce cited the racial differences at the parties' respective conventions. The Republican convention in Chicago was free of a color line in hotels, dining rooms, theaters, or public conveyances, but the same liberalism was not shown to black Democrats at the Baltimore gathering. The *Cleveland Gazette* doubted that Turner, an independent, and Democrats Peter H. Clark and Charles H. J. Taylor could draw blacks away from the Republican Party. Still, the Democrats had their black supporters. Former Republican, attorney, and clergyman T. McCants Stewart hoped that a Cleveland victory would lead to the end of the color line in political appointments, although he admitted that the American public was more concerned about the tariff than the race question.[33]

Two months before the election, the *Cleveland Gazette* suggested that blacks who supported the Democrats were "riveting the chains of slavery more firmly about their necks, and then misnaming it freedom, knowing it to be FALSE." The editor's blood boiled when he thought of those who had defected from Lincoln's party.[34] About this time, Bruce purchased an interest in the *National Leader* and promised that he and Magnus L. Robinson would "religiously and earnestly strive to make it worthy of its name."[35] His precarious financial situation, however, caused him to retain his correspondent position with the *Cleveland Gazette* and the *New York Age*.

Throughout September and October, Bruce continued to denounce the machinations of the Democratic Party in the *Age*. In the September 8 issue, he accused the Prohibitionist Party of being controlled by Democratic money. "[I]n making this statement I know what I am saying," he declared. Bruce accused President Cleveland of allowing ex-Confederate rebels and their children to hold political positions. A daughter of W. A. Jackson, a Confederate officer, was promoted from a $720 Patent Office clerkship to a position earning $900 annually. With tongue in cheek, Bruce wrote that there was no news that any of John Wilkes Booth's relatives worked for the government. One month before the election, a group of prominent blacks, including Frederick Douglass, John R. Lynch, P. B. S. Pinchback, and Robert Smalls, noted that the Democratic Party's vice-presidential candidate, Allen G. Thurman, did not believe that citizenship should be bestowed upon black men. They called upon northern black voters to use their power to defeat the enemy for "the eyes of our oppressed, persecuted and heart broken brethren of the south are upon you."[36]

A week before the election, Timothy Thomas Fortune declared that his love of race compelled him to point out that the hypocritical Republicans wanted the black vote without granting any benefits. He expressed disgust with his critics and vowed to continue to act in a wise manner. Fortune favored a tariff only for revenue. He opposed taxing poor southern farm laborers to benefit selfish northern manufacturers.[37] Bruce countered Fortune's tariff argument by stating that black Democrats believed that it did not apply to Negroes, who were not represented in the manufacturing industries as apprentices or mechanics. Bruce did not fault them for raising this issue, but he questioned their methods for redress as "unreasonable and impolitic." Bruce called upon black men to stop shooting off their mouths and to instead "organize for mutual protection." Learn not to be content with playing second fiddle, but understand that Negroes "can make as much music in politics as the white man." These were his final words on election eve.[38]

The election results shocked the nation. Cleveland outpolled Harrison by almost 97,000 of nearly 11 million votes cast, but the Republican candidate won New York and defeated his opponent by a margin of 233 to 168 in the Electoral College. The control of the national government went to Harrison and the Republicans. A jubilant Bruce rejoiced that the sons of Ham and Shem had removed from power "Grover the Fat, the chosen leader of the mugwumps and the doughface" (that is, a northern sympathizer of the South). Several of the nation's African American clergy assessed Cleveland's defeat. African Methodist Episcopal Bishop, Benjamin W. Arnett, in charge of an Episcopal district in South Carolina, thought it made no difference there who occupied the White House if the president was honest and just. Rev. B. F. Witherspoon of Mt. Zion AME Church in Charleston, South Carolina, believed that the South wanted fair play for the Negro and that Harrison would be so for all men. Rev. J. E. Hayne viewed Harrison's victory as the intervention of divine providence, and that God, through Harrison, would settle the race question. Racial prejudice would disappear, he argued, as whites noted the progress of the Negro.[39]

Despite his jubilation at Harrison's victory, Bruce still faced dire financial needs. Hoping that a change of location would improve his financial condition, Bruce moved to the Empire State shortly after the election and became the New York City correspondent for the Washington *Bee*. "J. E. Bruce is becoming strong in New York politics," reported the weekly that Bruce represented at Harrison's inauguration. Shortly before the inauguration, a delegation presented Harrison with resolutions, including one for his administration to protect southern blacks from lynch mobs. Harrison vowed to resign his office if that meant an end to injustice and led to interracial harmony. Delegate AME Bishop Benjamin T. Tucker reported that all thought "you are not president yet."[40]

Bruce's ability to ferret out information made him a valuable tool for the *Bee,* the *Cleveland Gazette,* and other papers he represented as a correspondent. He reported that politics in Washington and throughout the nation were manipulated in New York City.[41] Although Bruce's sojourn in New York was important for his career, his absence concerned his mother, who wrote him with complaints about her health. A concerned son soon returned to Washington.[42]

Harrison and African American Appointments

Upon returning to Washington, Bruce became embroiled in an appointment controversy that left many bruised feelings and strained personal relationships. Office seekers bombarded the political in crowd with requests for appointments for themselves, relatives, and friends. Responses to this quadrennial search were mixed. Frederick Douglass, whose political loyalty and elder statesman recognition was rewarded with significant appointments, ironically cautioned, "do not let us clamor for office, but rights." Sen. George F. Hoar advised Bruce that none should claim offices purely on the grounds of color or race but on the terms of character and public sentiment. Hoar believed that blacks would get diverse positions once whites respected them, but first they had to earn respect by becoming more industrious, temperate, and chaste. AME clergyman William B. Derrick called for many small appointments rather than the usual procedure of rewarding a half dozen or so big leaders. Derrick asserted that applicants should seek positions as Americans, not as Negroes. They should request nontraditional black appointments and forsake Haitian diplomatic appointments. There should not be one hundred seekers for the recorder of deeds position in Washington, D.C. Optimistically, Derrick believed that Harrison would give African Americans one-sixteenth of the appointments (more than 7,500 positions), because their vote represented the margin of victory in New York, Pennsylvania, Ohio, and Connecticut.[43]

William Calvin Chase, publisher and editor of the Washington *Bee,* concurred with Derrick's reasoning because he believed it was better to have five thousand officeholders than a half dozen diplomats with large salaries who were far removed from the people. Bruce complained that the capital city was full of office seekers who were competing instead of using their numbers to influence the appointment of those above the level of clerk, messenger, or laborer. He derided the popular wisdom that Negroes should accept positions as recorder of deeds, register of the Treasury, tax collector, and minister to Haiti or Liberia because these were the rewards traditionally bestowed upon them by Republican presidents. Like Derrick and Chase, Bruce wanted the administration to provide more various appointments, but he warned that the clique that controlled the appointment power for blacks needed to be disposed. Bruce and his allies detested the policy that rewarded men such as Frederick Douglass, John Mercer Langston, John R. Lynch, Blanche Kelso Bruce, and others for services that dated from antebellum or Reconstruction days, instead of honoring younger men who were on the front lines in the national struggle for equal rights. They also resented the white power structure, which felt comfortable with only a small select group of leaders and did not reach out to younger and more progressive men and women. Ironically, in light of later events that had the two men feuding, Bruce endorsed Chase's alleged interest in the position of Recorder because the *Bee*'s publisher was not a "chronic office seeker" but a faithful servant of the party.[44]

President Harrison was exceedingly slow in making black appointments. Nevertheless, Chase defended Harrison because he believed that the president would in proper time reward the race; he would not "endanger his party by failing to keep faith with the black man."⁴⁵ In April, the *Cleveland Gazette* declared that while Bruce deserved a Treasury position as a reward for his valuable service to the Republican Party, he was more qualified for the clerkship position than the current Democrat officeholder.⁴⁶

Bruce did not have Chase's patience. Despite his ambition, he was not discreet in his assessment of Harrison. In an April 6 *Gazette* essay, "How to Get Office," Bruce questioned the paucity of black female clerks in the national government. Bruce demanded that the Harrison administration recognize intelligent colored women or face the consequence of voters tired of seeing the same men given positions. He called upon the race to produce more manly men such as William Pledger of Georgia, who insisted that the U.S. attorney general not limit appointments to white men. Later, the appointment of a Pledger protégé convinced Bruce that voters were kings if they used their power wisely.⁴⁷ Bruce Grit reacted quickly in April when it was rumored that Harrison had replaced the black servants at the White House with white ones. E. M. Halford, Harrison's private secretary, replied that the Harrisons had brought with them "two colored servants [who were] in their employ for years . . . for duty here."⁴⁸

While appointments affected a few office seekers, African Americans were expressing more concern and alarm over Harrison's political agenda. A growing fear had slowly developed that Harrison supported an all-white southern Republican Party, a movement that had the support of some Republicans. For unknown reasons (though an appointment may have been in the works), in mid-April Bruce wrote that the president rarely expressed himself until he had given considerable thought to a topic "and then he takes his own good time in selecting an appropriate garment of English adjective [in] which to clothe it." Bruce noted in his column of May 4 that he, Robert Smalls, and Chase had consulted with Harrison but were unable to divulge the contents of their conversation. Hoping to allay fears, Bruce wrote that the race had no better friend in America than President Harrison. Bruce further declared that Harrison was a difficult man to either intimidate or mislead, adding that the president did not support the concept of a lily-white southern Republican Party. Bruce's assessment on this latter point proved to be wrong. Two weeks later, the *Cleveland Gazette* reported that Harrison had appointed a white man, Robert L. Houston, postmaster at Birmingham. Since postmaster appointments generally went to faithful black supporters, the *Gazette* questioned the decision, asserting that Harrison appeared to be in harmony with efforts to form a white southern Republican Party. This was a significant observation: Houston was chairman of the white Republican convention of Alabama. J. E. Rankin expressed a similar concern in a letter to Frederick Douglass.⁴⁹ Despite the growing suspicion that Harrison would do little or nothing to reward black voters, William Calvin

Chase (another aspirant to office) wrote in a May 11 Washington *Bee* editorial that Harrison would remember blacks in the distribution of patronage.[50]

At the time, Frederick Douglass was the acknowledged black leader in the country; yet his silence on the patronage question disturbed many, and some questioned his race pride. Douglass was a mulatto, a believer in humanism, and not one to openly discuss race pride. For these reasons, Bruce accused the old leader of wanting to get away from his race, an act he believed would not meet with armed resistance from Negroes. Bruce and others were still smarting from Douglass's 1884 marriage to Helen Pitts, a white woman, which they viewed as a betrayal of racial identity. Bruce's opposition to the Douglass-Pitts nuptial was based partly on a fear that an increase of marriages between black men and white women would cause white men to react violently against those who had access to "their" women. He also believed that too many black men who sought white partners settled for Irish servant girls who received the better of the bargain. This concern did not apply to Helen Pitts, who was an educated woman employed by Douglass before they wed. Despite his criticism of Douglass's marital choice, Bruce adamantly opposed prohibitions against interracial marriages. He used his influence in 1910 to successfully prevent New York State from enacting such a law, as marriage was in his opinion a personal decision. Bruce attacked Douglass for criticizing the black press for its "youthful imperfections" when black editors printed Douglass's ideas and agendas. Bruce was incensed that Douglass had condemned black solidarity as a vehicle that would alienate whites. Not one to suffer blows to his ego or one to take criticism lightly, Douglass dismissed Bruce by stating that he showed him mercy by his silence. An irate Bruce replied, "I do not fear his eloquence or his money." Joining Bruce in condemning Douglass's leadership was the *Cleveland Gazette,* which noted that Douglass had been lionized so long that it was impossible for him "to even dream that [he] ever did or could make a mistake."[51]

About this time, Bruce noted in an undated essay that he learned that blacks would not generally receive appointments in the South but would be appointed in the North, where they held the balance of power. Bruce calculated that the administration would opt for a lily-white southern movement in the hopes of luring dissatisfied Democrats to the Republican Party. Bruce denigrated this strategy because he believed that Harrison's first duty was to reward his faithful black supporters.[52] Remarkably, this frank and blunt assessment of Harrison occurred at a time when Bruce was seeking an appointment for himself. On May 20, New Hampshire Sen. William E. Chandler informed Bruce that he was soliciting a position for him and not to be discouraged. Unfortunately, Bruce had much to discourage him.

Bruce, Chase, and "We & Co."

While Bruce still wrote for the Washington *Bee* on occasion, his relationship with William Calvin Chase had become strained. Chase wrote cryptically on June 29, 1889: "J. E. Bruce is after the consulate at Jamaica, W. I., a good ways after it [but] he certainly will not get it as soon as Mr. Harrison examines the papers." It is not certain that Bruce was seeking a diplomatic position, and there is nothing in his papers to support this claim. Chase's sinister threat did not prevent Bruce's friends in Congress from attempting to help him. In March 1890, Rep. Byron M. Cutcheon informed Bruce that he was trying to find a position for him to replace his present employment in the Department of the Interior. On April 1, Sen. William E. Chandler wrote Rev. James M. Townsend, "I shall not get any other colored gentleman a place until I can get a suitable one for . . . Bruce."[53]

While Bruce's friends in politics sought to find him a suitable position, he did little to help his own cause. From late May 1889 until June 1890, Bruce, Henry C. Smith of the *Cleveland Gazette*, the *Bee*'s William Calvin Chase, and others engaged in a mean-spirited debate about the quantity and quality of Harrison's black appointments. Bruce and other dissenters questioned the leadership and challenged the right of Frederick Douglass and a few other old guard members to be spokesmen for the race. However, Harrison slowly began to make black appointments. The *Savannah Tribune* heralded Harrison's appointment of AME clergyman James M. Townsend, former member of the Indiana legislature, to the position of recorder of the General Land Office, and the appointment of former Congressman John R. Lynch as fourth auditor of the Treasury.[54] Unimpressed, Bruce wrote that these appointments were nothing to commend because neither Townsend nor Lynch had important positions. Again, Bruce called for an end of rewards for the old guard. The *Gazette* joined Bruce in questioning Harrison's appointments. After Harrison appointed Douglass as resident minister and consul general to Haiti, the black weekly noted that the president and the Republican leadership should understand that young black Republicans were neither followers of the old leaders nor blind party loyalists. "The sooner this is understood the better it will be for the party," Smith wrote.[55]

The *Gazette*'s disapproval was mild compared to the outrage Bruce felt when it was rumored that Harrison would appoint a white man as recorder of the deeds, a traditional plum for Negro patronage. Bruce was irate that by July 1889 blacks had received only seven minor appointments even though thousands of Democrat holdovers were still in office. Bruce faulted civil service exams because they discriminated against black applicants by asking them ridiculous questions such as "How far is Jupiter from Venus?" or "How many battles did Julius Caesar engage in?" Except for James M. Townsend, who came from Indiana, Bruce was upset that not a single black northerner was awarded a position, an affront to the balance of power they wielded in several states.[56] By the end of summer in 1889, eleven men of color had received appointments to positions with salaries ranging from $1,000 to $5,000 per annum. The *Gazette* reported in October that about twenty clerkships were given to blacks in Washington. A month later, the *Gazette,* incensed that none of the old guard black leadership had challenged Harrison on his accommodation to southern race hysteria, blasted Douglass and others as "miserable, fawning, cringing office seekers."[57]

Harrison's appointment of Blanche Kelso Bruce, a black former U.S. senator from Mississippi and one of the old guard leaders, elicited strong support from some and harsh criticism from others. The appointment of B. K. Bruce (no relation to John Edward Bruce) as recorder of deeds in early 1890 elicited praise from Chase. He viewed the new recorder as "a man of ability, sterling integrity, general and affable" whom "only the pot house politicians [would] abuse and try to traduce."[58] The *Bee*'s publisher's warm praise was motivated by his desire to entice B. K. Bruce to assist him in landing a government position. Immediate criticism of the appointment came from the *Cleveland Gazette,* which questioned the president's decision to ignore home rule and appoint a citizen of the District of Columbia rather than B. K. Bruce, who still voted in Mississippi.[59]

John Edward Bruce cautiously chose not to criticize President Harrison for the appointment. (He was still seeking a position for himself.) Instead, he castigated B. K. Bruce, John R. Lynch, Frederick Douglass, and other "leaders" for lacking race pride and backbone in light of racial oppression. He contrasted their collective silence with that of Sen. William E. Chandler, who appealed to Americans to give generously to seven mothers and their twenty-five children who were now without husbands and fathers after a lynching at Barnwell, South Carolina.[60] In March, Bruce Grit complained that B. K. Bruce had reduced Henry Johnson's salary, demoted him from his deputy recorder position, and replaced him with Colonel Schayer, a white German. Perhaps stung by the charge that he reduced Johnson's salary, the only black male employee in the office with a fixed salary, B. K. Bruce protested the criticism. Nevertheless, in the April 26 *Gazette,* a defiant Bruce Grit wrote his refusal to back down from facts that he considered irrefutable.[61]

The *Bee*'s editorial appearing in the May 3 issue claimed that Johnson was never a deputy recorder of deeds and that the man who started this rumor was "a liar, thief and poltroon." Bruce Grit responded in the *Gazette* that while Johnson may not have been a deputy in name, he was often in charge of the office as a de facto deputy under James M. Trotter, B. K. Bruce's predecessor. More to the point, Bruce Grit called on the *Bee* and B. K. Bruce to explain why a white Democrat was the deputy when Schayer's Democratic club passed resolutions opposing appointments of a Negro to the recorder's position. Bruce also demanded to know why the recorder was replacing some black female workers with white ones. The disgusted critic dismissed the *Bee*'s editor as a "brainless ass . . . truckling sycophant and toady." [62]

William Calvin Chase sought to dismiss Bruce Grit by reporting in the May 17 *Bee* that John E. Bruce, alias Charles E. Bruce, had been convicted in 1876 for forging the name of William J. Murtagh to a check for ninety dollars to Henry Roane. The felon served one year in the New York State penitentiary at Albany before President Rutherford B. Hayes pardoned him on April 14, 1877. Chase's accusation served no purpose except to raise doubts about Bruce Grit's character. An examination of the records did not indicate the race, color, occupation, or any description of the convicted individual that would confirm Chase's allegation.[63] Bruce Grit shrugged off Chase's forgery accusation because he expected nothing less from an "intellectual abortion evolved from mud, who thrives best on mud and whose name is mud . . . will seize me by the seat of my trousers and the nape of my neck and souse me in [mud]."[64] As much as he disliked Chase, Bruce Grit detested B. K. Bruce more because the latter represented himself to whites and blacks alike as a leader. Defending himself, on May 24 B. K. Bruce informed the *Washington Post* that he saw no need for two deputies. Henry Johnson was the confidential man of his predecessor; therefore, he decided to retain him in a lesser capacity. Angered that Schayer earned $1,600 more than Johnson for performing the same duties, Bruce Grit responded sarcastically in the May 31 *Gazette* that a white recorder would never appoint a Negro deputy

> because they believe
> a nought's a nought
> a figger's a figger,
> all for the white man
> and none for the nigger.[65]

Bruce Grit's hammer blows against recorder Bruce led the *Gazette* to speculate that some wanted their outspoken correspondent dismissed from his minor position in the Department of the Interior.[66] Throughout June and July 1890, perturbed that B. K. Bruce did not look out for his fellow black man, Bruce Grit offered no apologies for his relentless attack. "I spoke as a Negro, and I spoke in defense of my race," he declared. In the June 21 *Gazette,* Bruce Grit described how he visited the recorder's office and found it segregated, with Henry Johnson in a back room. Again, Bruce classified Schayer and the white female and male clerks as Negro-hating white Democrats. He condemned B. K. Bruce for not employing a single colored female, while Trotter employed two or three. J. E. Bruce was so certain of his charges that he vowed to apologize and make reparations for any injuries resulting from his accusations if, indeed, he was wrong. This he would do, he said, not out of fear of losing his position in the Department of the Interior but because it would be the manly thing to do. "I am not yet ready to make a recantation. I stand by what I have written," he added unapologetically.[67]

Believing that Bruce Grit was on the defensive, the *Bee,* in a July 5 editorial titled "Hold Up Viper, You Bite a File," hurled thunderbolts at Henry C. Smith and the *Cleveland Gazette.* The *Bee* accused Smith of jealousy because his candidate failed to get the recorder's position and because Smith was upset that his appointment as deputy coal inspector in Cleveland paid only one hundred dollars per year. Other black weeklies shared anger against Chase and B. K. Bruce. The *Gazette* responded that the *Agitator,* of Buckeystown, Maryland, reported that Chase flunked out of Howard Law School, cheated his employees, slandered males and females alike, and was a scoundrel. After Chase was appointed food inspector in the District of Columbia's Health Department, the *Virginia Lancet* commented that the job might teach him something about "cleanliness and decency." The *Pine Bluff Echo* in Arkansas was equally vicious in its attack on Chase. The weekly stated that B. K. Bruce was behind Chase's appointment as a reward "for dirty services" provided by one who had abused the trust of his race.[68]

While the saga over the appointment of Blanche Kelso Bruce finally came to near closure in September 1890, after the recorder dismissed Schayer from his position, bitter feelings between the principals continued for years. In June 1894, the *Bee,* without naming Bruce Grit, noted that a correspondent for the *Indianapolis World* (which Bruce then wrote for) was a former convict who had abducted his illegitimate daughter.[69] Again, Bruce Grit's admirers dismissed these speculations; but others, doubtful of his character, assumed the worst. A lesser man would have backed off from further controversy, but Bruce Grit proved that grit was a worthy description of his character. His battles against racism, political indifference on the part of the Republican Party, and ineffective black leadership continued.

Congress, the Race Problem, and Harrison's Failure of Leadership

Bruce's fight with Chase and B. K. Bruce about responsible leadership, while significant, was only one of many important battles that Bruce Grit was involved in during this period. In 1890, Congress debated two important bills to assist African Americans in education and voter rights. Sen. Henry W. Blair of New Hampshire proposed that the federal government provide for an equal distribution of funds for white and colored school districts in the South. This was a significant proposal to combat the machinations of southern racists whose control of all schools led to inequities for black youngsters. Not only did black districts receive less funding, requirements for black teachers were lower than for their white counterparts, which resulted in poorly prepared teachers making up the bulk of the teaching staff. Many black schools, particularly in rural areas, operated for only four months during the year, as youth were expected to tend to crops. Many whites looked on education for blacks with intense disfavor. They believed that education ruined blacks and made them unfit as laborers. Only federal intervention could guarantee equal access to quality education for hundreds of thousands of African American boys and girls. Bruce reported in the March 15 *Gazette* that his canvass of a number of senators indicated that many questioned the Treasury's ability to meet the extra demands the bill would place on it. Despite the good intentions of progressive whites, the bill was defeated. Senator Blair suggested that the opposition of the Roman Catholic Church led to the defeat. Bruce suggested that it was a combination of the Catholic Church, the Democratic Party, and the white press. He warned that the powerful influence of the Roman Catholic Church would someday "grab the United States by the nape of the neck and paralyze it from center to circumference." The Constitution, he cautioned, was in jeopardy because Catholics would subordinate it to the will of the Pope. The failure to provide equal funds for the South's dual school system left black schools segregated and unequal in buildings, supplies, and teacher preparation. This became part of the suit that culminated in the famous Supreme Court decision *Brown* v. *Board of Education, Topeka,* sixty-four years later.[70]

Granting the franchise to African American males was one of Reconstruction's greatest achievements. Redeeming the South under Democratic rule led to repression against blacks. Denying or suppressing the franchise for black males would be an issue that would help define the ugly nature of segregation until its demise in the sixth decade of the twentieth century. Massachusetts Rep. Henry Cabot Lodge introduced a bill in June for the federal supervision of national elections in southern states where fraud and intimidation made a mockery out of the concept of "one man one vote." Bruce demanded that Congress enforce the second section of the Fifteenth Amendment, which called for the proportional denial of seats in those states that prevented blacks from voting on grounds not related to residence or moral standing. Rev. C. N. Grandison, president of Bennett College in South Carolina, opposed the Lodge bill because its passage would embitter southern whites. Bruce countered by claiming that Grandison was concerned about offending conservatives who occasionally donated money to black churches or schools. "I rather not take a dollar of their money and be a man, than to take one and be a cringing, groveling, dependent upon their charity," Bruce exclaimed. In August, Bruce requested that Lodge's Federal Elections Supervision Bill be amended to place all questionable districts under control of the federal government. In February 1891, ex–Assistant Postmaster General James S. Clarkson predicted a Republican defeat in 1892, claiming that if the Lodge bill was not passed, one million voters would be disfranchised in the South. Clarkson believed that the party could not escape blame for its defeat because Harrison was a Republican and there was a Republican majority in both branches of Congress. Surprisingly, Bruce changed his mind about the bill after researching the subject for a debate. He decided that the bill should not become law because it was unenforceable. Inexplicably, Bruce argued that the passage of the bill would endanger the physical safety of thousands of southern Negroes who did not need to add more martyrs to the cemeteries. While Bruce did not question the sincerity of Lodge and his supporters, he deemed the measure twenty years too late. Bruce attempted to explain his abrupt change of heart by stating that he was responding as a Negro who would not desert his race, not as a party man. Instead of passing the bill and having blacks face extermination, he uncharacteristically claimed that his race had the patience to wait for the moment "when truth shall have a hearing and the muse of history shall open the book, when justice shall triumph over wrong and liberty shall be universal."[71] In contrast, Frederick Douglass argued that the problem was national indifference, not the Negro. The government, he insisted, must protect the rights of its colored citizens or admit its moral depravity and prepare to fall from God's grace. The Lodge bill passed in the House of Representatives, but a similar bill introduced in the Senate by George F. Hoar of Massachusetts was laid aside on a technicality.[72]

While it appears that Bruce wavered from his reputation as a race-first man and looked to providential intervention to solve the race problem, his retreat from proactive politics was based on his growing disillusionment with the Republican Party. A fellow dissenter was James M. Townsend, recorder of the General Land Office, who urged white Republicans to embrace death, if necessary, for their party. Townsend declared boldly in 1890, "I am a Negro. I am a Republican . . . but if its success in the South means ostracism and death for my people, I as a Negro say to them make terms for my people." Townsend's bluntness resulted in political heat for the outspoken officeholder. Bruce defended Townsend's assertion that John R. Lynch, fourth auditor of the Treasury, thought the race believed the cup was filled because he, Frederick Douglass, and Townsend had received office. Townsend took exception to Harrison's reliance on B. K. Bruce, Douglass, and Lynch for advice because he considered them cringers and apologists for the administration. These manly words from a government employee heartened Bruce Grit, who lamented that the same "leaders" that planned an assault upon the administration in the spring of 1889 had traded their silence for beef and five-cent cigars. He resented the influence of the "we & co." who basically had the right to approve Harrison's lesser black appointments. They were able to wield this power because Harrison knew so few blacks and he was ignorant of the Negro's diverse skills and talents. Bruce Grit bluntly declared that Lynch and company represented "decaying brains" who "would rather take crumbs from the white man's table than have a table of their own." Bruce called for real leaders instead of those who tried to convince the people and political parties that they led when they did not. In a personal dig at Douglass's interracial marriage, Bruce wrote in February 1891 that the people wanted leaders "who cannot be swayed by fawning white women."[73]

Others, besides Bruce and Townsend, openly questioned the failure of the Republican Party to defend its black supporters from atrocities. In March 1890, the *People's Advocate,* a Washington weekly, dismissed Douglass's often-cited axiom that the Republican Party was the ship and all else was the open and treacherous sea. Instead, the new image should be one of the Republican ship that "has gotten off her moorings and finds better sailing in the Democratic sea of blood, than in the open ocean of light and justice." Thus, he urged the Negro to "cast about for a raft which will drift into some safe haven." Alternatively, editor John Cromwell considered it wiser for blacks to boycott the 1892 election rather than have their "ballots neutralized by the [Republican] party."[74]

A combination of factors contributed to dissatisfaction with the Harrison administration. Republicans setbacks in local and congressional contests in November 1890 prompted Bruce Grit to blame the defeat on the party's poor leadership, which had "perverted, distorted and twisted beyond recognition" the party's original pro Negro platform. In Bruce's estimation, the party's failure to obtain a one-cent postage in 1880 to remove the internal tax on homegrown tobacco, to pass a national educational law, and to provide protection for southern black voters had cost the Republicans twenty-one congressional seats. To worsen matters further, Democrats captured state houses in New York, Massachusetts, and Iowa the following year. Stop reminding people that you are the party of Lincoln, if you expect to win in 1892, Bruce admonished Republicans. As James S. Clarkson suggested, Bruce insisted that they must put Negro newspapers on their campaign payrolls, just as they pay for campaign advertisement in the white press.[75]

Bruce and James Clarkson

The year 1891 was eventful as Bruce Grit continued his attack on the misguided racial policy of the Republican Party. Despite his harsh criticism of Republican leadership, Bruce still hoped to gain a better political position. Like the majority of aspiring blacks in the late nineteenth century, John Edward Bruce turned to a white benefactor to assist him in obtaining funds, an appointment, or both.

James S. Clarkson would not only play this role; he would also be Bruce's close and intimate friend until his own death in 1918. Clarkson, fourteen years Bruce's senior, a descendant of the British abolitionist Thomas Clarkson, was an Underground Railroad operator in Iowa from 1855 to 1861 and a zealous advocate for black civil and political rights. An assistant postmaster general from 1889 to 1890, he was now in charge of Negro appointments in the South. He had lived there for several years, and Clarkson was one of the few whites who felt at ease with blacks, regardless of their social status. Clarkson, who met Bruce in 1891, expressed to him that "the black race is the sympathetic race of the world." More than most white Americans, he understood that his generation should settle the question of race hostility; they should "not leave it to the next generation of white men."[76] Clarkson served the Republican Party as a member of its national committee from 1880 to 1896, as well as serving as its chair, and it was in these positions that he sought to serve Bruce and black Americans.

Clarkson's friendship was welcomed. He was a sympathetic insider who helped Bruce as often as he could. However, Bruce had other white benefactors. One was George Chandler of the Department of the Interior. While the facts are incomplete, Bruce became involved in 1891 in a work-related problem that called for an internal trial against him based on charges brought by a watchman in the Pension Office. Chandler informed Bruce on August 3 that he received his letter written two days earlier; and, although he was unable to dictate to the Commissioner of the General Land Office of the Department of the Interior, he promised to conduct a fair investigation. While the outcome of the investigation is unknown, Bruce felt unwelcome and contacted James S. Clarkson and others for assistance in securing a position elsewhere. In late August, A. B. Nettleton, assistant secretary in the U.S. Treasury, informed the embattled writer that there were no funds for hiring more inspectors for the immigration service in Washington. On September 11, 1891, Clarkson, now president of the National Republican League in New York, regretfully wrote his friend that he had not found him an agreeable position where he could show his true talent and "fidelity for work." Clarkson lamented that lesser men than Bruce received promotions, but that was the nature of political patronage.[77]

Bruce was desperate for additional funds to take care of his invalid mother, who had resided with him since 1890. Sometime in that year, Bruce, R. M. R. Nelson, and T. T. Symmons formulated a plan to send relevant items weekly to the politicians' constituents, for a five-dollar monthly fee, from the *Congressional Record* collated from newspapers and journals. The idea, Bruce lamented, was not implemented because it was stolen and put into operation by some white men. Choosing not to wallow in self-pity, on April 23, 1890, Bruce and associates organized the Associated Correspondent of Race Newspapers in Washington to provide subscribers a weekly newsletter of current social and political events. Bruce was the group's first vice president. Approximately one hundred black weeklies, and a few white ones, subscribed, but the endeavor went bankrupt several months later because too many subscribers failed to pay in advance. In the spring of 1891, Bruce formed a partnership with C. A. Johnson and Alex G. Davis in the National Capital News Syndicate to provide relevant news clippings to subscribers.[78] Later, in 1919, the idea of circulating news clippings among the black press led to the founding of the Associated Negro Press by Claude A. Barnett, a reporter for the *Chicago Defender*.[79]

Certainly Bruce's attempts to organize black press associations were commendable in themselves, but they underscored his desperate efforts to increase his earnings. Throughout the first half of 1892, he turned to James S. Clarkson for assistance. Bruce told Clarkson on July 1 (this letter is not extant) of his disappointment with the Republican Party, which prompted his mentor to reply on July 13 that the party's interests outweighed personal disappointments. Citing himself as an example, Clarkson noted, "I bear no scars . . . and have suffered no disappointments; and even if I had they should not weigh against anything of party concern or welfare." Clarkson advised Bruce to remember that intraparty rivalries would hurt Republican chances in November. He informed his friend that he had asked John W. Noble, the secretary of the interior, to give him the place he desired. "I hope you may find favor in his eyes and an appointment at his hands," he added.[80] It is not known whether Bruce received the promotion, but he was still employed at the interior a year later. Meanwhile, he supplemented his income in the fall of 1891 by establishing the National House Cleaning Bureau in Washington. It was located at 614 F Street Northwest (not his home address) and was patronized by Mrs. John A. Logan, who wrote him encouragement that his services were needed in the city.[81]

The Campaign of 1892 and the Triumph of Cleveland

As noted by Clarkson, triumph for the Republicans in November was crucial, and the black vote in several key northern states was needed for victory. The chairman of the Speakers Bureau for the Republican National Committee informed George A. Myers, a prominent black barber in Cleveland and a major ally of Ohio Gov. William McKinley, that it was crucial that loyalists keep the colored vote in line, as there were few stalwarts such as John R. Lynch or Fred Douglass who could be called upon.[82] Ironically, the chairman stressed the importance of younger black men stepping forth, an issue that had concerned to Bruce and others.

While there was the usual talk among dissenters of bolting to the Democratic Party, most blacks considered this an impossibility. Nevertheless, the

Cleveland Gazette warned that the Democrats represented "the devil let loose" and dismissed colored Democrats as "blind miserable, contemptible creatures . . . to be pitied rather than censured."[83] Unfortunately, the Republicans took the black vote for granted and underestimated their dissatisfaction with Harrison's neglect of issues of vital concern to African Americans. For example, the president alienated many when he sought to make lynching a federal crime to protect the lives of foreigners while at the same time ignoring the lynching atrocity perpetuated against American citizens. Former governor and U.S. senator William P. Kellogg informed Republican Party leadership before the election that the black vote was lost. Even the death of Carrie Scott Harrison, the president's wife, shortly before the election, did not provide Harrison with a sympathy vote. However, Bruce sought to console him by assuring the president that "a star in its brilliance has set but the light of its beauty we will not forget."[84] Grover Cleveland was able to recapture the White House because of the low black turnout in key states, the growing popularity of the Populist movement, and the angry defection of immigrants alienated by the antiliquor laws in the Midwest.[85]

During the waning days of the presidential campaign, Bruce dealt with the progressively worsening illness of his beloved mother, Martha Allen Clark Bruce. After suffering with a painful affliction for sixteen years, she died on December 8. He eulogized her as "a Christian without ostentation; she was an affectionate and devoted mother; she was loyal in her friendship; and I loved her with all the intensity of my nature, and honored her for her simple faith and rock ribbed integrity." Bruce wrote this public tribute to his mother's memory for "pleading with the master to save her boy." "God bless her. I loved her as I loved myself," he declared. Four years later, Bruce was still mourning her passing. Again, he praised her for sacrificing all for his well-being regardless of the burden it placed upon her. He viewed his unlettered mother as "the noblest work of God. May the Negro race continue to produce good mothers."[86] Rev. Alexander Crummell consoled Bruce by writing that all mothers were saints and that "if we could only . . . think day by day about our mothers, what noble and exalted men we could always be. [87]

Sometime in late 1892 or early 1893, Bruce moved to Cincinnati, Ohio, where he worked briefly for Perry S. Heath as a reporter for the *Cincinnati Commercial Gazette* before returning to Washington.[88] In February, Bruce sought an interview with James S. Clarkson on the topic of a recent lynching. Bruce urged him to speak out in order that the "chicken hearted" blacks might protest against the atrocities. "Certainly this condition cannot last much longer. How long O God! How long!" he lamented. Bruce was probably referring to an incident in Tyler, Texas, where a mob of five thousand watched a victim slowly roast for close to an hour. Bruce predicted that unless the national conscience halted the madness, anarchy and revolution might result. Eventually, he stated that God would have revenge because He made the Negro not to seek retaliation. Like the ancient Jew, the Negro is the lamb of sacrifice; but he will triumph over the bloody southern beast that seeks his extermination, Bruce declared.[89]

Bruce tempered his militant remarks with a nod to Providence. His strong religious faith and his unwavering belief in providential intervention showed that he would, at times, leave matters in God's hands. Since Bruce saw and judged most events or incidents from the perspective of an oppressed person, however, he usually reacted swiftly to condemn oppression. In this context, Bruce questioned in March 1893 whether Cleveland had removed the Negro servants who worked under Harrison from serving in the White House.[90] While this may appear to be a petty matter, for Bruce it represented race love to look out for the interests of all blacks regardless of class or social standing. Unfortunately, this type of persistence in defending the rights of his race created enemies who sought to exploit his precarious financial situation. Working mostly as a clerk or messenger, Bruce did not earn enough from his government position to afford to live in the same place more than a few months and rarely for a year. His newspaper writing paid little, if any, and he generally rented rooms. On April 12, 1893, James K. Jones, a "Dem[ocrat] Negro shylock," according to Bruce, wrote that L. D. Green of New York State provided him with two of Bruce's notes worth $16.20. Jones demanded that Bruce satisfy the two notes in full within three days and that the balance should be turned over to the secretary of the interior. Jones was true to his word. On May 10, Hoke Smith ordered the commissioner general in the Land Office of the Department of the Interior to discharge Bruce from his laborer's position paying $660 per annum. Bruce wrote in the margin of his discharge notice "mah walking papers," and, after Smith's signature, he inscribed "a Georgia viper."[91]

Upsetting as this setback was, Bruce kept up his spirits, and he sought employment to add to his meager earnings from writing assignments. By January 1894, Bruce had relocated from Washington to Albany, New York, where he took residence at 11 Congress Street. Encouraged by a Democrat in the White House and the lackadaisical race attitude of the Republicans, southern Democrats began the effort to remove protection for African Americans from the legal statutes. Bruce was extremely critical of the silence of American clergymen as the enactment of Jim Crow laws further eroded the civil and political rights of blacks in the South. He informed Alexander Crummell that he had no respect for white Christians with caste feelings. Indeed, he believed that "the new winter resort ... *Hades* would have to [be enlarged] to accommodate the large number."[92] Despite this strong censure of American Christianity, Bruce believed that the Negro's destiny was in the United States because God was in charge of "our destiny [which] is . . . linked to the chariot wheels of American civilization . . . and the nation's honor is pledged to protect us [as citizens]." Since it was Bruce's contention then that American Negroes were citizens (a claim he would later refute), he did not support programs for mass emigration to Africa or Brazil. He deemed this a "cowardly" policy that "ought not as it will not, find favor among the most intelligent and thoughtful men of the race."[93]

In 1894, two years before the presidential election, many black office seekers were hoping for a forthcoming Republican victory that would mean the possibility of patronage for them or their friends. Timothy Thomas Fortune, however, continued to criticize the Republicans for their habit of seeking the black vote only to ignore it after the elections. Bruce was close to journalist Fortune, whom he first met in 1874 when Fortune attended Howard University. They would remain friends until Bruce's death in 1924, though there were brief periods of estrangement. In an unidentified article, circa 1894, in Fortune's papers, Bruce expressed his admiration for the *New York Age* editor, noting that he was Fortune's friend "in sunshine and in shadow." Bruce did not even fault Fortune for flirting with the Democratic camp in search of something "outside of the great Republican ship." He added, "no truer race man lives than Tom Fortune." Bruce's respect for Fortune was genuine, although the *Age*'s editor was both an integrationist and assimilationist, while Bruce was a black nationalist and an evolving Pan-Africanist. Fortune thanked Bruce for defending him while others hurled their thunderbolts.[94]

The Campaign of 1896, McKinley's Victory, and the Patronage Clamor

Though Bruce sought a Republican victory in 1896, his barbed criticisms of politicians made it difficult for him to become an insider. That role was the domain of others. Jere A. Brown of Columbus, Ohio, suggested to Mark A. Hanna, McKinley's manager, that it was imperative to have five black Ohioans at the Republican convention to interview black southern delegates. This would convince them that McKinley was not racially biased. Brown urged Hanna to become acquainted with George A. Myers because southerners had confidence in him. Brown boasted that Myers never leaked confidential information but was a shrewd political tactician. He also urged Hanna to work out a plan with Myers for St. Louis, arguing that "then we will be prepared to capture the enemy, by carrying the war into Africa."[95]

In June, Samuel R. Scottron, an inventor and a member of Brooklyn's colored elite, informed John P. Green, a colored former justice of the peace and Ohio assemblyman, now a member of the Ohio senate, that he should do all he could to assure that "McKinley & protection" were nominated.[96] After McKinley easily won the nomination over Thomas B. Reed, Matthew S. Quay, Levi P. Morton, and William B. Allison, an Afro-American News Syndicate was formed to advocate the election of McKinley and Garret A. Hobart. Bruce was one of the twenty-one contributors, along with Timothy Thomas Fortune, Robert H. Terrell, John H. Smythe, Benjamin W. Arnett, and Richard T. Greener. Their mission was to enlist support for the ticket among the readers of more than two hundred black newspapers.[97]

Despite the formation of the syndicate, the Republican Party was indifferent to the active participation of black men other than John P. Green, John R. Lynch, or another of the "old" leaders. In August, Hanna informed Daniel Murray, an assistant librarian at the Library of Congress, that it was never the intention of the National Republican Committee to have colored men added to an advisory committee or any other committee. Bluntly, Hanna stated that McKinley could be elected without assistance of "some particular class" because he had no real competition from his opponent.[98] A mere six weeks before the election, Edward W. Blyden wrote the following to Bruce: "so the Negro has been eliminated from politics. The best thing that could have happened to him in the South." Blyden suggested the formation of a third party that would enable them to "sell themselves to the highest bidder." Understanding "the peculiarities of the colored people," Blyden concluded that such an organization would be impossible. Blyden added that if such an organization were formed, whites fearing its power would crush it. Though Blyden expressed dismay at the race's political prospects, he believed that America still offered hope. He cited Harvard awarding Booker T. Washington an honorary Master of Arts degree as an example that "the American people are too practical not to respect, honor and utilize a *man* of whatever race when they find one."[99] Ironically, a week later, Ernest Lyons, chief of the Republican National Annex, informed John P. Green that, as no colored delegation outside of Ohio had met with McKinley, a committee representing several states was forming to meet McKinley at his home in Canton, where he received delegations and responded to their previously submitted questions or concerns. Green agreed to be a delegate, but on October 15, Lyons canceled the trip because only sixteen of the one hundred invitees could afford to pay their own traveling expenses.[100] Shortly before the election, Bruce was invited to be one of the secretaries at an October 28 Republican mass meeting in Albany, thus facilitating the services of a potential maverick on behalf of the party.[101]

McKinley's victory over William Jennings Bryan elicited favorable editorial opinions from the black press. The *Freeman*, an Indianapolis weekly, gleefully noted that "mobocracy is rebuked, sedition is halted and populism is lame of gait." These theories, the editor suggested, would never again confront Americans.[102] Again, office seekers hoped to attract the attention of McKinley or one of his subordinates for the usual race appointments. For some, however, the stakes were higher. A public debate on the wisdom of placing a black man in the president's cabinet went on for several months. It was an idea that elicited both praise and horror. Eight months before McKinley's victory, James S. Clarkson suggested privately to Booker T. Washington that he wanted a president that had the courage to appoint a Negro to his cabinet. Clarkson conveyed the same message to Bruce several weeks after the Republican victory: that it was vital for the party to reaffirm its "apparently waning faith in the equality of men."[103]

Clarkson's suggestion was not original. The call for a black man in the cabinet dated back at least to 1880 when William Calvin Chase issued the charge. Chase reiterated this demand in July 1896. But it was a November 7 editorial in the *Washington Post,* a race-baiting Democratic paper edited by Beriah Wilkens, that would create a furor in the black press over the wisdom of the suggestion and the motives of the *Post*. The names of John Mercer Langston, Blanche Kelso Bruce, Richard T. Greener, and other leaders were bandied about, but it was Booker T. Washington that gathered the most support. Neither B. K. Bruce nor Washington publicly encouraged the clamor for a cabinet position, but the former privately requested Washington three times to inform McKinley of his interest in the position of register of the Treasury. Washington eschewed participatory politics and declared that under no circumstances should "Negroes . . . be appointed to offices involving personal contact with white people."[104] This was consistent with Washington's wish to avoid a controversy that would jeopardize his standing with the philanthropists who funded his Tuskegee Institute.

Neither McKinley nor the Republican leadership considered appointing a black man to the cabinet, but the usual lesser positions were kept available. This caused a scramble among the power brokers and their protégés. AME Bishop Benjamin W. Arnett, an Ohio politician, informed Myers on November 11 that "the colored contingent should not be 'left out' of the plum pudding." Ralph W. Tyler suggested to George A. Myers on November 14 that it would be a good idea to select men for a few representative positions. They could then use their influence to obtain "positions of minor importance for the lesser lights." Tyler stressed that those selected should be hard workers because the Democrats would unite in 1900, and there would be no defections to aid McKinley's reelection bid. Tyler insisted that it was important that these men be northerners, where "we have a voice in the elections," instead of southerners who came from where the black vote was undermined by fraud and intimidation. It was his contention that blacks should be given the positions of recorder of deeds, fourth auditor of the Treasury, register of the Treasury, and recorder of Land Office as rewards for loyalty. Tyler added that they should receive a consular post, but not Haiti, a traditional Negro assignment, which was an explosive mission that required a professional diplomat. Giddy with their role in McKinley's significant victory, defeating William Jennings Bryan by 195 electoral votes, many believed that the incoming president would, in the words of one job seeker, "recognize our people in more ways than we have had heretofore." Few could deny that black men should seek positions "not marked for colored men only."[105]

John Edward Bruce worked diligently for McKinley's victory and sought an appointment in his administration. He had married Florence Bishop in late 1895 and now needed funds. Once more, he contacted James S. Clarkson, then in private life serving as president of the board of directors of the Standard Telephone Company in Philadelphia. Clarkson responded to Bruce on November 26, "I believe there lies in you a great deal of latent ability of a superior sort which is not yet developed." Bruce had not found a position by the beginning of 1897, which he informed Clarkson on February 2. Two days later, Clarkson suggested that Bruce contact Louis T. Payn, a newly appointed insurance commissioner who would be Bruce's "best friend ... in New York if you could gain his friendship." Hard luck Bruce had lost an unidentified position and Clarkson was hopeful that Payn might get him reinstated or, "if not, [provide] some little position where you could earn bread for yourself and family." Bruce even contacted the White House for a position but was informed by John Addison Porter, McKinley's private secretary, that his letter with enclosures was placed in the file for the president's consideration.[106]

Others, who believed that they were entitled to eat high off the patronage hog sought appointments more aggressively. John P. Green believed that his loyalty warranted a presidential appointment. F. J. Loudin informed him in April 1897 that "McKinley [was] not falling over himself to appoint a black man or drop plums into his waiting mouth."[107] Green desired the recorder of deeds position and had the support of his close friend John D. Rockefeller.[108] By early July, Green's son, Will, suggested that Mark Hanna either reward Ohio's black politicians or the people would turn to other political parties. Hanna telegraphed the elder Green on July 10 with news that he had a position for him as superintendent of the stamp division in the Post Office Department. "Do you want it?" he asked. Green reluctantly accepted the minor position, but the coveted recorder's position went to Henry P. Cheatham of North Carolina. This decision disturbed many who believed that black southerners were being rewarded at the expense of northerners.[109] Blanche Kelso Bruce, still seeking the register of the Treasury position, wrote confidentially to Green on July 25 to tell Charles Dick, chairman of the Republican National Committee's Executive Committee, "that my appointment will be hailed with delight by the masses of our people ... and that they are expecting the appointment." After he got his desired position several months later, writer Charles W. Chesnutt wrote to Green, "I presume he had the longest pole, or the strongest pull." Green's position, the first for a person of color, required little work on his part. A minor controversy erupted when eight white clerks threatened to resign over his appointment, but Green's pleasant demeanor diffused the situation.[110]

Bruce did not receive a major federal position; his outspokenness made him appear untrustworthy to McKinley's inner circle. His disappointment was abated somewhat in early 1898 when he was elected a member of the Republican Party's executive committee in Albany's Thirteenth Ward. The *Colored American* newspaper in Washington hailed the election as a benefit both to Bruce and to local Republicans in upstate New York.[111]

The Spanish-American War and African American Responses

In early 1898, as the nation pondered a possible war with Spain, local politics took a secondary position. The sinking of the battleship *Maine* in Havana, Cuba, in February 1898 elicited the cry "Remember the Maine." Warmongers sought revenge; speculators and investors wanted to open the Cuban and Puerto Rican markets to Americans; and others adopted a "my country, right or wrong" attitude. Spain's defeat in the "splendid little war" created an American empire that stretched from Puerto Rico to the Philippines. In a few years, the United States would acquire the Panama Canal Zone and extend her economic and political influence into the Caribbean. Meanwhile, African Americans viewed the approaching war with ambivalence. Bruce Grit anticipated war and confidently predicted that "five or six of [Uncle Sam's] best Negro regiments will be more than a match for twice as many Spanish regiments." Bruce was so eager for a war that would allow black men "to vindicate themselves from the charge of cowardice and lack of patriotism" that he overlooked the fact that there were then only four commissioned colored regiments. Lewis Douglass, son of Frederick Douglass, believed it was hypocritical to fight for a nation that could not protect them from southern mob rule. AME Bishop Benjamin T. Tanner noted that President McKinley would not recognize a liberated Cuba because of its large population of people of African descent, a statement with which Bruce concurred.[112]

Black ambivalence did not abate during the brief three-month war that freed Cuba, Puerto Rico, and the Philippines from Spanish domination. George A. Myers expressed appreciation for Adm. George Dewey's victory in Manila Bay, which ended the hostilities, but he noted that the government needed to protect colored Americans from white mobs before interfering into the business of other nations.¹¹³ Myers had a point. A cursory examination of race relations during the war with Spain demonstrated the danger faced by black men in *uniform* in the South. The Colored Regulars—the Twenty-fourth and Twenty-fifth U.S. Colored Troops and the Ninth and Tenth Calvary—departed their western posts in April 1898 to Georgia and Florida to await orders. On April 10, Easter Sunday, the Twenty-fifth Infantry departed from Fort Missoula, Montana, with cheers echoing in their ears. At Chattanooga, they encountered segregation; they were placed in railroad "nigger cars" to travel to Chicamauga National Park in Georgia. There, and elsewhere in the South, the men encountered numerous incidents of racism until southerners learned that they would retaliate. Black citizens were amazed at the boldness of the soldiers. In Georgia, one civilian said, "Good lawd! jess wait till dey's all gone; den you'll see hard times about heah!"¹¹⁴

The mistreatment of black soldiers enraged F. J. Loudin, manager of a black touring singing and acting group, who wrote to John P. Green from Dublin, Ireland, that his blood boiled when he read about the racist treatment shown the Twenty-fifth Infantry. He wrote sarcastically, "I long to hear that the Spanish fleet has cast anchor off [our southern] hell holes and is pouring lead and iron so they will know the great day of [God's] wrath is upon them." Loudin wanted the war to last until the nation needed "the Negro so badly that they will treat him as a man and a soldier." In exasperation, Loudin added, "I don't see how the thinking Negro can hold his peace."¹¹⁵

Bruce dissented from Loudin's analysis of the war's impact on American race relations. He argued that it was suicide for African Americans to let their differences with the government override their patriotic duty. Those who held this conservative view hoped that the black man's bravery, heroism, and courage would defeat American prejudice and reinforce his claim to citizenship rights. Perhaps Bruce, who believed that the Civil War heroics of black soldiers led to citizenship and voting rights, hoped that African American participation in the war against Spain would yield similar civil and political rights gains. While some of Bruce's contemporaries saw the war with Spain as an example of American imperialism, he believed that it meant freedom for Cuba's predominantly black population. An inspired Bruce wrote Cuba Libre.

> O bankrupt, proud and haughty Dons!
> Your hour of doom is near;
> And the oppressed of Cuba's isle
> as freemen then will shout
> The stars and stripes for them will be
> a sure and safe defense;
> and o'er the land, and o'er the sea,
> they'll send their compliments.¹¹⁶

Ironically, Bruce saw gains for black Americans based on the heroics of black soldiers. However, he was willing to overlook the possibility of American prejudice enveloping Puerto Rico and Cuba. Instead, Bruce had been captivated by the prevailing anti-Spanish (and anti-Catholic) sentiment. In his May 14 *Colored American* article, "The Doom of the Spaniards," he characterized Spain's history as four centuries of "bloodshed, rapine and murder" that deserved condemnation instead of sympathy. The war, Bruce insisted, was the world's death sentence against the Iberian nation for its atrocities against the Aztecs and Incas.[117]

Some black critics of the war were not concerned about the morality of the war or the nation's imperialistic plans. For them, the war was a fact; therefore, appoint Negro officers for the Colored Regulars and particularly for the newly formed Negro volunteer regiments. During the summer of 1898, Congress passed legislation that formed ten black volunteer regiments known as "The Immunes" in the belief that Negroes were genetically exempt from yellow fever. Intense political pressure led to the commission of black officers in "The Immunes." Although this appeared to be a liberalization of the army's policy, it was, instead, a political compromise made because the military realized that placing black officers in the Colored Regulars would replace the white officers.[118]

The majority of the black press supported the idea of black officers for the segregated troops. John Mitchell Jr., an early critic of the war, initiated the demand for all black volunteer units to have Negro officers with the slogan "no officers, no fight." Bruce noted that the slogan would find a sympathetic response "in the breast of every Negro who has a spark of manhood in his anatomy." Bruce urged Mitchell to ignore criticisms of his slogan from the likes of the *Washington Post,* which he considered a "journalistic hermaphrodite." Accusing the Democratic paper of ignorance of Negro history, Bruce suggested that President McKinley would give the race "a fair deal . . . in the distribution of posts of honor to the army" because he read black writers and sought advice from John P. Green and George A. Myers. To hammer home his point that the president was fair, Bruce recalled the time when McKinley gave him a job endorsement, and while they were visiting the president displayed a copy of J. T. Wilson's *The Black Phalanx.*[119]

John P. Green, despite receiving a low-level federal appointment, agreed and instructed John M. Clark, president of the Colored Voters League in Pittsburgh, to postpone a convention demanding more representative positions in the Republican administration. Green argued that the race was treated better "both in civil office, and the army than ever before in the history of the nation."[120] This partisan view was unacceptable to Alfred Brewington, who was assigned to Camp Eagle Pass, Texas. A former member of the black

Tenth Calvary but now serving in a white regiment, Brewington complained that white enlisted men had vowed not to "salute a nigger officer." An outraged Brewington protested but was court-martialed and fined ten dollars. "We have a hard! hard time with these people! What has the poor colored man done that the white world looks on him with a frown?" Brewington asked. Believing that this racist behavior was conducted under McKinley's watch, a dejected Brewington added, "we had just as well make the best of it as we can, and make up our minds to take what they may choose to give us, for we will be oppressed by them for years! and years to come!"[121]

The defeat of Spain in 1898 quickly led to the United States acquiring territory in the Caribbean and in the strategically located Philippine Islands. Filipinos welcomed independence from Spain but resented American jurisdiction. Guerrilla units waged war for four years before being forced to yield to a superior military force and to acquiesce to American rule. Puerto Rico came under direct American control, and commonwealth status was imposed upon its populace. Cuba's politics and economics was strongly influenced by the United States until Fidel Castro's rise to power. In all these areas of American control, an emphasis on a rigid color line was introduced. It was feared by some observers in the United States that the American color line in postwar Cuba would result in a race war. However, Bruce hoped in early 1899 that the Maceo Party (named after martyred freedom fighter Antonio Maceo) would possess the strength and ability "to maintain all its legal and constitutional rights in . . . Cuba."[122]

Bruce's strong endorsement of American involvement in the Spanish-American War reflected a conflict in his race philosophy. As a race-first advocate, he viewed fighting in an imperialistic war acceptable if African Americans benefited by displaying their bravery or showing leadership as officers. He viewed their participation in the war as additional arrows to shoot down the racist utterings of bigots. It was Bruce's argument that the nation needed to recognize the fighting ability of black men, which would lead to recognition of their citizenship rights. This attitude, of course, failed to consider the larger picture. Just as the Colored Regulars had fought against Native Americans to benefit a racist nation, they now fought to spread American imperialism and, unwittingly, racism without any tangible benefits. Neither lynching nor the denial of civil and political rights of African Americans stopped because of the valiant efforts of black soldiers in the war against Spain.

The Rise of Booker T. Washington

The war proved to be a short diversion from the reality of American political life in the dawning days of the nineteenth century. In 1895, the most important black political figure since Frederick Douglass would appear on the scene in dramatic form. Within a few years, Booker T. Washington would become the most powerful and influential black man in America. His relationship with President Theodore Roosevelt and other influential whites would allow him to build a powerful "Tuskegee machine" that would stymie the efforts of African Americans opposed to accommodationism. Bruce's initial attraction to the racial policy of Booker T. Washington was not out of line with that of the majority of African Americans. Hindsight would suggest that Washington's call for blacks to assist whites in working for "mutual progress" while avoiding agitation for political and civil rights would result in an outcry against the educator. To the contrary, most blacks accepted his message because public segregation had not yet become all-inclusive throughout the South. Many naively believed that the changes in southern constitutions would only deny the franchise to the illiterates of both races. Within a few years, however, the franchise would be denied to African American males regardless of literacy. In his famous "Atlanta Cotton States Exposition Address," Washington's theme, "Cast Down Your Bucket," was a metaphor for both races to cast their lot among each other for the mutual benefit of the South. Washington's view that the Negro needed to earn respect before he was entitled to the franchise resonated with many in the nation. This abdication of equal rights (even if temporary) would later be known as the Atlanta Compromise. Not yet knowing or anticipating the horrors of the Jim Crow system of racial segregation, Bruce wrote Washington on October 14 thanking him for a copy of his speech. He added that the speech was "like old wine, it improves with age." Bruce agreed that black people must first improve themselves intellectually, industrially, and morally before seeking equality with whites. He denigrated those who spewed out an "interminable twaddle about Negro equality in the South to intensify the feeling against the black race and to retard its progress." Bruce praised the educator for holding the "key to the solution of the problem," and he assured him that he could do much to inculcate "the idea that *personal worth* is the one thing needful in the development of the Negro character." Here, Bruce was expressing a view shared by others that blacks had to overcome the obstacles and handicaps of slavery before they could be intellectually equal. Even W. E. B. Du Bois, who would in a few years become one of Washington's vocal critics, expressed favor with Washington's speech as "a word fitly spoken." Bruce, Du Bois, and others who initially approved of the speech agreed with Washington's call for black self-reliance; they did not or chose not to see the potential repercussions of accommodationism.

Washington's critics, who were few in 1895, lashed out at his compromising remarks. The Washington *Bee* castigated the speech in an October editorial as "an apology for the white Negro haters of the south." Editor Chase added several weeks later that the speech was "as poisonous to the Afro-

American Negro as that wasp that stung Cleopatra." They differed in ideology, but Alexander Crummell agreed with Chase that there was nothing to admire in Washington's outlook on industrial training. Long an advocate that civilization was attained by achieving a "higher culture" through literature, science, and philosophy, Crummell suggested that the Negro's educated elite, or "talented tenth," would lead the race forward.[123] Interestingly, Edward W. Blyden, then visiting in the United States, offered several perspectives both on Washington's speech and on race relations in the country. The Liberian informed Washington that his document compared to George Washington's "Farewell Address." Blyden shared Washington's belief that blacks should start at the bottom and find dignity in even the lowest position. The concept of social equality was derided by Blyden, who insisted that "it is a matter of taste which is not in our power to regulate." As an erudite man, Blyden frequently engaged socially with whites while traveling in Europe. Even in the United States, officers of the American Colonization Society entertained him. On September 15, Blyden wrote to Rev. Francis J. Grimke to cite his real opposition to social equality. He noted that, upon his return to the United States, America had become a materialistic nation that lacked an "appetite for true greatness and great achievements." Blyden asserted that instead of scholars, statesmen, and poets of the past, the new America had bowed down to the Vanderbilts, Astors, Goulds, and the other captains of industry who wanted to be American royalty. Elite whites coveted "record breaking steamships, fast sailing yachts, swift horses [and] political bossism" that, if attained, would lead to "enormous vanity and inordinate egotism." Blyden faulted the Negro for imitating a value system that made him "an imitator of imitators." The Negro is freed, Blyden noted, "but he has not yet found a way to clothe his naked liberty with the habiliment of self respect, good judgment and moderation, so as to make himself presentable and acceptable not only to his former guardian but to himself."[124]

Alexander Crummell, Bruce's mentor, provided a different perspective. Crummell informed his friend that it was his responsibility to correct "t[he] foolish & errant nonsense of ... unthinking men who presume to lead t[he] Negro race ... but who ... despise t[he] Negro." If this was a criticism of Booker T. Washington, whom Crummell did not like, Bruce did not respond to the reference. The aging Crummell boldly stated his criticism of false leaders because he recognized in Bruce a commitment that few men possessed. Crummell concluded that "God has given you [Bruce] great capacity for good ... but intellect is nothing without divine ... assistance for ... God plants t[he] highest motives."[125] Although Bruce heard his mentor's praise; as a pragmatist, he sometimes let financial concerns determine his choice of associates. Bruce's financial concerns led him into Washington's snare. On July 16, 1898,

Emmett J. Scott, Washington's private secretary, informed him that Bruce's piece in the *New York Age* (about Washington's Albany, New York, speech) was "a magnificent tribute." In the article, Bruce stated his surprise at Washington's demeanor. Critics had painted him as one who delighted white audiences with darky jokes as well as a man who "lacked moral courage and backbone." Instead, Bruce found Washington to be "the bravest and most outspoken young Negro orator I have ever listened to and he is true and loyal to his race." Bruce further noted that Washington was devoted to humanity and that he could count on his "public support from now on." It is possible that the two met in Albany because Washington had read Bruce's writings and indicated a desire to meet him at the event there if time permitted.[126] Bruce became one of the writers who shored up Washington's image in the twilight of the nineteenth century, and, according to Louis R. Harlan, Washington's biographer, Bruce may have been on the educator's payroll when he wrote favorably about the Albany speech. Harlan suggested that Washington might have employed Bruce as early as 1896. Washington wrote to him on April 21 of that year, telling him to "use your pen as much as possible. You help all along the line." It is also possible that Scott, Timothy Thomas Fortune, or Charles W. Anderson, all friends of Bruce, introduced him to Washington. In 1899, Bruce received one hundred dollars to write four pieces defending Washington against northern black critics that had met at the Afro-American Council Convention in Chicago that August. In his letter to the *Springfield Republican,* published in the September 11 issue, Bruce endorsed industrial education as the solution for solving the race problem. He praised the Tuskegee Wizard for eschewing the entanglement of political alliances. However, things were not rosy behind the public facade. Both Fortune and Washington found Bruce's demands for more money petty. Fortune informed Washington on August 28 that he had told Bruce four days earlier to provide only facts about the August 26 sessions and not to include his prejudices or preconceptions. According to Fortune, Bruce wrote some "splendid" letters to the editor but had withheld two from the mail because he wanted more money for "committing himself to our view." After some haggling over price, Bruce gave Fortune the third piece, which surpassed the first two. Bruce eventually wrote and submitted the four letters, but at a cost to his reputation. In a series of letters to Washington, Fortune described Bruce as a "scamp," a "cur," as well as an "Albany blackguard." After sending Bruce a check for eighty dollars, Fortune informed Washington, "I can't imagine a more depraved character than he is, *but his capacity for mischief is very great*. I think the $100 will cork him up, as he hardly let go a dollar when he gets hold of it." On September 7, Fortune informed Washington that he had discussed Bruce with Bishop Alexander Walters, head of the Afro-American Council, someone who considered Bruce "*a good man but* not *a man to trust."* Bruce's behavior also annoyed Edward E. Cooper, publisher of the *Colored American* newspaper in Washington, D.C., who refused to print some unfavorable pieces that he wrote about Washington. Cooper informed Bruce that he was a friend of both men but that he should "ring off . . . in his talk of [Washington]." Cooper promised Washington, "I shall control him [Bruce]." On September 16, Washington forwarded Bruce's favorable letter to the *Springfield Republican* to Fortune with the following note: "He is, as you suggest, a queer individual."[127] Evidently, Cooper or Fortune convinced Bruce to "get aboard." In the September 16 *Colored American,* and reprinted the following week, Bruce faulted northern Negroes for criticizing Washington at the Afro-American Council meeting. He praised the educator for training southern blacks for citizenship, for teaching them how to earn their living, for showing them how to be men, and for refraining from declaring politics as the only solution for race advancement. Bruce added that thoughtful race men (such as W. E. B. Du Bois, AME Bishop Henry M. Turner, and AMEZ Bishops Alexander Walters and George W. Clinton) repudiated the attacks against Washington. On October 28, Washington forwarded to Fortune galley proofs of Bruce's essay "The Wizard of Tuskegee," which was scheduled for inclusion in the November *Howard's American Magazine*. Pleased but perplexed by Bruce's changed demeanor, Washington commented, "he seems to be piling it on." Fortune responded a few days later that Bruce greatly admired Washington. "You get some queer fish in your net," he added.[128]

The uncertain relationship deteriorated more in 1901 when Bruce joined W. E. B. Du Bois and Monroe Trotter, two of the Tuskegee Wizard's principal critics. The lack of a Bruce diary for this period makes it impossible to understand his motivations fully. An assessment of the Bruce-Washington relationship must consider two factors. First, Bruce always attempted to ally himself with those who purported to advance the cause of the race. It was his hope that Washington had a solution to uplift black people from their myriad problems. Many of Washington's critics, too, were persuaded at first that the educator's self-help program would yield positive results. Like Bruce, they later became disillusioned. Although Bruce believed that Washington had the solution for uplifting the black masses; he left the relationship once he realized that Washington's efforts were aimed less at advancing the rights of blacks than at developing his own political machine, stifling opposing viewpoints, and representing himself as the only practical and logical spokesman for African Americans. Second, Bruce was motivated by a need for funds that Washington supplied. Unlike Fortune and William Calvin Chase, two who became dependent on Washington's largess, however, Bruce had enough sense to walk away when he realized that the loss of his integrity would be the price for his support. Washington clearly tolerated Bruce's "queer" behavior because

Bruce Grit was considered by many to be "the greatest Negro writer in America." Publisher Edward E. Cooper considered Bruce "a storehouse of racial information" who had the ability to get the attention of the Associated Press and the nation's large dailies. Charles Alexander, author of *One Hundred Distinguished Leaders* (1899) considered Bruce "the prince of Negro correspondents."[129]

Militant but Cautious

Bruce's entanglement with Booker T. Washington was not completely one of silver in exchange for ideological accolades for the educator. Bruce shared some of Washington's caution for radical change even as he continued his own pursuit for justice for African Americans. He sought to examine the issues of his day with a pragmatism that eluded agitators who saw a militant reaction as the only weapon in their arsenal. Bruce had a reputation for militancy, but he was also a cautious man who preferred intelligence to brute strength. On December 1, 1898, Bruce attended a mass meeting in Troy, New York, to protest racial atrocities in North and South Carolina. His message to the audience was a sober reminder to meet terror with brains for "the Negro is not prepared, or disposed, if prepared, to resort to . . . the torch, or dynamite, in retaliation for wrongs heaped upon him." By suggesting that "there is much heroism in bearing wrongs . . . as there is in resenting them with force," Bruce displayed the influence of Washington. He stated that Negroes should be patient and appeal to "the good heart and . . . conscience of the Christian white[s] . . . whose liberties and rights under these appalling conditions are no less safe than our own." Displaying almost a martyr complex, Bruce concluded that both Jews and Negroes were the sacrificial lambs whose ultimate victory would be attributed to "their calmness, in their resignation, [and] in their innocence."[130] While Bruce would utter firebrand comments on future occasions, his moderate view in the twilight of the nineteenth century met with the approval of others. Former Reconstruction politician Pinckney Benton Stewart Pinchback echoed Bruce's sentiments when he cautioned the Troy audience to avoid an impulsive rush to violence "or wholesale denunciation of the entire white masses." John C. Davey of Allegheny, Pennsylvania, wrote Bruce, "you are evidently looking ahead. The best minds in . . . both races endorse [your] attitude."[131]

Black militancy was met with swift criticism from the white press. *New York Age* editor Timothy Thomas Fortune's remarks on December 19 in Washington's Zion AME Church caused a furor. There is confusion over Fortune's actual comments, but his reported remarks included a condemnation of President McKinley for betraying his black supporters by not taking forceful action against bigots who killed innocent blacks in Wilmington, North Carolina. (Privately, he told Booker T. Washington that the president was "a thoroughly despicable character and I despise him.") Fortune stated, "I want the man whom I fought for to fight for me, and if he don't I feel like stabbing him." Fortune was bitter that McKinley had toured the South and observed "throwing daises over rebel graves." Fortune later attempted to explain that his stabbing remark referred to retaliation at the ballot box and was not a threat to assassinate McKinley. Nevertheless, the press condemned the outspoken editor. Bruce considered the criticism of Fortune's comments harsh but fair. In a January 7, 1899, editorial in New York's *Binghamton Chronicle,* he noted that Fortune's comment was more incendiary than those uttered by the wildest anarchist and that his remarks represent more of a threat to Negroes than that of a thousand white bigots. While Bruce did not believe that Fortune literally meant what he said, he advised him to repudiate the remark because nothing was gained from such "rash and indiscreet utterance."[132] Mrs. J. M. Holland, the Washington correspondent for the *New York Tribune,* confided to Washington that Fortune was drunk and could not "separate his own ideas from the others." While Fortune's words may have been intemperate, they reflected a strong anti-McKinley bias that worried the president's black confidants. George A. Myers wrote John P. Green ten days before Fortune's remarks that he had warned "uncle," his pet name for Mark A. Hanna, that the forthcoming December 29–30 Afro-American Council meeting needed to be controlled by the administration's supporters. Otherwise, Myers warned, McKinley opponents would dominate the proceedings and hurt the president's reelection chances. Myers advised Hanna to make plans to capture and control the council's agenda by consulting with George H. White, congressman; Henry P. Cheatham, recorder of deeds; Judson W. Lyons, register of the Treasury; John C. Dancy, collector of customs at Wilmington, N. C.; and Green. Myers suggested to Green that he persuade McKinley to push legislation to appease the outrage over the Carolina massacre. This, he expected, will show the Negro "that his confidence has not been misplaced." Myers again sent instructions to Green on December 20. Eight days later he advised his friend to get into the game of politics and play to win. Hanna conferred with Myers on the eve of the council's meeting and noted that things were under control. However, he asked, "what is the matter with John Green?" When Myers was evasive, Hanna replied, "they tell me John is a little sore because he did not get a better job." Myers passed this conversation on to Green and suggested that he see Hanna to tell him that "blood is thicker than water and the outrages perpetrated upon my people ... makes my blood boil." Although Hanna believed that he had the council's leadership under control, he expressed his concern about Fortune to Myers, who replied that he tell the president "to kick him out if he ever showed up at the White House again."[133]

The well-laid plans of Hanna to control the Afro-American Council's meeting failed to prevent discussion on a resolution to censure the president for his silence on southern lynching. Green tried to quiet the assembled body with a declaration that Elmer Dove, secretary of the Republican National Committee, had previously told him that black leaders advised the president not to act. Bedlam broke out, led by Fortune's indignant demand to know the names of the Judases. No names were volunteered. Green later learned that AME Bishop Benjamin W. Arnett, Judson W. Lyons, and Henry P. Cheatham had cautioned McKinley that mentioning lynching in the State of the Union address would lead to increased violence against blacks. Green saw McKinley on New Year's Eve and suggested that he ignore the criticism. The president replied that protest was "an old song."[134] Shortly after the new year, 1899, Jere A. Brown wrote a congratulatory letter to Green for his courage in standing up against the malcontents at the Afro-American Council gathering while the president's "friends" on the platform were mute. "Oh that you had told that T. T. Mis-Fortune to go and ask the president if he desired [the names of the Judases]. He would not have dared to have done so and I am sure you would have flattened him." Brown complained that Arnett and Lyons should not have been quiet since they received presidential favors. "Shame on Bishop Alexander Walters and Fortune," exclaimed Brown, because "black ministers, editors, and bishops have gone mad in their opposition to McKinley." "You are the only redeeming quality that participated," concluded Brown.[135]

The madness suggested by Brown was nothing more than a combination of disappointment and anger over the president's silence on southern racial atrocities. African Americans who believed that their support of the Republican Party deserved more respect elicited a variety of responses. Appeals were heard for providential intervention or retaliatory violence, while others suggested emigration to Africa or Cuba. Bruce denounced in the January 12 issue of the *Star of Zion* "all of these threats, schemes, and hysterical utterances [as] the children of folly and unworthy of men who are in reputation for wisdom." He excoriated Bishop Henry M. Turner's call for emigration to Africa as "impractical, impossible, utopian and visionary." Bruce dismissed Timothy T. Fortune's rhetoric as "revolutionary and dangerous." Nor did he condone AMEZ Bishop Alexander Walters's call for retaliation against white violence in Georgia. "I am no more a coward than is Bishop Walters, but I am not ready to subscribe to this sentiment." Unlike the bishop, Bruce did not think that progressive whites would join blacks in shedding "their family" blood. Bruce believed that whites were clannish and that, for his people, a race war would be suicidal. This does not mean that Bruce habitually eschewed violence. He noted that if blacks were truly united, retaliation might be justifiable; but unprepared and rash Negroes seeking revenge would be cannon fodder for every southern governor. Moreover, a mean-spirited white press would simply call blacks barbarians, brutes, and demons. He also feared that the southern accusers would fabricate stories of "black brutes [ravishing] fair flaxen haired victims before cutting their throats or dashing out their brains." These lurid but false accounts, he claimed, "would be published in northern papers by alleged eyewitnesses." Then, northern whites would join "their kinsmen by blood" and decimate defenseless Negroes. Rather than take this risk, Bruce advised that northern whites would sympathize with innocent victims by seeking federal laws for their protection. The religious Bruce suggested that people "keep cool, God is not dead, and his justice sleepeth not." Again, Bruce declared that the race should engage in an intellectual battle to prove their worth as citizens of the world. To follow visionaries, theorists, revolutionists, and anarchists would only widen the gulf between the races. Bruce faulted his people for not understanding that diplomacy (meaning accommodation) gained more than aggression. He emphasized that "the Negro is still a creature of impulse, an imitator, a braggart in debate and a procrastinator." Eschewing violence, Bruce contradicted an earlier held view and called upon the African American to use his potential political influence to seek favorable administration policies and not necessarily well-publicized but meaningless appointments.[136]

This sober analysis of the southern race problem was bolstered by Bruce's contention in February 1899 that because 40 to 60 percent of eligible black males there were denied the franchise, the second section of the Fourteenth Amendment to the U.S. Constitution should be enforced to reduce southern congressional representation. Daniel Murray, a black assistant librarian at the Library of Congress, wrote to Bruce on March 1 with the revelation that he wanted to do "something of . . . lasting benefit to my race." He confided that a census committee had brokered a tacit agreement. Murray had informed Illinois representative Albert J. Hopkins that an amendment to the census bill called for a proportional reduction in Congress for those states that practiced discrimination. Murray had hoped to keep this information secret, but the *New York Evening Post* had leaked it a week before Murray wrote to Bruce. The paper boldly proclaimed that the Republicans wanted to break up the solid Democratic South, increase the importance of the black vote, and return the Republican Party to its former role of protecting the rights of African Americans. Unfortunately, the Republicans chose not to enforce the Fourteenth Amendment but decided to urge the present Congress to authorize the census returns and perhaps have the next Congress use the census to determine patterns of voting discrimination.[137]

Bruce's Criticism of William McKinley

The Republican Party's failure to condemn the South harshly for its denial of civil and political rights to blacks disturbed Bruce, who placed the blame on the shoulders of President McKinley. Mindful that his assessment of the president's leadership might cost him, Bruce castigated McKinley for his visit to Thomasville, Georgia, hometown of Mark Hanna, within a week after the lynching of several blacks in South Carolina. Bruce classified this visit as an arrogant disregard for the feelings of Negroes, similar to Nero fiddling while Rome burned. Bruce added, "who will deny that [McKinley's] attendance at this Negro cakewalk while members of their race were wallowing in their own blood . . . was an insult to the Negro race. I say who will deny it?"[138]

Bruce's outburst against McKinley was motivated partly by his disappointment at not receiving a government position. Bruce would vacillate during this period between militant denunciations of the white political power and appeals to his white benefactors for an appointment. This approach caused him to appear undirected at times, as he sought a middle ground between the two positions. Bruce had walked into a quagmire when he became involved with Booker T. Washington. He sought to abate that dependency in late 1898 and the following year. His hopes were raised when nine members of a Republican organization from the Thirteenth Ward in Albany signed a statement endorsing Bruce for a position as head porter at the capitol. In mid-1899, James S. Clarkson, president of the New York and New Jersey Bridge Company, notified Bruce that he was seeking support for Bruce through New York Sen. Thomas C. Platt. Platt, the state's Republican political boss, dealt with patronage matters by counties, so Clarkson advised Bruce to go through a Mr. Coles. If Coles was receptive, Clarkson promised to inform Platt about Bruce's skills and capabilities. Clarkson thought Bruce suitable to work on the forthcoming 1900 census. A few weeks later, however, he expressed sorrow over Bruce's financial troubles and his inability to assist him immediately. Clarkson vowed to let Bruce know of any suitable position because of his deep affection and respect for the embattled writer. In late December 1899, Bruce's friend Sen. William E. Chandler promised that he would try to find an appointment "that will enable you to earn your living." In February 1900, Clarkson informed Bruce that he (Clarkson) had been considered for a position in the U.S. Senate but that his name had been withdrawn after several senators influenced by a large corporation objected. Clarkson declared that, if elected, he would have tried to find Bruce a "fine position as I fully appreciate your merit; capacity and needs." Clarkson was dismayed that the New York Republicans did not help Bruce and, if they were not careful, the Democrats would take advantage, as they had found places for colored men.[139] Some gossipmongers spread the rumor that Bruce's dismal job search was jeopardized by his criticism of McKinley's southern policy. An irate Bruce bluntly dismissed the "chicken hearted Negroes." "I don't happen to be a mealy mouthed politician, neither am I a poser," he thundered. "Neither do I say things for effect. Neither am I looking for office under McKinley." He was contemptuous of "body and knee benders [who] crawl and cringe and lie and fawn and slobber over President McKinley." Bruce praised former President Ulysses S. Grant, who had provided federal protection to the former slaves. McKinley, in contrast, was interested only in using the Negro vote for his political ambition. Vowing not to vote for McKinley in 1900, Bruce boldly declared that "if this treason make the most of it." Bruce was becoming so dissatisfied with Republican leadership that he considered the possibility that dividing the black vote was an answer to the southern race problem.

This sentiment, if only an expression of a disappointed office seeker, was a significant gesture on the part of Bruce. Once a staunch Republican, Bruce vowed in 1899 to vote for James C. Matthews, a black incumbent Democrat, for Albany County recorder. He subsequently urged some blacks to desert the party to give more leverage to those who remained. Those who left could always return, he noted. He justified this shift in his political allegiance by declaring that even President McKinley sought an alliance with southern Democrats by endorsing a sentiment to bury former Confederate soldiers in national cemeteries. To the dismay of many, McKinley advocated pensions for ex-Confederates and even wore on his lapel a Confederate button, a gift from a former rebel.[140]

The dawn of the new century saw Bruce standing at a crossroads. His brief courtship with the Tuskegee Wizard provided him with needed funds but at a cost to his reputation as an uncompromising ideologue. His acrimonious attack on President McKinley took him beyond the pale of most black editors and certainly cost him favor among some Republicans who were in a position to help him financially. Bruce had ventured down the slippery path known as accommodationism, but he quickly retraced his steps. In front of him was the rocky path marked agitation. This was the road he chose to travel, but his desire for a position caused him to veer off the road at times.

National Politics, 1900–1923

Bruce may have flirted with the Democratic Party by vowing to support the candidacy of James C. Matthews, a politician he had opposed previously in a partisan contest; but this was more in the spirit of helping a "brother" than any manifestation of a switch in political allegiance. Bruce was angry with the Republican Party for its indifference toward the southern race issue, but he was astute enough to realize that black Americans had more friends within the party than without. Thus, he did not give up working with progressive Republicans to initiate progress on the racial front. Bruce was among the dozen guests of George Henry White, the nineteenth century's last black congressman, who met for dinner in Washington's Gray's Hostelry in early January 1900. The illustrious diners included Pinckney Benton Stewart Pinchback, a former Reconstruction politician in Louisiana; Bishop Alexander Walters; librarian Daniel A. Murray; and editors Timothy Thomas Fortune and Edward E. Cooper. The purpose of the meeting was to discuss the merits of the Crumpacker bill, which reduced representation in Congress in those states that used fraud or intimidation to disfranchise black voters.[1] Edgar Dean Crumpacker, an Indiana Republican, wanted to determine, from the 1900 census, the percentage of persons denied the suffrage because of race. It was a controversial proposal that Fortune advised Booker T. Washington to avoid.[2] Bruce declared that the federal government needed to enforce provisions of the fifteenth amendment to prevent southerners from revising their state constitutions to disfranchise Negro voters who were previously eligible.[3] Bruce wrote in the *Colored American* at the end of January that the Afro-American Council's financial committee (of which he was the secretary) needed funds for a test case in Louisiana over the disfranchising of black voters. It was his suggestion that churches set aside a Sunday for a special collection, that school children donate one penny each, and that all Negro societies tax members five to twenty-five cents to aid the cause. Bruce noted that it was imperative for the race to rally around this issue because "this question of 'rights' is the most important question of the present century." He declared that whites would start treating blacks with respect if they saw African Americans donating funds for their own liberation. Bruce exhorted members of the race to use their vote as a weapon to pressure Congress to respond positively to George Henry White's antilynching bill. "Sentiment to the dogs! Stand by your race and your rights. If you do not, you won't have influence enough to elect a dog catcher," admonished Bruce.[4] Bruce was forceful in his language because bigots in 1900 rejected the argument that the United States was the rightful home of black Americans. Their suggestion that blacks should emigrate or face extermination made him livid. Upon learning that Alabama Sen. John T. Morgan, a former Confederate general, favored black emigration to Africa, Bruce retorted that black men had voted in five states when the U.S. Constitution was ratified. Bruce challenged Senator Morgan to study history to learn that the civilizations of the world were indebted to the African race [5]

Bruce and the Antilynching Movement

The lynching of black Americans plagued former slaves who were helpless in the face of a hostile South, where lawlessness reigned. Increasing Republican disinterest in atrocities committed against African Americans placed blacks in a precarious position. Calls for retaliatory violence were futile, as were efforts to persuade Congress to enact antilynching legislation. Still, Bruce's call for support for Congressman George H. White's lynching bill was fortuitous, for the lynching issue was widely discussed in the nation's black press throughout 1900. In April, the *Colored American* questioned the sincerity of America's tears over the Alfred Dreyfus Affair in France, its willingness to shed American blood for the liberation of Spain's subjected people, and its sympathy for the Boers in their struggle against the British in South Africa. The nation was silent, noted the *Colored American,* when they read of mobs butchering and burning innocent black American citizens. Few whites demanded that Congress or the president take action to prevent the wholesale slaughter. Bruce satirized lynching in "A Southern Pastime" by suggesting that southerners who were bored with the routine practice of lynching "niggers" should enliven things by requiring that "first class" lynching parties include all of the state's elected officials. Bruce recommended that handbills advertise the coming attraction with the promise to use only the "best pitch pine and bush wood ... 95 proof standard . . . oil [for] saturating the [victim]." After the burning, "choice cuts of roast darky" could be made available for sale, as well as teeth, heart, and liver of the deceased. He wrote that it should be a family affair with affordable fees that would allow all to enjoy coon songs, "Dixie," and cakewalks. Photographs of the event could be sold and a percentage of the proceeds used to benefit heathens in foreign lands. Tragically, this satirical account closely resembled some newspaper accounts of actual lynchings. In a more serious vein, Bruce wrote the pamphlet *The Blood Red Record* in 1900, a critique of the lynching epidemic since 1893. Placing America's moral laxity in an international perspective, Bruce noted in a letter to Wu Ting Fan that hypocritical American Christians could profit from the Confucianism tenets of brotherhood.[6] The editor of the *AME Church Review* sarcastically expressed happiness upon learning that some whites had been victimized by lynch mobs as "we have for a long time waited for." "There is no reason," he suggested, "why the best citizens . . . should not command the best victims in the market." Tongue in cheek, he concluded, that it would be preferable to lynch one honorable Caucasian than five hundred "ignorant trembling Negro[es] of no social standing."[7]

The lynching question also attracted the attention of Americans traveling abroad. Frederic J. Loudin, manager of the Loudin Jubilee Singers, wrote to Bruce from London in early 1900, reporting that Americans in England were spreading anti-Negro propaganda to discourage British resolutions against lynching. Loudin implored Bruce to inform the American public that Great Britain needed support in her conflict with the Boers in South Africa. (Hostilities broke out on October 11, 1899, after Great Britain sought to gain control of South Africa's gold reserves, which led to sympathy in Europe and the United States for the resisting Boers). Loudin informed Bruce that, if victorious, the Boers would enslave Africans. Events proved Loudin correct; many blacks were killed or died of starvation during the seven-month war. Like many Americans of African descent who lived in Europe (he toured there from 1898 to 1903), Loudin was moved by the lack of visible racism on the continent and the British Isles. From long distance, Loudin kept abreast of the American political scene. He had no love for McKinley and informed Bruce that he would give former President Grover Cleveland a thousand votes rather than "bloody McKinley" one. Loudin held those of his race who blindly voted the Republican ticket in low esteem because "nothing but a rebuke at the polls is going to arouse the party who *owned us body and soule* [sic]."[8]

The Reelection of McKinley and Bruce's Change of Heart

Loudin's remarks resonated with many in the United States, as McKinley offered little sympathy for the plight of African Americans. He and other Republicans refused to press the South on the race question. Bruce's initial misgivings about the McKinley's administration and his criticism of the Republican Party's stance on the race question would abate while he sought a government position. However, as a proud black man, he wanted the party to acknowledge its debt to his race. Bruce identified the eradication of lynch violence and the protection of southern black voters as the key issues (from a black perspective) in the presidential election of 1900. A twenty-five-man committee representing the Afro-American Council presented these two demands to the Republican National Convention that convened in June.[9] Both Bruce and Timothy Thomas Fortune, reported the *Colored American,* presented a clear analysis of the Philadelphia gathering.[10] Bruce's analysis, however, did not meet with everyone's approval. Bruce complained that the absence of African Americans on the convention's important committees and from the party's councils made them mere figureheads. As an example, he described an event that occurred while he was with a delegation that sought to meet with the resolutions committee. The chair sent out a black man, James Hill of Mississippi, with instructions to give them just three minutes to convey their sentiments. Disgusted, Bruce wrote, "this is the straw, and if it doesn't indicate which way the wind is blowing, what does?" He suggested that it was only the party's fear of losing the southern black vote that prevented it from reducing southern black representation at the convention. Bruce predicted that the party would ignore their southern Negro loyalists, if they could attract more southern white Republicans. William A. Pledger, the leading black Republican from Georgia, denied Bruce's claim that blacks had no influence at the convention and stated that black members served on all committees.[11] In a broader context, it was irrelevant to Bruce whether black men served in few or large numbers on convention committees. His concern was with the party's commitment to protecting the rights of southern blacks and rewarding faithful black loyalists.

To shore up McKinley's reelection chances, the Republicans selected Theodore Roosevelt, a popular Spanish-American War hero, as its vice president nominee. This decision pleased editors at the *Colored American* newspaper, who noted that the "Rough Rider" would bring to the campaign "the most striking personality that the country has seen in two decades."[12] Despite Bruce's criticism of the Republican Party, he had a keen interest in who would be selected as McKinley's running mate. Months before the Roosevelt's selection, Bruce praised New York Lt. Gov. Timothy L. Woodruff as someone who had the respect of the black community. Bruce's support for Woodruff influenced many black newspaper editors, who also backed him.[13] Still, Bruce was not completely disappointed with the choice of Roosevelt; two years earlier the writer had praised Roosevelt's "rugged honesty, . . . intrepid courage, . . . boldness of thought and utterance, . . . and his brilliant intellect." Roosevelt possessed, in Bruce's estimation, "great organizing ability, and the genius and the foresight of successful leadership." When some blacks interpreted Roosevelt's actions as president of the U.S. Civil Service Commission as antiblack, Bruce defended the Rough Rider. As proof that Roosevelt was not a bigot, Bruce cited his statement as police commissioner in New York City, "I shall not . . . discriminate against any man of color who applies . . . for appointment upon the police force [for] I know no man by his color. Merit, character and fitness count for more than color with me." Satisfied, Bruce called for 299,000 Roosevelts of both parties in office, which would assure African Americans a fair percentage of patronage. Others were not so benign toward the future vice president. In a letter written to Bruce dated June 22, 1899, an unidentified soldier stationed in Cuba wrote that Roosevelt's questioning of the courage of black soldiers during the recent war with Spain proved that he was not a friend of either black soldiers or the race. He, like other white men, this soldier argued, was capable of tricking black voters.[14]

The ambivalent feelings of the black community toward Roosevelt reflected their mixed feelings about the Republican Party itself. While many preferred to remain aboard the Republican ship, others were searching for lifeboats, even if they came from Democratic ships. Although some of those old enough to recall preemancipation days held the Democratic Party in contempt, a younger generation of blacks knew and cared little of the past wrongs. For them, the Republican Party did not offer the best hope for the realization of their dreams in 1900. The Democratic Party sought to exploit this latter group. Henry Y. Arnett, an employee in the Recorder of Deeds Office in Washington, informed George A. Myers two months before the election that there were hundreds of colored Democrats in West Virginia, Illinois, Indiana, and New York. "In short the Negroes seem to have gone mad," he confided. They complained that McKinley was silent on the race problem and was ignoring blacks on appointments. Bruce, who viewed deserting to the Democrats as a "new form of slavery," cautioned that blacks in West Virginia should not be seduced by Democrat suitors. He warned that the Democrats wanted new paramours while mistreating their black families in the South with segregated railroad cars and political disfranchisement. Bruce reminded them of Sen. Benjamin Tillman's boast in the Senate seven months earlier that Democrats stuffed ballot boxes and shot Negroes without any shame.[15]

Northern Democrats, too, sought to woo the black vote; but Bruce cautioned readers to reject the William Jennings Bryan–Adlai Ewing Stevenson ticket. Bruce urged African Americans to use their political power to gain respect instead of making "trash speeches at indignation meetings, after mobs . . . shoot down our old women and men."[16] One Bruce critic, J. R. Clifford of the *Pioneer Press,* commented that his militancy was fashionable at long range because there was no inherent danger. An irate Bruce responded that he had lectured and written from both long and short range "without fear or favor of the southern Democracy." As an illustration, he cited his criticism of Democrats in 1882 when he edited the *Portsmouth Republican* in Virginia.[17]

Oddly, Bruce, who had vowed not to vote for McKinley, softened his stance and became one of the president's defenders. In the August 18 *Colored American*, he stated that McKinley was a politician, not a king, and that upon researching the matter, he understood that the president lacked constitutional powers to interfere in state matters such as requirements for voting. It was highly unlikely that Bruce, who considered himself an astute political observer, simply "discovered" that McKinley's powers were limited. Again, he was motivated by the possibility of an appointment. Two weeks later, Bruce sought to silence McKinley's black Democratic critics by reminding them of the president's promise in his 1896 acceptance speech to deal with the "revolutionary assault upon law and order." McKinley, Bruce added, promised to "extinguish . . . the spirit of lawlessness . . . by the fires of an unselfish and lofty patriotism."[18] Bruce was not alone in retreating from previously caustic remarks about McKinley. *New York Age* editor Timothy Thomas Fortune considered the president to be a "despicable character," but he decided to muzzle himself and support McKinley's reelection in hopes of an appointment. Bruce defended Fortune (and himself) by dismissing the *Cleveland Gazette*'s denunciation of Fortune's shift, noting that it was unimportant what Fortune said or did previously. Besides, he added, "wise men change often, fools never."[19] Bruce's change of heart was more disturbing than that of Fortune, who, as a nominal Republican, had supported Democrats, Prohibitionists, and Independents during the past sixteen years. However, Bruce's desire for a position clouded his political judgment and muzzled his natural instinct to savage the pathetic race policies of the McKinley administration. It is interesting to note how much of a political reversal he committed from 1899 to the eve of the 1900 presidential election. Bruce had vowed in 1899 not to vote for McKinley because he was indifferent to black progress and was an obedient servant of business. Bruce even faulted the president's foreign policy, particularly his handling of the situation in the Philippines. Although he took pride in the patriotic service of black men during the recently completed Spanish-American War, Bruce now urged black civilians not to volunteer to fight Filipinos trying to prevent an American takeover of the archipelago. A month before the Republican National Convention convened, Bruce castigated America for being drunk with imperialistic power and motivated to subjugate the Philippines in the name of commerce. Bruce's bluntness takes on greater force when contrasted with the voice of the *Colored American*, which claimed that inferior races needed a superior race to guide them toward civilization.[20]

While Bruce softened his criticism of McKinley because he wanted consideration for an appointment, he was also motivated by disgust for the principles that William Jennings Bryan and the Democrats represented. He was genuinely alarmed at the prospect of Bryan being in power because he feared that the Nebraskan was no different than the vile racist Benjamin Tillman. On the local level, Bruce's concern that lawlessness would reign under a Democrat president was underscored when the police (under the control of a Democratic Tammany Hall) instigated a race riot in New York City, August 15–16, 1900. Bruce reported that the city's police department routinely blackmailed prostitutes and their pimps. On August 12, officer Robert J. Thorpe, believing that Mrs. Arthur Harris, a woman of color, was a prostitute, attempted to arrest her while her husband was in a nearby cigar shop. Upon his return, the irate husband intervened. In the struggle, the officer struck Mr. Harris, who in turn fatally stabbed Thorpe. Neither the police department, a grand jury, nor Mayor Robert A. Van Wyck took any action against this police officer or other officers who assisted civilians in brutalizing blacks following Thorpe's funeral. On September 3, the Citizen's Protective League was organized with Timothy Thomas Fortune as its chair. The *Morning Telegraph* blamed the riot on Fortune, who months earlier had urged black New Yorkers "to die in defense of [their] rights as citizens." Bruce defended the embattled editor and urged the black press to support Fortune because "blood is thicker than water." He was contemptuous of a delegation of black Democrats led by Edward E. Lee, who demanded trials for the accused officers. Bruce dismissed their action as a joke orchestrated by Tammany Hall. He urged New Yorkers to shun the wily Democrats who only believed in "elevating black men with a rope."[21]

Black politicians did not share Bruce's confidence that the Democrats would not make inroads into the black vote. Benjamin W. Arnett wrote on July 8 to Charles Dick, chair of the Ohio Republican State Committee, that the party needed a colored news bureau to offset the recruitment of dissident black voters by the Populists and the Democrats. On July 18, Cyrus Field Adams, editor of the *Appeal* in Chicago, notified George A. Myers that, if selected to be one of the two black members of the advisory committee, he could work well with either Bruce or W. A. Pledger, the two other potential members. Adams added that he desired "a chance to show that I am a hustler and that I can do effective vote making work . . . in Chicago [at the convention]."[22] Republicans were concerned that the Democrats would send anti-McKinley delegates to the August 28 Afro-American Council meeting in Indianapolis to try to push through their resolutions. Theophile T. Allain, founder of Southern University and a Bookerite, suggested to Charles Dick that Hanna should have AME Bishop Benjamin W. Arnett instruct the church to pack the meeting with McKinley men. "If Senator Hanna will send the boys, I will lead the army," he vowed. Allain sent a similar message to Myers.[23] Arnett, who considered himself the "bishop of politics," had dissenters who wanted him removed from the Republican Party inner circle. On August 15, John P. Green informed Myers of his displeasure with Arnett's advice in 1898 to McKinley to remain silent on the lynching question.[24] That questionable advice presented the Republicans with a dilemma: either mend their fences with their African American constituents or face the threat of a defection of the black vote to the opposition. A massive publicity campaign was needed, and the instrument was the black press. Bruce was the first vice president of the Afro-American Press Association (founded in 1899), and he considered it an ideal campaign tool to organize the masses.[25] Bruce's attempt to get the Republican National Committee to use Negro newspapers during the campaign was met with scorn. The committee decided that it would be less costly to send pamphlets and literature directly to the voters. However, not wanting to lose Bruce's unique talents, the Republican National Committee assigned him to its literary bureau in late August to furnish his political views weekly to the black press.[26] Bruce's selection garnered a mixed response. The *Colored American* lauded the selection because Bruce had a national reputation for describing "political plans and schemes in remarkable, forceful and readable language." New York's *Albany Spectator* suggested that only Bruce's skin color prevented him from being "hailed as a prince of writers." Albert B. George, a reader of the *Colored American,* believed that Bruce's appointment would cause hundreds of readers to take a fresh look at the Republican Party.[27] Henry C. Smith, editor of the *Cleveland Gazette,* opposed Bruce's appointment, observing that the party had shown its true colors when it previously ignored Negro writers and newspapers. The *Colored American* responded, "Smith would kick if he were hanging."[28] Cyrus Field Adams, hoping for an appointment, made available at his expense fifty thousand copies of an article, "Bryan Not Our Friend," for distribution to colored Democrats and fence-sitters. Adams projected that a Bryan victory would lead to a business panic resulting in the loss of at least $200 million in wages. The New York Republican State Committee decided in late September to shore up its position with black New York voters by appointing Charles W. Anderson as a committeeman at large. The *Colored American* heralded the selection of the erudite Anderson, who possessed the intelligence, campaign skill, and personality to converse with all social classes.[29]

In addition to Bruce, Timothy Thomas Fortune was another maverick whose militant prose was needed by the Republicans. He was appointed by the Republican National Committee to do in the West what Bruce was assigned to do in the East. This appointment annoyed Jere A. Brown, who told George

A. Myers that Fortune was a "loud mouth agitator" who lacked the confidence of the people. Cyrus Field Adams complained to Myers that he had written everything that Fortune sent to the black press. Nevertheless, the *Colored American* praised both Fortune and Bruce in late October for carrying "the literary honors of the campaign in magnificent style." McKinley's decisive victory caused a jubilant Adams to write to Myers that "the political bunco man, false prophet, charlatan, humbug and fakir, has been relegated to the background."[30]

McKinley's Patronage Policy Revisited

The petty squabbles for African American appointments began immediately. John P. Green, unhappy as a stamp agent superintendent, requested that Myers put in a word with McKinley for him to be given the position of recorder of deeds, fourth auditor of the Treasury, or an equivalent position.[31] Privately, Myers supported the ambitions of both Green and William Calvin Chase for political appointments. He informed McKinley on November 15 that while he was not seeking a position for himself or others, he believed it was imperative that the president reward loyal northern colored men, particularly with positions as recorder of deeds and register of the Treasury. He also considered it crucial that Congress enforce the Fourteenth and Fifteenth Amendments.[32]

The request was fair, and it was one that should have appealed to a progressive politician, but, again, McKinley disappointed black loyalists. Weeks after McKinley's victory, key black supporters were still wondering whether the president would reward their loyalty. Paradoxically, Bruce, who was looking for an appointment, had noted the year before the election that "just before election these 'white gods' to whom [Negroes] bow down and worship after election, are just as nervous and solicitous about their fate as the Negroes are after they decide their fate by voting them into office." Bruce urged office seekers not to grovel for appointments, as they were not favors but rights earned by "virtue of our citizenship, ability, moral and public worth and fitness to serve."[33] George A. Myers concurred with Bruce's advice to blacks not to beg for their rights. A sympathetic Jere A. Brown wrote to Myers on November 26 to express approval for his decision to quit politics after receiving "scant courtesy" from Hanna for his valuable support. William T. Anderson, chaplain of the black Tenth Calvary stationed in Cuba, wrote Myers on November 15, 1900, praising him for his service to the party. He added, ironically, "I hope that you have no bones broken." Myers bitterly informed Green on December 7 that McKinley wanted to dump Benjamin W. Arnett because he considered him a "bore" and an "intolerable nuisance" who had upset him by remaining silent at the 1898 Afro-American Council meeting. The president was angry that Arnett, Judson W. Lyons, and Henry P. Cheatham had behaved cowardly by letting Green take the heat over his silence on lynching. Myers added that he found out the names of the rascals because he was independent and could afford to be aggressive.[34]

Bruce, who had temporarily abandoned his independence to support McKinley, was disappointed that the president had not rewarded him for his campaign efforts. On December 29, G. F. Franklin, a Denver resident, wrote to Bruce, who had not yet been mentioned for a political appointment. Believing that Bruce was not interested in an office, Franklin offered his congratulations because "political preferment is like gold at the end of the rainbow seldom gotten and dearly bought at any price." Shortly after McKinley's inauguration, the weekly *Colored American* noted satirically that the president found positions for defeated Republican candidates as well as "their degenerate sons" but had was yet to find places for men of color. "What is the matter with McKinley?" lamented the editor. Several months later, the *Colored American* suggested that former congressman George Henry White be recognized with an appointment, preferably in the Treasury, for his contribution as the sole representative of ten million Negroes.[35]

Black leaders were disappointed and angered by McKinley's lack of significant patronage for them. With the exception of John P. Green, reassigned to the stamp division of the post office, Judson W. Lyons, register of the Treasury, and Henry P. Cheatham, recorder of deeds, there was little to shout about. McKinley was under no pressure to make significant black appointments, for they were wedded to the Republican Party and had no interest in a Democratic mistress or in seeking a divorce, despite the false nature of the marriage.

Roosevelt and African Americans

Despite his disappointment, Bruce was a patient man who was looking four years hence to a possible Theodore Roosevelt presidency. In April 1901, weeks after the vice-presidential inauguration, Bruce wrote that the Rough Rider was the logical Republican candidate for president in 1904 because he was a friend of the black soldier and citizen. Bruce considered Roosevelt to be "every inch of . . . a man." The *Colored American* said that Roosevelt was a friend of the race "without being a hypocrite, a poseur—or a juggler of honeyed phrases." From this period until Roosevelt's death in 1919, Bruce would remain faithful, even when other blacks denounced Roosevelt's perceived acts of racism and insistence on running as a third party candidate against President Taft in 1912.[36] Within six months of the inauguration, on September 6, 1901, McKinley was struck by an assassin's bullet. Writing from Camp Eagle Pass, Texas, Alfred Brewington informed John P. Green that he was glad that a black man, James B. Parker, had pummeled the assassin, Leon Czolgosz, and prevented him from firing a third shot at the stricken McKinley.[37]

After lingering for a week, McKinley died. Shortly after becoming president, Roosevelt and Booker T. Washington discussed plans to build a new southern Republican Party based on "character" instead of "patronage and bribery." Washington was reported in the press as stating that party lines should be broken down in the former slave states and that the inclusion of southern whites would broaden the party's appeal. Timothy Thomas Fortune and others found this news shocking. Their fears were realized when Roosevelt ignored E. A. Deas, a staunch black Republican, and appointed John G. Capers, a "gold Democrat," as a Republican national committeeman in South Carolina.[38] In reality, Roosevelt was carrying out the policy of his Republican predecessors who had skillfully organized factions of dissatisfied southern Democrats and lily-white Republicans. More telling was the Republican president's effectiveness in playing the factions against each other. The odd men out were loyal black Republicans who could count only on low-level positions.

James S. Clarkson, in private practice as president of the New York–New Jersey Bridge Company, wrote to Roosevelt suggesting that he find a solution to the country's race problem. Clarkson cautioned the president that Negroes were patient and would wait for justice, but not "under the lash or the torch, or under any new promise finally to be broken like all the old." He urged Roosevelt to provide justice, for "it is the white man who is on trial." In his reply to Clarkson, Roosevelt claimed to have been touched by the message.[39] Ironically, the conditions of black Americans might have improved considerably if Clarkson, a white man, had more influence with Roosevelt. Instead, Roosevelt depended on Booker T. Washington for counsel on racial matters. Where Clarkson was bold and forthright, Washington was pragmatic and cautious. Washington's influence with Roosevelt increased during the next seven years, leading African Americans to debate whether Roosevelt or Washington truly had solutions for their numerous problems.

Despite the aforementioned grievances, black Americans admired Theodore Roosevelt for his rugged individualism, and they considered him more of a friend than the late McKinley. Their optimism was reflected in a renewed interest in political patronage. "Reward the Faithful," declared the *Colored American* in a March 1, 1902, editorial. Bruce was singled out for an appointment by the weekly, which noted that even though Bruce never demanded "'loaves and fish' as a reward," the Republicans in New York should honor him for his campaign work. Give Bruce "a large and juicy slice of official 'pie,'" urged the editor.[40] It bode well for Bruce when Roosevelt appointed James S. Clarkson to the position of surveyor of the Port of New York in 1902. The former assistant postmaster general convinced Roosevelt to dismiss a few lily-white officeholders (a faction of Republicans in Alabama who sought to exclude blacks from party membership) as well as vow not to give patronage to Republican organizations that drew the color line. Still, Roosevelt's decision to replace dismissed lily-white Republicans with gold Democrats infuriated Fortune, who complained to Washington that the president's action was humiliating to loyal black Republicans.[41]

Not unlike his Republican predecessors, Roosevelt had to balance the support of black voters with the desire to lure more southern Democrats into the party. This political strategy angered black voters. Mindful of this, Roosevelt cautiously weighed the advantages and disadvantages of appointing southern blacks. To the delight of his black supporters, the president appointed William D. Crum as collector of the Port of Charleston, South Carolina, a decision that caused deep resentment in the white South.[42]

During the summer of 1902, Clarkson provided Bruce with a position in the correspondence division of the surveyor's office, which he retained until his retirement in 1922. The *South African Spectator* in Capetown expressed pride in Bruce's appointment because, unlike so many other appointees, he had no Caucasian blood in his veins. While grateful for the job, Bruce accused both the Republican Party and the white church of treating Negroes shabbily. He bluntly stated that blacks had less protection than did raw sugar.[43] Later in 1902, Bruce wrote that Roosevelt's bandwagon was heavy with supporters because the people loved a president who was "original, honest, fearless, loyal to duty and to truth."[44]

Nonetheless, there were signs that the love affair with Roosevelt was masking a growing African American disillusionment with the Republican Party. Besides the significant denial of patronage to Negroes in general, southern blacks, in particular, had to decide if they favored forming a segregated local Republican Party in opposition to the growing lily-white movement. James S. Clarkson informed Whitefield McKinlay, a Washington realtor and close ally of Booker T. Washington, that he had received a letter from the president advising black Republicans to be patient and to allow any local Republican parties they organized to be open to all races. Clarkson viewed the president's comment favorably, adding that he was the best friend that Negroes could have in the White House. On November 1, the *Colored American* reported that Roosevelt did not want a color line in the southern wing of the party. This reflected the influence of Clarkson's sage advice. However, Roosevelt's call for "patience" was unsatisfactory for those who preferred that he forcefully dismantle all lily-white organizations.[45]

Earlier, on October 16, Clarkson, who (with the president's advice) controlled Negro appointments and Negro political strategy, informed Washington of Roosevelt's surprise that there were no black New Yorkers on the list of African American federal appointees. Roosevelt asked for several names that would be suitable to New York Sen. Thomas C. Platt. "I feel too," Clarkson wrote, "that the appointment of one of your people . . . should be preeminently fit and as much for the vindication of the intelligence of the race as for the recognition of it by the president." Eventually, Charles W. Anderson was deemed fit by the triumvirate of Clarkson, Platt, and Roosevelt, and was appointed in 1905 as Collector of Internal Revenue at New York. The appointment was widely praised in the nation's press, but, more important, it silenced those critics who doubted that Roosevelt would entrust a black man with such a prominent position.[46]

Anderson's appointment was an example of Booker T. Washington's growing influence in the Roosevelt administration. In fact, Washington had acquired more influence with the White House than had his predecessors who had advised presidents on race issues. His ascendancy to power alarmed black activists who questioned the educator's reluctance to publicly advocate black civil and political rights. On November 9, 1901, William Monroe Trotter published the first issue of the *Guardian,* a Boston weekly that relentlessly attacked Washington's policy of accommodation. The first few issues convinced Robert W. Taylor, financial agent for Tuskegee Institute, that Trotter had unfairly labeled Washington as the race's arch enemy. Although in a few years Bruce would become a contributor to Trotter's paper, in 1902 he ridiculed the *Guardian*'s three staff members as disgraceful. He classified Trotter as "a janitor with an education, which he seems afraid to put into practical use." Bruce urged Trotter to "go west, or go south and be some body." It was quixotic to attack Washington and Tuskegee Institute, Bruce insisted. Besides, he added, Taylor is "their master in brains, ability, self respect and manhood." It is interesting that Bruce chose to defend Washington when the *Guardian* was offering an analysis that Bruce himself would express in a few years. There is no hard evidence to suggest what motivated Bruce to defend Washington, but it is possible he still saw much to admire in the Tuskegee model. Bruce certainly agreed in principle with Washington: that the race had to be more self-reliant and work collectively for mutual progress. However, Washington controlled federal patronage distribution, which was an effective deterrent against dissent. For these reasons, Bruce and others were conflicted in their feelings toward Tuskegee's founder. It would take W. E. B. Du Bois's famous essay,

"Of Mr. Booker T. Washington and Others," published in his seminal 1903 study, *The Souls of Black Folk*, to ignite a strong and consistent anti-Washington agenda. Meanwhile, black activists wanted Roosevelt to act more forcefully on their behalf as their rights were eroded by a combination of southern hostility and northern indifference. The president would at times accommodate their requests for federal intervention, but his inconsistencies troubled his supporters. At his best, Roosevelt was forthright and active in the cause for civil rights, but his decisions were often tempered by a stubbornness that caused him to lose the support of a significant segment of the African American community. Roosevelt acted swiftly and positively when Mrs. Minnie M. Cox, postmaster in Indianola, Mississippi, resigned because she feared white ruffians who sought to remove all black officeholders in the area, even though blacks in Sunflower County outnumbered whites (12,070 to 4,006). President Roosevelt closed the post office in Indianola and had the mail forwarded to Greenville, twenty-five miles away. Postmaster Cox was kept on the federal payroll pending an investigation.

Bruce praised the president for his willingness to take on the southern Bourbons, but he expressed disappointment that blacks were reluctant to retaliate. This, he felt, provided cowardly white mobs with a mask of invincibility.[47] Bruce generally derided violence, but on occasions he considered "an eye for an eye" to be a proper response to premeditated southern violence against African Americans. Bruce called for retaliation because he understood that the white supremacist ideology in the South made it impossible for African Americans to obtain justice. Nonetheless, a call for retaliatory action was an aberration for Bruce. In this case, however, his appeal was an indication of his frustration with Republican politicians who lacked both the will and resources to confront southern racists. Despite this display of militancy, Bruce still believed that intelligence was the best weapon against southern bigots.[48] This can be seen in his response to the Dancy affair. In late summer 1902, John C. Dancy, former collector of customs at Wilmington, North Carolina, and now recorder of deeds in Washington, attempted to have dialogue with southerners to improve race relations. His efforts led many northern blacks to brand him as a conservative. However, Bruce defended Dancy's actions with the observation that they proceeded from a desire to promote better race relations. Bruce believed that men like Dancy could reach conservative whites who would respond to the appeal for justice. Therefore, in Bruce's estimation, Dancy was "one of the most useful young men of the race." Still, Bruce was inconsistent in his assessment of working with the South's "better" white element. When it was rumored in 1903 that some blacks in Alabama were to convene to express their love for their white southern friends, an astonished Bruce wrote that "every mother's son of these cringing, cowardly and subservient darkies ought to be lynched, or have their black backs whipped." Bruce questioned any alliance with whites. These "good whites," he noted, lynch Negroes every year for "the white man is the biggest liar, and the biggest thief on record [and] . . . as a criminal he will make a barbarian turn green with envy."[49] Evidently, Bruce considered alliances with whites desirable if both parties were respectable and honorable—or if the black initiator of meetings was one who shared Bruce's sense of manhood or racial identity. Nevertheless, Bruce's sometime-conservative views mirrored Booker T. Washington's emphasis on appealing to the South's elite whites to curb the racist excesses of the masses. This again suggests that Bruce had a difficult time extracting himself from the influence of the Tuskegee Wizard. Professor E. A. Johnson of Raleigh, North Carolina, concurred with Bruce's assessment of Dancy and southern reality. He wrote Bruce in late September, "the only sensible thing to do" would be "to make terms [. . . .] the better the terms the better the conditions." Johnson urged Bruce to use his influence to encourage northern blacks to spend less of their funds on picnics, lavish displays at conventions, and building fine churches. Instead, they should forward funds to the South to build schools and support missionary activities in "the back woods . . . where the light of civilization has scarcely gone."[50] Whether Bruce responded to Johnson is not known, but it is clear that he was in conflict over the appropriate solution to the race problem. While he had prophesied that the battle between the races would be on an intellectual level, or that revenge for racial wrongs would come from God, Bruce was not above using (and approving of) violent rhetoric. In his view, it was no more "incendiary or revolutionary than Patrick Henry's . . . 'give me liberty or give me death' [speech]." Bruce added that whites respected fighters, not cowards.[51] It was this erratic display of allegiance to competing ideologies that makes Bruce difficult to assess, but it may help to explain his initial support for Washington's accommodationism.

Bruce wanted the races to work out their differences because he thought it would be a major benefit to American democracy. Unfortunately, his optimism for a peaceful resolution waned. Bruce expressed fear in his column "Gotham Notes" of March 21, 1903, that since neither statesmen nor ego-driven so-called leaders could solve the nation's race problem, the crisis might lead to mutual slaughter unless God intervened. In "The Negro and His Future," an undated draft written about this time, Bruce contradicted himself by stating that the Negro must have race loyalty to survive and that he had "no weapon save his tongue with which to do battle."[52] Despite his earlier fatalistic observation, Bruce joined several thousand progressive individuals at the Brooklyn Academy of Music on April 3 to voice opposition to the disfranchisement of black male voters in the south.[53]

While Bruce did not think that statesmen had the answer to the race problem, he was absolutely unwilling to let paternalistic and racist thinkers dictate solutions to the treatment of southern blacks. On April 14, an illustrious group of whites attended a fund-raiser for Tuskegee Institute at New York's Madison Square Garden. The list of distinguished guests included James S. Clarkson; William H. Baldwin Jr., president of the Long Island Railroad; Edgar Gardner Murphy of the Southern Education Board; Rev. Dr. Lyman Abbott, pastor of Plymouth Congregational Church in Brooklyn and editor of the *Outlook*, one of the nation's most influential journals; Andrew Carnegie; George Foster Peabody, a banker and a Tuskegee benefactor and trustee; Oswald Garrison Villard, editorial writer and president of the *New York Evening Post;* St. Clair McKelwaly, editor in chief of the *Brooklyn Eagle;* and former President Grover Cleveland. Booker T. Washington remarked that "freedom . . . must be a conquest" achieved by sacrifice and discipline and that the race problem could be solved by racial cooperation. Although Bruce considered Washington's speech to be his "ablest and manliest deliverance" to date and approved of Clarkson's remarks (that no tolerance should be given to politicians who treat black Republican voters as though they were lepers), he held most of the other speakers, particularly Grover Cleveland, in contempt. The former president stereotyped blacks as lazy, vicious, thriftless, and ignorant people who would become acceptable to whites only as they acquired education at Tuskegee and similar industrial training schools. Bruce swiftly condemned Cleveland's remarks as "cowardly and brutal slander." Oddly, Bruce was not critical of Washington's silence on Cleveland's comments, even though the $600,000 worth of U.S. Steel bonds raised for Tuskegee's endowment by the event might have been considered "hush money."[54]

The 1904 Election Campaign, Roosevelt, and Brownsville

For Bruce, the stakes in the 1904 presidential election were clear: a Democratic victory would mean a complete reversal of black progress. Although Bruce would welcome a Republican victory, he cautioned that blacks should not wait for the Republican Party to fight their battles. Thus, he urged African American voters to fight the racists with their ballots. Alarmed that some dissatisfied blacks might bolt to the enemy, Bruce warned that a vote for Alton B. Parker, the Democratic standard-bearer, was a challenge to their manhood. "Let Roosevelt and victory be the slogan from now until election day," he urged.[55]

Roosevelt's black critics questioned his lack of enthusiasm toward solving the race problem. Displaying confused reasoning, Bruce defended the president by noting that he was only completing McKinley's term; therefore, a Roosevelt victory would result in a change of cabinet officers and policies.[56] Lost in Bruce's reasoning was the fact that Roosevelt was not compelled to retain McKinley's cabinet appointments or follow through on his policy initiatives. Still, other black loyalists agreed that a victory by the Democrats would be disastrous for African Americans. George A. Myers confided to John P. Green that he "would rather be a 'has been' in the house of the Lord (Republican Party) than to wear silken raiment in the camp of the enemy."[57] Even Booker T. Washington, who publicly avoided partisan politics, confidentially informed Edwin Doak Mead, editor of the *New England Magazine,* that a Parker victory would result in the southern ruffians terrorizing the region's black population. Henry A. Williamson informed the *New York Sun* that any race man who would vote for Parker "should be ashamed to call himself a man and a voter."[58] The majority of African Americans expressed joyous relief after Roosevelt's election. "The deed done. Roosevelt reelected by the Negro vote," Bruce confided to his journal on December 17, 1904.[59]

The next four years of the Roosevelt administration would be bittersweet ones for African Americans who questioned his commitment to their civil and political rights. An incident at Brownsville, Texas, in the late hours of August 13, 1906, provided Roosevelt and Washington critics with an opportunity to attack both men. Soldiers of the Twenty-fifth Infantry Division, recently arrived at Fort Brown, were assigned to the border area from Fort Niobrara, Nebraska, where they had served without any racial problems. Neither the men nor officers wanted to go to Texas, which regimental Chaplain Theophilus Gould Steward considered a "maelstrom for colored regulars."[60] One fateful day, a soldier was beaten and threatened by a customs official for inadvertently brushing against a white woman's dress. Later, unknown party or parties shot up Brownsville, then only separated from the fort by a fence. One resident was left dead, and the chief of police was severely wounded.[61] Although a military inquiry showed that all the soldiers and ammunition were accounted for, President Roosevelt was incensed that not a single soldier came forth with names of guilty men. Consequently, he issued an order to dishonorably discharge 167 men, including six Medal of Honor recipients and thirteen who had received citations for bravery in the war against Spain. (In 1972, the secretary of the army issued the men posthumous honorable discharges).[62]

To avoid antagonizing black voters, Roosevelt issued the discharge order after congressional elections, which led to criticisms from the black press and clergy. Critics were angered that the president punished the men because none would inform on their comrades. Only a few days before issuing the discharge order, Roosevelt praised his own son for not implicating his friends in an incident in Boston that called for a police investigation.[63] Timothy Thomas Fortune used the editorial pages of the *Age* to severely criticize Roosevelt over Brownsville. This embarrassed Washington, who had over the years used funds and recommendations for political positions to keep Fortune in line.

Washington attempted to maintain a low profile concerning the Brownsville affray, but he understood that his closeness to Roosevelt could further undermine his leadership. A pragmatic but cautious Washington sought privately to find out the facts in the case by contacting the regiment's chaplain. He refused to publicly condemn Roosevelt, even though he knew that his enemies would blame him for the president's action.[64] Washington was concerned about his own position as "the voice of the Negro," and he was eager to assure the president that bitterness over Brownsville would soon dissipate. On December 16, 1907, he wrote Roosevelt that the Brownsville matter would not prevent blacks from supporting William Howard Taft in the fight for the nomination or in the presidential election if he was the Republican nominee. Washington's true feelings about Brownsville were revealed in a confidential Christmas 1907 letter to Arthur Isaiah Vorys, an Ohio attorney and insurance executive who managed Taft's presidential campaign in that state. Privately, Washington admitted that it would be difficult to convince black voters in the North and in doubtful states to support Taft. Therefore, it was important that Taft not associate himself with any of the lily-white movements in the South and make "the effort to overcome the Brownsville influence any more difficult than it is."[65]

The Brownsville affray remained a sore point for years and led some black Republicans to defect to the Democratic Party. It also soured many on William Howard Taft's candidacy when he ran for president in 1908 because, as secretary of war, he had carried out Roosevelt's discharge order. While Washington tried to protect Roosevelt by his silence, an enraged Fortune lashed out at the president with unbridled fury for his unprecedented action and for appointing southern Democrats to positions in his administration. These bold attacks, his vow not to support either Roosevelt or Taft, and his increasing alcoholism and erratic emotional state led Washington to dismiss Fortune as editor. The operation of the *Age* was turned over to Fred Moore. On September 3, 1907, Ralph W. Tyler, auditor for the navy department, informed George A. Myers that Fortune was out as editor and that he (Tyler) would be in charge of the editorial page. The October 3 issue of the weekly "regretfully" announced the "retiring of its editor."[66]

While his firing was not entirely unexpected, Fortune was crushed. He had taken significant flak from activists for his close relationship to Booker T. Washington as a ghostwriter and an apologist for his accommodationist policy. A bloodied but unbowed Fortune wrote in November to William Monroe Trotter urging his former nemesis not to "let up on Roosevelt or Taft." He encouraged Trotter to "lay it on them thick as usual. They are the sinners who have provoked the thunder and should get the lightning." In December, Fortune informed the Indianapolis *Freeman*, "when President Roosevelt and his people are endorsed by me I will be a dead man. Am I dead? Here I am."[67]

The Election of 1908

Fortune's defection was not entirely unexpected; he had attacked Roosevelt's racial policies intermittently for the past several years. However, the dissatisfaction of other African Americans with Roosevelt and Taft delighted Democrats and caused alarm among black Republican loyalists, who expressed no interest in the presidential campaign. Even a staunch Republican like George A. Myers succumbed to the rationalization that American politics was a white man's game. While this sentiment was made in 1899 and was meant for Ohio, it was apropos for 1908. Myers wrote to John P. Green that "the political caldron is bubbling over, but bubbling without me. I cannot afford to mix in these bitter local fights, if perchance poor old darky is on the wrong side—when the white folks get through quarreling and make up—poor old darky he gets left. No white man's fight for me." Others agreed that politics had left the black voter in its wake. Such was the sentiment of Ralph W. Tyler's Christmas 1907 letter to Myers. "The fight is now a white man's fight, and they will settle it, while we hoe the corn." Tyler added that black men were not needed until it was time to defeat the Democrats. His blasé attitude was due to the common belief that because Roosevelt would dominate the convention, William Howard Taft had the Republican nomination "sewed up." Tyler claimed to have inside information and wrote to Myers on January 12 with news that Taft would receive a first-ballot nomination.[68]

Meanwhile, a stop-Taft group was organized early in 1908 by William Monroe Trotter, editor of the *Guardian* and president of the New England Constitution and Suffrage League; Bishop Alexander Walters, president of the National Afro-American Council; and Rev. William H. Scott, president of the Suffrage League in Boston. In February, bishops from the African Methodist Episcopal Church, the Colored Methodist Episcopal Church, and the African Methodist Episcopal Zion Church met in the nation's capital to warn the Republican National Committee not to make Roosevelt or Taft the party's nominee and risk the loss of northern black voters.[69] Tyler dismissed the clergymen as supporters of Sen. Joseph B. Foraker, an outspoken critic of Roosevelt's handling of the Brownsville incident. Again, Tyler informed Myers that he had inside information that guaranteed Taft's nomination.[70]

The accusations against Roosevelt and Taft did not escape Bruce's attention. He had been disturbed by rumors in late 1907 that three southern former congressmen wanted to abolish the colored regiments that they blamed for the Brownsville mess. Bruce dismissed them curtly: "they will all be dead before this happens." More immediate and serious, however, was the anger many black Republicans felt toward Roosevelt and Taft. Despite his reputation as a race-first man, Bruce was unusually loyal to Roosevelt. Instead of castigating the president over the dismissal of the soldiers, he supported him. As the editor of the *Yonkers Standard,* Bruce wrote a letter to the editor of the *New York Tribune* in April declaring that despite the unfairness of the discharges it was time to move on. Without naming them, Bruce criticized the Trotter group for "their sensational methods and their bombastic oratory," which would not "right the wrong of which they justly complain." More was expected of the reputable race-first man, but Bruce feared that the Brownsville hysteria would harm the Republicans in 1908. Rejecting Trotter's and Du Bois's call to switch party affiliation, Bruce proclaimed, "I could not vote a Democratic ticket without insulting my manhood and the memory of my father who was sold like beef by the pound during ... Democrat ... James Buchanan['s] ... administration."[71]

Bruce was influential, but others, angered by the president's arrogance in dismissing the soldiers and upset that the Republican nomination appeared to be Taft's, met in Philadelphia on April 8 to form the National Negro American Political League. The coalition consisted of representatives from the National Afro-American Council, the New England Constitution and Suffrage League, the Niagara Movement, the Constitutional Brotherhood of America, and the National Independent Civil and Political League of America. The mission of this decidedly anti–Booker T. Washington faction was to have the discharged soldiers reinstated, to prevent the nomination and election of Taft (or Roosevelt, if he chose to run again), and to secure the Republican nomination for Sen. Joseph Foraker. (Du Bois and Bishop Alexander Walters vowed to support William Jennings Bryan, an enemy, rather than Foraker, an alleged friend). Additionally, they wanted to organize blacks to use their political muscle to defeat anti–civil rights candidates and to fight against Jim Crow laws and southern disfranchisement amendments.[72] Despite their valiant effort, Taft was considered unbeatable. It was understood that Roosevelt would handpick his successor if he chose not to run, and all indications were that he would not seek another term for himself. Roosevelt's choice for a successor rested among Taft; Elihu Root, secretary of state; and George B. Cortelyou, secretary of the Treasury. James S. Clarkson was fond of Cortelyou and told Bruce "I think our brunette brother will have a fair show under Cortelyou in whatever office he hold or may hold." Strangely, in 1940 Whitefield McKinlay informed F. D. Patterson, president of Tuskegee Institute, that Washington had convinced Roosevelt that Taft was the best choice. Thus, according to McKinlay, "for the first time in history a Negro judgment named a president of the United States."[73] We will never know for certain if Washington influenced Roosevelt's choice of successor, for neither left any writing to validate this statement. Meanwhile, on June 6, 1908, Ralph W. Tyler informed George A. Myers that Taft would be swiftly nominated by acclamation. Taft was nominated on the first ballot with 702 votes to a combined 274 votes for his six opponents. After a motion, the nomination was made unanimous.[74]

Bruce did not support the effort of Trotter and Du Bois to disassociate black Republicans from Taft's candidacy, and it was during this period of soul searching that he distanced himself from Trotter and stopped contributing articles to the *Guardian*. Shortly before the election, Bruce informed the editor of the *New York World* that black Americans would do the right thing in the forthcoming presidential election. They wanted, he argued, a "heterogeneous citizenship" that would recognize the contributions of people like Crispus Attucks, who was the first to die in the 1770 Boston Massacre.[75] During the waning weeks of the campaign, Bruce put race aside and closed ranks with Roosevelt and Taft. A vote for Taft was essentially an approval of Roosevelt's tenure in office and a vote of confidence in his handling of the Brownsville incident. Normally, Bruce would have severely castigated a politician for his callous dismissal of so many innocent men. However, there are several possible explanations for Bruce's failure to join forces with the anti-Roosevelt coalition. Bruce, like others, may have been blinded by Roosevelt's manliness, forthrightness, and the potential he represented. Thus, he may have overlooked the president's egocentrism, his paternalistic treatment of people of color, and his racist handling of the men of the Twenty-fifth Colored Infantry. In part, Bruce was also influenced by his good friend Edward W. Blyden, who advised him three years earlier that "it is the dawn of [the Negro's] day [because] the spirit of Roosevelt is not a dying spirit, his influence . . . is 'the spirit of the years to come yearning to mix itself with life.'"[76] It is also possible that Bruce may have had a genuine fear of losing his government position in New York City. Several years earlier, on March 12, 1906, Charles Anderson had written to Booker T. Washington that a recent issue of the *Guardian* contained a letter from Bruce endorsing Bishop Henry M. Turner's assertion that the American flag was a dirty rag. This was a statement that President Roosevelt deemed treasonable. Anderson mused that it would be interesting if Roosevelt knew that Bruce was a federal officeholder. Anderson added that in the same article Bruce accused Washington of never having voted. "Thus, you see, there is an opportunity for some reprisals," Anderson suggested. On October 21, 1907, Anderson informed the Tuskegee Wizard that Bruce had probably written an unsigned letter in the previous week's *Guardian*. The accusatory article claimed that Timothy Thomas Fortune had made Washington famous and was repaid by being replaced as editor of the *New York Age* (which Washington secretly controlled). Again, Anderson suggested that Roosevelt be notified that Bruce was writing anti–Roosevelt and William H. Taft articles. Anderson cautioned Washington not to inform the president by letter, fearing it would be forwarded to James S. Clarkson, who would then turn it over to Bruce. This happened before when Emmett J. Scott, Washington's private secretary, sent a Bruce letter to the White House. Anderson added that Clarkson's action made Bruce hate Washington even more, and it did not affect his government position.[77]

Meanwhile, Bruce, intent on suppressing defections to the Democrats, informed the *New York Tribune* a month before the election that blacks did not intend to punish the GOP for Roosevelt's Brownsville action. Bruce asserted that a black vote for Bryan was the vote of fool Negroes who had forgotten the racist history of the southern Democrats.[78] In contrast, The *Guardian* urged black voters to maintain self-respect and vote for either Bryan or the socialist Eugene V. Debs or for the prohibitionist Eugene W. Chafin. The *Guardian* pushed its readers to defeat Taft and end Rooseveltism. The collapse of Roosevelt's control was expected to lead to a reorganization of the Republican Party, "which will recognize our particular race disabilities, and set about remedying them in earnest." Voters were encouraged to vote against the Taft-Roosevelt ticket so that they could tell their children and grandchildren how they defeated the man who was not a friend of the Negro at Brownsville.[79]

Bruce would have nothing to do with these naysayers. It was not expected that he would bolt the Republican Party to support the Democrat's nominee, but, based on his militant reputation, it was expected that Bruce would at least warn Taft not to ignore black voters. Instead, Bruce was so confident of a Taft victory that he wrote him on October 30, three days *before* the election, "as I shall be busy hurrahing for you and enjoying myself next week I take advantage . . . to offer you my heartfelt congratulations upon your election to the presidency. . . . I picked you for a winner and . . . I know as my redeemer liveth thou art the *man*."[80] Bruce was looking to gain an appointment for his support of Taft, but his lavish praise went for naught. Despite a letter from Thomas L. Woodruff, chair of the New York Republican State Committee, thanking Bruce for his "splendid service during [the] recent campaign," the party denied him access to the patronage trough.[81]

Taft's victory proved to be bittersweet; the seeds of discord had been planted for a division within the Republican Party. An indication of the lingering black dissatisfaction over Brownsville emerged during the 1910 New York gubernatorial campaign. Many were incensed over Roosevelt telling delegates to the National Negro Business League Convention that the league taught them "not to whine and cry about principles you do not have." Black Democrats and dissatisfied Republicans argued that a vote for Henry L. Stimson was a vote for Roosevelt. "Mr. Colored voter, are you a man? Remember Brownsville, and bury Theodore Roosevelt so deep on Election Day that his advice to 'stop whining' will be buried with him," urged the United Colored Democracy. The organization's membership was elated when 50,000 African Americans helped elect John A. Dix governor.[82]

America's Unsolved Race Problem: Proposed Solutions

Taft, former military governor of the Philippines, was a skilled administrator who lacked Roosevelt's leadership skills and charisma. He was ineffective in combating America's race problems as the color line—so eloquently defined by Du Bois—extended northward into areas previously not tainted with blatant colorphobia. The migration of southern blacks to the North to seek relief from low wages, political disfranchisement, the convict lease system, inadequate schools, and lynch mobs all contributed to increased hostility toward African Americans. Their increased numbers led to a rise in tension between them and European immigrants seeking their economic liberation in the United States. A race riot in Springfield, Illinois, the boyhood home of Abraham Lincoln, alarmed William English Walling, Mary White Overton, and Dr. Henry Moskowitz. They issued a call for a meeting on the race question, which was subsequently held on February 12, 1909, in New York City. From this meeting came the National Association for the Advancement of Colored People (NAACP).[83]

By 1910, Washington's influence had waned. President Taft did not hold him in the same esteem as his predecessor. The NAACP, whose early leadership and financial support came from white reformers and socialists, vigorously challenged Washington's leadership. This made it impossible for Washington's spies to infiltrate or to control the organization. Washington sought to shore up his image by serving as a trustee of Howard and Fisk Universities (to indicate that he was not opposed to higher education) and by gingerly speaking out against racial discrimination. It is possible that Washington attempted, through one of his lieutenants, to enlist Bruce as a writer. However, Bruce wanted to avoid involving himself again in a messy alliance with the often-maligned Washington. In March, Bruce wrote to Daniel Murray, "I do not think I shall touch Booker Washington. He has Boswells (ghost writers) enough among his satellites to lie about him. I don't believe in him and I am not going to fracture my conscience about writing about him what I cannot make myself believe. This isn't narrowness. This is plain unadulterated honesty. [He is] a crafty and cunning opportunist." Bruce dismissed Washington by acidly noting, "if Tuskegee had a manufacturing instead of a servant factory I might find something in its inventor to commend." In contrast, Bruce praised Du Bois for being a man of convictions, unlike the man from Tuskegee who gained wealth and fame by pleasing white men. James S. Clarkson concurred with Bruce that Du Bois, not Douglass, was the leader of the race.[84]

Criticism of Washington's leadership also came from abroad. Joseph C. Lundy wrote Bruce from England's Jersey Channel Islands to say that Washington's "hog and hominy policy = dollars," whereas Du Bois's "intellectual and ethical policy = free and equal manhood & womanhood." Lundy recommended that Bruce and Du Bois should organize their own national political party in those states with large African American populations.[85] Neither Bruce nor Du Bois, however, had the resources or the inclination to follow up on this suggestion.

It was clear that Taft lacked the political skills and the moral commitment to do anything significant about the rising tide of American racism. Several prominent individuals offered their opinions on the sad state of the nation's racial situation. Civil War hero and politician Robert Smalls believed that African American progress had led to white prejudice based on fear and jealousy. Whites, insisted Smalls, wanted the rising Negro to stay in the rear "before he becomes too powerful and strong." Maritcha R. Lyons, a Brooklyn schoolteacher and a member of that borough's colored elite, argued that segregation had to be eliminated or the nation's progress would be retarded. Bruce blamed white arrogance for contributing to the race problem. He was critical of white clergy, press, and politicians who were "*squeamish* about *admitting* that Negroes are capable of thinking along the same lines as white men." Bruce urged his readers to emulate the Jews who protested the slogan "America for Americans" because it implied limited inclusiveness.[86]

Bruce had insisted for years that Negroes were American citizens; but the government's abandonment of blacks since Reconstruction and the various Supreme Court decisions that denied blacks equal citizenship and voting rights led him to qualify that statement. As 1909 came to an end, Bruce noted in draft notes of a speech, "Disadvantages of Negro Citizenship," that blacks were mistaken to view themselves as American citizens. Technically they were not, and the government had not reciprocated their unconditional allegiance and loyalty. While he believed that it was time for the nation to decide if African Americans were entitled to full citizenship rights, he understood that blacks would not resort to anarchy or violence in pursuit of these rights. Therefore, he believed it imperative that they emulate ethnic European and depend on their own resources to achieve success.[87]

Despite his isolated and intemperate remarks demanding retaliation, Bruce eschewed violence because he knew that it was futile. Instead, he again argued that the battle between the races was an intellectual one. He called upon his friend James S. Clarkson to assist him in finding a solution to the problem of disfranchisement. On January 22, 1910, Bruce wrote confidentially to Daniel Murray with information that Clarkson needed to learn the estimated number of black voters in the country and other information relative to their disfranchisement. Bruce explained that Clarkson had interested some influential New Yorkers in the issue and that, while he (Bruce) was checking New York figures, it was vital for Murray to use his position in the Library of Congress to provide the national statistics. After hearing from Murray on February 18, Clarkson quickly informed him that he would meet with him soon in Washington, D.C. Clarkson reminded Murray that blacks held their own destiny in their hands, providing they were determined and organized.[88]

Clarkson's point was well stated; there were pessimists who questioned the ability of blacks to organize. Richard T. Greener, the first black graduate of Harvard College, complained to Murray in December 1910 that the Negro was inured to "kicks, insults, [and] rebuffs, that he has come to like it," and, thus, lacks race consciousness. Pan-Africanist Edward W. Blyden wrote in 1910 to Rev. Edward W. Cooke in Snow Hill, Alabama, with the admonition that southern blacks should follow Jesus Christ's example: *"He eschewed politics."* Blyden enunciated this extraordinary view because he believed, according to his biographer, that participation in politics was irrelevant since the black man's destiny was in Africa.[89]

Wilson and African Americans

Millions of African Americans sought their American destiny in civic and political activities, and they were determined not to be cast aside. Although the majority of them had supported the Republican Party, a small but growing minority was tempted by the siren's call of other parties. For some, the possibility of supporting a Democrat for president began to seem practical. The 1912 election offered options for black voters; they pondered the candidacies of President Taft, Democrat Woodrow Wilson, and former President Roosevelt, the Progressive Party candidate. Taft had alienated them during his term in office by appointing an ex-Confederate Democrat to the Supreme Court; Roosevelt undermined his chances by refusing to have black delegates seated at the Progressive Party's convention, and the southern-born Wilson offered only the vaguest outline as to what his administration might mean for African Americans. Blacks were divided over the trio, and there were supporters in each camp, with illustrious figures such as Du Bois supporting Wilson. Loyal black Republicans were appalled that Roosevelt entered the contest as a spoiler. (When Roosevelt perceived that some of Taft's appointments were meant as insults, a quarrel ensued. It ended after Taft sent a sympathetic letter to Roosevelt during an illness. In May 1918, the men met and settled their differences.) Cyrus Field Adams praised Taft for having 22,000 blacks on the government payroll. Adams was particularly pleased that Taft had appointed William H. Lewis in 1911 as an assistant attorney general in charge of Indian depredation claims—then the highest appointment held by an African American. (Lewis could pass for white.)[90]

Others were dismayed at the prospect of a second Taft term. Robert H. Terrell, a municipal judge in Washington, D.C., suggested to George A. Myers on August 10 that Taft would be "unmercifully beaten" if the election was held that day. Terrell did not believe that Roosevelt's exclusion of southern blacks from the Progressive convention would hurt him because northern blacks resented their southern brethren who, reportedly, sold their votes at Republican conventions. Whitefield McKinlay, a Taft appointee, and P. B. S. Pinchback, a former Reconstruction politician, shared the fear that many blacks would vote for Wilson. George A. Myers agreed, suggesting that Roosevelt could get few black votes in either Ohio or throughout the United States. Even James S. Clarkson, a Republican, declared that it was time for African Americans to divide their votes and desert the Republicans for their betrayal of their most loyal supporters.[91]

The election returns indicated that while Roosevelt and Taft together won nearly a million and a half more popular votes than Wilson, their combined popular vote was nearly seventy-five thousand fewer than Taft received in 1908, and their combined electoral votes paled in comparison to Wilson.[92] Roosevelt, who polled a quarter of the popular vote, was blamed for the Republicans' loss of the White House. Criticism against the Rough Rider was swift. Charles Purvis complained to Rev. Francis J. Grimke that Roosevelt's "diabolic ambition" destroyed the party's chance for victory. Whitefield McKinlay offered a different assessment. He informed Purvis that a Roosevelt victory would have benefited black America: "I know you will say tut, tut; but I was on the ground and in a position to know what I speak," he argued.[93]

Many blacks were willing to give Wilson the benefit of the doubt before judging him and his administration. Grimke kindly informed the president-elect on November 20 that he was impressed with the views he expressed in *The Importance of Bible Study*. Grimke believed that Wilson's sincere Christian character would assure blacks that they would have no reasons for complaints. AMEZ Bishop Alexander Walters, head of the National Colored Democratic League, expressed a similar optimism before the election. Walters expected that a Wilson presidency would extend "justice . . . executed with liberality and cordial good feeling" to African Americans.[94]

Lack of evidence makes it impossible to determine how Bruce viewed Wilson's candidacy. Bruce was staunchly Republican, but still the Democrats sought to use his name to their advantage. Prior to Wilson's inauguration, A. H. Underdown, chair of the subcommittee for public comfort, indicated that

Daniel Murray had suggested Bruce for consideration as auxiliary chair of the subcommittee for public entertainment and accommodation (for black visitors to Washington). It is not known whether Bruce agreed to take part in the festivities, but his consideration for the position suggests that, like Du Bois, he may have considered Wilson to be a progressive Democrat.[95]

William Calvin Chase, publisher and editor of the *Bee* in Washington and never one to mince his words, wrote Wilson shortly after the inauguration to inquire if it was true that he would use color to keep Negroes out of federal positions. The president's reply was the dismissal of Assistant Atty. Gen. William H. Lewis and auditor of the U.S. Navy Ralph Tyler, who were replaced by white Democrats. Wilson was the first Democrat in the White House since early 1897, the end of Cleveland's second term. This did not bode well for the civil and political rights of southern blacks. Tyler informed George A. Myers that discrimination in the South was on the rise because that region "is in the saddle" with Wilson in office. Since most of Taft's black appointees were southerners, Tyler predicted that "Ham is sure to get it good." Wilson's reactionary policy was hammered home when he appointed a white man to the Haitian diplomatic post, generally a secure black position since 1869, except for a brief four-year period.[96]

Rev. Francis J. Grimke, pastor of Washington's most prestigious black Presbyterian church, no longer believed in Wilson's "Christian character." He wrote a scathing letter of protest to the president on September 5, 1913, after Wilson segregated the races in various government departments.[97] Wilson was forthright on many issues but extremely cautious when it came to making a few black appointments. After he appointed A. E. Patterson to be register of the Treasury, another traditional "Negro position," Thomas Dixon, author of *The Clansman,* informed Wilson that he was "heart sick" that a black man would "boss white girls." Patterson eventually declined the position amid intense southern criticism.[98] Concerned that Wilson's conservatism would jeopardize his reappointment as a municipal judge in the District of Columbia, Robert H. Terrell informed George A. Myers by letter on December 19, 1913, that he was "sitting on a can of nitro-glycerin, likely to explode in a week or two." W. H. Clifford expressed his hope that Terrell would win his confirmation fight because the "slight recognition of our class by the administration might do the race some good." Terrell was confirmed by the U.S. Senate, but his appointment did little to convince African Americans that Wilson would be fair to them.[99]

Whatever favorable sentiments Bruce may have harbored for Wilson were quickly dissipated by the president's callous treatment of black officeholders. It was understandable that Wilson would dismiss black Republican holdovers, but his appointment of white Democrats galled those who saw in him, however fleeting, the hope for a better day. Bruce noted two months after Wilson's inauguration that the policy of white nations was to subjugate the darker races even to the point of rebellion. The African American, asserted Bruce, lagged behind the militant Japanese and Chinese. He urged blacks to emulate them and to stand up for their rights or be kicked about by "pigeon breasted white men [who are] the biggest bluffer[s] in the world." Call his bluff, he demanded.[100]

For African Americans, Wilson's presidency proved disastrous. The Virginia-born chief executive dismissed them from government service, ostracized them in civil service positions by segregating washrooms and dining areas in Washington's government buildings, and maintained a silence concerning the lynching and disfranchisement of black voters in the South. W. E. B. Du Bois, who had supported Wilson in 1912, sharply rebuked the president weeks before the 1916 election. He wrote Wilson on October 10 to express disappointment at his failure to honor his promise of justice for Negroes. Wilson replied that he stood by his assurances and tried to live up to them, but had been defeated in some cases. To Du Bois, these remarks spoke volumes about Wilson's arrogance. Bruce joined Du Bois and others in an attempt to restore the White House to a Republican. Initially, the Republican Party's nomination of Supreme Court Justice Charles Evans Hughes for president did not please Bruce, who considered the jurist a candidate of the nation's ruling class. He characterized the Republican convention in Chicago as "the beginning of the end" of making Negro rights a campaign issue. Instead, Bruce saw the issues of peace, preparedness, and protective tariff begin to occupy the nation's attention. However, the enactment of the Beef Inspection Act, the Pure Food and Drug Act, the passage of child labor laws, and the attacks against capital punishment demonstrated that concerned people could improve life in America. Unfortunately, little was being done to improve the lot of blacks or to enforce their constitutional rights. The old guard Republican reformers who fought to end slavery and racial discrimination were no longer on the political scene. Bruce lamented that Hughes was "neither a Lincoln[,] a McKinley or a Roosevelt in his attitude toward the Negro," which made him "hardly a man to enthuse over." Despite his reservations, Bruce informed Charles W. Anderson that he wanted to "render some service" in the fight. At first, the election was thought to have been a Hughes's upset. Late returns from the West provided Wilson with a close victory, however, as he amassed 277 electoral votes to 254 for his opponent.[101]

Wilson's reelection was a bitter pill to swallow for African Americans and their supporters. Bruce had observed American politics for more than forty years and was perturbed by the lack of interest shown by both major parties toward the race problem in America. While he was not willing to turn his back on the party of his youth, he was becoming slowly but increasingly disillusioned with the Republicans lack of sensitivity. He addressed this issue in 1916 with the publication of a sixty-two-page fictional account, *The Awakening of Hezekiah Jones,* which depicted a black former Civil War colonel, now a confidential bank messenger, who consistently brought out the black vote. The local Republican leadership declined to place any black candidates on their ticket and, fearing that Jones might entice blacks to the Democratic Party, offered to buy his loyalty with a lucrative appointment as well as provide for fifteen to twenty minor positions. While Jones surprised the Republicans by giving them a $250 campaign donation, he requested a square deal in return for the black vote. Jones convinced his followers that their vote deserved two or three clerkships and twenty-six municipal appointments, not only the promised minor positions. Bruce explains in his conclusion that his story, "it is hoped, will teach a lesson to black men everywhere who seem to have lost faith in the self redeeming power of the race and in the honesty and integrity of those whom they have chosen to be their leaders." Ultimately, the moral of the story was "follow your leader, give him your confidence, and your loyal support."[102] Again, Bruce's writing was simplistic and quick to point out the prowess of black men. Less than one hundred black men were commissioned as officers during the Civil War, but Bruce could do no less than make his character of Hezekiah Jones a colonel.

Nevertheless, his account struck a chord with the nation's African American population, who saw little hope for advancement through traditional politics. For decades, Bruce had advocated black voters to use their political muscle to force change. He understood profoundly, however, that racist machinations in government prevented many of his people from exercising their franchise.

African Americans and World War I: Patriotism or Pessimism?

For years it had been Bruce's hope that the participation of African Americans in the nation's wars would show white America that blacks, too, were patriotic souls who held the republic's salvation in high esteem. It was for this reason that he exulted in the exploits of the colored troops in the Civil War and in Cuba and Puerto Rico in the brief war against Spain. Since he fervently believed that battlefield heroism and sacrifice would eventually translate into citizenship rights, even if not immediately, Bruce welcomed the coming of war in 1914. With prescience, Bruce predicted that whites would have to alter their opinion of the darker races, "for in the next war . . . every man here of every race capable of bearing arms will be needed for the struggle." He foretold that it would not be a minor conflict "like the Spanish-American War but a war spelled out with a [capital] W." In such a war, America would "emerge with the loss of a great deal of conceit and cocksureness as to their ability to win . . . without the aid of *alien* races." Bruce also argued that America could not win a war without black men, for "this is his country and he is going to fight for it whether Mr. Wilson believes he has [the courage] to do so or not."[103]

Bruce saw the war as God's retribution for the injustices Europe committed against her colonial subjects. He explained, "we are approaching the end of a cycle of wrong and injustice, but before it arrives rivers of blood will flow." Bruce was so sure of this belief that he cautioned the race to be patient and wait for God to bring "mercy, justice [and] righteousness" to the world upon the cessation of hostilities. Walter Everette Hawkins also subscribed to this viewpoint. Germany was doing to Belgium, he argued, what King Leopold did to the Congo. America is next, thundered Hawkins, for "her garments are filthy in the blood of Afro Americans crying for justice at her gate." In 1915, Hawkins predicted that the war would expose "the white man's . . . savagery and barbarity, his venality and lust, his . . . depravity and moral and innate debasement." Agreeing with this point, Casely Hayford informed Bruce that the war would bring astonishing changes. "Out here [in West Africa]," he added, "we are going steadily to work to make good use of the opportunity, and I am quite certain that there is going to be a tremendous advance forward."[104] Despite his call for blacks to wait on God, Bruce wanted black and brown men to prove their mettle on the battlefield. As the American representative of the *African Times and Orient Review,* Bruce suggested (to an unidentified newspaper editor) that readers wanted to hear about the black troops on the European front. Bruce noted that Duse Mohammed Ali had sought permission from the British war office to send a representative to the war zone to report on the fighting. Since funds were limited, Bruce suggested that syndicated articles should be sold for a minimum of five dollars per week. Bruce thought the proposition would appeal to black publishers because their readers wanted to read about the bravery of West Indian and African soldiers. Bruce may have been seeking a war correspondent position because he noted in an unpublished piece, "Getting By the Censor," that the British typically censored outgoing mail to keep out unpleasant or uncomplimentary war news. Bruce claimed that when he corresponded with his British contacts, he used coded messages written on five stamps that covered most of the envelope, which the censor overlooked.[105]

In April 1917, after the submarine sinking of American merchant ships, the United States declared war on Germany and her allies. The outbreak of war received mixed reactions from black Americans. Representing the radical voice was the *Messenger,* edited by Asa Philip Randolph and Chandler Owen; these socialists considered it "slavish to fight for a government that would not protect their basic rights of citizenship." Instead, they argued, "fight to make

Georgia safe for the Negro."[106] Many agreed with William H. Crogman, a college president, who wrote to Rev. Francis J. Grimke, "they tell us it is a war for 'democracy'! This war is largely a war for commercial supremacy with Africa as the chief prize." Grimke confided in his journal that the colored people did not care whether the kaiser or Uncle Sam was victorious as long as the nation's capital remained a segregated city. Grimke was so opposed to the war that in 1918 he vowed not to donate any money to the Liberty Bond drive or lend his name to the cause because "it is a lie that we are fighting for democracy in the world." He promised not to speak about loyalty to the government while the nation showed no appreciation for the Negro's past military contributions and as long as the Red Cross continued to discriminate against black nurses and physicians. "I hope I have some little self respect left . . . not to allow myself to be insulted and to acquiesce in it. No! I have not spoken, and it is not my purpose to speak," he thundered.[107]

The black community was not monolithic when it came to the war, nor to most controversial subjects. In July 1918, W. E. B. Du Bois shocked and outraged many when he called upon blacks to temporarily put aside their assault on civil and political discrimination and close ranks with the government to defeat Germany. Many viewed the editor as a sellout in search of a military commission, for he had noted three years earlier that the war was a fight among Europeans for Africa's vast mineral wealth. Responses to Du Bois's "Close Ranks" editorial were so hostile that he declined the offer of a military commission.[108] The majority of African Americans, however, eschewed radicalism and displayed their patriotism by buying liberty bonds. Nearly two hundred thousand blacks served in the military despite the cries of "Negro cowards" made by bigots and the army's unwillingness to commission blacks as officers in the segregated regiments or to protect them from hostile southern mobs. Most recruits were assigned to the most difficult assignments and were initially denied an opportunity to engage in combat. In contrast, the French provided them with opportunities to prove their mettle on the battlefield. There they created fear among the Germans, who called them "hell fighters," and adulation from French military and civilians alike.[109]

John Edward Bruce did not join those who called upon blacks to refuse to support the war effort. Instead, he emphasized the past loyalty African Americans had shown in the nation's wars and his readiness to demonstrate his prowess on Europe's battlefields. In an undated essay, "The Negro and the Coming War," he noted that President Wilson was concerned about the loyalty of ethnic European Americans but gave no thought to African Americans. Bruce indicated that he did this "as though [we have] no interest in the government, and no right to share in the burdens and benefits of citizenship . . . among which is the right to bear arms in defense of [our] country." Bruce emphasized that the American Negro was the nation's truest patriot.[110] Once again, Bruce took up the issue of citizenship. He clearly understood that, if considered as an alien race, African Americans would have no reason to fight for the United States. However, as citizens, it would be their duty to fight and, if necessary, die in defense of "their" country. Several months after the United States entered the war, Bruce informed readers of the *African Times and Orient Review* that Negro troops were still being denied opportunities to become commissioned officers. He urged black enlisted men to prove their undying patriotism and take advantage of the officers' training camp the military had established at Des Moines, Iowa. Bruce wrote a pamphlet, *A Defense of the Colored Soldier Who Fought in the Rebellion* (circa 1917), to show that black troops helped preserve the Union during the American Civil War as well as to counter the vicious anti-Negro message presented by Thomas Dixon in *The Clansman*.[111]

Early in 1918, Bruce wrote *A Tribute for the Negro Soldier*. This important piece was a study of black soldiers from ancient history to World War I. His account was well received, even earning praise from Congressman Walter M. Chandler of New York, who published it in the Congressional Record. Chandler even offered to mail copies to all black voters in New York City who could be located "if [Bruce's] race pride suggests this." The supportive legislator noted that a million copies, if sent to whites and blacks, "would tend to lessen race prejudice." Bruce sent a copy to Theodore Roosevelt with a request that the former president mention the work in his public writings. Roosevelt politely acknowledged receipt and promised to read the book. Bruce solicited donors to provide from fifty to one hundred free copies for distribution to sick and disabled soldiers.[112]

Bruce was wise to salute the exploits of black soldiers. American racism limited black soldiers and sailors to positions as bakers, butchers, stevedores, and laborers. This continued until, eager to prove their mettle, they were assigned to French combat units (the 369th Infantry) where their combat prowess earned them the coveted Croix de Guerre, France's highest military honor. Others were awarded the Distinguished Service Cross for their battlefield exploits. Bruce addressed this issue in a synopsis of a proposed play, *Somewhere in France,* which described battered British troops urgently pleading for reinforcements. In the play, the horrors of war lead to the integration of white and black troops and dissolves the race prejudice of white American soldiers.[113] This fictional account of an integrated military unit expressed Bruce's hope that someday the world would judge men by their character and abilities, not by their color or race.

The American military did not embrace Bruce's concern for an integrated force, but the war experience exposed many black soldiers to the liberating knowledge that, in France, the restrictions of the American color line did not exist. Ralph W. Tyler, a black war correspondent, had three sons in military service in Europe. Putting aside parental concern, Tyler reported on the activities of America's segregated black troops in France. After the defeat of Germany and her allies, Tyler wrote to George A. Myers on December 21, 1918: "I feel ... [unequivocally] free. Were I a young man I would never return ... were it not for the fight I ABSOLUTELY KNOW we face on returning." The correspondent added that there was real democracy in France. "No color line ... absolute social equality, as well as political and civic equality." The only thing that caused him to return, noted Tyler, was the fear of being labeled "a coward, which I am not."[114]

Cowardice did not prevail among the returning black soldiers, either. In early 1919, black American troops experienced a bittersweet return. They had helped to make "the world safe for democracy" but saw continuing bigotry and prejudice in the land of their birth. In April, Rev. Francis J. Grimke urged returning soldiers to fight American injustice. He ridiculed the racial ideology that made segregation the rule in the American military. "I know nothing," he wrote, "that sets forth this cursed American prejudice in a more odious ... light than the treatment of our colored soldiers." The Presbyterian minister urged them to fight homegrown racism and make America safe for democracy. At a mass meeting in Philadelphia for returning black troops, also in April, an unidentified speaker proclaimed, "We died in France ... we will die in America. Justice we must have it now." Methodist minister H. F. Butler told the audience that America, not Africa, was their home. We "cleaned up" France "and we are going to clean up home," he concluded. Even Du Bois was no longer willing to close ranks with the racist Wilson administration. In a *Crisis* editorial, "We Return Fighting," the erudite scholar lashed out at a nation that treated its darker citizens as "dogs, monkeys and whores." He vowed that the black man would now turn his energy to fighting against bigotry and racism.[115]

Ralph W. Tyler had returned to America hoping that the contributions of black soldiers would diminish if not eradicate prejudice. He was rudely awakened from this dream. Tyler's nostrils were assaulted by the odious stench of racism in Springfield, Illinois, when he and returning veterans were refused service at the railroad station's dining room. An irate Tyler sued the establishment and pledged never to "forget" the insult nor be silent because he feared that "the spirits of the dead [black] heroes would arise from the battlefields" and call him a traitor. Bruce had previously believed that battlefield heroics would lessen American prejudice. Now, he, too, took umbrage at the mistreatment of the returning soldiers. Declaring that justice would be denied "until white men learn to do *justice* and *to live it,*" the pessimistic Bruce noted that "the day of reckoning between the children of the sun and the white race is... inevitable." While Bruce may have anticipated racial violence, curiously, he dreamed that the pope had remarked that America was not a Christian land because of its mistreatment of Negroes, whose contributions were documented in the Vatican's archives. Bruce was so moved by the dream that he wrote it down, along with the note "what does it mean?"[116]

"The day of reckoning" came in mid-1919 when twenty-five race riots broke out and blacks struck back with a fervor that heightened race pride and alerted whites that a New Negro was on the scene. The loss of seventy-six African Americans to lynch mobs led Bruce to declare that "the time for cringing is over." He called upon black men to respond "MAN FASHION." "If we go forward we die; if we go backward we die. Better to go forward and die. We are going forward," he vowed.[117]

Ironically, while the races fought so fiercely in the streets that the period became known as the Red Summer of 1919, others sought to honor the bravery of the black heroes, dead and alive. Bill H.R. 5131 was introduced into the 66th Congress on June 6. Among other things, it called for a commission to design a monument or memorial in Washington to the memory of Negro soldiers and sailors for their contribution in the nation's wars. The National Memorial Commission was composed of Walter E. Edge, Isaac Sherwood, L. C. Dyer, Ferdinand D. Lee, James H. W. Howard, J. Thomas Hewin, and John Edward Bruce. Later, Judge Robert H. Terrell became the president of the National Memorial Association. The association's goal was to raise $500,000 to cover the expenses of the design and construction of the memorial. In 1920, the governors of several states, including New York, appointed Bruce to represent them in the National Memorial Association. Happily, Bruce thanked Marcus Garvey's Universal Negro Improvement Association (UNIA) for its help in raising the desired funds. This effort, he noted, showed the world that the UNIA was "not a body of grafters & race patriots," a significant observation at a time when the Pan-African organization was coming under intense scrutiny.[118]

Wilson and Harding

The year 1919 witnessed an incremental rise in Bruce's racial chauvinism that was fueled, in part, by the contemptible foreign policy of Woodrow Wilson. The American president arrogantly dismissed African and Asian people in his proposed plans to reshape the national boundaries of eastern and central Europe around the cry of self-determination. Neither Wilson nor European leaders envisioned independence for colonial subjects in Africa, Asia, or the Caribbean. For these reasons, Bruce predicted a coming race war. Like others, he was angry that black soldiers were mistreated by the American military in France and discriminated against in the United States. He cited the shabby treatment of Col. Charles Young, who, despite riding a horse from Ohio to Washington, D.C., to prove his fitness for service, was denied an opportunity for active duty during the war. Bruce told an audience of masons in 1919 to gain respect and stop exhibiting slave traits by acting like mammies and uncles. Understanding that after blacks had shown their fidelity during time of war, whites pushed them back to their subordinate positions when the conflict had ceased, Bruce cautioned, "we should school ourselves to resist the flattery and blandishment of white people." He called for the creation of a brotherhood of Negroes who adopted the motto "one aim and one destiny" to combat white oppression and repression. In "The Significance of Brotherhood," a speech delivered on May 23, 1919, Bruce called upon masons to be the catalyst for the organization of African Americans to fight caste and race prejudice and demonstrate the proper way to control their destiny in the coming years.[119]

The Wilson administration's segregation of black civil servants, the humiliating treatment of black soldiers, the race riots of 1919, and the rising tide of racism in the North made many African Americans pessimistic about their future in America. Before the death of Theodore Roosevelt in 1919, Bruce informed the former president that he had voted to put him in "every elective office [he] had ever held and expect to vote for [him] in 1920, if alive." African Americans in 1920 saw little hope for racial progress in the presidential campaigns of the two major candidates. The Democratic ticket remained mute about the concerns of blacks, and the Republican ticket of Harding-Coolidge left much to be desired, although Harding noted in his July 22 acceptance speech that "Negro citizens . . . should be guaranteed the enjoyment of all their rights." Somewhat encouraged by his remarks, black voters wanted a possible Harding administration to guarantee voting rights in the South and to remove segregated facilities in government offices in Washington. They also wanted laws that would make lynching a federal crime, provide federal aid to education to ensure all children free common school education, and eradicate Jim Crow railroad cars in southern states and in interstate travel. Harding's inaugural address of March 4, 1921, did not mention Negroes and did not address any of their most vital concerns. However, Harding praised women, who had recently won the constitutional right to vote. (Most black southern female eligible voters were disfranchised by southern racism.) Soon thereafter, Bruce called upon women to urge Harding to appoint civil rights activist Mary Church Terrell, founder of the National Association of Colored Women, as recorder of deeds in Washington. By the fall of 1921, Bruce bitterly declared that Harding had also drawn the color line in appointments, as did Wilson, and that it had been a crime for Negroes to vote for him. Bruce wrote several open letters to President Harding criticizing him for his policies and for lacking the courage of Reconstruction Republicans such as Charles Sumner, Thaddeus Stevens, and Ulysses S. Grant, who defended the rights of black Americans. Once a staunch Republican, Bruce was now convinced that the concept of Negro political equality was a joke, as the Republican Party no longer represented a safe ship in the open sea. Instead, Bruce lamented that the Negro "has been chucked overboard."[120] Bruce wrote in 1922 that blacks were "political outcasts" who could only hope that "maybe in 1923 or 1924 somebody who [knew] us well in the old days will be jacking for 'we.'"[121] Embittered by the indifference of white America, Bruce saw the future of the race in self-reliance and not upon the goodwill of the nation. He urged blacks to "root hog or die." Their survival, he declared, depended upon their ability to make terms with the leaders of all parties and to use their vote as a weapon to secure their rights. It was during this period that Bruce embraced the racial chauvinism of Marcus Garvey's Universal Negro Improvement Association and vowed that the black man's destiny was in Africa. While racism spurred others to increase their agitation, Bruce decided that American racism was so entrenched that nothing short of God's almighty hand could cause its immediate termination. It took years of agitation before Bruce reached this conclusion.

John Edward Bruce, circa 1922. Courtesy Photographs and Prints Division, Schomburg Center for Research in Black Culture, New York Public Library, Astor, Lenox and Tilden Foundations.

Marcus Garvey, Christmas 1919, taken on the occasion of his marriage to his first wife, Amy Ashwood. Courtesy Photographs and Prints Division, Schomburg Center for Research in Black Culture, New York Public Library, Astor, Lenox and Tilden Foundations.

Alex Crummell, circa 1890s. Courtesy Photographs and Prints Division, Schomburg Center for Research in Black Culture, New York Public Library, Astor, Lenox and Tilden Foundations.

Marcus Garvey, in handcuffs, being taken by a U.S. marshal from court to the Atlanta federal penitentiary, 1925. Courtesy Photographs and Prints Division, Schomburg Center for Research in Black Culture, New York Public Library, Astor, Lenox and Tilden Foundations.

Mourners at John Edward Bruce's grave, 1924. Left to right: Mrs. Bruce, Marcus Garvey, and Arthur Schomburg. Courtesy Photographs and Prints Division, Schomburg Center for Research in Black Culture, New York Public Library, Astor, Lenox and Tilden Foundations.

Arthur Alphonso Schomburg, 1900s. Courtesy Arthur A. Schomburg Photograph Collection, Photographs and Prints Division, Schomburg Center for Research in Black Culture, New York Public Library, Astor, Lenox and Tilden Foundations.

From Civil Rights to Pan-Africanism, 1890–1920

Garvey's association, the largest black membership organization ever, was part of a tradition of African American organizations that had existed since before the establishment of the United States. Between 1800 and 1861, a growing number of free African Americans sought their salvation in church, mutual relief, and benevolent societies. These organizations and institutions that they formed emphasized self-reliance in the schools, lyceums, debating clubs, and reading rooms. African Americans joined antislavery societies to combat the evils that held in captivity millions on southern farms and plantations. With emancipation came colleges, banks, insurance companies, labor organizations, and publishing houses. In short, black people organized themselves in various organizations to demand civil, political, and economic rights in America.

The Afro-American League and National Afro-American Council

Bruce devoted a considerable portion of his adult life to supporting organizations that he joined or founded. They all welcomed his pen, which he wielded with a ferocity that earned him accolades. It was through Bruce's columns in the black press that he emphasized the need for organized and intelligent group activity in order that the race could successfully make gains in the struggle to overcome America's race problem. Unlike some who shared Bruce's strong ego and personality, he did not let these qualities exclude him from joining in organizations as a follower. His first concern was always whether the organization promoted the interest of African Americans. If the answer was affirmative, Bruce willingly gave his time and writing talent in behalf of that organization.

His earliest known participation in a race organization began with the Afro-American League founded by journalist Timothy Thomas Fortune. The origin of the league dates to 1887 when Fortune suggested its formation. A call went out two years later for a founding convention to meet in January

1890. At the appointed time, 147 delegates came from twenty-one states and the District of Columbia. A critic of the Republican Party, Fortune told the Chicago gathering that the league should stand for the race and not for any political party. He outlined the grievances that penalized blacks educationally, economically, and politically. The league, argued Fortune, should be more than a protest organization. High among his recommendations was a call for an Afro-American national bank, a bureau of immigration to locate desirable spots in the country for relocation of willing participants, a bureau of technical industrial education, a bureau of cooperative industry, and lobbyists to influence legislators in the federal and state legislatures.[1]

John C. Price (of North Carolina) and Fortune were elected president and secretary respectively.[2] Bruce joined the Afro-American League because it appealed to his interest in racial self-reliance and activism. Its emphasis on civil and political rights for blacks attracted many of the most progressive black thinkers. Bruce remained active in the league during its near decade-long existence.

Bruce's talents, however, also drew some white leaders to him. Albion W. Tourgee, for example, sought to recruit Bruce for the National Citizens Rights Association. The radical Tourgee, a former Reconstruction judge in North Carolina, advocated a raceless and classless society and suggested that atrocities should be met with retaliation. He informed Bruce on November 17, 1891, that he had received more than two hundred applications for the association and, outside of headquarters, the membership was secret unless an individual wished to divulge his own name. There were no meetings, thus no discord, and no talk of social equality to cause unrest. Assured Tourgee, "We have only to be prudent, active and sensible and we shall not only have the strongest following but the best backing a good cause ever had." It is not known how Bruce responded to Tourgee, but it is clear that he preferred organizations that had black leaders and members. Despite the militancy of his writings, Bruce generally eschewed retaliatory violence. At this time, he was also involved with the Equal Rights League as secretary of the District of Columbia's chapter as well as with the Afro-American League. He had a legitimate excuse to evade Tourgee's overture, which probably involved some clandestine, if not illegal, activity.[3]

Despite its good intentions to eradicate racial prejudice and discrimination, The Afro-American League lacked cooperation from black elected officials who were reluctant to confront the Republican Party for its neglect of African Americans. For this reason, others decided in 1898 to form the National Afro-American Council. Organized under the leadership of AMEZ Bishop Alexander Walters, the objectives of the council nearly matched those of the defunct Afro-American League. Bruce was for a time financial secretary of the new organization. However, it lost its effectiveness around 1902 after

Booker T. Washington's spies infiltrated it and effectively undermined its efforts to publicly criticize President McKinley's ability to uphold the rights of southern blacks.

Bruce was an active council member and often delivered messages of self-reliance. For example, he presented in late 1899 a paper titled "The Concentration of Energy" before an Afro-American Council meeting in Albany, New York. This far-ranging lecture touched upon many subjects. Bruce believed that disorganization prevented progress and generated contempt from whites who viewed the Negro as shiftless, aimless, and spineless. Bruce urged his audience to stop enriching white businesses while ignoring their own. Disdainfully, he dismissed the pretty boys on the street corner "with their hair done up in ox marrow or quinine juice and their faces plastered with corn starch." He suggested that blacks form cooperatives for economic development. It would be better, he argued, to have five men each invest one thousand dollars in a business than have one man invest the same amount without any surplus capital. "The experiment is worth trying," Bruce noted. "All it needs is experience, confidence, courage and application. Is the Negro equal to the demand? We shall see."[4]

Bruce wrestled with his question over the next several years as he watched Booker T. Washington's influence increase among white America while many blacks militantly denounced his accommodationist policies. Bruce was searching for solutions to the race problem. He, of course, could not completely accept accommodationism, although he alluded to it in some of his speeches and writings. Bruce dismissed anarchy as antithetical to the black man's worldview. He was, indeed, more comfortable during this period placing things into the hands of God because he believed that He had a special role for the Negro. Bruce addressed this in "The Hour of Prayer":

> Gather to your so'emn meeting
> ye who weep for human woe;
> God is never tired of greeting
> those who seek his face below
>
> Pray for those who've felt the power
> of a race whose proud boast is,
> that this Christian land of ours
> unto all doth justice give . . . Heaven hear us,
> and defend us, help, o, help our blind belief
>
> ■ ■ ■
>
> Pray with tears for proud oppressors
> Trampling on the North they hate.[5]

While this sober reflection was indicative of Bruce's yearning for a solution to the race problem, it was also a plea to the Republican Party and the nation not to abandon African Americans to the mercy of southern tyrants. It was a harbinger of a period so eloquently named by historian Rayford Logan as "the betrayal of the Negro." While Bruce's plea captured the faith of a devout Christian, he would slowly abandon his conviction as the new century rapidly approached. Meanwhile, as the century neared its end, Bruce sought answers from his mentors. Edward W. Blyden advised the American Negro to eschew politics. Alexander Crummell thought that intellect was the proper weapon to take into battle against bigotry. During the next several decades, both views would capture Bruce's interest as his disillusionment with his native land grew.

Meanwhile, the National Afro-American Council's weakness was the presence in the organization of men with different ideologies and political persuasions. Some were pro-McKinley; others were in the opposition. Some supported the accommodationist views of Booker T. Washington; others denounced them at every opportunity. Integrationists and assimilationists argued with black nationalists as to the fate of African Americans. They even argued whether *colored, Negro,* or *Afro-American* was the most appropriate nomenclature for people of African descent. Few had the simple luxury to call themselves American, with its implication of full citizenship. All of these differences undermined the effectiveness of the organization. The color issue became a tempest in a teapot in January 1903 when a frustrated Bruce criticized the colored elite who attended a White House reception where all but President Roosevelt snubbed them. He asserted that dining with the president had done nothing to put nails into the coffin of caste prejudice. Bruce was upset with those who cackled when they received appointments because this only played into the hands of the white bigots who resented boasting Negroes. Emulate Jews, he demanded, for "they do not crow about the religious faith of Jacob Canter, yet they have the borough President of Manhattan." Bruce cautioned the race to be discreet, not to boast; to check their speech and not to "embarrass [whites] who are endeavoring to secure to us ... the blessings of liberty and equality before the law." He concluded that nothing they could say or do would hasten change. However, his postscript was that slavery had been destroyed by the violence of war, not the moral efforts of abolitionists. This exposed his confused reasoning. Bruce had difficulty in articulating a consistent strategy for racial advancement, and this inconsistency led others to question his leadership.[6]

While it was clear that Bruce believed that blacks were equal to whites in intellectual capabilities, it was less certain why he was so hostile toward those whose intelligence, wit, and culture earned them an invitation to one White House function. Others pondered this enigmatic reasoning. In the February 7,

1903, *Colored American,* George McBane wrote that the attendance of Henry P. Cheatham and other members of the black elite at the White House had done the most to break down racial barriers since the freeing of Bruce and other slaves. McBane attributed Bruce's outburst to jealousy because he had not been invited and that, if invited, he would have attended. He asked God to "reconstruct 'Bruce Grit' and make many more 'misguided colored people' to keep his company." Clearly, the argument was over class and political difference. Bruce did not possess the degrees, bank accounts, or real estate holdings of the invited elite, and he may have assumed their presence at the reception was merely for their personal aggrandizement. Ida D. Bailey, a resident of Washington, criticized Bruce's tirade. She noted that blacks should not feel that their presence was embarrassing to whites at a White House function when Chinese, Turks, Jews, Italians, and others also were in attendance.[7] A beaten but unbowed Bruce admitted that he did not mean to condemn the attendance of Negroes at White House receptions. Rather, he questioned the wisdom of their attending in light of the race question. He dismissed the idea that such attendance was the wedge to open the door to racial harmony. Instead, Bruce urged the race to obtain political and civil rights and to seek "his social rights both inside and out, of the White House." Bruce added that even the most refined and cultured whites considered themselves superior to the colored elite because the enslaved and the enslavers cannot have an equal social or political status.[8]

Although this view mirrored the message of Booker T. Washington's famous Atlanta Compromise speech, Bruce's negative response to the attendance of colored elite at Roosevelt's reception went beyond the issues of social equality. In a larger sense, it represented a quarrel with the ideological position of some black elite who were unwilling to confront the president on the sorry state of race relations in the United States. This view was confirmed after Atty. James H. Hayes, president of the National Negro Suffrage League and an opponent of Booker T. Washington, expressed before the Afro-American Council his opposition to the adoption of the 1902 Virginia constitution and its restrictive voting and public accommodations clauses. Hayes's manly view, as noted by Ida D. Bailey, was in contrast to that of Henry P. Cheatham and others who had attended the White House reception and had suggested that Roosevelt be spared the embarrassment of nominating "troublesome candidates for office." This was an indirect reference to William D. Crum, who was being considered at the time for a custom collector's position in Charleston. Instead, they recommended that before reaching the president for consideration, black candidates for federal appointments should first be recommended by the Afro-American Council. This meant, of course, that only individuals approved by Booker T. Washington—and who were not rabble-rousers—

would have an opportunity for an appointment. (Washington had minions who were members of the Afro-American Council). Ida D. Bailey promised that women planned to protest these backroom decisions because they undermined the race's civil and political rights, and they were tired "of these self appointed apologists speaking for them or telling them what to do."[9]

Hayes's remarks elicited a hostile reception from the Afro-American Council. AME Bishop Charles S. Smith castigated him for stating that murderous mobs in the South would "breed a race of Nat Turners and the sword and torch will devastate and dissolve the South." An outraged Smith noted that Hayes did not speak for the race because "the American Negro is the best ally that the white man has." A February 7 editorial in the *Colored American* declared that, despite his good intentions, Hayes's intemperate remarks left him "discredited and despised as a senseless agitator."[10] Bruce, however, offered a ringing defense of Hayes. He considered his statement a warning, not a threat, but "an appeal for justice and fairness." Critical of Bishop Smith's call for an alliance with whites, Bruce dismissed "good whites" as liars, thieves, and criminals who lynch blacks every year.[11] Here, Bruce would distinguish between whites such as James S. Clarkson, who had consistently supported equal rights and justice, and the majority of Christian whites, southern and northern, who remained silent in the face of atrocities against African Americans.

Bruce's strong reaction to the anti-Hayes forces underscored his concern that race leadership in America was, at best, floundering. At worst, it was under the control of Booker T. Washington, the political manipulator. The faction-ridden Afro-American Council was virtually fruitless by 1903. The gathering that met in Louisville, Kentucky, in that year was beset by intrigue, as reported by the *Colored American* in its July 4 and July 11 issues. Some of the delegates, including Bruce, broke away and organized the National Afro-American Association and elected George Wibecan president. Bruce explained in the July 11 issue that the association had developed from James H. Hayes's plea to legally oppose disfranchisement of black males but that the thirty members decided to merge with the Afro-American Council to jointly battle discrimination.

The attempts of Bruce and others to undermine the Afro-American Council created a brouhaha. The editor of the *Colored American* branded Hayes "an ill balanced agitator." Charles W. Anderson, an ally of Booker T. Washington, wrote him on July 6 that Bruce was involved with the opposition group and added that Hayes probably paid for Bruce's trip to Kentucky because he usually avoided paying for himself. Upon hearing the news about Bruce's involvement, James S. Clarkson promised Washington that he would scold his friend. In the July 18 weekly, a badgered Bruce sought to defend himself and the suffrage association. He claimed that it had not been their intent to antagonize the Afro-American Council; they meant merely to draw up a constitution because the council had offered overtures that were accepted "in the interest of harmony and peace." Bruce denied that he and other dissenters were agitators or beggars. His contention that his group had arrived in Louisville completely ignorant that the council was also meeting there was ludicrous. It also lacked credibility, since the suffrage movement was associated with William Monroe Trotter, Booker T. Washington's most outrageous critic.[12] Bruce's lame excuse was attributed to his dependency on his position in the surveyor of the Port of New York office under James S. Clarkson.

Bruce's effort to undermine the Afro-American Council was a clear indication that he no longer admired Booker T. Washington or wanted to maintain his affiliation with the organization. He severed his ties with both when he assumed the editorial responsibilities of a new magazine, the *Impending Conflict*, published by Melvin J. Chisum. The publication, according to Bruce, eschewed force or "a resort to arms" and preferred to present "a clash of opinion, of intellect, of intelligence, and a final statement fair to the Negro and fair to the whites."[13] Unknown to Bruce, the magazine was in the Tuskegee camp. Determined to keep their spy's identity secret, Emmett J. Scott, Washington's private secretary, wrote as "R. C. Black" on July 23 to Atty. Wilford H. Smith (J. C. May) that an enclosed editorial from the *Impending Conflict* "ought to draw out [William Monroe] Trotter if any thing does. You say not to fear Bruce. *I do fear Bruce.*" His fear was based on Bruce's mercurial behavior as well as the suspicion that he could not be trusted. Scott (Black) warned that Bruce should not know about a probable lawsuit against Trotter nor of their involvement in it. "I think, however it is going to be a royal scrap to see Bruce, as he will be represented as doing, fighting the Trotter gang when they have been trotting together so much," he concluded. A week later, Smith (May) replied, "I do not mean in speaking of Bruce that he would be trusted with any of our affairs whatever. He knows absolutely nothing and will not be told anything. All my dealings with Chisum are in a very private and confidential way."[14] Meanwhile, Chisum informed Scott by letter on July 23 that the magazine was neither a corporation nor a partnership and that Bruce had signed an agreement not to write, publish, or cause to be published letters or articles hostile to Washington's policy. An irate Chisum complained that Bruce wrote this "blasted stuff" for the *Denver Statesman*. Chisum promised to keep Bruce to the contract; therefore, Scott should not expect to see any more of his "tommy rot." Chisum believed that he could control Bruce Grit because he had never been employed regularly on any publication's payroll and because of his dependency upon Clarkson. Chisum requested that his letter remain confidential between them and Washington. A concerned Washington wrote to Scott on July 25 advising Smith to avoid all confidential dealings with Bruce, "who is very unreliable."

Despite assurances from Chisum, Bruce was unpredictable and not easily controlled, but Charles W. Anderson sought to gain Clarkson's assistance to curb him. In February 1904, Anderson, who was Bruce's "friend," visited Clarkson and found Bruce in the outer office. Anderson informed Washington that Bruce begged him to put in a good word for Chisum but that he replied that he thought the two had parted over the breakup of the *Impending Conflict* several weeks earlier. Bruce replied that Chisum wanted a letter stating that the magazine folded because Bruce refused to let it be turned over to Washington. Anderson suggested that perhaps the two were close friends and that Chisum needed the letter to do business with Washington. (No evidence suggests this.)[15]

Washington had to contend not only with a mercurial Bruce but also with William Monroe Trotter, who was the educator's most vocal critic. On July 30, Trotter and his followers instigated a riot to prevent Washington from speaking before the Boston branch of the Negro Business League. The incident embarrassed Washington, who had his adversary arrested, leading to his incarceration for a month. While Trotter's antics shocked many of the city's African American middle class, Washington's reaction exposed him as someone who would go to extremes to silence his critics. The unflappable Washington informed Francis J. Garrison, grandson of abolitionist William Lloyd Garrison, that the "riot" was a "painful and disagreeable . . . experience" that he compared to "a severe surgical operation." The Tuskegee educator expressed a mixture of pity and anger toward the Trotter clique. Confident that Trotter had been removed as an irritant, Washington confided to Garrison that Trotter's action destroyed his credibility and influence with Boston's black middle class. Six months later, Washington gloated over Trotter's "downfall." He informed inventor Lewis H. Latimer that his critics were undeserving of his attention or sympathy because they were seekers of cheap notoriety who did not have "the welfare of the race upon their hearts." Washington suggested to Whitefield McKinlay, his close friend in the District of Columbia, that Trotter, George W. Forbes, Archibald H. Grimke, and several others had killed their influence with both races and that Trotter had been removed from the meeting "in handcuffs, yelling like a baby."[16]

Despite his earlier rejection of Trotter's anti-Washington rhetoric, Bruce now fully supported the editor of the *Guardian*, but it is not clear what role he may have provided behind the scenes in the Boston incident. His views of the riot are unknown. Edward E. Cooper, publisher of the *Colored American*, probably refused to print any of his anti-Washington tirades, and many of the other papers Bruce wrote for are no longer extant.

The Niagara Movement

Bruce's involvement in the Trotter-Washington debate would lead to him joining forces with Trotter, W. E. B. Du Bois, and other activists to form the Niagara movement. The ineffectiveness of the National Afro-American Council, Du Bois's failure to accommodate a rapprochement with Washington in 1904, and the jailing of Trotter caused thoughtful men to seek an organization to take on the race's civil and political battles and confront Washington's sway over the nation's white power structure. In February 1905, Rev. Charles S. Morris, pastor of New York's Abyssinian Baptist Church, wrote to Bruce that advocates of racial justice had to organize to remove Washington from his influential leadership role because he begged for money from whites to buy black men.[17] On June 13, Du Bois planted the seeds for the Niagara Movement when he proposed the formation of an organization to stop the Tuskegee educator from using money and influence to prevent criticism and to manufacture public opinion. Du Bois also wanted the organization to insist on "manhood [voting] rights, industrial opportunity and spiritual freedom." From July 11 to 14, twenty-nine men from fourteen states met on the Canadian side of Niagara Falls to organize the Niagara Movement. While some of its goals, such as universal male suffrage, economic and educational opportunity, and eradication of discriminatory practices on the public carriers were similar to the objectives of the Afro-American Council, the Niagara Movement was not in Washington's orbit.[18] Not unlike Booker T. Washington, Du Bois valued Bruce's prestige as a disseminator of information, and he enthusiastically sought the writer's support for the movement. Du Bois wrote to Bruce shortly before the holidays in 1905, "merry Christmas, and a new year devoted to effective work for our race and nation." Acknowledging that work falls on the shoulders of a few, Du Bois inquired, "with the New Year won't you be sure you are giving a reasonable part of your time and purse to the cause? Remember the Niagara Movement is going to be judged by its deeds. After the rest of the holidays—DEEDS."[19]

Booker T. Washington's supporters were correctly concerned that the Niagara Movement potentially represented a major threat to the educator's leadership. They realized that his white supporters might distance themselves from Washington if his standing in the black and white community was seriously threatened. *New York Age* editor Timothy Thomas Fortune defended Washington against the radicals of the Niagara Movement. In an April 1906 editorial, Fortune rebuked the critics by asserting that Negroes were no better off under the militant Frederick Douglass than they were under Washington's leadership. Moreover, those who now denounced the Tuskegee educator had previously castigated Douglass. He attributed the anti-Washington rhetoric to the race's refusal "to follow any leadership . . . [which] is the . . . misfortune of the race in the past and the present."[20] Fortune's critique aside, Washington's critics were intent on invalidating his leadership.

In August, the *Guardian* published an unsigned letter from New York, probably written by Bruce. The piece praised the call for the Niagara Movement as a "manly, courteous, dignified and emphatic statement of the Negro's case [for] equity."[21] Bruce's dedication to racial uplift led his friends and associates to plan a testimonial dinner in his honor for the evening of September 28, 1905. Bruce still did not believe that Charles W. Anderson was a spy for Booker T. Washington, adding that Anderson wanted to discuss the testimonial with Schomburg. "He is a *real* friend and will cooperate with you heartily in the matter," commented Bruce. Ironically, Bruce so valued Anderson's friendship that he wrote to Trotter on April 17, 1905, that a *Guardian* editorial attacking Anderson was full of lies; he was not a knee bender, flunky, or a white man's Negro. Bruce demanded a retraction. Trotter refused and dropped the bombshell that Anderson was Washington's chief spy in New York. Therefore, "to H[ell] with 'Charlie.'" Bruce appealed to Trotter, "I ask you . . . to publish this defense of [Anderson] who is my warmest, truest and loyal friend." Bruce declared that he was not a "holiday friend." Bruce's loyalty to his friends was undeniable. His credo was "a true friend is the medicine of life" and that friendship based on interest does not last because it is insincere. This attitude explains why Bruce later broke off his relationship with Trotter.

Bruce's circle of loyal friends extended around the globe. Invitations were sent to his admirers in Africa, Europe, and throughout the United States. Twenty-seven guests attended the testimonial, but among those absent was Bruce's "good friend" Charles W. Anderson, who conveniently vacationed in the Adirondack Mountains from September 27 to October 5. Distance kept many other invitees from attending, but those who did were a reflection of Bruce's international contacts. Bruce urged the assembled body to agitate the race because "the satisfied Negro will never advance." Emphasizing self-reliance, Bruce declared that those who constantly accept favors are never the equals of their patrons. In his toast, Bruce declared the following: "the Negro, may he ever be right, but right or wrong . . . he is a bone of our bone, flesh of our flesh and . . . we are indissolubly linked together . . . wherever . . . one of our race and blood is found."[22] Bruce received honors because his love of his people knew no bounds. In his unpublished papers is located this rare self-description, dated August 5, 1905:

> I bow only to the inevitable-fate
> I am master of all things else.
> I acknowledge no power beyond myself

or that is not contained in myself.
Being made in the image and likeness of God.
I am inferior only to Him.
I am the peer of my equals
... I am God's noblest work. *A Man.*[23]

American Negro Academy

Bruce was best known to contemporaries as a militant writer who challenged racial bigotry and self-important misleaders. While this was an accurate assessment, it does not fully describe the man. Bruce was also interested in uncovering the past of the black man and woman. He believed that his people's history did not begin on the slave ship or in the cotton, rice, or tobacco fields of the American South. Science, technology, mathematics, and civilization thrived in Africa long before the slave trade brought Africans to the Americas. Bruce understood that ignorance of their past caused many African Americans to possess low self-esteem.

In 1897, Bruce teamed up with Alexander Crummell and other intellectuals from academia, the clergy, and the professions to form an American Negro Academy. The ANA sought to "foster black literature, scholarship and the arts" to counter the materialism symbolized by industrial education.[24] The erudite Crummell contrasted with the earthy Bruce, but the two became close friends. Crummell, an Episcopalian priest, had resided in Liberia many years before returning to the United States because of health reasons. He offered Bruce sage advice about life in West Africa, as well as prescriptions for conducting his personal life. The two shared an intense pride in being Negroes (meaning dark complexioned), and both strongly opposed using the terms *colored* and *Afro-American*. They felt such terms too often were preferred by the lighter complexioned to identify people of African descent.

The American Negro Academy was perhaps Crummell's greatest legacy to his people. Its immediate origins date to 1893 when Richard R. Wright, president of the State Industrial College near Savannah, Georgia, suggested to William H. Crogman, a professor at Clark College in Atlanta, that scholars needed to solve the race problem. Crogman contacted Rev. Francis J. Grimke, who recommended that he contact Crummell. In 1894, Crummell suggested to Crogman that an African Institute of about fifty scholars engage in "literary, statistical, ethnographical, [and] folk lore investigation" concerning the African race worldwide. An effective organization, noted Crummell, would exclude "mere talkers and screamers"; the validity of the work would attract applicants who would clamor for membership, and the resulting scholarship would "command the respect of the scholarly element outside."[25] The plans for a scholarly organization moved forward. Excited by its possibilities, Crummell wrote to Bruce on October 30, 1896, that he was contemplating a project he hoped "may serve toward [a] coalescence of superior power among us." He requested Bruce's "presence & assistance." The reply was succinct: "the civilization under which we live is white," and a scholarly Negro organization was necessary. Crummell reminded Bruce that, even if whites wanted to appoint blacks to prestigious positions, few had the scientific minds. The race must absorb civilization in all its respects "as a prerequisite for civil functions & the use of political power," declared Crummell. Otherwise, he would remain "a puppet & a tool of white demagogues & black sycophants."

On March 5, 1897, the American Negro Academy (ANA) was formed with eighteen members. Bruce joined W. E. B. Du Bois, William S. Scarborough, Richard R. Wright, Robert H. Terrell, Kelly Miller, Paul Laurence Dunbar, T. McCants Stewart, John H. Smythe, AME Bishops Benjamin T. Tanner and Benjamin F. Lee, Theophilus G. Steward, Levi J. Coppin, William H. Ferris, Rev. Francis J. Grimke, William H. Crogman, Crummell, and others in the organization.[26] From its inception until its demise in 1928, the ANA sought to be the voice of the race and to protest injustice in a period of accommodationism. It attracted members from much of the race's elite, but it failed to galvanize either it or the masses enough to bring about substantial change in America's racial climate.[27]

The Nomenclature Question: Who Are We?

Arguments over the proper name for African Americans contributed in part to the inability of the ANA to fight successfully on behalf of the race. Bruce declared that *Negro* represented "national hope" and was a name that would "stick . . . as long as God rules the universe." Timothy Thomas Fortune preferred *Afro-American* because he understood *Negro* to mean "unmixed," and he felt that its usage would cause a split between "blacks" and those of mixed race. Another critic of the term *Negro* argued that the name did not apply "to the intelligent, educated men of mixed blood" but rather to those with distinctive African features such as Booker T. Washington. Bruce was extremely critical of Dr. James E. Henderson, a Springfield, Illinois, physician and surgeon who wrote a series of newspaper articles in 1895 that denigrated full-blooded Negroes. He called upon mixed-bloods to free themselves from the Negro race and lift the weight of inferior status from their shoulders. C. H. J. Taylor, recorder of deeds, assured Bruce that he was right not to apologize for calling Henderson a "pterodactyl hybrid neither bird nor bat." Bruce's scathing remarks prompted J. Robert Love to write from Jamaica, "you are a pitiless writer—so caustic and sarcastic, so impertinent and persistent. Your last unmerciful castigation of Dr. Henderson might properly be characterized as 'cruelty to animals.'"

Adding to the dissension among members, Crummell and Bruce believed that the ANA should support the concept of Pan-Africanism, which they considered essential for the formation of a race literature not dominated by "white thinking." Unimpressed, Fortune declared that Pan-Africanism could not be attained in the United States because the Anglo-Saxon dictated taste in art, philosophy, literature, and politics. As an aside, Fortune criticized dark-complexioned Crummell and journalist John W. Cromwell for marrying mulatto women.[28] Crummell was in Europe and did not hear about Fortune's remarks until he received a copy of the article from Bruce. An enraged Crummell notified Bruce that Jeannie Crummell was not a mulatto, and even if she were, "do I lose my race devotedness if I marry a mulatto, any more than the Prince of Wales loses his robust British feeling ... by marrying a Danish woman?" Fortune was a "pitiful creature [who had] for years [wiggled in and out] of one fanatical theory to another," asserted Crummell. The Episcopal priest confided that he feared that the prejudice of complexion (of which he was guilty) would lead to a caste fight among the race. Crummell considered an increase of more "pure" Negroes into the membership of the ANA to be the remedy. He asked Bruce to nominate several to offset the current membership, 50 percent of whom were mulattos.[29] Meanwhile, Fortune, who had sided with Bruce on other issues, wrote in December 1897, "I shall regret to see the color question become an issue among us because it is senseless ... and because we have more issues now than we can successfully wrestle with."[30] Bruce was in an awkward position. He admired Fortune for his willingness to confront the enemies of the race, but he strongly believed that Fortune was seeking to use the color question as a wedge to divide the race. Bruce could not respond to Fortune because he had written a month earlier to Crummell, "the forces of evil and ignorance are ... trying to create a new Negro with the assistance of drunken Tom Fortune[,] the chief apostle of the new religion of color caste among white men's disowned varicolored children." Bruce may have been referring to an organizing effort for what became the Afro-American Council.[31]

Crummell, who took pride in mentoring the younger Bruce, cautioned him to beware of opportunistic leaders who were shams, not statesmen. The color conscious Crummell placed many of the nation's mulatto leaders in this category, but he insisted that they were a dying breed. As "proof," he cited the ANA's December 1897 meeting where every speaker was a "pure & unadulterated ... Negro." Crummell did not suffer those he believed were fools or race traitors. The acerbic priest brushed aside Richard T. Greener's assertion that he wanted to deny membership in the academy to mulattos. Crummell confided to Bruce that he opposed Greener's appointment because the former Harvard College graduate and Howard Law School dean had passed for white for years before deciding that being a Negro would get him a political position. The color issue, which has yet to be resolved, was a major factor in dividing African Americans a century ago. It was an issue that was not limited to the United States. J. Robert Love, a Jamaican physician who had previously lived in Haiti, informed Bruce in 1893 that the intracolor issue had plagued Haiti but it was subsiding. There, blacks outnumbered mulattos 100 to 1, and more blacks were being educated to love their African features. "Don't *neglect* to fight" the color issue in the United States, urged Love, who warned Bruce that Crummell needed more "Bruce Grits" to sustain him on the issue of intraracial caste prejudice. In 1899, Love urged his friend to chastise a Reverend Davenport, who, referring to Bruce in *The Star of Zion,* had written "on the Negro (color) question, . . . I thought the fellow is spoiling for the severest spanking by *black* hands he ever got." Love and Crummell's concern with the spreading color line was not simple paranoia. The color issue between mulattos and darker complexioned individuals in Liberia had driven Crummell out of the country. Crummell was concerned with those would-be mulatto leaders who repudiated their ancestry by considering Negroes to be the "dead weight" that kept the mulatto, quadroon, and octoroon out of white-owned hotels and saloons because they were viewed as "black." Agreeing with his mentor, Bruce believed that lighter-complexioned individuals sought to escape by calling themselves "colored" and by establishing social clubs, fraternities, sororities, and political clubs that catered exclusively to the blue-vein societies. These organizations were so named because their members' blue veins could be seen through their fair skin. It was Bruce's contention that a Negro who ranged in complexion "from fast black to Nile green" may be classified "colored," although "he won't stand for anything racially if he insists on calling himself 'colored.'" "Colored men" have no history, Bruce declared, but the term *Negro* "stands for a race to whom God Almighty has given a mission" and whose glories extend throughout an ancient world that was influenced by African achievements."[32] In summary, both Bruce and Crummell loathed those whom they believed sought a mulatto escape hatch to avoid identification with their darker-complexioned race members.

Throughout the years, the color question would remain a source of contention among ANA members. In 1919, Bruce was one of the dissidents who questioned the leadership of President Archibald H. Grimke, who Bruce described as "a man of *large* Caucasian reinforcement." Francis J. Grimke, Archibald's brother, alienated some members with a derogatory reference about John W. Cromwell's dark complexion. Whether out of sympathy or solidarity, the membership voted 10–6 on December 30, 1919, to make Cromwell their president. Moreover, Bruce's distinctly Negroid features did not prevent his election to the academy's executive committee.[33]

The color question may have even caused Bruce to temporarily turn against his close friend and confidant Arthur Schomburg. Schomburg was president of the ANA in 1922 when Bruce joined the dissenters who resented the lackadaisical leadership of Schomburg, who was better at collecting books and rare documents than he was in concerning himself with the duties of an administrator. Corresponding Secretary Robert A. Pelham was extremely lax in corresponding with members and often neglected to make copies of occasional papers written by the academy's members, which were to be made available to the membership and the public. Bruce wrote John W. Cromwell on October 14 that "our half br[e]ed brothers have dual minds and they are not expected to think black as did Alexander Crummell. The head of the Academy should be a *seasoned* well equipped [sic] mentally black scholar soaked from his toes to the outer surfaces of his [cranium] in the ideas and ideals which Dr. Crummell held." It is not clear why Bruce questioned Schomburg's racial allegiance or raised the color issue. Despite Schomburg's obvious racial mixture, the two were close friends. The Bruces lived briefly in Schomburg's Brooklyn home, and they often kidded each other about liquor smuggling during Prohibition. Perhaps there was a tension below the surface. Schomburg could be extremely testy when Bruce annoyed him. On one occasion, Bruce failed to return a prized book. Irate, Schomburg wrote, "a collector cannot afford to give away ... the like of his desire unless it is safe guarded with an original." He added that he did not care if the reminder irritated Bruce. On another occasion in 1916, Schomburg advised Bruce that, while he accepted his criticism in the spirit in which it was given, Bruce got upset when criticized. "Too bad," he noted. "You claim I am a book worm with spectacles [and] grouchy [and that] I am more interested in gluttony ... You say I am obtuse," but "Ralph Tyler said you were square headed. All glory to you." Another possible explanation for Bruce's behavior was that his interest in advancing the race through its organizations clouded his judgment. In the case of the ANA's seemingly indifferent leadership, Bruce attacked with whatever weapons were handy, regardless of the consequences. Both Schomburg and Pelham were reelected despite the efforts of Bruce and Cromwell. Fortunately, Schomburg never learned of Bruce's spiteful comments, and their relationship remained publicly cordial until Bruce's death in 1924.[34]

Bruce's antipathy to mulattos carried over to whites in general. While he considered James S. Clarkson a true friend, Bruce eschewed association with white-dominated organizations, lest the Negro remain a subordinate. Despite his sympathies for the objectives of the National Association for the Advancement of Colored People, Bruce did not join the organization because, in its infancy, it was led by whites. W. E. B. Du Bois was the lone black representative in a leadership position. Du Bois, editor of the *Crisis,* the organ of the civil rights organization, hoped to obtain 25,000 subscribers. He asked for Bruce's assistance in this matter in September 1911 and asked him to take out membership. Bruce was one of many who received the appeal to increase readership and to "prove that colored people are interested in their own future." Bruce teamed with Du Bois earlier in the Niagara Movement and admired the younger man for his intelligence and militancy, but he was displeased initially with the writing style of the *Crisis*. In 1913, Bruce confided to Alain L. Locke, the first black American Rhodes Scholar, that the publication was "too stiff in manner and liv[ing] too much in the upper ether." However, Bruce later subscribed. In 1918, he actually praised a Du Bois essay: "I have never read a more fascinating and beautifully written contribution in any number of *The Crisis*."[35]

The Negro Society for Historical Research and the *Journal of Negro History*

Proslavery propagandists noted that Africans were a people incapable of building civilizations and thus had no history. This message took hold. Many African Americans believed that all achievements and contributions to world civilization were the properties of whites, particularly the Anglo-Saxons. In 1911, Bruce and Schomburg sought to dispel this malicious falsehood and to create pride among the black masses by organizing (in Bruce's Yonkers home) the Negro Society for Historical Research. Others had previously sought to do the same by establishing lyceums and reading clubs, but Bruce and Schomburg hoped to place their society on a larger scale. Bruce had sought the same objective previously when he formed the Alexander Crummell Historical Club in 1899. He had wanted to honor his recently deceased mentor by forming a club highlighting "the achievement of the Negro in letters, art, science, medicine and all industry that dignify labor, whether it be of head or of the hand." While some of this duplicated the ANA's objectives, Bruce would have personal control over its direction. From his experience with the Alexander Crummell Historical Club, Bruce decided to make the objectives of the Negro Society for Historical Research broader.

Bruce aimed to make black New York City the cultural and intellectual center for research by forming libraries and art collections to collect data, pamphlets, books, and other pertinent materials chronicling the race's achievements in the African diaspora. Members, honorary members, and corresponding members represented a Who's Who of the African world ranging from King Lewanika of Baratseland to Majola Agbebi of Nigeria to Alain L. Locke of the United States. Many members were black nationalists and amateur historians who would later join Marcus Garvey's Universal Negro Improvement Association. C. A. Franklin, editor of the *Denver Statesman,* was so pleased with his selection as a corresponding member that he wrote the following to Schomburg: "research will furnish ample refutation of the 'nobody' claim, [and] it will . . . encourage us to strive for the eminence that once was ours."[36]

In early 1912, Schomburg, the secretary treasurer, informed President Bruce that the Negro Society could be incorporated as soon as funds were available to pay New York State. More pressing, however, was Schomburg's concern about selecting members. He informed his friend that correspondent members "should show the ability to do some good for the society because he is with its life & should do something to support it." Schomburg made a distinction between honorary members who lived far away and regular members who were close enough to New York to be active participants. He advised Bruce to draw a line clearly distinguishing between corresponding, honorary, and regular members to avoid conflict.[37]

The Negro Society for Historical Research possessed about three hundred books and pamphlets, including some rare items. Like Schomburg, Bruce had collected books, manuscripts, newspaper articles, and other items relating to the history of African people for years. In 1900, Bruce located an 1859 copy of the *Anglo African Magazine,* an important Civil War–era New York City newspaper, in a bookstore. He described it as "the richest treat I had in years." Bruce also had an autographed Phillis Wheatley poem dated 1778. At some unspecified date, Bruce purchased an 1833 theological work by a Reverend Cannon, which he vowed never to loan or sell "durin my nacheral life." Bruce encouraged Rev. Charles D. Martin, pastor of Harlem's Morovian Baptist Church, Arthur Schomburg, and Henry P. Slaughter of Washington to collect books. It was through the instrumentality of the Negro Society for Historical Research that other authors were able to borrow photographs and data for their own publications. The society encouraged its members to go to museums and libraries to search for the glory of Africa's past. For example, in 1913 Schomburg informed Bruce and others that the American Museum of Natural History in New York had on exhibit African curios which "bespeak the ability[,] industry and mental possibility of the African."[38] John W. Cromwell, a corresponding member, agreed with Bruce that the study of history was an important tool for racial empowerment. He asked Bruce in 1912, "Don't you know the Negro is asleep? Or, if awake[,] does he deserve to be treated like a man?" Cromwell lamented that "we have not *one* educational magazine . . .

that can reach our ... teachers.... If we can not ... [get that] before the American public and the world we are doomed and damned. God will not go out of his way and help a race that will not employ the agencies in their grasp." Cromwell's pessimism was caused by his rereading of back issues of his publishing endeavor, the *People's Advocate,* of thirty-five years earlier. It elicited this comment: "I am amazed to see that we have done so little of what was clearly in our power."[39]

Bruce was determined with the help of friends to take the study and celebration of African American history from a marginal state to the mainstream of American educational institutions. Bruce understood that all major rivers had many tributaries. In this case, one significant tributary was the free library system. Bruce joined forces with Library of Congress librarian Daniel A. Murray, James Weldon Johnson, Robert T. Browne, and Arthur Schomburg to form the Negro Library Association in 1914. Housed in the Brooks Branch Library in Brooklyn, the purpose of the library group was to collect, preserve, and encourage literary and artistic attainments among the city's black masses. It also proposed to acquire a building where youth would study Negro history and literature, develop a magazine to disseminate knowledge, publish monographs, books, and other materials, and establish an endowment fund to organize branch libraries throughout the nation. The Negro Library Association's ambitious plans were undermined in 1915 by the establishment of the Association for the Study of Negro Life and History under the leadership of Carter G. Woodson, a Harvard Ph.D. In the following year, Woodson published the scholarly *Journal of Negro History,* followed by the *Negro History Bulletin* for public school teachers. In 1926, Woodson established the week of February 9–14 as Negro History Week.[40] In many respects, the Association for the Study of Negro Life and History duplicated the objectives of the Negro Society for Historical Research. This prompted Schomburg to exclaim that while the *Journal of Negro History* was "credible," he was dismayed because Woodson and associates "are stealing our thunder in which we are pioneer." Still, neither Bruce nor Schomburg resented the competition because both men wanted to see more members of the race acquire knowledge that would make them proud of their African ancestry. Despite his commitment to the Negro Society for Historical Research, Bruce contributed his time and finances to increase the subscription rate of the *Journal of Negro History.* In September 1917, he informed Woodson that he had loaned his copies of the publication to white associates in the hope that they might subscribe. Bruce was pleased that many of them spoke of it with "fulsome praise." Impressed with the scholarly articles, Bruce exclaimed, "I most certainly consider it *helpful* and you may send it to me until one or the other of us dies."[41] Bruce found the

Journal of Negro History so helpful that in January 1919 he sent the one-dollar subscription fee on behalf of Samuel R. Wood of the Gold Coast in West Africa. Wood had forwarded funds to Bruce to purchase or subscribe to race publications. During this period, Bruce promised C. G. Woodson to aid the association financially, but his and Florence's poor health eroded their meager savings. Bruce eventually contributed ten dollars to Woodson, although he regretted that circumstances did not permit him to be more generous, for he was "in full sympathy." He promised in a later period to provide "substantial proof of [his] interest." Bruce requested in July that Woodson send his letters to Schomburg's home at 105 Kosciusko Street in Brooklyn, where the Bruces now took up residence. In November, Bruce thanked Woodson for an autographed copy of his book, *A Century of Negro Migration,* which he promised to read with pleasure.[42]

From 1921 to 1923, Bruce actively contributed funds to Woodson and solicited subscribers to the *Journal of Negro History*. Although, during this period he relocated three times in Harlem after vacating Schomburg's home, and both he and Florence suffered illnesses that wiped out their cash reserve. He was generous with his limited funds because he considered the *Journal of Negro History* a valuable historical source. Bruce informed Woodson in February 1922 that a sample copy of the *Journal* should be sent to R. T. Brady of New York, who was interested in Negroes but ignorant of their accomplishments. "He may loosen up. He is going to Europe [soon] so go after [him] now," Bruce argued. On New Year's Day, 1923, Bruce wrote Woodson that he would send him his long overdue twenty-five dollars after a debt to him was repaid. Bruce was eager to assist Woodson, and the historian was anxious to receive donations because the Association for the Study of Negro Life and History had only a $658.78 surplus as of June 30, 1923. It was no wonder that after Bruce's death the following year, Woodson acknowledged that Bruce was one of the first subscribers to the *Journal of Negro History* and, indeed, "one of the main supporters."[43]

Bruce's generosity toward Woodson was unconditional, although on one occasion he complained that the historian failed to acknowledge the loan of rare photographs in his 1922 publication, *The Negro in Our History*. Bruce added that perhaps this was due to Woodson's haste in printing the book and that an acknowledgment would appear in the *Journal of Negro History*. (No acknowledgment came, however). Schomburg, the owner of the photographs and prints in question, was not as magnanimous. He spitefully panned *The Negro in Our History* for poor scholarship and overreliance on secondary sources and for omitting essential facts and offering loose interpretations of such topics as cannibalism in Africa.[44]

Woodson, who had a well-deserved reputation for imperiousness, and who presented an unfriendly face to associates, did not, on at least one occasion, reciprocate Bruce's kindness. On January 14, 1923, Bruce informed Woodson that he had received a manuscript from Africa on Edward W. Blyden. Bruce lacked "an angel with a fat wallet," therefore, he asked Woodson's Associated Press to publish the manuscript with all rights in exchange for four hundred copies. Woodson rejected the offer unless someone else besides his publishing house would underwrite the cost of printing.[45] Unperturbed by Woodson's snub, on January 17, Bruce wrote his intention to review *The Negro in Our History* in the *Negro Daily Times*. On February 1, he forwarded Woodson a list of possible subscribers to the *Journal of Negro History* with a request that he try to get Casely Hayford, an author and lawyer in West Africa, to write for the *Journal*.[46]

Loyal Order of the Sons of Africa

Bruce's correspondence with Hayford, one of many West Africans he exchanged news clippings and other printed materials with, reflected his growing interest in joining forces with Africans. His interest in Africa reflected that of a small but growing number of African Americans who, for the past century, had displayed a desire to know more about Africa's peoples and cultures. Bruce's earlier interest in Africa was whetted by letters and conversations with Edward W. Blyden and Alexander Crummell. During the first two decades of the twentieth century, Bruce would correspond with Africans and West Indians, some with affiliations to the Negro Society for Historical Research. These conversations convinced him that there was a dire need for a Pan-African organization. Bruce suggested, in an unpublished essay, that the headquarters be situated in Africa with officers divided proportionally between Africa, the Caribbean, and the United States. He recommended that a fund be organized by taxing American supporters three cents per week. The money would be placed in escrow to pay Negro attorneys to confront acts of bigotry or injustice against African people. This action, insisted Bruce, would force "the governing race [to] not hesitate to respect the wishes and honor the demands of an organization of blacks united for self defense." Bruce noted that membership should be divided into units of ten or twenty persons, with a captain for each group. He concluded that their motto be "the injury of one is the injury of all."[47] On September 17, 1913, Bruce organized in Harlem (65 West 134th Street) the Loyal Order of the Sons of Africa to unite in one brotherhood the black and colored races of the world. This was actually an outgrowth of a 1912 secret benevolent society known as the Sons of Africa, which emphasized mutual help and paramilitary training. The Loyal Order of the Sons of Africa was also a secret organization. The officers included Bruce, president; James E. Kwegyir Aggrey (Gold Coast), first vice president; Rev. C. D. Martin (Antigua), second vice president; Professor W. H. Butler, third vice president; D. B. Fulton, secretary; Harry Martin (Antigua), assistant secretary; Rev. Dr. E. G. Granville Sutton (Sierra Leone), corresponding secretary; and Arthur A. Schomburg (formerly of Puerto Rico), treasurer.[48] In a lecture sometime in 1914, Bruce offered a rationalization of the new organization. The First World War had led Bruce to proclaim that this was the right psychological moment for Negroes and colored men worldwide to organize "to secure uniformity of utterance and action among the darker races and to meet organized [oppression] with intelligently organized resistance." Bruce viewed the Caucasian as a "treacherous biped . . . selfish and hypocritical." Therefore, he urged people of color to play the white man's game "but upon a loftier plane in the hope of saving to a future generation . . . the heritages bequeathed to us by our fathers." He reminded them that, like the oppressed American colonists, they should understand that "eternal vigilance is the price of liberty."[49] Despite Bruce's previous assertion that "the battle of the darker races is an intellectual one," he may have begun thinking about other alternatives for African liberation. Ten days before he organized the Loyal Order of the Sons of Africa, Bruce informed Schomburg that in Harlem he had met James A. K. Aggrey, a linguist who was teaching at Livingstone College in North Carolina. Impressed with the young African's intelligence, Bruce wrote to Schomburg, "ask him to tell you *sub rosa* whether or not the West African native understand the manufacture of fire arms and whether they are now doing anything of that sort. He tells me that intelligent Africans are sustaining friendly relations with the Japanese and East Indian and that the *entente cordiale* between the black and brown is more than encouraging." Bruce added, conspiratorially, "he is a 33 mason, therefore you may talk with him freely."[50]

It was no coincidence that Bruce mentioned Japan, for he, like others, was tremendously impressed by Japan's defeat of Russia. The rapid rise of the Asian country from feudal state to modern nation convinced Bruce that African people could achieve the same results and gain world respectability. Bruce was encouraged from reading clippings from West African newspapers that nationalism was on the rise in Nigeria and the Gold Coast. He eagerly followed their nascent quest for political independence. There is no evidence that Bruce encouraged talk of "revolutionary action," and the fate of the Loyal Order of the Sons of Africa is unknown. Bruce's clandestine talk about revolution may have been rhetorical because he consistently argued that the battle of the darker races was an intellectual one and that violence was the dominion of God.

The Hamitic League

Bruce's interest in African affairs would prepare him for his later alliance with Marcus Garvey's Universal Negro Improvement Association (UNIA) and his scheme for African redemption. Meanwhile, Bruce was still in search of an organization to lead the masses of black people out of the wilderness into the promised land of racial equality. In this quest, he had joined or led numerous organizations since the early 1890s, including the Afro-American League, the National Afro-American Council, the American Negro Academy, the Niagara Movement, the Negro Society for Historical Research, and the Loyal Order of the Sons of Africa. Now, in 1919, he joined another. In July, the New York branch of the Hamitic League of the World was organized. Besides Bruce and Schomburg, its most illustrious supporters were West Indian intellectuals, most notably Cyril V. Briggs, who appeared Caucasian. The Hamitic League had an Afrocentric perspective and affiliated briefly with Garvey's UNIA. That was before charges and countercharges of race treachery dissolved the relationship. Bruce was attracted to the Hamitic League because its founder, George Wells Parker, wrote *The Children of the Sun,* a study that extolled the African as the first builder of civilizations.[51] Despite his busy schedule, Bruce gladly contributed essays to the Hamitic League's organ, the *Crusader,* which he described as "champion of the dark sad millions," who, if unified, would achieve "victory o'er the oppressor" despite "doubt and fear."[52] Bruce's praise for the *Crusader* reflected his deep racial pride in publications that addressed the concerns of the Pan-African community. In turn, others displayed their respect and love for Bruce. Andrea Razafkeriefo, a black humorist, poet, and songwriter praised Bruce in the *Crusader*'s inaugural issue as a bold speaker "who hates the coward and the hypocrite" whose person is looked upon by "Ethiopia['s] . . . smiling face" because "his name reads in the book of fame-'Bruce Grit.'" Others shared Razafkeriefo's admiration for Bruce. A representative voice was that of D. E. Headley of England, who wrote Bruce on July 12, 1919, lamenting that his sons in New York lacked ambition and self-respect and were now derelicts in the metropolis. He further complained that "that is for running away from your good home, where everything intellectual [and] of the best decorum was obtainable. May they see their mistakes before it is too late is the heartfelt wish of a sadly disappointed father."[53] What Bruce sought to do for Headley's sons was a microcosm of his efforts on behalf of people of African descent to create a praise song for a maligned race.

Bruce's Racial Ideology, 1883–1919

Bruce's contemporaries viewed him as a race man, as someone who valued the advancement of the race above all else, even personal achievements. While Bruce labored to be true to this assessment, he did not always live up to this goal. At times, Bruce was intent on doing what was best for his self-interest. Despite those lapses when Bruce sought to promote his own interests over those of the race, he remained steadfast in his praise of Negro identity. At no time did he consider white Americans morally or racially superior to members of other races. Bruce understood that Caucasians used "whiteness" to extol their "superiority" in beauty, intelligence, and creativity. He was harshly critical of those African Americans who bent their knees and sang the praise of whiteness out of a false belief that science, technology, and all displays of intelligence emanated from the brains and souls of Caucasians. At the time, most of white America deemed "black" anyone with a drop of Negro blood. Yet many fair-complexioned persons readily identified with their white parent's blood and repudiated that of their black parent. Bruce was a lifelong foe of those within his race who sought to use a light complexion to escape from a "Negro" identity. These "milk bastards" and their rejection of black culture became the particular objects of his scorn. He would lash out viciously against those African Americans with class bias who sought to distance themselves from the masses. This explains his earlier ridicule of Washington's colored society and its stress on straight hair, fair complexions, and non-Negroid features.

Bruce was also mindful of the insults hurled against his race by white bigots. He never let an opportunity pass to venomously attack white Americans who questioned the intelligence or capability of black people. Bruce understood that the failures of African people could not be attributed to a lack of innate intelligence. Rather, they resulted from the conditions imposed on them by slavery. He believed that these conditions had caused some to lack self-reliance, self-pride, and self-love. In part, Bruce believed that blacks were confronted with these failures because their history had been denied to them. In the waning years of the nineteenth century (and until his death), Bruce sought to promote the study of Negro history. This represented a significant psychological step forward because many African Americans—former slaves and freeborn—accepted Anglo-Saxon values as paramount. Bruce was one of several race-conscious individuals who in the late nineteenth century sought to undermine the psychological damage caused by the racist assumption that African people had no history. Bruce joined Rev. Henry Highland Garnet, Greek scholar Rufus Perry, AME Bishop Benjamin T. Tanner, explorer Martin R. Delany, and other pioneers who insisted that science, art, religion, and philosophy came out of ancient Africa and, moreover, that the credit for these accomplishments had been falsely given to Europeans.

Pioneers in African American History

It was widely known by scholars that history could be mythological, polemical, or propagandistic. While in the nineteenth century some European scholars had chronicled the achievements of African and Asian people, many others, unfortunately, wrote that people of color, particularly Africans, had no history. Race-conscious individuals of African descent were determined to correct these falsehoods. Scholars such as Edward W. Blyden were able to write about Africa's achievements. Other proponents of Africa's glorious past chose to concentrate on the contributions of black Americans to American history and culture. In 1883, George Washington Williams published *The History of the Negro Race in America* and, two years later, *The Negro in the American Rebellion*. Both books addressed significant omissions, but Bruce viewed Williams's first effort as inaccurate, more a literary effort than true scholarship. In 1893, local black leaders in Cleveland sought to get the city's schools to adopt E. A. Johnson's *School History of the Negro Race in America*.

Not entirely satisfied with these books, Bruce decided sometime in 1896 to write a history book for school children. This project came to the attention of Robert H. Terrell, a trustee of the educational board in Washington, D.C., who offered his support. Terrell agreed with Bruce that it was lamentable that black children were ignorant of the achievements of their ancestors and their role in the development of the United States. "If you can do anything to increase the respect of our people for their own[,] you will be a benefactor to the race," he noted.[1]

As the year approached its end, an impatient Alexander Crummell suggested to his protégé that Bruce make his reader "a real literary historical book. [I]f for nothing else[,] it will pay. [I]t will make a sensation in the white world, & do a great good for the race." On Christmas Eve, Crummell suggested that Bruce secure five hundred subscribers before seeking a publisher. He added that Bruce could make his book a classic by supplying speeches, orations, and poems by black writers throughout the world who are "solid men." "You can do it & do it thoroughly & well, with restraint & sober rhetoric," Crummell noted. Finally, Crummell recommended that Bruce associate Paul Laurence Dunbar's name with the book since "he is a young man after my own heart, in all race devotedness & aspiration. I look upon him and yourself as the rising hopes of our people." Aware of his own frailty, Crummell warned, "I shall rise up in my coffin when I have departed, if you two do not quit yourselves well for the needed people."[2]

On November 5, 1897, Crummell inquired about the forthcoming publication of the reader. He suggested that Bruce take twenty or thirty of his (more than one thousand) newspaper articles, turn them into essays, and publish a volume. Bruce, who had collected two hundred pages of writings by Negroes covering the period from 1800 to 1896, had expected to published his book six months earlier. However, the project was delayed by the lack of five hundred subscribers and his depression over the outcome of the New York City mayoral race. Along with the defeat of Bruce's candidate came the loss of "a [potential] first class position with a gentleman's salary and a four year lease [on a residence]," he informed Crummell. Bruce decided to publish his collection, now known as "The Elliott Reader" (in honor of Robert Elliott, a former black congressman), after the 1898 New York gubernatorial election. He had money in the bank for self-publishing but did not want to take the risk until he had been financially secure for a year or longer. In mid-May 1898, Charles Dudley Warner, an essayist from West Hartford, Connecticut, informed Bruce that he was wrong to attempt a school reader from the materials collected because "a school reader should contain only the best literature." In 1902, Moses Da Rocha of Edinburgh University in Scotland wrote an introduction to a Bruce book that was a compilation of Negro literature from Peru to China, 1800 to 1902. Da Rocha noted that the author "has won our eternal gratitude by his brilliant vindication of the race." It is not known if "The Elliott Reader" manuscript was ever published because Bruce wrote in the margin of Da Rocha's letter that he "couldn't make it go."[3] Evidently, Bruce had difficulty in obtaining subscribers to help pay for the publication.

It was during this period that Alexander Crummell's failing health brought him closer to Bruce. Crummell saw qualities in Bruce that his own son, Sidney, lacked. Bruce was forthright, proud of his blackness, and a defender of the race. In contrast, Sidney was an alcoholic who refused to abide by Crummell's autocratic control, and, in retaliation, he publicly humiliated his father. Crummell was in England during part of 1897. On June 1, he informed Bruce by letter, "I know of no man of our class so thoroughly respected, looked up to & followed as yourself. If it doesn't pay to be right, & do right & to speak right; it is nevertheless, most glorious to *be* & to speak right & [that] is always better than '*pay*.'" Soon after, an old and tired Crummell, believing that he might never see his friend again, advised him to "be good, true, faithful [and] heroic." In better spirits by July 4, Crummell ascribed his recovery from the grippe to Bruce, saluting the younger man as the "Negro 'satirist' of the time: I thank God for it." Crummell expressed his disgust with politicians whom he characterized as brazen, impudent, and opportunistic. He saw in Bruce a leadership capacity that the race needed for the coming century. In an earlier note to Bruce, Crummell wrote, "God has given you a clear head & a facile pen; & you seem to live under a sense of stewardship." He encouraged Bruce to continue speaking for both the present and future generations.[4]

Crummell's letters touched Bruce. He was pleased that his friend and mentor thought so highly of him, but he was distressed by the news of Crummell's poor health. Bruce believed that no man was better to advise the race than Crummell. He sought to amuse Crummell by saying that the improvement in his penmanship proved that he was a brat compared to those who lived for several centuries in the Bible, and that his ears should be boxed for impersonating elders.[5]

Next to Edward W. Blyden, Crummell influenced Bruce most to consider *Negro* a term of race pride. He questioned the integrity of journalists who failed to use the appellation in the title of any of the two hundred race papers in circulation. Crummell was appalled that they failed to emulate European immigrants who routinely used their German, Irish, English, and other national names in the titles of their papers. Soon thereafter, Bruce forwarded Crummell a copy of the *Prospect,* a new magazine with which he was affiliated. Crummell gently scolded his protégé by suggesting that a better title would be "The Prospect: A Negro Journal of Literature" because "the battle of the race is an intellectual one."[6]

Crummell was pleased with Bruce's decision to become involved because he considered the *Prospect* an outlet for Bruce's genius and talent. However, Crummell recommended that Bruce devote a few months interpreting to the public the historical portions of his letters and articles. Crummell informed Bruce that his advice was not so much to assist him as to aid the Negro race, "who through centuries, in his parents and grandparents, had helped make him what he is." Bruce found Crummell's advice rewarding. The old priest saw in Bruce's eyes a reflection of his own interest in racial uplift, and it gratified him to have a protégé with energy and time to carry forth the torch. Bruce seriously considered publishing some of his letters, as he informed William H. Council, who wrote back on November 25, 1898, that he was "glad that your able letters may go . . . public."[7]

Alexander Crummell's death on September 10, 1898, left a void in Bruce's life; he had lost an intimate friend, mentor, and father figure. Bruce's eulogy honored the great scholar as "a prince among men." Crummell, he added, was not afraid to be known as a Negro because he knew the history of the Negro, both ancient and modern. Crummell's influence on Bruce was immeasurable. As noted by another admirer, the Episcopal priest was a "great soul . . .

who did more to give character, dignity and unity to the race than any other man." Crummell's passing was more poignant in light of the earlier death of Bruce's cousin, Charles A. Douglass. Although Bruce saw him only twice after they were separated during slavery, he concluded, "I learned to love him as a brother. I sincerely deplore his sad death."[8]

Bruce and the Theater

Bruce emulated Crummell's devotion to the uplift of his people in many respects. Besides educating people with his astute political analysis, Bruce also sought to broaden their interests by exposing them to theatrical performances that entertained and educated. He collaborated with Henrietta Vinton Davis, the gifted elocutionist, in June 1898 to develop a five-act drama, "Our Old Kentucky Home." The main characters are Clothilde, a Creole slave woman who becomes a heroine in the Union army during the Civil War, and Basil, a runaway slave who also enlists in the military. Later, Basil purchases his former owner's plantation.[9] This was the beginning of Bruce's fictional writings, which included short stories. All of his stories heralded Africans or African Americans as the moral or intellectual equals or superiors to Caucasians; but these works were devoid of the racial tension of American life. Blacks who were considered intellectually deficient or untrustworthy were not highlighted in Bruce's stories. His message was simply that blacks were just as interesting, intelligent, and brave as their white counterparts. Interestingly, the whites in his stories all came to this conclusion and readily admitted that prejudice had blinded them to the genius of African people. Despite the sobering effect the display of intelligence had on his white characters, Bruce did not cater his stories to white readers. Instead, he wrote for a black audience that he criticized for being imitative of white societal values. Instead of the Negro duplicating "the great professional [white] celebrities on the stage," Bruce demanded to know "why can't the Negro stand on his own merits, and create his own ideals? Why cannot he be great as an actor or singer, without advertising some white man or woman, who, perhaps is no better artist than himself or herself?"

Racial Solidarity versus the Self-Hating Views of William Hannibal Thomas

Others also demanded what black playwrights or performers should accomplish. Bruce was pleased in 1898 that African Americans in Albany would soon have a first-class Negro hotel that would advertise positive Negro entrepreneurial achievement. This hotel would be a haven for those who faced rejection at white hotels. Bruce acknowledged with pride that the new hotel would not be a typical Negro hostel with air befouled by vile tobacco smoke and a lobby with penniless men ogling women.[10]

On June 18, 1898, Edward E. Cooper, editor of the *Colored American,* criticized the ninety thousand African Americans of Washington, D.C., for spending their funds with white merchants who did not hire them or advertise in their journals. Bruce concurred with Cooper: the money would be better employed in developing black-owned businesses. "I wish you could set this editorial up in black type and keep it standing in your columns," exclaimed Bruce.[11] Bruce understood that the lack of race pride prevented many blacks from engaging in business or cooperative race practices. Concurring with this sentiment was G. F. Franklin of Denver, Colorado, who wrote Bruce, "We are now making a fight for more business and for more business like methods among our people." The dawn of the twentieth century represented to progressive African Americans "the awakening of Ethiopia." The editor of the *Freeman* in Indianapolis wrote in 1896 that the twentieth century was a crossroads. African Americans could find themselves permanently "fixed in [their] standing as the caste class of India" unless there was "a revival in [their] hopes, aspirations and accomplishments."[12] A preview of the race's saga for respectability came in March 1901 when the *Cleveland Gazette* printed James S. Clarkson's letter to Bruce. Clarkson's commitment to racial equality was unimpeachable. He vowed to do whatever he could to honor the covenant made to the slave by both Abraham Lincoln and the Union army. Clarkson, unlike most whites, visited the homes, churches, and businesses of blacks and knew that they had much to teach whites about patience, forgiveness, and the capacity for life. These words might have been dismissed as paternalistic if a less-sympathetic individual had uttered them, but Clarkson had intimate relationships with Bruce and other black men. Clarkson believed that God had much in store for the Negro who, despite his own trials and tribulations, has sympathy for the world's oppressed and maligned people. Clarkson confided to Bruce that the day of the black American was coming. The white man should be ashamed and fear God who would in His time cast aside both "[D]emocratic opposition [and] Republican cowardice."[13]

Paradoxically, while Clarkson sought to honor an oppressed people for their belief in universal justice and equality, a self-described mulatto, William Hannibal Thomas endeavored to defame his mother race. Thomas, who claimed military service in the Civil War, a stint in South Carolina's Reconstruction government, and a law degree, wrote *The American Negro: What He Was, What He Is, and What He May Become; a Critical and Practical Discussion* in early 1901. Ironically, this diatribe was written by one whose middle name was glorified by Afrocentric individuals for his military prowess. Thomas, who was severely injured in the Civil War and suffered constant pain, caused anguish and hatred in others with his statement that "Negro nature is so craven and sensuous in every fiber of its being that a Negro manhood with decent respect for chaste womanhood does not exist." Not only did Thomas assert that it was impossible to find a Negro male or female virgin over the age of fifteen, he provided lynch mobs with ammunition with his declaration that Negro men craved carnal knowledge of white women.[14] Thomas's rambling account, typical of the utterings of racist whites, might have been dismissed as the ranting of an unbalanced person except that the reputable Macmillan company published it.

Black critics and their white allies were shocked that Thomas's diatribe followed so closely the 1900 publication of *The Mystery Solved: The Negro a Beast*. The author of this work claimed that Eve had been seduced, not by a snake offering an apple but by an African-looking creature lacking a soul. This and other works offered justification for lynching black men whose alleged rapacious lust would be visited upon chaste white women. Criticism of *The American Negro* was swift and widespread. James Hulme Canfield, a Columbia University librarian, informed Booker T. Washington that the work was "a terrible book—terrible if false, and far more terrible if true."[15] From Europe, an irate F. J. Loudin wrote to John P. Green that Thomas should be lynched. Realizing that lynching was harsh punishment, he instead suggested "tar and feathers."[16] Novelist Charles W. Chesnutt considered *The American Negro* a poorly written book that read like a collection from a scrapbook. He accused Macmillan of being ignorant of Negro life; otherwise, the editors would not have published the manuscript. Chesnutt wrote to Bruce, "I hope that we have spiked Mr. Thomas' guns. Our own work is the best answer to his complaints, & the best antidote for his libelous statements."[17] Another critic, Rev. C. T. Walker of New York City, informed Bruce that he would attempt to have the book banned from libraries.[18] Bruce wrote to Whitefield McKinlay that he intended to encourage the public to reject Thomas "as an authority on the moral ethics of the Negro race."[19] Bruce was one of the few critics who had personal knowledge of Thomas. He admitted to working with Thomas for about three weeks in Boston on a magazine, *The Negro*, but that they soon parted. Bruce confided to Booker T. Washington that Thomas was an unsavory character who consorted with courtesans, "jumps bail for debt[,] dishonors his [bank] notes, and lives on the earning of women to whom he is not married."[20]

Bruce was motivated to discredit Thomas completely. His additional research indicated that Thomas had been expelled in 1868 from Western Theological Seminary in Allegheny, Pennsylvania, had engaged in criminal intercourse with a woman he later married, and had been indicted in 1877 for "seizing and selling [stolen] property."[21] Even though Bruce viewed Thomas as "the worst onion that ever came out of the loins of the black race," he was concerned that the sensational book would assist in lighting "the torch about many innocent Negroes in peril of the hunger of a mob for blood." An angry Bruce considered Thomas a "TRAITOR!" who should follow Judas's example and hang himself.[22]

White Racism and Black Responses

The pain and anger emanating from Thomas's book coincided with the rise of racism in the North. Long considered a southern problem where nearly 90 percent of African Americans lived, de facto discrimination was spreading to northern hotels that formerly catered to black guests. Bruce complained in March 1901 that Philadelphia hotels excluded blacks who experienced no discrimination during the 1900 Republican convention. Citing Benjamin Disraeli, who noted "race is the key to history," Bruce suggested that blacks build and operate their own hotels to compete directly with the white establishments. He urged blacks to patronize James L. Goodall, who recently obtained a liquor license to open a first-class hotel for Negro visitors to the City of Brotherly Love. Emulate him and other members of the race, Bruce advised: "We cannot merge our destiny with that of the white man [for] the white man is cunning and crafty." Bruce found it annoying that whites would sell blacks anything they wanted but were unwilling to employ them in moneymaking positions.[23]

Bruce's bitterness and anger was not simply academic; it was also fueled by his personal encounters with racial discrimination. When he lived in Washington, a white landlord refused to rent a six-room house to him despite endorsements from prominent whites. In 1901, he booked a room in an Albany, New York, hotel for the singer Harry Burleigh, but the next day the management claimed that no rooms were available. Governor Odell was among the elite who reveled in Burleigh's performance; after hearing of the discrimination, he invited the singer to be his guest in the governor's mansion. Bruce noted sarcastically that Burleigh "ate breakfast with the governor and his family, and none of them took the measles or had an attack of the St. Vitus Dance; the dishes were not cracked and not a spoon was missing." Sarcasm aside, Bruce again urged blacks to pool their funds to establish businesses, restaurants, and hotels instead of trying to force recognition. This does not mean that Bruce acquiesced to segregation. Instead, he called for action against the most degrading and insidious forms of segregation. His immediate concern was the Afro-American Council's fight against Jim Crow railroad cars and disfranchisement laws. Instead of spending hard-earned dollars on inaugural balls and emancipation parades, Bruce recommended that members of the race set aside funds to support the council's effort. Bruce was upset with his own people's disinclination to organize for their betterment: "What a booming set of idiots we Negroes are! And how the white man must snicker as he contemplates us in our mad ambition to secure outward conformity to his race, even to straighten our hair, bleaching our black faces and emptying our purses in the struggle to be like him. Bah!"[24]

While Bruce admonished his race not to "force recognition" from whites, he sadly understood that it would take several generations, at least, for black Americans to achieve economic independence. Just as he was dependent upon James S. Clarkson and other white friends for positions, the race needed white employers for their daily bread. Unfortunately, the labor unions that offered an opportunity for better wages and working conditions often denied membership to black men. Bruce was a working man, but he had disdain and antipathy for white strikers. In 1901, he urged African Americans to shun the white unions in favor of their own "big union." In May, impoverished European immigrants in Albany, New York, struck for ten days against the United Traction Company, leading Bruce to predict a bloody conflict between capital and labor. While Bruce did not sympathize with racist strikers, he did condemn the labor barons who refused to employ blacks as motormen or conductors for fear of a white backlash. Still, both Bruce and the *Colored American* were in agreement that the prejudice of white workers caused the Negro to befriend John D. Rockefeller and J. Pierpont Morgan, capitalists who eschewed race and were "for merit, pure and simple."

Others also condemned the refusal of white workers to ally themselves with African Americans. Editor Benjamin T. Tanner, of the *AME Church Review*, advised black workers to strike when white workers struck and settle when they settled. However, Tanner believed that black workers should shun prejudiced whites and seek to take their jobs permanently.[25] Bruce's opposition to striking white workers extended to the 1902 Pennsylvania coal strike, which he dismissed as a group of "tyrannical . . . half educated white men . . . who imagine that . . . they will dictate terms . . . to capitalists [and] to government itself." Bruce added that he opposed strikers "because they are against my race," and as a menace to society they should be silenced by the sword. The *Colored American* called upon wealthy corporations to employ blacks in skilled positions in order to force unions to submit to fair hiring practices. Many considered the tactics of strikers to be anarchy. "The anarchist," observed Bruce, "may become the safety valve and prevent the destruction of the Republic at the hand of those who are now denouncing whether their theory of government is right or wrong." This statement should not suggest that Bruce relished violence as a means to a political end, nor should it be taken to imply that he supported socialism. He considered socialism an impractical solution to the problems of African Americans. Bruce was suggesting that anarchy would provoke enough attention to the problem that it might be dealt with more quickly. In 1907, street riots disturbed the serenity of Yonkers, New York, when the poorly paid conductors struck for a two-cents-per-hour raise to twenty-three cents per hour. Yonkers had a large immigrant population, with nearly a third of its residents coming from Austria, England, Germany, Hungary, Ireland, and Italy. Thrown into this mix were African Americans who accounted for nearly 2 percent of the city's population. Mayor John Henry Cooper's reluctance to intervene resulted in property damage and seriously injured strikebreakers. Bruce blamed the strike and the melee that followed on the failure of white workers to accept as equal partners their black counterparts. He had firsthand knowledge of this insidious racism. Bruce was the business representative of an unidentified union (probably a sugar-refining union), and when he first accepted the position, workers who had known him for years avoided contact with him. As the only black agent in a body of two hundred delegates, Bruce worked hard to get benefits for men who often worked for twelve to sixteen hours, including Sundays and holidays, for low wages. His efforts paid off because sometime in 1908 he told the Yonkers Men's Sunday Club that "today . . . I have the respect of every employer . . . [and] the men are recognized as union men. Wages increased to 68 [cents] per [hour], hours reduced to 8, double time for Sundays and holiday work." Bruce noted that both the ignorant Italian and the Negro needed to unite around their common labor exploitation. There would not be black strikebreakers if unions organized all workers, not just white ones. Bruce added that capitalists hoodwinked whites into believing that industrial equality was the same as social equality that, for different reasons, neither race wanted. He cautioned black workers not to seek special favors because they were descended from slaves. Instead, they must create a demand for their labor by becoming proficient mechanics and laborers. This cogent Bruce "Gritism" elicited support from Pauline E. Hopkins, who wrote, "I have argued the union of the Negro with labor for a number of years, but being only a woman have received very small notices." It is unknown why Bruce remained silent on the 1905 formation of the Industrial Workers of the World (or "Wobblies"), which sought to organize One Big Union for workers regardless of race, color, creed, gender, national origin, and skill. Benjamin Harrison Fletcher, a black longshoreman in Philadelphia, was one of their major organizers. Perhaps it is because Bruce accepted the then popular view that they were anarchists that prevented him from endorsing their platform.[26]

    Bruce's argument that blacks should make themselves so competent that others would demand their service or skills was similar to Booker T. Washington's exhortations. However, Bruce differed from the educator in his insistence that blacks organize themselves against the evils of racial discrimination, labor ostracism, and other ills imposed on his people. This thought led him and others to establish the American Protective League (APL) on March 16, 1898. The league was incorporated in 1901, in direct competition with Booker T. Washington's National Negro Business League, formed in 1900. The APL exhorted Negroes to pay a fifty-two-cent annual membership fee. If 10 percent of them complied, they would raise $520,000 annually to develop businesses. Thus, the organization, with its collective influence, would be in a position to demand respect and an end to barbarous practices. In a sense, the APL was a reaction to Washington's insistence that industrial education would guide the race out of the wilderness and into the promised land of freedom and opportunity. Bruce countered that industrial education alone would not solve the race problem but that a combination of industrial and literary education would provide blacks with the skills and intelligence to engage in business among themselves in the nation, the Americas, and throughout the world. Unfortunately, the APL was unable to match Washington's well-oiled Tuskegee machine and proved unable to compete successfully with the better-organized National Negro Business League.[27] Bruce's refusal to support Washington's National Negro Business League underscored a problem that plagued black America then and continues to plague it now. Those with different political agendas found it impossible to form coalitions to seek solutions to their economic problems. Unfortunately, these political differences, while significant in their own right, prevented the African American population from advancing economically like other ethnic or racial groups supportive of each other.

Bruce on White Supremacy and Black Cultural Superiority

While Bruce had many ideas for racial advancement and helped develop many race-based organizations, he lacked skills to make these organizations financially independent and viable for a long period. Often, others would capitalize on Bruce's efforts and develop similar organizations that had more finances or better leadership. Nevertheless, his greatest contributions were his writing and oratorical skills, which proved to be valuable assets as he advocated justice for African Americans. While Bruce's writing skills were widely praised, he also had a well-earned reputation as an engaging speaker who employed wit, charm, and sarcasm to inform audiences about history. On July 2, 1901, while enjoying himself on a brief respite to Asbury Park, New Jersey, Bruce spoke satirically at a local church on "The White Man's Burden." Rudyard Kipling told a generation of Britains that their burden was to spread civilization to the "new caught sullen peoples [who] were half devil and half child." Bruce challenged this imperialistic and racist message and retorted that the burdens taken up by white men were no different from those that challenged brave men everywhere. "Then why the white man's burden[?] What more doth he bear than we[?] The victim of his power and greed from the Great Lakes to the sea."[28] On another occasion, Bruce amused audiences with his interpretation of a "white" heaven where only docile, meek, orderly, and musical Negroes were permitted to enter. Upon entrance, good "darkies" sang "Give me Jesus, *you may have all the world.* Give me Jesus," or "Look up yonder. What I see. A milk white angel after me. Glory, glory, glory hallelujah." Such views satisfied bigots that, as on earth, heaven was also segregated.[29]

Whether Bruce confronted racism with sarcasm or humor, he understood clearly the pain that the ideology of white supremacy brought to his people, and he was determined to expose America as a hypocritical and barbarous nation. It angered him that the professed land of Christian idealism failed daily to conform to the dictates of the Ten Commandments. Bruce's 1900 pamphlet, *The Blood Red Record,* chronicled lynching since 1893. It described a nation that went into a frenzy over the murder of an American in other countries but tolerated orgies of lynching against black citizens within her own borders. Bruce's depiction of America as a bloodthirsty land "not far from barbarism" made the pamphlet, by his admission, a bestseller throughout North America, the Caribbean, Africa, and Australia.[30] Bruce was in solidarity with Ida B. Wells, the famed antilynching crusader. As editor of the *Free Press* in Memphis, Wells's pen was as trenchant as Bruce's ever was. In 1892, the militant female journalist argued that "nobody in [the South] believes the old thread bare lie that Negro men assault white women." Wells's comment was based on southern gossip and observation that some southern belles fancied black men. This statement would have caused little reaction from the South if Wells had stated that white men fancied mulatto, quadroon, and octoroon women or their darker sisters. Southern men believed their own myth that black men were better lovers or had larger sexual organs and were determined to prevent sexual congress between white women and black men. Enraged by Wells's heresy, a mob stormed the offices of the *Free Press* and forced her partner to flee. Fortunately, Wells was away from the city and wisely decided not to return after the *Memphis Daily Commercial* editorialized "the fact that a black scoundrel is allowed to live." Wells's outspokenness on lynching and her challenge to the leadership of black men alienated many in the conservative and progressive camps. Lafayette M. Hershaw, a clerk in the Department of the Interior, could not comprehend why black politicians and the press sought to "shackle her efforts to arouse the moral sentiment of the world against a great evil." He commended Bruce in 1894 for endorsing Wells's trip to England to rally international support against lynching.[31]

Despite the widespread problems of white racism, racial segregation, and vicious lynch mobs, Bruce took solace in the belief that "the dark race is the last race." His unquestioned belief that "Ethiopia [shall] stretch forth her hands unto God" led him to conclude that someday there would never be a white man's government or a government ruled by black men. Rather, there would be God's country, where race and class would cease to exist. That was a utopian view even Bruce realized would probably not occur in his lifetime. Like others of his religious faith and generation, he accepted the controversial viewpoint that God brought the African to America to endure slavery and discrimination while at the same time "absorbing and assimilating and digesting the lessons" of the so-called superior Anglo-Saxon. This view may vex today's generation, but it was widely accepted a century ago by the devout black religious community. In contrast, Army Chaplain Theophilus G. Steward argued in 1900 that "the day will dawn when it will be wicked to be *white*."[32]

Bruce agreed that many whites were wicked; he also understood that they colonized and exploited the world with their awesome displays of technological superiority. He argued that not only should blacks emulate this technology (for different purposes), they should never overlook their own glorious history. In an early version of the "sun people versus ice people" theme popularized by late-twentieth-century Afrocentric scholars, Bruce described Europeans as cold creatures that relied on technology to subjugate the world's people of color. In contrast, his many references to Africa's ancient civilizations were a reminder to African Americans that their ancestors were a warm and hospitable people who shared their technological skills with others.

Africans as the Proper Race Model

Except for missionaries and a few travelers, Americans of both races were generally ignorant of Africa's diversity in terms of climate, topography, peoples, and cultures. The uninformed considered "the Dark Continent" a land of wild animals, poisonous snakes, and semibarbaric heathens who were not above cannibalism. Bruce joined others in trying to improve the popular image of the African. Although he never realized his earlier desire to go to Africa, Bruce kept abreast of developments on the continent through his extensive correspondence with Edward W. Blyden. He subscribed to African newspapers in English and developed relationships with African intellectuals and businessmen from the Gold Coast (Ghana) and Nigeria. As one who was proud of Africa's glorious kingdoms and civilizations that predated the rise of European technological supremacy, Bruce was pleased whenever he heard of individual or collective African achievement(s). For the next two decades, Bruce would maintain a close relationship with either Mojola Agbebi or his family. At the end of 1902, Agbebi, president of the African Baptist Union of West Africa, delivered his inaugural sermon at the celebration of the first anniversary of the establishment of the African church in Lagos, Nigeria. Agbebi was an ethnic Yoruba whose father was a Christian missionary, but, unlike some Western-trained African theologians, Agbebi recommended that West Africans worship in an African style with original songs and tunes for an African Christianity. He urged Africans to eschew the hymn book, the prayer book, pews, and "the white man's style, the white man's name, the white man's dress." His criticism of white Christians extended to African American Methodists and Baptists missionaries who came to Africa to establish "civilizing missions" and to eradicate "heathenism" among the indigenous people. Agbebi saw hypocrisy in Western Christianity because its followers drank liquor, smoked tobacco, and danced with the spouses of others. "We have to cease to preach men into heaven and begin to preach heaven into men. We have to cease to preach men out of hell fire and damnation, and preach hell fire and damnation out of men. We have to be supremely earnest in teaching men *how to live* and be carefully indifferent as to *how they die,*" asserted the pastor. He added that sermons should be given in African languages, not English.

Edward W. Blyden was pleased that Agbebi spoke as an African and not as a trained parrot. Bruce was so impressed after reading the sermon in the *Sierra Leone Weekly News* that he requested a copy to publish for an American audience. A very pleased Bruce wrote Agbebi in April 1903: "I am a Negro and *all Negro.* I am black all over and am [as] proud of my beautiful black skin . . . as [is] the *blackest* man in Africa." He requested that Agbebi forward him a photograph and an autograph to add to his collection of great Negroes.[33] Bruce met Agbebi on November 8, 1903, when the pastor, Arthur A. Schomburg, and R. H. Brown were guests in his Yonkers home. Agbebi's commitment to Pan-Africanism so excited Bruce that in 1907 he attempted to have October 11 observed annually by black New Yorkers as Mojola Agbebi Day. Agbebi's friends and family in Nigeria were so moved by Bruce's gesture that they sent him a letter of appreciation with the expressed hope that Agbebi would be the link between Africans and their American cousins. The 110 signers were illustrative of Bruce's ability to develop feelings of solidarity between people who had never met each other. Bruce was so saddened by Agbebi's death in 1917 that he informed his widow that he loved her husband like a brother.[34]

Agbebi represented a small but growing population of Africans who had been converted to Christianity by white and black missionaries. Bruce was pleased to learn that West Africans were not just gullible believers of Western theology. John P. Jackson, editor of the *Weekly Record* in Lagos, informed him that the indigenous population rejected European Christianity for their own practical Christianity, which they considered nearer to Christ's teaching. Bruce probably seconded Jackson's comment that "Africa will have to teach this white man's Christianity and show him the way to God." In a twist of interpretation, Justice R. B. Richardson of the Liberian Supreme Court wrote Bruce in 1903 that local people felt miserable when they dreamed of white objects because white represented wicked things; whereas, in America, it was a sign of degradation to be black.[35] These letters from educated Africans encouraged Bruce because the image of Africans in popular magazines or travelers' reports was one of ignorance, heathenism, and superstition. Bruce knew that these adjectives did not apply to his erudite friend Edward W. Blyden, but he was happy to realize that it was also untrue of many others.

Bruce's pride in contemporary African achievements did not lessen his interest in the ancient contributions of that continent. He was thrilled when he read that Egyptian monoliths were to be installed in Manhattan's St. John the Divine Cathedral. A letter to the editor from Bruce informed the *New York Tribune* that the world's largest monoliths were in Egypt and, in comparison, made the ones in St. John the Divine resemble toothpicks. Noting that the United States was still a young nation, Bruce observed that in time the country "may be able to do some of the remarkable things which have eternized the name and fame of the ancient Egyptians, but not now." In two unsigned pieces printed in the *Guardian* during the summer of 1907, Bruce declared that Blyden had correctly proven that ancient Egyptians were black, not white. Bruce considered this information vital, for, as he noted, "fixing the racial identity of the Egyptian is an important step in the direction of fixing the racial identity of their descendants in America." Of course, Bruce was making a huge leap in logic and geography to suggest that most African Americans, a hybrid of African, European, and Native American, were direct descendants of the Egyptians when the majority of their ancestors had come from West Africa. More significant, however, was Bruce's declaration that some white scholars had acknowledged that Greece and Rome were indebted to African civilization. If whites knew this, then so should blacks, he asserted. On July 15, 1907, Bruce accompanied Charles Arthur Franklin, editor of the *Denver Statesman* and Rosetta Douglass Sprague, Frederick Douglass's daughter, to view Cleopatra's Needle in Central Park. Awed by its majestic prominence and its inscriptions, Bruce wrote "and yet the white man who knows everything finds here a puzzle which he cannot solve." An excited Bruce informed members of the Yonkers Men's Club, circa 1907, that blacks had built the pyramids and that there were some idols in Japan that resembled "wooly haired Negroes." The same, he noted, applied to idols elsewhere in Asia. Proud of African achievements, Bruce told his audience to study their history, for then none could rob them of racial pride and self-respect.[36]

Since Bruce exalted blackness, it was not difficult for him to create his own version of the Adam and Eve story. He wrote in a series of tracts around 1903 that the couple migrated to Ethiopia after their banishment from the Garden of Eden. This made the inhabitants of the biblical world black, not white, as taught by American theologians and depicted by Western artists.[37]

Bruce understood the psychological need all people had to create myths to explain their origin and enhance their historic pasts. He clearly recognized that American slavery not only denied to the enslaved the knowledge of their heritage but also sought to make whites the standards of heroism. This denial of self-authenticity led many blacks to hate their wooly hair, thick lips, dark complexions, and "Africaness" because they were unaware of heroes who looked like them. Bruce was aware of this loss of spirit, and he sought to provide authentic African and African American role models. From 1907 to 1909, Bruce's story "The Black Sleuth" was serialized in *McGirt's Magazine*. The Eton College–educated hero Mojola Okukenu, who headed an international detective agency in West Africa, was a linguist fluent in Arabic, English, German, French, and Italian. In the story, the black hero is hired by a ship captain to investigate the theft of uncut diamonds. The hero quickly solves the case to the amazement of the white man, who decides that Europeans are not superior to Africans. Through the protagonist in this example, Bruce sought to show that racial pigmentation did not determine intelligence. In his formulaic writing, Bruce's hero is superhuman, not unlike the larger-than-life white heroes. However, although he has whites praising black intelligence, Bruce's audience comprised African Americans who saw nothing positive in their race. This was evident by the comments of Moses Da Rocha of Edinburgh University, who informed Bruce that the African sleuth resembled Mojola Agbebi very much. He was impressed with Bruce's account, considering it "immeasurably superior to the serials that one comes across in the popular magazines of the day." Making certain that Bruce did not misunderstand, Da Rocha concluded, "I do not write . . . to merely flatter you. I am quite, quite sincere."[38]

Blyden, Scholarship, and Activism

Bruce's friends appreciated his labor on their behalf; but many who knew him only as a correspondent, such as Da Rocha, were not aware how fragile his health was. Nor did they know that Bruce was working diligently at two jobs and still finding the time to write and lecture. Bruce was employed in the early 1900s at the Port of New York under James S. Clarkson and by a sugar refinery in Yonkers. Bruce's Yonkers residences were often rented rooms in stuffy attics or damp basements lacking central heating or proper ventilation. From late December 1902 until early into the new year, he was laid low by a bout of typhoid fever. Despite his illness, his wit did not desert him. He informed the *Star of Zion* in Charlotte, North Carolina, "as Tom Hood once said: 'I have been so near death's door, that I could almost hear the creaking of the hinges.'" From May 24 to June 3, 1904, Bruce suffered from the effects of congestive fever and kidney trouble. He ate his first square meal of "a chop and milk toast" on June 2. The following day he went to his job at the sugar refinery, but his legs were too weak for him to work. Bruce suffered intermittently from various illnesses that taxed his health.[39] His serious illness prompted Bruce to express gratitude to God. He wrote to his journal, June 8, 1904: "I give grateful thanks [to God] for all [H]is mercies . . . in bringing me back to health and happiness." This period of sickness convinced him that man was impotent and that God, indeed, ruled the universe. He also comprehended that since money could not buy happiness nor health, it was foolish to hustle for it when one day it would "be as cheap as dirt and . . . of no value." Bruce often consulted his Bible during those trying times because it represented "our rock in the mighty storm, [and] our shelter in the weary land."[40]

Bruce shared his strong religious faith with his good friend Edward W. Blyden. Blyden had many private conversations with Bruce about American politics, race relations, and the need for selective emigration to West Africa. While Bruce was not then interested in seeking his destiny in Africa, he willingly assisted his friend in disseminating his writings among African Americans. In March 1910, Blyden requested Bruce's help in promoting *The Arabic Bible in the Soudan: A Plea for Transliteration*. Blyden also asked Bruce to present a manuscript to the *North American Review* for publication and to become Blyden's American agent, helping circulate books in the South among "both races [who] need light on the so-called Negro problem." A month later, a mutual friend wrote Bruce from England that Blyden was extremely feeble and deeply in debt after a 1909 operation for an aneurysm in his knee. Blyden had worked for the British in West Africa, but not long enough to warrant a pension. Blyden's money situation worsened with the death of Sir Alfred Lewis Jones, his financial mentor. Friends in West Africa were hoping to persuade Sierra Leone to provide Blyden with a hundred-pound special pension, although two hundred pounds annually would have made him comfortable, suggested Joseph L. Lundy. The intervention of Blyden's friend, Sir Reginald Antrobus, a former under secretary at the colonial office, led the British colonial secretary to instruct the governors of Sierra Leone, Lagos (Nigeria), and the Gold Coast (Ghana) to provide the aged African with twenty-five pounds each from 1910 until his death on February 7, 1912.[41]

The news of Blyden's death was a major blow to Bruce. He had lost his father figure. Although the two men met infrequently, and only when Blyden's American visits allowed him time to visit New York, they had engaged in a long friendship via the mail and had exchanged clippings from newspapers and magazines. A memorial meeting was held for Blyden on April 4 in New York's St. Marks Church on West 53rd Street, sponsored by the St. Marks Lyceum, the city's oldest black literary organization. Bruce enlightened the audience with a talk on his friend's life and work.[42]

Bruce's assistance in helping to disseminate Blyden's writings represented a significant contribution to Pan-Africanism. The African's sage thoughts reached a wider audience. In this vein, Bruce and Arthur Schomburg also helped William H. Ferris complete his two-volume study, *The African Abroad*. They provided valuable data and photographs, including one of the father of Alexander Dumas, the great black French writer. Bruce was particularly pleased with Ferris's call for black writers to return to their cultural roots, for in "assimilating the culture and traditions of Anglo Saxons they . . . [had lost] their rich and luxuriant African heritage."[43] Bruce also extended help to Alice Moore Dunbar, widow of the poet Paul Laurence Dunbar, who informed him in 1914 that she had compiled a reader for young students, *Masterpieces of Negro Eloquence*. In one letter, she asked, "May I call upon you for help again—I mean this time in finding just the kind of extracts I need, and the biographies to go with them?"[44]

The letters from Blyden, Dunbar, and Ferris illustrate Bruce's generosity in assisting others even when their works might compete with his own projects for public attention and acclaim. It was his keen devotion to promoting black achievers that led him in early March 1910 to inform Daniel Murray at the Library of Congress that he planned to write seven or eight volumes on notable race personalities. He asked the librarian to locate sketches of scholars and thinkers but no "Jim Crow Negroes." He added that, next to writing, he liked "nothing better than . . . an occasional drink" of Madeira. Bruce confided to Murray that he had joined the Haklyut Society in London and he believed that association might facilitate the publishing of his book. Ultimately, the Haklyut Society did not publish his work. The Gazette Press in Yonkers did publish *Short Biographical Sketches of Negro Men and Women in Europe and the United States in 1910*. The title suggests that Bruce recognized no gender bias in highlighting achievers. In contrast, similar books highlighted either men or women but rarely both in the same publication.[45] Bruce's publication was "inscribed to the Negro youth of America in the humble hope that they may stimulate a reverence for the virtue and an imitation of the examples here set forth." In the preface, Bruce noted his wish that the book would "awaken race pride" because "'race,' said the Earl of Beaconsfield, 'is the key to history.'" To test the readers' knowledge, Bruce added a series of questions after each sketch.[46] Like many contemporary black authors, Bruce sought to promote his book by selling copies to friends or at churches and other organizations. Robert Smalls, a Civil War hero and now a customs collector in Beaufort, South Carolina, informed Bruce that he was trying to get his book into the public schools. He doubted that this would prove successful, as the board of education preferred books written by southerners or those partial to the racial ideology of that region. Alice Moore Dunbar reprimanded Bruce for not providing her with the price of *Short Biographical Sketches*. The schoolteacher sarcastically added, "I need the book[,] false and fickle man." A. J. Gary of the Standard News Company in New York acknowledged the receipt of Bruce's book, adding that it belonged in the homes of intelligent colored people but especially in the hands of whites to "help to allay the perpetual race prejudice." Unimpressed, Bruce wrote in the margin, "this is a specimen business letter from a concern . . . which failed largely because of its failure to properly express itself."[47]

Daniel Murray, the assistant librarian at the Library of Congress, knew how to express himself. He proposed an ambitious project for thirty associate editors (including Bruce, Arthur Schomburg, John W. Cromwell, and Wilberforce scholar William S. Scarborough) to write 25,000 biographical sketches covering the history, music, art, and culture of the African diaspora from antiquity to 1912. Excited by the project's enormous potential to develop race pride, Bruce wrote to Murray on November 21, 1910, with a promise that his contributions would be accurate. He was "proud" and "pardonably jealous" of his reputation and prepared to deal with white critics with their egotistic opinion "that the average Negro is inexact in his thinking and unreliable in his statements." For example, Bruce was dismayed to learn that a Yonkers teacher had informed his students that the Sphinx was the work of whites. Bruce urged Murray to make the proposed encyclopedia successful. "It must be," he cautioned, "because we Marylanders are different from other Negroes as all history show[s]." Unfortunately, the ambitious project was not published because it did not attract enough subscribers willing to pay twenty-four dollars in advance for the six-volume set to satisfy the demands of the intended publisher, The World Cyclopedia Company.[48]

Bruce was equally supportive of unknown writers and activists alike, for he believed that each in his own way was contributing to the advancement of a race. Poet Walter Everette Hawkins of Warrentown, North Carolina, wrote to Bruce on March 10, 1910, stating his appreciation for his mentor's support and encouragement. Noting that he wanted to live as a free man, Hawkins confided, "you have come to me as a voice whispering good cheer in a darkened hour in a still more darkening land, pointing out to me the heights with a giant's shoulders to stand upon." Hawkins, who was awed by Bruce's accomplishments, added the following: "push me all you can. I need such as you." The young poet vowed to live up to Bruce's words of encouragement, although he did not believe that he would ever "be of equal value." However, he added, "I may grow, who knows." In gratitude, Hawkins promised to emulate Bruce and live an "unpurchasable life devoted to all that is grand, true and exalted in race ideals and devotion." The aspiring poet requested that Bruce judge the forty-six poems he forwarded because he considered his mentor to be "the fulcrum upon which I am to rest my lever to move the world."[49]

Bruce's prescription for life in a "darkening land" was to exult in the achievements of African people regardless of their language, cultural affinity, or geographical area. This is why he was always excited to read about Africa's greatness. Speaking as a freemason and editor of the *Masons Quarterly,* Bruce delighted a Prince Hall audience in New York with the observation that King Solomon's temple was built by Hiram, an Ethiopian king and master builder. Masons, according to Bruce, had the potential unity and skill to lead black New Yorkers. Citing Japan's rise to prominence from feudal society to the world power that defeated Russia five years earlier, Bruce called upon Masons in 1910 to raise $100,000 to erect a temple in memory of Prince Hall, America's pioneer black Mason. He declared that black Masons needed to set examples and be a moral force to uplift the race, not by seeking legislation but rather by exalting a scientific education. This would compel others to recognize intelligence as an equalizer. Like others, including W. E. B. Du Bois, Bruce saw in Japan's rise a triumphant model for all persons of color to emulate. He reminded African Americans that their African ancestors had bestowed upon the world mathematics, an alphabet, religion, navigation, astronomy, the arts, fraternal organizations, and legal jurisprudence. Thus, they needed to read and obtain facts to increase their racial pride. Noting that a fusion between the Caucasian and the African was impossible because the "black race is the race expectant," Bruce urged the black Masons to help regain the race's lost moral and intellectual superiority by forming a Negro brotherhood to fight against caste and race prejudice. As Bruce was well aware that blacks often prematurely announced their intentions to gain publicity, he cautioned them to unite but "without the flourish of trumpets or the blare of brass bands, or press notices." In this, Bruce reflected the influence of Blyden, who had cautioned African people not to compare their progress to whites but rather to discover their true place in the world.[50]

Besides Blyden, Bruce developed close relationships with other activists. Among them were Frances Ellen Watkins Harper, the former Abolitionist, feminist and writer of poetry, prose, and political essays who was a leading voice in the nineteenth century against racial oppression. Harper's death in

1911 touched Bruce, who eulogized her as one "who pleaded, prayed and cried until nation was aroused and the [enslaved] released." Similarly, he honored Alexander Crummell in 1911 when a school in Washington, D.C., was named in his memory. Bruce described him as "every inch a man."[51]

In 1912, Bruce began an association with Duse Mohammed Ali, editor of the newly formed monthly journal the *African Times and Orient Review*, whose motto was "devoted to the interests of the coloured races of the world." The journal's inaugural editorial, "A Word to Our Brothers," called upon black, brown, and yellow activists and intellectuals to submit essays because it was their "very own journal." Bruce became a contributor and corresponded with the Egyptian editor for years before meeting him in person. Eventually, both men joined the Garvey movement.[52] Bruce's collaboration with Duse Mohammed Ali was typical of how the writer dealt with progressive individuals. He immediately contributed his writing skills and, whenever he could, his money.

Bruce's reputation as a fighter against injustice prompted Oswald Garrison Villard, chairman of the NAACP's board of directors, to seek his assistance on August 3, 1912. Villard requested that Bruce write the governor of Virginia to stay the death sentence for Virginia Christian, a sixteen-year-old black girl who claimed she had killed her employer in self-defense. Villard enlisted Bruce's support in the hope that his writing would galvanize a sympathetic public to send in donations to offset the expenses of an appeal.[53]

It was Bruce's dedication to the race that in early January 1914 led James S. Clarkson to write to Lafayette Young, editor of the *Capital* in Des Moines, that Bruce "is the best writer of his race in America." Clarkson also added that Bruce wanted to submit articles to the paper without compensation because he appreciated Young's stand on the race question, unlike many other Republican newspapers that had abandoned the struggle for equal rights.[54] Despite their differences in background, social standing, and color, the two men were close and intimate friends. Clarkson's admiration for Bruce is revealed in a moving letter to Florence Bruce shortly before his friend's fifty-seventh birthday on February 22, 1913. Clarkson expressed joy in the knowledge that the Negro Society for Historical Research was planning a surprise party for its cofounder. He heaped praise on Bruce for his diligence during the past thirty years in gathering the scattered pieces of African diaspora history to share with a doubtful world. Clarkson added that the black race needed to show more faith in themselves and "more pride in its own past and more ambition for its future." He vowed to attend the birthday celebration.[55] Among others, Clarkson admired Bruce for his race love and for his insistence that the progress or achievement of one represented vertical movement for the race.

A case in point was the election of J. R. Archer, the first man of color to the position of chief magistrate of the borough of Battersea in London, England. Bruce sent Archer his congratulations and in a subsequent correspondence sent him a copy of George Washington Williams's *History of the Negro Race*. In January 1914, Archer notified Bruce that he had received the Williams book and informed him that Bruce held the honor of being the first black American to recognize his historic achievement.[56] Archer's accomplishment was impressive, but with it came financial obligations that were beyond his means. James Wilson, a London resident, wrote confidentially to Bruce on January 28, 1914, that Archer lacked funds to host receptions. Asking for assistance, Wilson requested that Bruce discreetly seek funds to aid Archer. Wilson sought to emphasize his message by adding that, without funds Archer would be criticized by whites as a poor excuse for an official. Dr. York Russell, a Harlem resident, cautioned Bruce that money was needed in New York for race initiatives. Thus, he advised Bruce to be evasive in his reply to Wilson: "*Put* him *off. Play* for *position,*" suggested Russell.[57] Bruce would have given Archer money, if he had it, but his inability to comply illustrated his willingness to be generous even when his own precarious financial situation dictated otherwise.

Bruce was rich, however, in willingness to assist others to choose the right path for racial advancement. In late October 1914, Bruce welcomed to Yonkers alumni from the Virginia Theological Seminary and College with these remarks: "character and culture in the Negro will constitute the saving qualities of the race." He again called for the study and teaching of Negro history and joined Arthur Schomburg in demanding the establishment of a chair in Negro history. Such a radical demand came decades before the establishment of departments of black studies in colleges. Bruce and Schomburg understood that both races could benefit from a more comprehensive understanding of the contribution of African people to world civilization. As noted by Schomburg, much of the ignorance could be attributed to white writers who treated blacks as "flotsam and jetsam." Bruce urged blacks to stop thinking white and to study their own history because "race is the key to history."[58]

Understanding that propaganda sometimes passed for history and that most white American scholars falsely depicted the role of blacks in Reconstruction, Bruce joined forces with other progressives in 1915 to protest David W. Griffith's film *The Birth of a Nation*. Griffith's glorification of the Ku Klux Klan depicted blacks as corrupt lawmakers or ignorant and savage freedmen. It led to calls for boycotts and censorship. Bruce criticized the filmmaker for encouraging racial antipathy and prejudice among Americans who were fast forgetting the bitterness of the Reconstruction era. The rising tide of racism was aided by President Wilson's praise for the film as an accurate depiction of black misrule. An angry Bruce noted that Negroes would never be true American citizens unless God bestowed upon American whites "a larger measure of justice[,] a greater love of truth [and] a keen conception of his duty to his fellow man."[59]

If nothing else, *The Birth of a Nation* revealed that reactionary whites would use any means to discredit black involvement in American politics and that blacks and their allies had to organize their struggle against racism better. Even before the public outcry against the film, Bruce sought to stimulate activism among black New Yorkers. In February 1915, he became editor of the *Phalanx Hornet,* organ of the Phalanx Club, a newsy four-page pamphlet that argued that "we must have [peace] at any cost if the organization is to live and prosper." The organization hoped to raise funds for a clubhouse by having as many as 250 members contribute the miniscule fee of three cents per week to raise about twenty-five hundred dollars in six years. Bruce was elected a presiding officer in November. He joked that he accepted the position under his "sincere protest for I am naturally diffident and retiring." More seriously, he warned the members to stick together and not succumb to the love of money and power, as did whites. He cautioned them that a worsening of race relations had them "sitting on the edge of a seething volcano." With venom, he added that he had studied white men since 1875 and "the more I see of white men the more I like dogs."[60]

Editors who noticed Bruce's efforts on behalf of his race welcomed his commentaries. Earlier, in April 1915, Bruce consented to submit occasional articles to the *Washington Sun,* which welcomed him by writing "no man knows Negro history better than . . . 'Grit Bruce,'" noted the editor, who reversed Bruce's nom de plume. The *Star of Zion,* organ of the African Methodist Episcopal Zion Church, considered Bruce and Richard W. Thompson to be one and two among secular writers legitimately able to claim the title of "best." Both men were praised for the "irresistible magnetism and charm in their writing that arrest the attention of the multitudes."[61] Other editors also heaped praise on Bruce. Philip H. Brown, editor of the *Saturday News* in Hopkinsville, Kentucky, informed Bruce in 1915 that his white readers were devoted to his weekly column. He thanked Bruce for forwarding to him African newspapers and informed him of his decision to place the *Weekly News* of Freetown, Sierra Leone, on his exchange list.[62] Editor George W. Harris of the *New York News* noted, "words are inadequate to express my deep appreciation of your loyal cooperation and superior work."[63] Editors at the *New York Times* were less supportive; they claimed that lack of space prevented them from publishing Bruce's antilynching letter. Bruce, who viewed the rejection as "delightful evasion," wrote in the margin, "I didn't expect it to appear in this southern owned journal. Fortunately, I have other medium in which to voice my view."

Notwithstanding the *Times*'s dismissal, Bruce's work was highly appreciated by race activists. Andrew B. F. Perry, an AME pastor in Clarksville, Arkansas, informed Bruce in 1915 that he kept his photo, clipped from a newspaper, hanging over his desk. Perry was so inspired by Bruce to fight injustice and Negro corruption that he read one of his letters two hundred times. He reminded Bruce that they had met in Yonkers and that Bruce had "begun to dry up the many deep waters of ignorance by the powerful heat from the rays of life which you held out in your hands." Moved by Bruce's interest, Perry addressed him as "my dear father and friend." Similarly, Chicago attorney George W. Ellis applauded Bruce for assisting others. He predicted that someday the entire world would give Bruce proper "historical consideration."[64]

Hubert H. Harrison, a native of St. Croix in the Caribbean, who would later join Bruce in the Garvey movement, wanted Bruce to write a book to preserve "for the next generation your flawless English, big heart and fine Negro personality." "Please do it. Talk it over with me when we meet again," he concluded. Bruce had a prodigious appetite for work. In addition to his employment, he organized activities for the Negro Society for Historical Research and the Loyal Sons of Africa and wrote to a large number of friends and associates around the globe. Unfortunately, he did not have time to research and write a book. He also was working closely with Schomburg in Ye Sons of Shakespeare to discuss the bard's work with enthusiastic audiences in Yonkers. Schomburg wrote his friend on January 13, 1915, that their organization could be of assistance to the Shakespeare Tercentenary by arranging a local production of *Othello*. In June 1916, Bruce assumed the presidency of Ye Friends, and told the followers that he would tolerate no cliques. In the study of Shakespeare, Bruce saw an opportunity for New Yorkers to learn something about the bard's "incomparable genius" that would inspire them to emulate his intelligence and imagination. He sought to attract both scholars and laypersons to the organization regardless of status or education. Bruce encouraged members to "write your names where all ages may believe them and all time cannot efface them."[65]

Bruce was willing to support all race organizations that endeavored to uplift the masses, particularly those that emphasized knowledge about the race's achievers and historical accomplishments. In September 1915, he spoke at St. Marks Lyceum, one of New York's oldest lyceums for African Americans. He heaped praise on St. Marks for its proposed library of books, pamphlets, manuscripts, and photographs of noted race men and women. He urged his audience to *"think black"* while they "dig deep for hidden treasures

... which reveal the greatness and glory of a race that was born to scholarship." Impressed with the lyceum's potential, Bruce urged them to develop a grand library collection with books in Arabic and Spanish that would validate ancient and medieval African history. At the same time, such a library would placate "the doubting Thomases in our own and in the white race."[66]

Near the end of 1915, Bruce told children at the Antonio Maceo Cuban Club (in Harlem's St. Marks Church on West 138th Street) that they needed to learn about the great Cuban freedom fighter for which their club was named. Language, geography, and culture, Bruce argued, should not separate descendants of enslaved Africans. While Bruce sought to enlighten the audience with tales of Maceo's military exploits during the war against Spain, he did not ignore the raging European conflict. On Christmas Day, 1915, he and Florence spent the day at their Yonkers residence going over cards sent by friends on three continents. He lamented that there "can be no merry xmas when half of Christendom is in tears." Bruce devoted part of New Year's Day to rereading letters, manuscripts, and papers dating back twenty to thirty years. He noted in his unpublished writings that the rereading convinced him how "shallow and insincere is the friendship of some people who wrote 'sincerely yours.'"

A happier occasion was Bruce's sixtieth birthday, February 22, 1916, when a contingent of friends surprised him at his residence at 146 Warburton Avenue in Yonkers. One couple was resplendent in period dress and powdered wigs as George and Martha Washington. The next day, he received ten dollars in the mail from a young man whom he had introduced to a friend in Africa, which led to employment in the import-export business. Bruce reflected upon reaching four score in age with a vow to "make good use of [his] remaining time." He expressed hope that God would permit him "to die in harness fighting for my race[,] defending its good name and urging it ... to ... attain ... unity, cooperation [and] race loyalty." Bruce was thankful to be mentally alert and not physically impaired. "How great and good is God! I feel that I cannot do enough for Him ... nor for my race."[67]

Bruce was willing to work for his race even if it meant swallowing his pride. A case in point was when Emmett J. Scott requested in April 1916 that Bruce support efforts for a Booker T. Washington memorial. Despite his major ideological differences with Washington, Bruce acknowledged that the Tuskegee Wizard had aided the race, particularly in the area of education. Bruce responded with the suggestion that the committee solicit potential supporters in the Caribbean and Africa by publicizing an appeal in the *African Times and Orient Review*.[68]

Not all of Bruce's efforts to help his people proved successful. In early 1916, Bruce failed to organize a recital in Yonkers for the famed elocutionist and dramatist Henrietta Vinton Davis. Davis, who was in Bermuda, wrote Bruce on April 30, "I know you did your best, but I am well acquainted with my people. I know their lack of cohesiveness—and it is that very lack that the white man takes advantage of. He knows the Negro better than the Negro knows himself." She encouraged Bruce to revise a play, *Double Trouble,* that he was working on in order that it could be rehearsed in August and produced that September.[69] Davis's letter underscored the obstacle Bruce and Schomburg faced in 1916 in developing a race consciousness among a people ignorant of their contributions to world history and culture. On March 30, he informed an audience at St. Marks Church in Harlem that although Christianity began in Africa, where Jesus spent his youth, the popular belief was that the African was not in the Bible. Bruce considered true Christianity, with its emphasis on brotherhood, to reside in Africa, not Europe or white America. He urged the youths to read Negro history, although he realized that precious little could be found in New York's libraries. He admonished them to read in order to raise their race consciousness. In his estimation the ignorance of whites was as much a problem as black ignorance. He noted that God would see that their posterity would "reap the whirlwind." Despite Europe's thousand years of civilization, Bruce predicted that "the clock of God is about to strike the hour of her doom for she has been a harlot among nations, [and] a hypocrite." For proof, he cited the awful destruction of European youth on the battlefields.[70] While Bruce believed that God would avenge the wrongs whites inflicted upon people of color, he also advocated that African Americans aim for greater race love and self-respect. These attributes, he believed, came from proper home training, something he considered the proper domain of women. He noted that "children like the men ... cannot rise any higher in the scale of morality, and good breeding and pure thinking than the womanhood of the race." Bruce thought highly of women as a force to raise the race from the depths of ignorance and depravity. While some of his writings emphasized the essential role of women as homemakers, Bruce did not deny that activists such as Mary Church Terrell, Frances Ellen Watkins Harper, or Ida Wells Barnett were necessary. He indicated in a June 1916 essay, "The Negro Woman," that the race's future rested in the hands of liberated women who would oversee the liberation of men.[71]

Bruce understood, however, that race pride was an essential factor in the uplift of a people who had known the horrors of the slave owners' whips, the terror of Ku Klux Klansmen, and the humiliation of the Jim Crow system. He also knew that an oppressed people had to see themselves in a positive light before they could exult in their racial pride. In September 1916, Bruce hoped to work out a deal with an artist to sell lithographs of notable figures such as Nat Turner, Dred Scott, and Paul Laurence Dunbar at $1.25 each. Bruce saw in the potential sales of hundreds of lithographs and thousands of color prints a safe and profitable investment, as well as an opportunity to develop black race pride. In August 1916, Bruce sent out a mass mailing announcing his invention of "an improved clip or clasp binder" that served the dual purpose of creating race pride and, hopefully, securing sales for him.[72]

On Christmas Day, 1916, John and Florence celebrated Christ's birthday in their new Harlem residence, 2109 Madison Avenue. Adding to their pleasure was the news that Bruce would receive a promotion and a salary increase of $120 in his position in the office of the surveyor of the New York Port. Bruce welcomed 1917 with praise to God for his restored health. Months earlier, Henrietta Vinton Davis unsuccessfully urged him to winter in Bermuda with its filtered rainwater as a treatment for his undisclosed ailment. His journal entry for January 1 reads: "the year just past has been one . . . [of] embarrassment but in every crisis God's blessings have been showered upon me. In the darkest of hour . . . the Lord . . . has been . . . my friend."[73] (The embarrassment Bruce referred to was probably a reference to failed investment ventures.) The happiness he did have was overshadowed by his concern that black Americans needed to act in unity for racial progress. In March, in a speech before the city's Episcopal Mission, he took exception to Dr. Lymon Abbott's remark that the two races could not live together harmoniously in the nation. Abbott's statement aroused concern because the respected clergyman and attorney was also editor of the *Outlook*. Abbott had touched on white America's concern that there were few persons of color worthy enough to integrate into the mainstream of society. Like Booker T. Washington and countless other blacks who called for racial uplift, Bruce counseled African Americans to behave in a modest, reserved, calm, and dignified manner or bring shame to the race. Bruce urged his listeners to emulate the Jews, who did not make noise until they were ready to act. Citing an inaccurate but popular viewpoint, he added that "commercial America is controlled largely by these meek and patient and plodding people." Bruce called upon three hundred race-conscious individuals to pledge two dollars monthly for one year to raise funds to purchase one or two apartment buildings and others later. Confronting his audience, Bruce challenged them to "put their hand to the plow and follow it to the end of the row."[74]

While Bruce preached racial solidarity, he was sometimes negatively judgmental of the intentions and motivations of others. One such case was his reaction to Joel Augustus Rogers, who, according to Bruce, was "a West Indian of the type . . . who draw the color line in his own island home and who came to America to be disillusioned as to their social status." Enraged, Bruce added, "they make good fighters in us who have felt the iron in our soul." He faulted them for not being "*true* to their black *mammies* and to the race." Bruce concluded his diatribe with the observation that the British had men like Rogers thinking that they were white until they arrive in America and discovered that they were Negroes who could write about the "Negro problem." There are several possible explanations for Bruce's anger. First, immigrants from the Caribbean thought of themselves as primarily West Indian and chose not to be identified with black Americans who differed from them in culture and experience. This caused conflicts with African Americans who resented being called "lazy" by Caribbean immigrants who were shocked to find themselves viewed by whites as "Negroes"—with all its negative connotations. Those who claimed that race was not a concern in the islands were dismayed upon learning how pervasive race was in the American consciousness: that their color lumped them into a category that defined them as inferior. They resented this, and they exhorted black Americans to seek more education, own more homes, and establish business enterprises. Second, Bruce overreacted to what he perceived as Rogers's racial ambivalence. Having never traveled to the Caribbean, and under the influence of the antimulatto sentiments of Edward W. Blyden and Alexander Crummell, Bruce was not prepared to be sympathetic. He did not understand that in the Caribbean multiple categories of racial identities existed, unlike in the United States, where one was "black" if one looked "black" or had the proverbial one drop of African blood in one's veins. Third, Bruce probably was unaware of the role of class in British Caribbean society, and he attributed the privileged positions of West Indians in the islands to their alleged withdrawal from their "people." In fact, these individuals rose to the top because of superior education, a trait that meant less in the United States, where educated blacks were often marginal individuals. It is probable that Bruce assumed that immigrants like Rogers wanted to be considered white. In reality, many stood shoulder to shoulder with their darker brethren in the struggle against racism and colonialism while also fighting for Pan-Africanism. Ironically, this point was displayed throughout the coming years in Rogers's prodigious output of literature proving that Africans had a rich history. Bruce admitted as much and declared that Rogers's 1917 publication, *From Superman to Man,* was "clever, vigorous in style, [and] audacious in utterance." In 1919, Rogers confided to Schomburg his "ardent desire to write something big for the race in a literary way" because the race had not "produced even a good one of the third rank." Rogers vowed "to write one that will rank with the masterpiece of the world." His later studies on race and culture indicated that he identified completely with the African race. That he was willing to go door to door in efforts to sell his books indicated his tenacious desire to educate his people about their contributions to world history.[75]

In 1919, Bruce was keeping up with his diverse newspaper writings, renewing acquaintances, making new international contacts, participating in the activities of the American Negro Academy, and contributing to the *Crusader,* the organ of the Hamitic League of the World. On New Year's Day in 1919, he entertained E. J. Braithwaite, an old friend from Trinidad and uncle of the poet with the same name. Arthur Schomburg and William W. Weeks, a pianist from British Guiana, were also there. Before retiring, Bruce thanked God for all the blessings bestowed upon him during the past year. He also asked that "God grant that we may be worthy and privileged to record the brief happenings in our humble lives during the [new] year . . . [for] who can tell what it may bring forth."[76] Bruce continued his busy schedule throughout the year, writing, lecturing, corresponding with friends abroad, and involving himself in African investment schemes before joining with Marcus Garvey's UNIA. Bruce wrote in his journal for New Year's Day in 1920 that "we are still alive thanks be to God and have our health, a crust of bread, and a corner to sleep in." Thinking of the year ahead, he wrote, "may the new year bring to us all the joy and happiness and prosperity which we deserve and may [God] . . . bless and keep us in His holy keeping until the [Judgment] Day." The following day, Bruce wrote a New Year's resolution to "[b]e kind [and] helpful to others-charitable in deed and thought, to be true to [my] race and do everything in my power to prove it worthy of respect and the consideration it seeks at the hands of those in power, to at all times and in all places be a man—a *gentle* man."[77]

It was Bruce's faith in the limitless possibilities of African people that encouraged him to write short stories that extolled the greatness of his people. A representative selection was *The African Aeroplane,* written circa 1918. In the story, a crowd in the western United States is startled to see an airplane hundreds of feet larger than a German zeppelin glide noiselessly into a field. The pilot, an African, has made a stop to make some minor repairs. The crowd is amazed upon learning that the thousand ton aircraft was built by Africans of African wood and metal not available outside that continent. They are shocked to learn that a white powder derived from the kernel of an African nut propelled it. The pilot warns the curious group that aboard he carries a sleeping powder made by African doctors to stop enemies from stealing their cattle or gold. To their disbelief, the crowd soon learns that the pilot expects to arrive in Tokyo, six thousand miles away, in just five days. As the plane flies into space like a rocket, a white man on the ground admits, "I hate the idea of Negroes being in possession of such valuable secrets, and exercising such power over white men. It is a menace to our civilization." His friend replies that they should seek the source of the secret but that it will be difficult, as "they are thoroughly awake now."[78] The story, of course, was Bruce's way of encouraging black Americans to be proud of Africans who would one day repeat their earlier successes as builders of civilizations. His reference to Japan was clearly a suggestion that the darker races of the world would unite to overthrow worldwide white supremacy. In another short story, published in the Omaha *Monitor* in early 1919, Bruce described how Dr. McDendon, a black physician, came to treat Silas, the faithful servant of a white family whose physician was unavailable. In her effort to assist Dr. McDendon, lifting Silas off the floor, Mrs. Flint twists a muscle in her arm. The excruciating pain is quickly alleviated by McDendon, which pleases Mrs. Flint so much that she renounces her former race prejudice. "I had no faith in Negro doctors but you have converted me. You have skill, culture and ability." In gratitude, she pays Dr. McDendon twenty-five dollars, the same fee her white doctor would have commanded. Mrs. Flint even decides that McDendon will now become her family physician, and even Silas, who had considered whites more competent, is converted and arranges for the black doctor to become his lodge's physician.[79] Bruce's version of life did not reflect reality, but it was his contention that blacks had skills comparable, if not superior to, whites and that prejudice would be eliminated if blacks were judged by their character and ability. All of his fictional heroes were erudite, proud, courageous men of action and were modeled after Martin Delany, Frederick Douglass, Edward W. Blyden, and Alexander Crummell, each one an important father figure for Bruce. Now, in the twilight of his life, Bruce would become a father figure for so many others who continued to look to him for leadership.

African Emigration and Economic Investment, 1889–1919

Early Interest in Africa

Of all the suffering slavery inflicted on African people, possibly the worst was the physical separation of people from their ancestral homeland. While the vast majority of American slaves and their descendants lived and died in the New World, some emancipated slaves and free persons of color longed for a return to the motherland even before the birth of the United States of America. Lack of finances and sponsorship prevented many from achieving their goal until black seaman Paul Cuffee's 1817 journey to Sierra Leone convinced some that Africans in America could be repatriated. Inspired by Cuffee's journey, the American Colonization Society (ACS), founded in 1817, sought throughout the nineteenth century to enlist blacks to sail to Liberia, the society's colony that became an independent republic in 1847. Many leading Americans, including presidents and members of Congress, supported the goals of the ACS; but the vast majority of African Americans rejected the society's efforts to repatriate them. They vehemently argued that they were entitled to rights of free citizens despite the efforts of bigots to deny them. Additionally, many refused to leave their enslaved brethren without a voice for emancipation. Some blacks, however, saw emigration as an opportunity to achieve complete political, social, and economic freedom. Approximately fifteen thousand emigrated to Liberia by 1870 under the auspices of the ACS. Others were enticed to brave the ocean voyage to do mission work among the indigenous "heathens," while some hoped to find their wealth by exploiting West Africa's mineral resources.

In 1877, Martin Delany, a black Civil War officer and advocate of emigration, joined others to form the Liberian Joint Stock Steamship Company. The following year, *The Azor* made its first and only voyage; unfortunately, the incompetence of its white ship captain led to the seizure of the vessel in debtor's court. Southern atrocities against blacks in the 1890s led to a proliferation of emigration schemes. Sen. Matthew Butler proposed a bill to provide free transportation to African Americans who departed from the South to become citizens of another country. White southern conservatives supported the bill, but it never came to a vote in Congress. Efforts to transport blacks to Africa by the Afro-American Steamship and Mercantile Company, organized in 1893, failed for lack of investors. The International Migration Society was formed in the following year; but it, too, soon failed. The ill-fated arrival of *The Horsa* in Liberia left migrants stranded, without provisions or long-term support from a financially stressed Liberian government. Edward W. Blyden made many trips to the United States during this period in the hope of attracting limited emigration to the West African republic. His biggest American supporter was AME Bishop Henry M. Turner, who became an irritant to those who insisted that they, too, were American citizens and that their destiny was in America.[1]

The Influence of Blyden and Crummell

Bruce's interest in Africa would develop gradually from an initial curiosity about the continent to an interest in African history. What followed was a desire to invest in the land's natural resources and ultimately to an expressed desire to claim it as the rightful home of blacks in the diaspora. This evolution in thought took place over a half century. Bruce worked as a file clerk in the Washington office of the ACS. There he met Blyden, a vice president in the ACS, on one of his trips to the United States in the late 1870s or early 1880s. William Coppinger, ACS secretary, introduced the two and suggested that Blyden take Bruce to Africa because he had expressed interest.[2] Most African Americans before the Civil War who sought ways to end slavery, not to emigrate, shunned the ACS. Resentment still existed two decades after emancipation. Many were deeply offended by the organization's effort to repatriate them to Liberia, a land they neither knew nor to which they wanted to emigrate. Bruce offered no explanation in his personal papers to explain why he would work for such a despised organization. In this instance, Bruce placed his desire for funds above the interests of the majority of his people. As a file clerk, Bruce probably had access to correspondence from and to Liberia that undoubtedly whetted his appetite for knowledge about Liberia. No evidence exists suggesting that Blyden sought to encourage Bruce to emigrate, but Blyden found much in common with Bruce and was impressed with his fervor. Originally from the Danish West Indies, Blyden had lived in West Africa for decades. His battles with Liberia's mulatto class resonated with Bruce, who despised the fair-complexioned elite who dominated African American politics and culture. Blyden's blatant appeal to full-blooded Negroes to seek their destiny in Africa angered many who claimed they could overcome America's ingrained racism and find a destiny in the United States.[3]

Besides the guiding tutelage of Blyden, Bruce began at this time to correspond with a small group of men who fervently held out the possibility of Africa's rejuvenation through the efforts of black men. Some of these men had lived in Africa; others had intellectual and spiritual interests in the "Dark Continent." Rufus L. Perry, editor of the *National Monitor,* a black Baptist publication, mailed Bruce a copy of his book *The Cushite.* In his book, Perry, also a Greek scholar, argued that much of the credit Caucasians claim for ancient glories "rightfully belongs to the black man." In this respect, Perry was in agreement with explorer Martin R. Delany, Rev. Henry Highland Garnet, and AME Bishop Benjamin T. Tanner, who argued that Ethiopia influenced Egypt, whose scientific knowledge spread to Greece, Rome, and eventually to the Anglo-Saxons.[4]

Alexander Crummell, an Episcopal priest who had lived in Liberia as a missionary for nearly twenty years and who shared Bruce's antimulatto bias, was instrumental in furthering Bruce's knowledge about Africa. They first met around 1878 and remained close friends until Crummell's death in 1898. Along with Blyden, Crummell would provide Bruce with useful information about Liberia's political and cultural history. Writing from Washington in November 1893, Crummell thanked Bruce for sending him an article from a Lagos, Nigeria, newspaper and a letter from J. Robert Love, a physician who resided in Jamaica. "How strengthening, how assuring this solidarity of leading minds of t[he] race in such wide & distant quarters of t[he] globe! [is]," declared Crummell.[5] In the summer of 1895, Blyden visited the United States and presented Bruce with letters of introduction to the *Lagos Record* and to the *Sierra Leone Weekly News.* Bruce began to submit articles to these publications that acquainted West African readers with the passion and wit of Bruce Grit. In 1896, Blyden forwarded to Bruce some submissions for various American newspapers, including the *North American Review.* In this respect, Bruce assisted Blyden in getting his message of limited emigration to Liberia to a wider audience.[6]

Bruce was proud of his blackness, both as a color and as an ideology. He wrote to Love that he may have been "too black" for some. However, the West Indian responded, "you are not 'too black' for me." Love took the same amount of pride in his own color: "there are very few of you who can beat me in *blackness.* I am foolish enough to be a little vain of being *so* black." Love expressed pride when he recalled how strangers in Haiti would remark *"quel bel noir* [what a handsome black man]." Love ended his letter by informing

Bruce that he was preparing to lecture on Phillis Wheatley to encourage the girls in Jamaica to aim for racial unity. "It makes me so proud that I am a Negro," he declared.[7]

Between Blyden and Crummell, who educated him about the culture of West Africa, and Love, who provided him with useful information about Haiti and Jamaica, Bruce's Pan-Africanist perspective began to develop rapidly. Bruce's awareness of Africa's diversity of people, culture, and natural resources increased during the next two decades due to his voluminous correspondence with Africans from the Gold Coast, Liberia, and Nigeria. Bruce's Pan-Africanism was in a nascent stage during this period. It primarily consisted of trying to understand the continent's historical contributions to civilization. While Bruce enjoyed corresponding with Africans and reading clippings from the continent's newspapers, he was initially opposed to wholesale emigration. "What does the Negro know about Africa?" he inquired. He added that they should not heed the call of cranks to leave the land that their ancestors' labor and blood had enriched. Bruce noted in 1902 that, outside of Africa, the so-called Negro was "no more a Negro than a [Comanche] Indian is a Turk." He sarcastically added that blacks in America had been so acculturated that they considered African Negroes as much a joke as did the white man.[8] In his honest appraisal, Bruce was merely stating the obvious. The vast majority of Americans of African descent considered themselves culturally American and ignored African culture. Not even vocal advocates of emigration such as Bishop Henry M. Turner deemed African culture worthy of emulation. They viewed traditional African culture as primitive, barbaric, and heathen. Despite his hostile opposition to emigration, Bruce momentarily broke with the anticolonizationists in 1900. Disillusioned and embittered by the rapid decline in civil and political rights following the rise of Jim Crow segregation in the South and the spread of racial prejudice and discrimination to the North, Bruce asked the editor of the *Planet,* a black weekly in Richmond, Virginia, "Why do we insist that our destiny in America is coordinate with that of the white man? Is it because we were born here? Do we think the ties between the races can't be broken? Vain delusions." Calling Booker T. Washington's accommodationist ideology more a hindrance than a help, Bruce declared that blacks were "sitting upon the edge of a ... volcano." Thus, citizenship in Africa would ease their problem, for it would provide African Americans with a homeland and status among the nations of the world. This pessimistic statement represented an aberration in Bruce's thinking that was probably influenced by Blyden, who believed that the destiny of the American Negro would eventually be fulfilled in Africa.[9] The idea that Africa was greener grass, however, did not hold his vision for long. Bruce was, at that time, too committed to fulfilling the race's destiny in America to sustain interest in African emigration. However, on a deeper level, this sentiment would slowly grow on Bruce, and he would advocate it after he accepted Marcus Garvey's vision for African emigration.

Even Blyden, who made periodic trips to the American south to encourage limited emigration, understood that America had much to teach her citizens of "darker hue." He noted by 1895 that "there are lessons to be learned in the house of bondage, both by the Negroes and their former masters, before a large exodus to Africa would be anything but a peril and stumbling block to the cause of genuine African progress." Blyden had convinced Bruce that British imperialism in West Africa would prove beneficial to the region's inhabitants because they would provide the indigenous population with education and training for self-government. In contrast, according to Blyden, the French and Belgians would attempt to colonize the region with their citizens. And the French, in particular, would annex a large section of the continent to prevent the rise in the future of an independent black West Africa.[10]

Blyden's influence is noted in an undated Bruce essay. Sometime after 1900, Bruce described the European presence in Africa as a necessary evil. "The African is an observant and apt pupil," observed Bruce, "and he is absorbing, assimilating the good the white man brings to Africa, chiefly for his own benefit and protection, and is eliminating the bad, as rapidly as his understanding of the white man permits." Bruce argued that it would be a mistake to expel Europeans from the continent. In a conservative tone that was incongruous with his later views, he stated that American slavery was not as harsh as white slavery in England or Jewish slavery in Egypt. Without the institution of slavery, he argued, the American Negro would be "a g[i]bbering ignoramus." The latter portion of the statement reflected the influence of both Blyden and Crummell. Many others believed that God brought the African to America to receive Christianity and the fundamentals of democracy so they might return to Africa to teach the "heathens" about their savior, Jesus Christ. Needless to say, later generations called this theory preposterous.[11]

Bruce was unwilling to support any mass emigration to Africa, even if he believed that the mosquito would render West Africa the "graveyard of European civilization." Despite tremendous opposition from black politicians, ordinary citizens, and even fellow bishops, AME Bishop Henry M. Turner undiplomatically declared in 1903 that "every Negro who is not a natural born fool, and a servile cur, must see that there is no future in this country for the colored man." Bruce dismissed Turner with the observation that "we ought not to be persuaded that our only safety and hope for better things lies in flight to Africa . . . on the contrary we would show ourselves arrant cowards by running away." This harsh indictment of Turner was fueled by two passions. First, Bruce believed at this time that the black American's demand for citizenship rights would prove fruitful; therefore, why run to a land that they knew only as a romantic sentiment? Second, Bruce was disgusted with the "so-called Negro leaders who preached *deportation* as a way out" because of fear that bigots would attempt to seek that as an answer to the problem of race in America. Turner was widely respected by African Methodists, although the council of bishops remained steadfast in their opposition to his emigration schemes. Although Turner was not one of those leaders appointed by the white power structure, Bruce attacked him as one who reflected the desires of bigots to rid America of her darker citizens. He urged people not to follow "the professional Negro leaders in America [who] are a standing joke," but rather rally around those persons who "intelligently organize resistance" to the efforts of demagogues to deny blacks their citizenship rights.[12]

By 1915, war had embroiled Europe and her colonies in Africa, Asia, and the Caribbean. Anti-imperialists saw the war as an opportunity to organize for eventual self-rule throughout the world. In a few years, Marcus Garvey would outline his program for "Africa for Africans at home and abroad," but during the war years Bruce ridiculed the prospect of a Negro confederation forming a nation in Africa. He viewed such a scheme as "chimerical and utopian," something that could not occur for a hundred years, if even then. Bruce noted that it took Germany four hundred years to become an important nation; therefore, it was "nonsense and flub dub! . . . a waste of time and energy and intellect . . . to excite . . . the unthinking masses" who believed that Negroes fifty years out of enslavement had the resources to form a nation in Africa or form an army and navy to militarily defeat the British. The "scheme" he referred to may have been that of Chief Alfred Sam, who tried in 1913 to enlist blacks to emigrate to the Gold Coast. Two years later, Sam solicited Booker T. Washington for an introduction to influential whites, presumably to ask for financial assistance.[13]

While Bruce did not support African emigration at this time, he resented that the continent's wealth was being divided among Europeans. Others shared this viewpoint. African Americans had sought unsuccessfully during the last quarter of the nineteenth century to develop investment schemes in West Africa. Both John H. Smyth and Henry Highland Garnet, U.S. resident ministers to Liberia during the 1880s, urged Americans to invest in Liberia's gold, silver, iron, cotton, coffee, tobacco, and forest products. Both diplomats realized that failure to invest in Liberia would eventually result in English businessmen filling the void. From his contacts with Blyden and others, Bruce knew that it was feasible for African Americans to develop trade relationships in Liberia, where some of their countrymen had gone to settle. There is in Bruce's papers an unsigned letter, circa 1907, that requests the development of a trade relationship between Liberians and African Americans. The letter requests assistance in establishing "terminal and transportation facilities with

America." The writer mentioned that he had resided for years in West Africa and considered America "our best market for all lines of manufacture."[14] There were no follow-up letters, and it is unknown how Bruce may have responded to the solicitation. While Bruce was receptive to investment offers, he took exception to unscrupulous individuals whom he believed were corrupt or incompetent. Bruce wrote in early February 1907 to Arthur A. Schomburg complaining about a phone message he received on February 3 requesting funds for three thousand shares of stock, with instructions to forward a check the next day. Bruce decided not to comply because the caller, a "Mr. Cowan is . . . a *rusher*." Bruce had attended a few meetings but was surprised to learn upon receiving a letter and blank subscriptions that he had been made vice president without his consent and against his wishes. He confided to Schomburg, "it seems a hard thing to do to get American Negroes to do the square thing in business transactions. I am too old a bird to let any salt get on my tail feathers."[15] Bruce mailed his complaint to George W. Ellis, who was with the U.S. legation in Monrovia, Liberia. Ellis wrote back in late April that he was sorry about Bruce's disappointment but that Cowan would return money to all dissatisfied parties. Nevertheless, a troubled Ellis notified Bruce that he had asked Cowan to include intelligent colored men in the venture who understood the risks of investing in African mining in the Gold Coast (Ghana). Ellis held out hope that the race could get together "and not make this effort another striking example of the inability of colored men to work together." Ellis also requested that his letter remain private and not published, adding that Bruce should let the matter rest until he arrived in New York. In the meantime, he requested Bruce to "use [his] influence for harmony and success to those interested and the race."[16] The outcome of this investment scheme is unknown, but Bruce would continue to involve himself in African mineral and agricultural investment ventures.

Investing in Africa's Wealth

Bruce's economic and political interest in Africa was nurtured by his many personal contacts with West Africans and his correspondence with many of the continent's leading activists. In April 1908, Edward W. Blyden provided a letter of introduction to James Jenkins Dossen, vice president of Liberia, and later that nation's chief justice of the supreme court, to meet Bruce upon his business trip to the United States. On June 26, Bruce hosted a reception in his Yonkers home, at 228 New Main Street, for Dossen, former Liberian President Garretson W. Gibson, Liberian Sen. Charles B. Dunbar, and T. J. Franklin.[17]

Desperate for loans, the Liberians had come to America as commissioners to seek Booker T. Washington's assistance in meeting with President

Roosevelt. In June, Ernest W. Lyons, U.S. minister and consul general to Liberia, arranged for Liberia to award Washington the Knight of the National Order of "African Redemption." In mid-June, Washington notified Secretary of State Elihu Root that the African envoys had asked him to become their chargé d'affaires in the United States, a position he believed would give him weight to speak on their behalf. Washington added that he wanted to assist Liberia in developing its natural resources as well as have some of the nation's youth study at Tuskegee. Root replied that it would be unwise for Washington to accept a low-rank diplomatic position that would hinder Washington's independent effort to speak on their behalf.[18] Washington's flirtation with the Liberians alarmed some, but an unworried Bruce wrote Schomburg on October 31, 1908: "I do not think that the Wizard is dangerous in Africa or that he will be able to deliver the goods he is offering. If the president and his cabinet in Liberia find out that BTW is playing with the hands of the white speculators there'll be some doing." Liberia was desperate for foreign assistance and had no qualms about asking Booker T. Washington to persuade the American Department of State to protect them from British and French encroachment. In early 1910, the educator informed Dossen that he and Ernest W. Lyons had urged the secretary of the Navy to send a war vessel to patrol the Liberian coast occasionally. In April, Washington informed Dossen confidentially that Sen. Henry Cabot Lodge had assured him that the United States should use her rapport with England, France, and Germany to settle the border issue. Eventually, Washington was able to convince the American government to form a Liberian commission composed of Washington's private secretary, Emmett J. Scott, and two whites, George Sale and Roland P. Falkner. The United States established a protectorate over Liberia but did not provide financial aid or funds for economic development because the African republic allegedly wasted funds in importing foodstuffs that they could have produced themselves.[19]

Liberians also hoped that a surge of investors from America would invigorate the county's sluggish economy. In 1908, Dossen wrote to Bruce from Cape Palmas, Liberia, with information about possible investment schemes in mining, fishing, and lumbering. Dossen invited Bruce to come visit for two weeks. We "will kill the fattest calf for you and give you such a welcome as only the African can," Dossen promised. The Liberian also provided Bruce with surprising news. President Arthur Barclay had conferred upon Bruce the "Humane Order of African Redemption" in recognition of his hospitality when Dossen visited New York. Dossen closed his letter with the hope that Bruce "will take a deeper and more energetic interest in the struggling Republic." Late in August 1909, Dossen apologized for a delay in forwarding Bruce's bronze medal because "the order is very popular in Europe and will take you into circles there where you will otherwise might not be permitted to enter."

Dossen's letter had a serious intent. Liberians wanted Bruce to help organize an African American petition to President Taft and Congress to support the African republic in her border conflicts with French Guinea and British Sierra Leone, as well as persuade European powers to restructure Liberia's loan payments. Dossen promised to memorialize Bruce's name if he could persuade John D. Rockefeller or Andrew Carnegie to provide funds for education.[20]

Liberia needed scientific, technical, and industrial workers that loans alone could not provide. Bruce was unable in 1910 to provide such assistance, but the request convinced him a decade later that Marcus Garvey's UNIA could provide the necessary technical skills that would make the small African republic a showpiece for the African world. Bruce urged Negroes in 1922 to provide Liberia with a $10 million loan and to emigrate there in order to develop that struggling nation's mineral and agricultural wealth.

African Americans had sentimental reasons to invest in Liberia's future. It was founded by former slaves and free blacks that left the United States in pursuit of freedom and opportunity. The ruling class, the Americo-Liberians, was culturally similar to America's colored elite in taste and education. Despite these inducements, Liberia was far away. Mail between the two countries took months to arrive, and the distance between the nations made it difficult to keep an eye on investments. For these reasons, some were enticed to earn profits in the nearby Cuban market. Members of the U.S. Army who had fought in Cuba during the war with Spain wrote glowing reports to the black press about investment opportunities as farmers, dentists, physicians, commission merchants, and shopkeepers in Cuba. Edovardo Rodriguez, a Cuban member of the Odd Fellows, urged Bruce and other Freemasons to support a movement to send ten thousand African Americans to that island nation to grow tobacco, sugar, and other crops. Rodriguez informed Bruce that if he could persuade one thousand to emigrate, he "would never again feel the need of a dollar. What a bonanza if I can get 10,000 here!!" He urged Bruce to make haste to promote the project. It is unlikely that Bruce supported the endeavor, because he wrote on the margin that it was a scheme of R. M. R. Nelson. Bruce also noted that an editor from *La Lucha,* a Spanish-language newspaper, had visited him on February 21, 1912, and offered him space for a column to write supporting black American investments in Cuba.[21] It is not known if Bruce took up this offer, but the intent was clear: African people throughout the world needed to eliminate the barriers of language, geography, culture, and color distinction and join forces for their mutual benefits.

In late 1915, Bruce contacted James J. Dossen, now chief justice of the Liberian Supreme Court, about importing animal skins. Dossen's reply, though it indicated that it was not a feasible project, did not discourage Bruce, who would continue during the next half decade to engage others in various

African investment endeavors. Bruce's interest in investing in Africa's wealth resonated with Africans who saw in the African American a source of cash. In August 1916, Bruce went to the Brooklyn home of Adolph Nassay, an immigrant from British Guiana, where he met C. D. B. King, recently elected president of Liberia. King hoped to attract American investment by promoting Liberia as the gateway to the development of the continent's vast reserves of minerals and agricultural products. Bruce believed that it was the duty of black Americans to make Liberia the center of Negro culture. This was the rebuke he sent to the *New York Evening Sun* for suggesting that King's visit aroused no interest in him or in Liberia. The following month, Bruce learned more about investing in Liberia when the Grand Lodge of Prince Hall Masons of New York (of which he was a member) hosted a banquet to honor President and Madame King. Bruce's interest in investing was further whetted in February 1917 after hearing a lecture by M. J. Highes of Lagos, Nigeria, on intraracial cooperation for economic development. Highes's call for cooperatively owned ships to export African goods to America and import American products to Africa appealed to Bruce. In early 1918, James E. K. Aggrey, a professor at Livingstone College in Salisbury, North Carolina, informed Bruce that Samuel R. Wood, manager of the General Shipping and Commission Agency of Axim in the Gold Coast, was looking for American investors. Aggrey sought to entice Bruce, whom he referred to as "Dad," by letting him know that he and others had twenty years earlier helped several dozen chiefs and kings save their lands. The grateful royalty were now willing to provide American investors with cocoa, despite the tactics of foreigners seeking to dominate the market. J. P. Brown, a former president of the Gold Coast Aborigine Society, allied with Aggrey. Eager to move, Aggrey informed Bruce, "I mean business and can deliver the goods." He added that Bruce and Arthur Schomburg should make contact with a business firm to received cocoa, rubber, mahogany, palm oil, and gum arabic. Aggrey was so eager to get Bruce involved in the project that he wrote him again on the same date suggesting that Brown and Wood divide the Gold Coast between them for investment purposes. Urgent to get started, he reiterated, "any way I am ready to talk real business and trust you too will do the same." Intimating that he was on close terms with several Gold Coast kings, Aggrey instructed Bruce, "tell the firms for I am to the manor born in Africa and to the manor born in dealing with the natives there. Besides I have [favor of the majority] of the native kings and chiefs." Aggrey was even willing to take a leave of absence from his teaching position to travel to England to make financial arrangements for the scheme. "Let us hit while the iron is hot," he pleaded. In an undated 1918 letter, Aggrey wrote Bruce, "Dear Dad, push the business you and Mr. Schomburg, we can deliver the goods." Upon hearing from Bruce and Schomburg, Aggrey responded that he shared their letters with J. P. Brown and others. He closed his letter with the hope that soon they would bring to "our fatherland economic liberty."[22]

Bruce and Schomburg were unable or unwilling to join forces with Aggrey and Brown, and there are no letters in Bruce's papers to suggest any further discussion of this particular scheme. Nevertheless, if Bruce felt pressured by Aggrey's aggressiveness, it did not interfere with his personal opinion of the African's character, for Bruce was extremely proud of one he referred to as "son." On July 28, 1920, Bruce wrote three letters in praise of Aggrey's capabilities. To Moses Da Rocha in Lagos, Nigeria, Bruce indicated that Aggrey was his "warmest friend and I want you to know him well." Bruce was excited about Aggrey's scholarly achievements at Columbia University, where he studied each summer. "Could you expect anything else of an African?" he quizzed. To James J. Dossen in Liberia, Bruce noted that Aggrey represented the Phelps Stokes Fund and would be surveying West African missions and schools. "We claim him as an American since he is a professor. *He is an African* of the Africans and *working* for Africa. Help him," he requested. A similar request was sent to Professor Abayoni Cole in Freetown, Sierra Leone. Several years earlier, Bruce considered Aggrey and other African scholars as the "host to the son of God—to the Olympian gods who consider them . . . the only fit company for [themselves]."[23]

In early 1919, Bruce made arrangements with Leilia Walters, widow of AMEZ Bishop Alexander Walters, to host a reception at her Harlem home, 208 West 134th Street, for officials of Liberia's national college. Bruce encouraged James J. Dossen to have the country's professors instill race pride in students by teaching them Negro history, past and present. He urged "expatriated Africans in America to create a fund of $1,000,000 to build a great school of learning" in the West African republic. He also suggested that Liberia College reach out to the African world for its growing faculty.[24] In this endeavor, Bruce understood that an educated nucleus of Africans would contribute in the long run to the continent's economic and political independence. African Americans had over the years gone to West Africa as missionaries for both white and black denominational mission boards. Now, Bruce saw the real possibility of blacks in America emigrating to Africa to address Liberia's dire need for teachers, engineers, surveyors, skilled craftsmen, and professionals. In this quest to make the Liberian republic the model for African development, Bruce would soon join forces with Marcus Garvey's Universal Negro Improvement Association.

The Garvey Movement, 1918–1922

By 1918, Bruce had known many significant African American leaders. Edward W. Blyden and Alexander Crummell shared his love of race and mentored him on African affairs. He joined forces with others, such as Monroe Trotter, Booker T. Washington, and Timothy Thomas Fortune, for strategic reasons while maintaining off-and-on personal relationships. Bruce was a man of strong passions who did not tolerate those whom he considered race traitors or apologists for a system that discriminated against African Americans.

Frederick Douglass was one of America's most forceful agitators against slavery. He was a giant among men, but in the decades before his death, younger men, some of lesser talent, sought to discredit his leadership with accusations that success had made him complacent and indifferent to the struggles of the masses. At times, Bruce led this group's efforts to diminish Douglass's stature. Despite his early criticisms of Frederick Douglass, Bruce came full circle in his attitude toward his former foe. Once, he had attacked the old leader for his alleged lack of race pride. Now, Bruce found much to emulate in Douglass, who had died in February 1895. Bruce memorialized "Mr. Republican" with love, and his admiration for the race leader grew with the passing years. In an undated draft (written after 1900), Bruce characterized Douglass as one who was "more loyal to his race than it ever was to him." He faulted the American Negro for shameless showing of "lip loyalty . . . to its best and truest and ablest men." Ironically, in light of Bruce's own previous attacks, he lamented critics who were too concerned with Douglass's social and domestic affairs. On December 31, 1916, a reflective Bruce wrote that Douglass's "memory is the shrine at which we bow and lay our offerings [for] the laurel wreath rests on thy sable brow and men who loved thee sing thy praises, now Douglass farewell." Bruce wrote these passionate words of respect because he believed that Douglass was not "an opportunist, a genuflexionist nor a sycophant" but "the greatest man the race has produced." Douglass demonstrated "to the world the possibilities that be hidden in a black skin."[1]

This change of assessment was characteristic of Bruce's personality. His judgment was mercurial. At times, Bruce was hasty in judging others, rightly or wrongly. Nevertheless, to his credit, he did not let his ego interfere with his judgment either to break with someone—as he did with Booker T. Washington—or to support a person that he had initially rejected.

An Initial Response to Garvey

Bruce's first reaction to Marcus Garvey was negative, but his response would later change to admiration and complete allegiance to Garvey's agenda of economic development and African redemption. Garvey came to the United States in April 1916 to visit Tuskegee after exchanging letters with Washington, who had died in November 1915. The UNIA was then interested in self-help and advancement programs and would not raise its controversial African redemption and emigration schemes for several years. Bruce was not initially impressed with either Garvey or his organization, but Garvey was eager to meet prominent black Americans who might assist him while he was in New York. Garvey met Bruce in 1916 or 1917 and immediately the Jamaican held Bruce Grit in high regard as "a true Negro," on the same level as antilynching crusader Ida B. Wells-Barnett; Dr. Richard R. Wright Jr., editor of the *Christian Recorder* in Philadelphia; Dr. William S. Parks, vice president of the National Baptist Convention; and AME minister Rev. J. C. Anderson. Bruce was not impressed, but he agreed to provide Garvey with some names and addresses, including that of W. E. B. Du Bois, editor of the *Crisis*. He also gave him five dollars to aid in establishing a school in Jamaica along the lines of the Tuskegee Institute. Despite his reservations about Garvey, Bruce agreed in 1917 to chair an advisory board to the UNIA.[2]

Never one to mince words, Bruce's first unflattering, published accounts of Garvey appeared sometime in late 1918 or early 1919. Bruce wrote, "Garvey is a *glib* phrase maker and a dreamer" who has about as much influence with Africans as does "the Statue of Liberty, or a deaf and dumb Choctaw Indian." He accused Garvey of fooling gullible individuals who represented "a pretty good meal ticket until the period of disillusionment wanes." Bruce admitted that he liked to listen to Garvey speak because "the music of his mouth . . . is amusing." When Garvey demanded that the powers at the Versailles Treaty table allocate some of the partitioned parts of Africa to Negroes as a reward for their wartime allegiance, Bruce declared that most thinkers do not reveal their strategies or plans, "but Garvey *tells all* and some have his number." Sarcastically, he added, "you won't do Mr. Garvey. Too *muchee talkee*."[3] Bruce went further in a 1918 essay in *The New Negro*. Writing under the nom de plume "Argus," Bruce raised a series of questions for Garvey. He wanted to know if he was an American citizen, his means of financial support, whether or not he had put into writing the sources of his fund-raising schemes, and, if not, why. Bruce asked for an explanation of the whereabouts of the $7,500 that Garvey had raised in Jamaica to establish an industrial school. "What Africans . . . are cooperating with you to establish a great Negro commercial center?" he demanded. Bruce wanted to know if any African chiefs or kings supported Garvey or authorized him to speak for them or for their subjects. He requested that Garvey show in writing the endorsements he had allegedly received from prominent Africans. Suspicious, Bruce asked, "are you aware that you are playing with fire and may get your fingers burned!" Bruce also remarked that Garvey's criticism of black Americans would be more credible and effective if he were an American citizen instead of "an unknown wandering alien with a grudge against toil." Finally, a skeptical Bruce demanded, "who are you anyhow and what is your game?"[4]

British military intelligence also had an interest in Garvey's "game," as well as in Bruce's possible involvement with the UNIA. On November 5, 1918, Col. Vernon George W. Kell, director of the Special Intelligence Bureau in London, wrote to Lt. Col. H. A. Parkenham, Military Intelligence Branch, War Department at Washington, D.C., that Bruce regularly corresponded "with a mongrel Soudanese-Egyptian named Duse Mohammed, who . . . dabbles in any sort of mischievous agitation . . . [in] which a little money is to be made." The British were concerned that Garvey was trying to correspond with West Indian and African soldiers to lure them into joining the UNIA.[5] On December 6, Col. John M. Dunn, acting director of U.S. military intelligence, wrote to Emmett J. Scott, special assistant to the secretary of war, for information on Garvey and Bruce. Scott responded five days later to Maj. Wrisley Brown that Garvey, who was visiting in Washington, came to see him at Scott's request. He understood from their conversation that articles and editorials in the *Negro World,* organ of the UNIA, might be considered disruptive for congenial race relations. Garvey promised to make changes, but Scott dismissed him as "a soap box orator" incapable of building a serious movement. Bruce, noted Scott, had a wide circle of correspondents but lacked "widespread influence . . . and is one of those . . . seeking . . . to redress the wrongs of the Negro people of the world." On December 16, Parkenham informed military intelligence division Section Four that London had advised him that Garvey was a fraud and that "it would be interesting to know who Mr. John E. Bruce is . . . and why he is interested in this fraud." Parkenham added that he had questioned Duse Mohammed, who explained that he had met Garvey in London in 1913 but had discharged him from a messenger's position for unsatisfactory work three months after hiring him. Parkenham added that Mohammed had discovered that Garvey was a fraud when he received a circular in 1917 from

Bruce stating that Garvey was a graduate of Oxford University, which the facts did not bear out. Further damaging evidence was supposedly presented when Bruce informed Mohammed that he had attended a lecture by Garvey on January 13, 1918, and had told the Jamaican to "clear out." Mohammed told the interrogator that Garvey was hustling for money and that the UNIA represented no danger to British colonialism.[6] (Garvey scholar Robert A. Hill noted that there is no evidence of such letters between Bruce and Mohammed).

The U.S. government was also curious about Bruce's possible involvement with Garvey. Either someone in the government contacted Bruce or he was persuaded by Emmett J. Scott to volunteer information about his dealings with Garvey. On January 13, 1919, Bruce wrote to Retired Maj. W. H. Loving of the military intelligence branch that he had resigned as chair of the UNIA advisory board because Garvey had deviated from his original goal to establish an industrial school for the broader goal of redeeming and regenerating Africa, "and to relieve gullible Negroes of their surplus cash." Garvey's scheme was in Bruce's estimation "impracticable, utopian, and jackassical." Bruce insisted, "I am . . . too good an American to join hands with any alien black, or white against my country. Certainly I would not be such a simpleton to line up with . . . Garvey." To prove his point, he added, "when I discover a fake, I make the discovery known." He requested that the government not associate him with Garvey because he was a "100% 'merican, red hot Republican, and a shouting Methodist. If you can manipulate a traitor out of these 'ingredients,' send me [the] formula; suh!" Bruce further sought to distance himself from Garvey by noting his membership with the Societe Internationale de Philalogie et Beaux Arts and the African Society of London, indicators that he was not a wild-eyed radical but rather a sensible and responsible citizen.[7] Bruce certainly exaggerated his anti-African redemption tone. His earlier investment schemes in Africa and his founding of the Loyal Order of the Sons of Africa represented a much stronger interest in Africa than he was willing to admit to Loving. It is more likely that his hyperbole was lip service to satisfy an official who, despite his Negro identification, was known for his loyal service to the military intelligence branch.

Metamorphosis

Ten months after writing to Loving, Bruce's opinion about Garvey underwent a metamorphosis after hearing Garvey speak in Harlem on a cold October 1919 night. Garvey did not say anything that Bruce had not heard before, but in the chill of the evening came the realization that no one, not even W. E. B. Du Bois or Asa Philip Randolph, offered a better plan to aid the masses of blacks in America and throughout the African diaspora. Du Bois was faulted for his dependence on white financial support and, although socialists were more liberal than other whites, Bruce questioned those who sought an alliance with them. Bruce had heard Randolph speak about "The New Radicalism and the Negro," which criticized the older black leadership for their undying support of Republicans, Democrats, and capitalism. Randolph's argument for socialism was both eloquent and brilliant, but Bruce did not deem socialism to be the best solution for the race's myriad problems. "I have no faith in socialism nor in its propagandists." It had not solved society's problems despite its centuries of existence. His main concern, however, was that "socialists are themselves divided and there can never be unity in division."

Garvey was able to capitalize on the disillusionment of Bruce and thousands of others who saw a nation lacking the courage to make them full citizens. Bruce decided to stop opposing the Jamaican in writings and speeches because Garvey did not consume liquor or tobacco and was not a thief of UNIA funds. The *Negro World,* Bruce noted, named crooks in the UNIA after Garvey removed them from the organization.[8] Bruce now found Garvey to be a man worthy of his devotion. The next five years would represent a transformative period in his life. He began to shift his attention away from reforming America to articulating support for Garvey's emigration program to Africa, which he expected would achieve full equality for the black American. Bruce would become one of Garvey's faithful defenders despite the accusations of William Monroe Trotter, who derided Garvey's race ideology; the shouts of fraud from Asa Philip Randolph, William Pickens, and others; and W. E. B. Du Bois's verdict that Garvey was "either a lunatic or a fool."[9]

Bruce's conversion was shocking but understandable given that he stood at a crossroads. For years, he had diligently sought to reform America to where it would accept the Negro as an equal citizen. While his finances were always limited, he relied on James S. Clarkson and other patrons to provide him with positions and a modest income. They were now dead or no longer men of influence. Several decades earlier, Bruce hoped to gain financially from his relationship with Booker T. Washington; but he became disillusioned once it became clear that Washington's conservative ideology was the price he paid for white philanthropy. Alexander Crummell and Edward W. Blyden, possessors of great intellect, strongly influenced his outlook on Pan-Africanism, but neither had the personality or the skills to organize the masses.

While Garvey would soon display remarkable organizing skills, there was much in his emotional makeup that should have kept Bruce at a great distance. Garvey was an autocratic megalomaniac who tolerated no dissent, employed incompetents who dared not challenge him, and considered himself to be wiser than others. Perhaps a less embittered and disillusioned Bruce would have seen the minefield that Garvey represented. Instead, he actively joined forces and, throughout the next five years, became one of the Jamaican's most devoted defenders and a supporter of his ill-fated economic development plan.

Bruce had fought long and hard to convince the nation that African Americans were also citizens who deserved all the benefits of full citizenship instead of the crumbs granted them as aliens and merely tolerated by those who valued only their prowess as laborers. If America was unwilling to fully integrate blacks into the society as full citizens, Bruce was willing to look to Africa as the solution—although Garvey would not deliver on his promise to make Africa the land where the black man's dreams were fulfilled. There had been a time when Bruce would have dismissed this view as nonsense, but now he was ready not only to accept it but also to urge others to seek their destiny in the land of their ancestors.

Garvey vainly sought to fulfill the prophecy of Charles A. Emanuel's 1916 poem "Africa, Arise!" The native of St. Thomas, then a part of the Danish West Indies, wrote in his first stanza: "Africa, arise! The dawn of truth is breaking. Thy ransomed children come from lands afar, following their leader in the soul's awakening." Bruce and Garvey shared a dislike for the mulatto who celebrated the "whiteness" of their fathers and rejected the "blackness" of their mothers. Both argued that the product of these unions should run to their mothers' people with money, education, and culture to assist the race in regaining her status and respect from others. Despite accusations to the contrary, neither man had problems with lighter-complexioned persons who accepted their "proper" race identification. Garvey had mulattos in his organization, most notably Henrietta Vinton Davis, a fair-complexioned international organizer and staunch supporter who publicly proclaimed the beauty of blackness.[10] Bruce expressed a willingness to collaborate with mulattos, quadroons, and octoroons providing they emulated Davis and allied themselves completely with their darker "family" in their search for "one common destiny, one aim, one hope."[11] Bruce called upon this group to stop living in "a fool's paradise," believing that skin bleachers and hair straighteners would make them acceptable to the white majority. He expressed contempt for the kinky-haired southerners who came to the North and straightened their hair hoping to pass for a Cuban or East Indian "until it rains" and the moisture reverted their hair back to its natural nappy state.[12]

Garvey's message of race pride reflected Bruce's. Both blamed the black race for its hardships suffered at the hands of whites in the Americas; for it was in their estimation that black "taught the white how to discriminate against the Negro by doing it himself by his silly class [and complexion] distinctions and pretensions to excellence which he never possessed." They both understood the power of propaganda. Bruce and Garvey used poetry to politicize the UNIA membership, and Bruce's play *Preaching vs. Practice* expressed Garvey's hostility toward unscrupulous black preachers. But Bruce was more than just a disciple in the Garvey movement. The Jamaican came to the United States with an ideology much more conservative than one espoused by Bruce. During the next few years, Bruce would, in his capacity as Garvey's private secretary, direct the younger man to be more like Bruce Grit in his outlook and actions than like Booker T. Washington, whom Garvey admired.[13]

Bruce had endeavored through his affiliation with various organizations, notably the American Negro Academy, the Negro Society for Historical Research, and the Loyal Sons of Africa, to raise the consciousness of African people in the diaspora. For various reasons, none of these organizations fulfilled this mission. A spiritual man, Bruce believed that the carnage that emanated from the battlefields of Europe during World War I was God's plan for the darker races in China, India, and Africa to see their future advancement based on the unity of oppressed people of color. He declared that whites were a bleached race that had failed in their stewardship due to their unwillingness "to love mercy and to deal justly and to walk upright before [God]." Bruce believed that the time for "Ethiopia to stretch forth her hands unto God" had arrived. All that was needed to lead the darker races to the forefront of world supremacy was effective and organized leadership.[14]

Bruce saw in Marcus Garvey's UNIA an instrument to raise the worldwide consciousness of African people while at the same time removing from them the dominance of white supremacy. Nevertheless, he cautioned people to eschew individual advancement as an antidote to white racism, for such an objective would cause anger and hatred from the lower class of whites whose policy was to dominate the darker races. While Bruce believed in the dynamics of group solidarity, he also understood that the whole is made up of many parts. In a group, each individual must see salvation coming from pride in knowing that the Negro was the foremost race in the past, if not now. Since Bruce believed that Jesus came from the loins of Ham, black people should cease thinking "white." Instead, he urged them to organize racially and politically to take the "iron heel of power" from white control. It was this declaration of manhood that inspired Andrea Razafkeriefo to proclaim that "Ethiopia looks with smiling face upon . . . 'Bruce Grit.'"[15]

Redemption of Africa

The carnage of the war not only left parts of Europe in ruin; it led to a reconfiguration of empires and kingdoms. Both the Ottoman and Austro-Hungarian Empires were destroyed. New nations were formed in Eastern Europe that reflected the cultural and political identities of formerly subjected people. Self-determination was the watchword for Europeans, but it did not apply to colonized people in Africa, Asia, and the Caribbean. Seeds of nationalism were planted in all three regions. Garvey's cry of "Africa for Africans at home and abroad" met with applause from UNIA members who fervently declared that he was correct in demanding the redemption of Africa from European colonial rule. The feasibility of this project was the subject of an editorial—"Can Garvey Win in Africa?"—that appeared in the September 10, 1920, Baltimore *Afro-American*. The Maryland weekly viewed Garvey's aim to form an African confederation impractical, since British ships would keep the UNIA's navy out of Africa. Despite this bleak assessment, the *Afro-American* declared that Garvey had created race enthusiasm and that he was an organizing genius.[16] Enthusiasm for Garvey's program also came from Monrovia. The *Commercial Intelligence Bureau Liberian Bulletin* declared in January 1920 that it was time for African people to support Garvey because the black man's position was contemptible in the white dominated world.[17]

While Garvey's critics did not expect much beyond bombastic rhetoric from his movement, Garvey's message of self-rule resonated throughout the Caribbean. He had enthusiastic supporters in Panama. Etta Marie Duchatellier, a friend of Bruce, wrote him on January 12, 1920, that she and Cyril Henry had their ship stopped at Panama City by United Fruit Company and Panamanian authorities who did not want them to disembark. She noted that if authorities prevented their ship from landing, local and imported Jamaican workers threatened to stop work on the Canal Zone and to burn down the city of Colon. "Everywhere I go I have large audience," she wrote. Duchatellier was proud of the workers' actions, but she understood that Garvey's rhetoric was disturbing to the authorities. She acknowledged Bruce's request to get Garvey to curb his rhetoric, but she admitted that she might as well "stop the flowing waters of Niagara Falls" or have "the Ethiopian change his skin or the leopard his spots." She added that Bruce's letter to Garvey on the matter should prove sufficient.[18] (I have not located this letter in the Bruce or Garvey papers, but, if it was written, it shows that Bruce was beginning to experience Garvey's stubbornness.) While Garvey's rhetoric was too pompous for some, others took pride in knowing that a black man could arouse so much anxiety in others. George Wells Parker, one of the founders of the Hamitic League of the World, wrote Bruce in early 1920 that he was satisfied with Garvey's honesty and sincerity despite criticism from the black press. "I will hereafter be a Garvey booster. He is . . . the kind of man the Negro race needs at this time," noted Parker.[19] Parker was just one of the many contacts Bruce had made over the years that he attempted to draw into the UNIA. This point cannot be underestimated. Bruce was able to bring into the Garvey movement many race-conscious men and women because of his contacts in West Africa and the Caribbean.

Black Star Shipping Line and African Economic Development

While Bruce's recruitment cannot be underestimated, his most significant contribution to the spread of Garveyism was the political and economic astuteness his writings brought to the pages of the *Negro World* and the *Negro Daily Times,* organs of the Universal Negro Improvement Association. Bruce wrote in the *Negro World* that his West African contacts were enthusiastic over the Black Star Line, Garvey's hope for commercial success. Garvey vowed to establish a successful shipping line to engage in trade as well as transport emigrants to Liberia. Although others had failed to operate a profitable shipping line, Bruce glowingly predicted that a dozen trips to Africa would make the Black Star Line wealthy because African merchants and traders eagerly awaited the arrival of the ships to carry their products to the Caribbean and the United States.[20] Bruce was so excited over the prospect of black-owned vessels engaging in a triangular trade between Africa, the West Indies, and the United States, that he wrote a short story about a Mr. Ajai who went to Nigeria as a representative of the UNIA. A month after his arrival, Ajai sent UNIA headquarters in Harlem a packet containing the names of twenty-five hundred new members, subscriptions for the *Negro World,* and a contribution of one hundred pounds for the African Construction Fund.[21]

Sadly, fiction was not reality. It was difficult to organize new members for the UNIA in Africa as well as undertake a massive commercial enterprise of transporting African raw products to the Americas. Both efforts would prove taxing to the organization's energy and purse, as well as take a toll on Bruce's declining health. On April 3, 1920, Bruce wrote to his friend James J. Dossen, a Supreme Court justice in Liberia, with the sad news that age and the advice of his physician prevented him from visiting Liberia as part of a forthcoming UNIA delegation. Bruce added that the letter was meant as an introduction of Hubert H. Harrison, chair of the delegation. A similar letter of introduction was sent on the same day to President C. D. B. King of Liberia.[22] It was a painful decision for the sixty-four-year-old Bruce to decline the offer to visit Liberia; he was certain that Africa would soon "stretch forth her hands unto Him." Bruce also regretted the opportunity to be the recipient of African hospitality, because he had entertained Liberians when he served on the reception committee that celebrated Liberia's seventy-second anniversary of independence in 1919.[23]

Bruce was a tireless worker for the UNIA, which led appreciative delegates in August 1920 to propose his candidacy for president of the American sector. Unfortunately, age and poor health caused Bruce to decline. He informed Garvey that he needed to "save [his] wind for another kind of fighting."

However, Bruce assured Garvey that he would do whatever he could to promote the UNIA's "welfare and success," for he understood Garvey's vision "to lay the foundation broad and deep" to realize "African nationalization."[24]

Bruce's service to the UNIA went beyond recruiting members and writing essays for the organization's organs. He was also responsible for writing the prayer that opened every meeting of the UNIA.

> Not by might, nor by power, but by
> my spirit, saith the lord of hosts
> God of the right our battles fight,
> Be with us as of yore.
> Break down the barrels of might,
> We rev'rently implore.
>
> Stand with us in our struggles for
> the triumph of the right,
> and spread confusion ever o'er
> The advocates of might.
>
> And let them know thy righteousness
> [is] mightier than sin.
> That might is only selfishness
> and cannot, ought not, win.
>
> Endow us, lord with faith and grace,
> and courage to endure
> the wrongs we suffer here apace,
> and bless us ever more.[25]

Bruce's pride in this prayer did not extend to the organization's opening hymn, *From Greenland's Icy Mountains,* with its admonition for Christians to propagate the Gospel among heathens. Nevertheless, the hymn was popular among black Christians.[26]

Bruce believed that the African American's willingness to overcome racism and discrimination would assist the UNIA in making the Black Star Shipping Line not only a financial success but also a source of intense race pride. Every black person in America knew that ocean vessels segregated African Americans whether they were poor or wealthy, the sons of sharecroppers or of luminaries.

Bruce suspended his disbelief and assumed that black Americans would support the shipping line out of pride. He concerned himself, however, with encouraging Africans to invest in the Black Star Shipping Line. Despite the lyrics to a popular UNIA song, "Hurrah for the Black Star Line! Over to

Africa, where I shall dine, digging of gold,"[27] it was not easy to convince Africans to collaborate commercially with African Americans. Nor was it expected that the British or the French would permit Garveyites to interfere with their political and economic control in West Africa.

In its eagerness to establish contacts in Africa, the UNIA made bad choices. Illustrative of this is a series of letters written by E. M. E. Agebi, nephew of Mojola Agebi, whom Bruce befriended in 1904. On February 20, 1920, Agebi wrote Bruce complaining that his cousin, Akinbami Agebi Jr., had been appointed an agent of the Black Star Shipping Line. He regretted that Akinbami had gone to America, where he expected to be maintained by others, and had signed a contract that Bruce witnessed. Agebi considered Akinbami unfit for his position and believed that disaster awaited him and the UNIA. The letter concluded with a request that Akinbami be released from the contract with the promise that all funds he received would be returned. The letter writer chided Bruce and other friends of Africa who naively viewed all African visitors as worthy. "Only a miracle would make him a good agent," he stressed. Agebi's concern was that Akinbami lacked the skill to engage in the import and export business.[28] For unknown reasons, Bruce forwarded the letter to Akinbami, who deemed it merely "annoying." He informed Bruce in an April 8 letter that, while he received hundreds of pounds daily, he was prevented from accepting any because British law required that he sell from a registered office, which he could not do until documents were forwarded to Lagos. Akinbami hoped to borrow funds to sail to New York to get the documents from Garvey. He confidently predicted that there were investors in Nigeria who "are afraid to send their money direct to N.Y. on account of the rate of exchange." Still, they wanted to buy shares in the shipping line and in the Negro Factories Corporation.[29] Akinbami wrote on May 15 to a dear "sir" (probably Garvey) complaining that white firms in Nigeria were merging and acquiring land with long and expensive leases. Optimistic, he noted that there were many potential investors but that he could take no action until he had a charter of corporation for registration. He acknowledged receipt of one hundred dollars. However, he could not understand why he had not been sent the requested five hundred pounds to cover manifold shipping dues, government fees, expenses for loading and unloading Black Star Line ships, and money for rent and salaries.[30] Three days later, Akinbami wrote Bruce that Garvey had not yet sent him any funds. Hoping to interest Bruce in a private business deal, he informed his "father" that, while sixty thousand loaves of bread were baked daily in Lagos, the industry was contained in sixty-one small female bakeries. Akinbami urged Bruce to seek investors by selling stock in a proposed African Baking, Ltd., to build a plant whereby twenty thousand loaves would be baked daily. He offered to make Bruce president. Lacking business acumen, Akinbami asked Bruce to mail catalogs of "bread baking machines and the best literature of baking industry."[31] On June 25 Adeotan Agbebi wrote to Bruce with confirmation (Bruce had written to him on May 8) that Akinbami needed funds and official documents to operate in Lagos. Acknowledging that Akinbami had not sold a single share, Adeotan urged the UNIA to strike while the iron was hot. On a personal note, Adeotan indicated that African cloth for a suit, presumably for Bruce, would be sent on the next ship. The irony was not lost on either person that the next ship leaving Lagos would be European and not black owned.[32] An agitated and disappointed Akinbami wrote to the president of the Black Star Line on August 4 that he had to returned hundreds of pounds to potential investors because he still lacked documents to open a registered office. He complained that he would have to borrow £115 to sail to New York for the required documents. Akinbami expected to depart on August 22. "Do you approve?" he asked.[33]

This fiasco undermined the potential trade between Africans and African Americans. While fiscal mismanagement and incompetence prevented the Black Star Line from realizing its objective of sending passengers and finished products to Africa in exchange for the continent's valuable resources, individual Africans continued to seek Bruce's cooperation in facilitating trade between Africans and African Americans. S. Okagoo Logemoh, a resident of Monrovia, Liberia, wrote to "Father Bruce" on June 15, 1922, that he had acquired the two hundred pounds of Liberian coffee that Bruce requested, but that he needed one hundred dollars to cover the cost of shipment. Logemoh noted that he had lumber and animal skins for tanning. He added that he had several friends who were willing to cooperate with Duse Mohammed Ali and Bruce to develop trade in Africa. In this letter and one following a week later, Logemoh indicated that he had a collection of curios he wanted sold in a Harlem curio shop.[34] Curios were interesting, but Logemoh was primarily interested in sending coffee, which he indicated in the June 22 letter. He requested that Bruce get about six investors to advance money as "the hour is really here for the Negro to act and cease talking." Eager for business, Logemoh wrote on June 24 that he was ready to ship two bags of coffee as a sample for Bruce to establish a wholesale and retail business among African Americans. " I have set the ball rolling if you over there will open the necessary credit even with three hundred dollars to test my business capacity," challenged Logemoh. Logemoh sent Bruce two pieces of cowhide to use to start a tannery. The Liberian appreciated Bruce's interest and declared that he wanted blacks to be producers instead of consumers. In early January 1923, Logemoh acknowledged Bruce's letter of October 7, 1922, with its enclosure of fifteen dollars for coffee. Again, he urged Bruce to seek viable investors to compete with Europeans who were grabbing Africa's resources.[35] It is unlikely that Bruce was able to put together an investment group, as his health was deteriorating in 1923; and there are no more letters addressed to Logemoh in his papers.

There are two significant observations that can be made based on these letters to Bruce. One, Liberia had coal, gold, diamonds, forests, rubber, coffee, and animal hides available for profitable exploitation, but most African Americans lacked the business acumen or funds to take advantage of the opportunities. Some, as noted by Logemoh, lacked patience and quickly tired of a project if results were not immediate.[36] Second, in the effort to have African agents represent the Black Star Line, Garvey and his associates put faith in *any* African who claimed that American blacks were "cousins and brothers." This was noted by A. S. Wynter Shackleford, president of a UNIA division in Lagos. Shackleford informed Bruce in 1921 that Madorikan Denoyi Deniyi, a self-declared prince, was an impostor. Shackleford told Bruce that Americans were gullible and willing to believe anyone who claimed to be of royal blood. The British, noted Shackleford, kept tight control over the children of royalty and would not let them leave Africa without permission; those that did leave were chaperoned by "white emissaries of the government." He beseeched Bruce to warn people "about these impostors who come back boasting of their conquest and the stupidity of foreign Negroes, and when foreign Negroes come to Africa you do not get the least chance or sympathy, let alone help from the blithers." Deniyi had gone to churches in Harlem praising Garvey hoping to raise funds to enable him to return to Africa. Bruce heeded Shackleford's warning and informed readers of the *Negro World* to disassociate themselves from the fake prince who was criticizing the UNIA after the organization refused to have him as a representative.[37]

The Black Star Line was plagued with many problems besides unscrupulous African con artists. Garvey's poor judgment, and the incompetence of subordinates, caused him to pay too much for decrepit and unseaworthy ships. Critics within the UNIA accused him of building "from the air down instead of from the ground up." By 1922, Garvey's hopes for a commercial shipping empire had lost more than $1 million for its investors. Eventually he would be indicted on charges of mail fraud when he attempted to sell shares in the Black Star Line for ships that were not legally his.[38]

Often overlooked in the examination of the demise of the Black Star Line is the potential it offered for black Americans to emigrate to Liberia. An independent African republic since 1847, the nation was dominated politically by Americo-Liberians, who were the descendants of American slaves and free blacks who had migrated there in the nineteenth century. One prominent émigré, T. McCants Stewart, a clergyman and an attorney, left Brooklyn in 1882 for Liberia, where he became a professor at Liberia College. A frequent visitor to the United States, Stewart departed from Liberia in 1913. He informed Rev. Francis J. Grimke in 1920 that the racial situation in America was "a hard fight" that they could not win "except through such amalgamation as has taken place in San Domingo and some of the South American countries." Stewart advocated the need to build financial and commercial enterprises in Liberia that would empower the race to fight the cause for equality in the Americas. He supported emigration to Liberia, not as individuals but as "communities, or we will go under when we get there." Stewart was author of "Liberia, the Gem of West Africa." The first two lines appealed to Garveyites. "Liberia, the gem of West Africa. The land where the Negro is free." Stewart planned to return to Liberia but, unfortunately, he died in 1923 without realizing his goal.[39]

Stewart's advocacy for emigration to Liberia was echoed by President C. D. B. King, who was honored by Bruce and Schomburg at a banquet they hosted in New York in September 1920. In his remarks, President King noted that Liberia wanted black Americans to help develop the country's resources. King's reception was favorably reviewed. Robert T. Browne wrote in the *Masonic Quarterly Review* that "in Liberia lie the hope and the future of Africans [for] it is the key to the domination of African affairs by Africans for Africans."[40]

Defending Garvey

Rhetoric aside, it was difficult to attract African American pioneers to Africa. Many were unwilling to undergo an arduous sea voyage to a land lacking in conveniences and comfort. Rather than accept the reality of their reluctance to emigrate, Bruce chose to criticize them as misguided self-hating Negroes, believing that many would shun emigration even if conditions in Africa were perfect. Bruce observed that "we have among us Negroes who are *of the race, but not with it.*" Bruce considered these individuals "neither Negroes at heart, in feelings, nor in aspiration." He contemptuously dismissed them as race haters who "would give . . . a king's ransom to be admitted into the white race."[41] Bruce was unfair to millions who were unwilling to reject the land where their fathers were buried and who still awaited recognition for their ancestors' assistance in building America. Their belief that America could become a nation where all races would be recognized as equal was one that Bruce had previously shared. However, a colorblind society meant that the races had assimilated, a concept that Bruce contemptuously dismissed. Nor was he tolerant of white paternalism or the ideology of the white man's burden. Bruce faulted the white man for his conceit in spite of the fact that civilization and science had been appropriated from the darker races. Bruce dismissed the Caucasian claim of racial supremacy as "the biggest joke in the world today." God, Bruce vowed, will humble them "before the eyes of those races whom he regards as inferior to his own."[42]

Determined that racial equality in America was unattainable, Bruce continued to advocate for African emigration and investment. As a newspaperman, Bruce understood the power of the press to sway public opinion. He faulted the white press of America for its silence on race prejudice and the British press for its refusal to condemn politicians for denying British subjects their self-determination. Although some members of the black press were shallow imitators of their white counterparts, Bruce was pleased that throughout the world the black press was beginning to catch Garvey's vision and "to see . . . that it has a mission and a duty to perform for the race." He called upon the black press to adopt the slogan of the *Negro World* that the "black race may it ever be right, but right or wrong, our Black Race!"[43] (It escaped Bruce that this chauvinistic sentiment was the same ideology that he lambasted when practiced by Caucasians.) While Bruce wanted to believe that the world's black press subscribed to Garvey's vision, he exaggerated the point. He understood the power of the white press and knew that, too often, African American readers accepted the reports of white writers as infallible. For instance, Bruce knew the harm the white press had created when they tried to paint the UNIA red with the brush of Bolshevism, which was a political ideology antithetical to Garvey's black nationalism. It upset Bruce that gullible blacks believed every negative word printed by white newspapers against the Garvey movement even though white reporters and editors knew nothing about black life or had any black friends.[44]

However, not only naive and gullible readers questioned the motives of Garvey. The *Crisis,* edited by W. E. B. Du Bois, represented the better-educated class of African American, and Du Bois often ridiculed the UNIA's financial situation and Garvey's leadership. In turn, Garvey questioned the validity of Du Bois's racial leadership. He wrote that Du Bois's "association with an alien race, size of his pocketbook and the writings of a few books favorable to Negroes is not enough recommendation for us. He must be 100 per cent Negro. We do not care two pins for Dr. Du Bois; when we think of big Negroes we do not think of men like him."[45]

Garvey's criticism of Du Bois was all the more meaningful in light of Bruce's former close relationship with the scholar. Bruce had joined forces with Du Bois in 1905 to organize the Niagara Movement; he subscribed to the *Crisis;* he marched with Du Bois in the 1917 silent parade against lynching and mob violence; and he congratulated him in 1918 on the occasion of his fiftieth birthday with words of admiration: "I have looked into your soul this morning and have seen a *man.*" Now, however, Bruce put Garvey before Du Bois.

In March 1921, Du Bois invited Bruce to attend the Pan-African Congress meeting scheduled to meet in Paris the following September. Bruce wrote in the *Negro World* of his regret at his inability to afford the ship passage and related expenses. He wished Du Bois success for his forthcoming Pan-African Congress, but he hoped there were enough Negro millionaires in the United States to make up a respectable delegation, as the expense would be beyond the means of most African Americans. Privately, Bruce curtly replied that he did not represent any organization "that would be likely to be interested in this movement or that could afford the expense [eight hundred dollars] entailed to send a delegate." Bruce's refusal to endorse Du Bois's Pan African Congress indicated how far he had come from the teachings of Blyden and from his own earlier perspective. Du Bois's call for a gradual transferal of power from European to African rule was in line with both Blyden's and Bruce's previous contention that a period of European tutelage was needed before self-government could be established. Now Bruce chose to abandon his earlier conviction in favor of the UNIA party line. Believing that Du Bois was the tool of white business interests, Bruce supported Garvey's vicious attack of the *Crisis* editor. The *New York World* reported in late 1921 that Garvey opposed the Du Bois–led meeting "because they seek to bring about a destruction of the black and white races by social amalgamation of both." In 1923, Garvey wrote, "Du Bois had no more right or authority to have called a Pan-African Congress than a cat had to call together a parliament of rats."[46]

Garvey's misrepresentation of Du Bois's racial views was challenged. Cyril V. Briggs, editor of the *Crusader,* organ of the African Blood Brotherhood, a black auxiliary of the American Communist party, asked, "was there ever such servile surrender of a principle vital to the dignity and well being of the Negro race and such absolutely rotten logic as contained in Mr. Garvey's statement?" Briggs accused Garvey of twisting Du Bois's words to make it appear that he favored the mixing of races. Social equality as espoused by Du Bois meant equal opportunities, explained Briggs. Garvey, Briggs argued, interpreted the expression to mean race mixing, intermarriage, or amalgamation in the same manner as the Ku Klux Klan, who would deny blacks citizenship rights. "Hadn't his friends better appoint a guardian for Marcus Garvey—a guardian that will exercise an intelligent censorship over his unintelligent and maniacal ravings and servile surrender of Negro rights?"[47]

Throughout 1921 and into 1922, anti-Garvey criticism would emanate from black integrationists, socialists, and communists, factions within the black community that were often at odds with each other but who managed to form a tenuous union to combat the "Garvey menace." Bruce defended his leader, referring to his critics as "crabs that wanted to pull Garvey back into the basket." He added that their lack of success had caused them to strike out maliciously against Garvey because they envied him as a true leader who, unlike them, sought to uplift the masses.

Garvey aimed to convince blacks to consider Africa their homeland. Support for Garvey emanated from Liberia, where R. Johnson Clarke, editor of the *Liberian News,* declared that, for solving the race problem, Garvey was a better leader than was Du Bois. Clarke chose not to join either the UNIA or the NAACP, but he believed that American blacks should work together for African redemption and the founding of a great African empire.[48] An editorial in the October 1920 *AME Review,* "Back to Africa, a Militant Call," viewed the UNIA's Declaration of Rights for the Negro People of the World "bold enough to make the late Bishop Henry McNeal Turner appear like a mild conservative." Without endorsing the UNIA, editor George W. Forbes welcomed the declaration because it demonstrated that Negroes had awakened from their slumber to show more assertiveness and militancy than previously displayed. Prophetically, he noted that the British would pay attention to the declaration, for "it will inspire black people throughout the world to preserve their national and territorial inheritance in Africa." However, in January, Forbes adopted a more critical perspective on Garvey after reading an article by Truman Hughes Talley that appeared in the December 1920 *World's Work.* Now Forbes declared that racial progress should not be abandoned for Garvey's plan, for the black race's future would not be credible "anywhere outside of a mad house." Forbes added that, despite his "rot," Garvey had found the world's richest district of Negroes in Harlem upon whom to prey."[49]

These statements troubled Bruce, and he dismissed them as merely the voice of a jealous man. After Herbert J. Seligman, director of publicity for the NAACP, wrote in a December 4, 1920, *World* magazine article that Garvey was "the green and purple robed provisional President of Africa with a navy of three rickety old ships." An outraged Bruce responded that since Jews were victims of persecution, they should be more sympathetic. "But Mr. Seligman," he declared, "seems to have forgotten his history" and has joined with those gentiles who want to deny the black race independence and manhood.[50] When John Crosby Gordon wrote in July 1921 that if the Negro was taken out of the Negro problem, there would no longer be a problem, Bruce declared that Gordon should have written "take the Negro out of the mind and thought and consciousness of the governing white race . . . who has made him a problem." Bruce confided to Arthur Schomburg that Gordon and Du Bois wanted race absorption through intermarriage and that they whined, yearned, and reached out for social equality with whites. He added that Gordon was incorrect in stating that the UNIA practiced a color line in its membership because the organization did not concern itself with questions of color, class, or hair texture, which was the domain of self-hating snobs such as Du Bois, who resented their

African heritage. Instead, Bruce insisted that the UNIA, unlike other race organizations, past or present, ignored the color line and made it unpopular among its ranks. "There is absolutely no . . . intention to encourage this crass nonsense," he declared, as the UNIA welcomed anyone with one-sixteenth Negro blood who was willing to work for the advancement of the race.[51]

Bruce was outspoken in his defense of Garvey and the UNIA because he believed that Garvey's name and deed would be acclaimed for decades because he had begun upon a work that aimed to lift the black masses from self-hatred and dependence upon white America.[52] John W. Cromwell noted Bruce's passionate defense of Garvey, although he did not share his friend's admiration. He wrote cryptically to Bruce, "I am glad that the interest in the Garvey movement continues even though he is not on the ground."[53]

It did not matter what Cromwell or anyone thought, for Bruce believed that Garvey stood solidly on the ground with shoulders wide enough to support the weight of the black world. What critics saw as Garvey's ego-driven authoritarian leadership, Bruce saw as a needed forcefulness to guide the race out of the racial wilderness. Since the end of Reconstruction in 1877, Bruce had witnessed an unholy alliance between "crafty politicians, and . . . spineless *leaders* who have used the mass[es] . . . to lift themselves into office and temporary power." Now he saw in Garvey a true leader who eschewed deals with both black and white politicians. Garvey, to Bruce, was a man whose vision for the fulfillment of the Negro's destiny in Africa reminded him of the sage advice of his good friend and mentor Edward W. Blyden to learn the ways of civilization from the whites and then use them to develop Africa as the black man's rightful home. In 1921, Bruce boldly stated, "we have no illusions as to our status here in America or in any other country dominated by the white race and we have no quarrel with the white man who wants to and will continue to dominate in his own country."

This assertion that Liberia was the African American's true home was a complete reversal of Bruce's earlier belief and a clear representation of his complete estrangement from the land of his birth. In 1899, he emphatically noted that "the Negro is here to stay" in America.[54] Bruce was so steadfast in his defense of the UNIA that he suggested that the Bureau of Investigation (predecessor to the FBI) leave the organization alone, since there had never been in the United States a black assassin, anarchist, or traitor. He blamed the anti-Garvey hysteria on "jealous and spiteful Negroes who failed to catch the vision" and old leaders who "have been asleep at the switch and [have seen that] their glory has departed."[55]

Bruce's spirited defense of Garvey and the UNIA belied his chronic health problems. Advancing in age, the sixty-five-year-old self-described "gadfly" fell down the stairs in late summer 1921. This alarmed E. D. Thompson, a Chicago friend, who suggested that he take Nu tablets to help retard age and improve health. Thompson, pleased that Bruce had been inducted in August into the Knighthood of the Sublime Order of the Nile, noted that "the race is reaching a stage now where it needs you more than ever." Bruce suffered throughout September from swollen feet that prevented him from walking long distances. From Nigeria in late September came concern about Bruce's recent illness and indisposition because his weekly column in the *Negro World* was "food for the yearning sons of Africa at home."[56]

During this busy period of writing a weekly column, defending Garvey, and other commitments, Bruce's wife, Florence, was also experiencing bad days. Arthur Schomburg suggested that Bruce find Florence an elderly woman to help her around their home at 260 West 136th Street. "Cheer her up & the hours won't be so lonesome," he advised. While this may imply that Bruce was neglecting Florence, he was actually very considerate and loving toward his wife. Their relationship was comfortable enough for him to address her in a letter as "good morning fatty!" Bruce may have been thinking about Florence when he wrote in 1919 the words to "A Love Song" with music by Harry T. Burleigh. "I have never told thee darling, how my heart is yet as true." In an undated poem to Florence, Bruce wrote of his love for her:

> Heart of my heart, I love thee more than ever.
> Thy loyalty and trust, thy innocence and faith
> Are links in the great chain which nought on earth can sever
> While life remains nor even after death.
> We two have been together in sunshine and in shadow.
> And trod the path which many before have trod.
> And we have braved the storms as well as others.
> And fought our battles with a firm trust in God.[57]

The relationship between John and Florence would become closer during the next three years as his health concerns reminded them both how precious little time he had to arouse public support for Garveyism. These years would be both taxing and lonely ones for Bruce because his unyielding defense of Garvey's program would take its toll on his health and distance him from many former friends.

The Final Years, 1922–1924

Starting in May 1920, Bruce used "Bruce Grit's Column" in the pages of the *Negro World* to defend Garvey from his critics. His task was an arduous one as the UNIA was thrown into chaos in 1921 and 1922 when external criticism threatened its image. While answering critics, Garvey had to respond to a potentially greater problem. Widespread defections by formerly staunch members undermined his credibility. Chief among the defectors was George McGuire, who resigned the chaplain general's position in October 1921 to join the African Blood Brotherhood. Two years later, the breach between McGuire and Garvey healed and the former returned to the UNIA. McGuire's return restored some stability and credibility to the UNIA; however, the dissatisfaction of departed members had caused significant damage.

Response to Garvey's Arrest

Defections had an immediate impact on the organization's morale, but it paled in comparison to the reaction European powers had to Garvey's call for African redemption. Throughout 1922, colonial powers fearing the political power of the *Negro World* to encourage unrest banned the publication in French West Africa, Nyasaland, Nigeria, Gambia, and the Gold Coast. The cash-strapped and mismanaged Black Star Line was declared insolvent on August 15, 1922, a crushing blow to the UNIA's propaganda machine.[1] After an unidentified Harlem Baptist minister referred to the UNIA as a dangerous organization, Bruce criticized "white men's Negroes, who, hat in hand, beg white men for money to fight Negroes." He complained that too many black members of the clergy lacked backbone and elected instead "to pose as mendicants." Defiant, Bruce noted that the UNIA would be around when the "race varmints are dead and rotten."[2] Yet, as Randall Burkett has shown, not all black clergy opposed Garvey or the UNIA.[3] Bruce had seen many leaders in the past fifty years, and he was critical of those who did not worship with the average man or woman or live with them and of those who held the masses in contempt. In contrast, he praised Garvey as a man who understood the needs of the average person. Bruce declared that those who believed in the Black Star Line, the UNIA, and Marcus Garvey were "notable people who have been fast asleep for 50 years [but] are just waking up."[4] Prodded by Garvey's critics who claimed that the Jamaican was a fraud, federal authorities arrested him on January 12, 1922, and indicted him soon after for mail fraud in selling shares of the Black Star Line.

Five days later, Bruce wrote in his column that there was not a white man in New York who had firsthand knowledge pertaining to the objectives of the Garvey movement. He castigated white reporters for printing malicious "facts" from disgruntled former employees who left after realizing that they could not easily steal from the organization. Bruce contended that since the stockholders trusted him, critics should leave Garvey alone. As proof, Bruce noted that the membership raised $4,400 the night Garvey was arrested and were prepared to raise $1 million in sixty days for his defense.[5] Privately, Bruce viewed whites as more ominous than ignorant. On January 18, he confided to an attorney in Washington, "I fear that . . . the white man . . . is wide awake and preparing to eliminate us . . . because we are aspiring to attain to his levels intellectually and politically."[6]

Despite the public display of bravado, Bruce understood the seriousness of Garvey's arrest. In his capacity as special secretary to Garvey, he lectured the executive secretaries of the UNIA branches on February 11 that Garvey needed their aid to make the organization function properly. Meanwhile, he noted, they needed Garvey until racial consciousness, vision, and race pride were "more than *mere* words." To protect Garvey, Bruce cautioned them to check their books to make sure that there was no theft or shoddy accounting. He advised them to be patient, firm, and thorough. "Don't strut. Don't lose your temper, nor sight of the fact that you are examples . . . to teach [others] efficiency in transaction of business; accuracy in keeping their accounts; [and] punctuality in the discharge of their financial obligations to the Parent Body." Bruce recognized that these officials were in position to stem panic within the ranks, but he warned them to be tactful in their dealings with others within the UNIA. "Don't swell up like *cushion fish* because you carry the title 'Executive Secretary.' Be humble, but never obsequious . . . and be . . . THOROUGH," he stressed. Do this, he added, and "the great hope of Marcus Garvey . . . will find realization."[7]

Bruce sought to calm UNIA members elsewhere who found communication from New York slow, unreliable, or incomplete. On February 16, he wrote to J. Raphiel Ralph Casimir, a UNIA leader in Dominica, West Indies, informing him of Garvey's innocence. According to Bruce, the trouble started when Garvey permitted New York City Democratic mayoral candidate John F. Hyland, the incumbent, to address a UNIA audience at Liberty Hall. Henry H. Curran, the Republican candidate, came later, but Garvey, who claimed to be neutral, did not attend. Bruce believed that the Republican leadership blamed Garvey for their defeat and thus, in Machiavellian fashion, had framed him on mail fraud charges. This was a dubious defense. Garvey's greatest enemies were African Americans, not white politicians or, initially, the federal government.[8]

Since Bruce contended that politicians were out to get Garvey, he reasoned that they could also end the legal mess that entailed the Jamaican. He attempted to capitalize on relationships that he had developed over the years with many politicians. Bruce went to the Washington office of New York Sen. William M. Calder. The senator was allegedly promised a large UNIA vote if he could successfully delay Garvey's mail fraud case, or so reported a confidential informant in his report to Bureau of Investigation agent George F. Ruch in late April 1922.[9] This observation is interesting but flawed. The UNIA did not possess the political muscle to influence the outcome of elections because Garvey considered American politics a white man's game and urged his supporters not to vote.[10] It is more likely that Bruce approached Calder seeking to convince the senator that Garvey was a victim of unscrupulous Negroes who resented his leadership. Although Bruce understood that a powerful black voting bloc could bring change, he was pessimistic that anything would happen until the race obtained economic independence and stopped believing "in the infallibility of the dominant race." Again, he called for racial unity and unwavering support for Marcus Garvey.[11]

In 1922, Bruce wrote a sixteen-page pamphlet, *The Making of a Race*, which contained his ideas for a solution to white domination. *Negro World* editor William H. Ferris considered the tract a remarkable tribute to the great achievers of the Negro's past. Bruce declared that both Jews and Africans had fallen from their lofty heights and been "reduced to the plain level of races." Agreeing with Benjamin Disraeli that race "is the key to history," Bruce called for the protection of female virtue since the pollution of women would doom a race. Recognizing that blacks had overcome the horrors of slavery and the atrocities of the postslavery period, Bruce urged people to read ancient history, such as Felix Dubois's *Timbuctoo: The Mysterious* or Hiob Ludolph's *History of Abyssinia*. Reading these works, Bruce believed, would awaken them to the realization that their salvation depended upon "the spirit of cooperation, unity and brotherhood." Again, he noted that the UNIA provided the basis for the greatness of the African race.[12]

Garvey and the Klan

Garvey was indicted on February 15, 1922, but his trial would not begin until the following year. Garvey outraged his critics during the interval by associating himself with bigots. Two days before his indictment, Garvey praised Mississippi Sen. T. S. McCallum's resolution of February 13, which called upon the U.S. Congress to acquire African territory for black Americans as a solution to the nation's race problem. A week later, the resolution was adopted by Mississippi's senate. This action was a prelude to the revelation that on June 25 Garvey had met with Edward Young Clarke, Imperial Kleagle and acting Imperial Wizard of the Ku Klux Klan. Shocked civil rights advocates were dumbfounded by Garvey's claim that the Klan "represented the invisible government of the United States." Garvey's invitation to Clarke to speak at Harlem's Liberty Hall resulted in strong protest from the integrationists.[13] Even Garvey's supporters within the UNIA were taken back by his bold overture to a white supremacist.

Months earlier, William H. Ferris questioned why the current Klan (revived in 1915 by William Joseph Simmons) took the name of its predecessor, which killed and tortured blacks during Reconstruction. Bruce knew firsthand the horrors committed by the Klan against African Americans. Certainly, his reputation suggested that he would repudiate Garvey's meeting with Clarke, but he was caught on the horns of a dilemma. A strong repudiation of Garvey's action would destroy his credibility within the UNIA, but his defense of Garvey would further drive the wedge between him and his moderate friends. Bruce remained silent for two months, perhaps hoping that the matter would die away; but when it did not, he offered a response that reiterated the editorial policy of the *Negro World*. He could not join the anti-Klan chorus. To do so would be a criticism of Garvey's overture. Instead, Bruce attacked Garvey's critics by declaring that his leader was not a race traitor or "a moral coward with a backbone made of jelly" but one who wanted to know firsthand the Klan's position on the Negro. He dismissed the NAACP's William Pickens and other Garvey critics as "egotists and ... asses" who had done nothing "to deserve the title leader." Bruce's defense of Garvey meeting with Clarke is one that perplexes a biographer; for no one, particularly not Bruce, who had castigated the Klan for years, could offer any plausible rationale for Garvey's overture to Clarke. It was not Bruce's finest moment.

The Klan had more than 100,000 members by 1921. Their anti-Catholic, anti-Jewish, and anti-Negro ideology appealed to many, not only in the South but also as far west as Oregon. Their floggings, cross burnings, and threats were well known. Bruce had no love for the Klan, but his blind allegiance to

Garvey overrode his disgust of Klan's principles, which he privately repudiated. This latter point was illustrated in November 1923 by Bruce's admission that the Klan wanted to make the Negro "an alien [and] a sojourner" in the land that his blood and sweat had enriched. Furthermore, Bruce approved, in 1923, of Hubert H. Harrison's strong denunciation of the Klan menace. To some degree Bruce's race-first instinct was muted by a belief that blacks could not overcome American race prejudice. It was only in Africa that the Negro could be free, Bruce argued. This viewpoint, and his insistence that whites were determined to "dominate every foot of land which we now proudly call 'our country,'" demonstrated how far he had changed from his earlier conviction that America was the African American's rightful home. Instead of repudiating Garvey's association with the Klan, Bruce opted to warn Garvey's critics against planning to harm the UNIA leader. The hostility displayed by the black press and civil rights leaders against Garvey alarmed Bruce, who feared that violence might ensue. Bruce had reason to be alarmed. There was an assassination attempt against Garvey in October 1919 and rumor of another one in late summer of 1922. A defiant Bruce vowed that "the *hired* assassin who attempts to kill Marcus Garvey, *had better have wings.*"[14]

Garvey's Black Critics

In turn, Garvey's black critics, notably Asa Philip Randolph and Chandler Owen, coeditors of the *Messenger;* Cyril V. Briggs of African Blood Brotherhood; and W. E. B. Du Bois and William Pickens of the NAACP, considered the Jamaican a menace, a fraud and an obstacle preventing the development of positive American race relations. Garvey, however, sought to make an ally of Pickens in 1922 by inviting him to attend the third annual UNIA convention. It was a surprising request and suggests how eager Garvey was to gain allies among the middle-class black establishment. Pickens, an NAACP associate field secretary since 1920, was dissatisfied with his salary and explored the possibility of working for Garvey. Despite flattering Garvey with a positive article praising the UNIA, Pickens used Garvey to extract more money from the NAACP. In May 1922, unaware that Pickens had decided to remain with the opposition, Garvey again offered him a position. The following month, Pickens wrote that Garvey was not a crook, that his program was not a menace to the white world; however, he decided to remain with the NAACP because he believed "in the EARLIER FRUITIONS of the sowings of the [organization] for the good of Negroes in the U.S.A." He urged Garvey to rid the UNIA of crooks "and [to] speak plain about [the] ORGANIZATION of the racial group, and try not to fool anybody about the 'back to Africa' myth."[15] On July

10, Garvey invited Pickens to accept an honor at the August UNIA convention. However, Pickens, now securely in the "Garvey Must Go" camp, refused. Bitterly, he informed Garvey by letter on July 24 that he was "just about the wrongest black man that ever tried to lead American Negroes anywhere." He added that Africa was for Africans, black and white, and America was for Americans, "native, naturalized and all colors." It would be foolish, he asserted, for anyone to give up American citizenship "for a thousand year improbability in Africa or anywhere else."[16]

Keeping the Faith

While Garvey underwent his struggle to ward off criticism, he had loyal support from Bruce, Lady Henrietta Vinton Davis, and others who visited branches to shore up support for their leader. Bruce traveled in late June 1922 to visit with UNIA members in the Boston area, but his health was failing. He wrote Florence on June 21, informing her that he came from Fall River, Massachusetts, three days earlier to Cambridge, outside of Boston. Mr. and Mrs. William H. Wilkes hosted Bruce at their home, and he was pleased to have freedom of the house. Bruce informed Florence not to worry about his health because his breakfast of whole wheat bread, grapefruit, fried egg, bacon, steamed onions, and coffee with rich cream was helping him keep up his blood sugar. Despite his health concern, he kept up his humor. Bruce threatened to "hang [Florence] out the window for 2 nights" if she did not write to him. He requested that she give his regards to Duse Mohammed Ali: "Tell him I got his impudent letter this A.M. and will smash him when we meet." The following day, he wrote his wife to confirm the receipt of her letter and that it had improved his spirits. He expressed regret that he was unable to express in words "the deep love I bear to my noble little wife for her many [efforts] to promote my happiness." He wrote Florence on June 27 with the news that he had an appointment to see Massachusetts Gov. Channing Harris Cox the following day. He requested that she forward fifty copies of *A Tribute for the Negro Soldier* for distribution at a forthcoming reception on June 29. Bruce added that he was scheduled to address the UNIA Boston branch on July 2.[17] In his final letter to Florence, Bruce informed her that he and five friends were to be guests of Mayor Quinn in an auto tour of Cambridge and, later, dinner guests at Boston's oldest and most fashionable hotel.[18] Bruce's letters did not indicate what he said to the assembled UNIA members, but, evidently, he used the time with them to persuade wavering members to stick by Garvey and the organization. Certainly, he spoke to Governor Cox and Mayor Quinn as well as the editor of the *Boston Chronicle* about Garvey's situation.[19]

Bruce's efforts to assist Garvey explain his willingness to cooperate on racial matters with two of his critics, James E. K. Aggrey and W. E. B. Du Bois. Aggrey, who was once so close to Bruce that he referred to him as "Daddie Bruce," denounced the Black Star Line and questioned the sanity of the slogan "Africa for Africans." Instead, he offered thanks to the missionaries who taught him not to be a pagan with a dozen wives.[20] Aggrey was a member of the commission on educational mission work of the Phelps-Stokes Fund, and he used this position to attack the Garvey movement while traveling in Africa. If he was critical of Bruce's involvement in the UNIA, he kept his feelings to himself. He wrote the following to Bruce on June 28, 1922: "I can never forget your loyalty to the race is genuine. Dad, this mission in behalf of my country and my people of African descent lies so heavily upon my heart—I make it my daily prayer." Aggrey had met some wealthy men in Canada who were interested in mission work in Africa. He confided to Bruce, "I know you cannot now say much about me, as [the *Negro World*] may not permit it but I know your heart Dad and I want you to pray for me that I may not fail my people." Aggrey wrote to his father figure "so as to cheer [his] heart, and to show [him] that God is more ready for us than we are ourselves. I wish I could convince my people that cooperation of all the best of all races were the best method of reaping God's kingdom." The last statement was meant for Bruce to ponder.[21]

Although Bruce no longer counted himself among Du Bois's admirers, he put aside his differences with the editor of the *Crisis* to work with him and Charles W. Anderson as a member of the Fair Play League Committee. On June 2, New York City Police Commissioner Richard E. Enright appointed Bruce to a committee whose objective was to visit station houses in Harlem and Manhattan's black West Side to see that prisoners were fairly treated. Bruce participated because it not only benefited black New Yorkers but gave him the opportunity to show others that he and the UNIA, despite their call for African redemption, were concerned about the welfare of African Americans.[22]

While Bruce and others were speaking around the country on behalf of Garvey and the UNIA, their leader wrote to the League of Nations on July 22, 1922. Garvey informed them that at the forthcoming Third Annual International Convention of the Negro People of the World scheduled to meet in August he was instructed to present a petition calling for the right of people to live under "the protection of their own racial government." It would make for a happier humanity, argued Garvey, if Palestine was a Jewish homeland and if Negroes were given former German territories in East Africa (now Tanzania) and Southwest Africa (now Namibia) for their loyalty during the past war. "We are no longer disposed to hold [our]selves as serfs, peons and slaves," noted the petition. Bruce was among the signers.[23]

The Issue of Identity

To assist with Garvey's defense and disseminate information faster than that provided by the weekly *Negro World*, the UNIA launched the *Negro Daily Times* in the fall of 1922. The newspaper was edited by Timothy Thomas Fortune and Bruce. Ironically, the two men, who had differed two decades earlier over Washington's leadership, joined forces in spreading Garvey's propaganda. Fortune, the dean of black journalists during the late nineteenth century, and Bruce, praised as one of the nation's best writers, sought to produce a lively, well-written, and well-edited newspaper. The prospect excited Bruce, who lamented the decline of the black press. He complained that one could read the typical race weekly in five minutes and within minutes forget what was read. The black press he noted had little news beyond advertisements for hair straighteners and skin-bleaching creams. While he exaggerated, his point was well taken; too many black publishers eschewed the hard political analysis that was the staple of Bruce's newspaper writing. The concept of a daily newspaper instilled race pride in Bruce. It showed how far the race had come since 1899 when he dismissed talk of a Negro daily as foolish because blacks lacked the financial wherewithal to support first-rate weeklies let alone a quality daily.[24]

Unfortunately, Bruce's 1899 sentiments proved correct. Insufficient funds led to the demise of the daily six months after the publication of its maiden issue. Even while the *Negro Daily Times* was slowly expiring, Bruce hoped that Garvey could make it solvent. Months after the dissolution of the *Negro Daily Times*, Bruce reported in the *Negro World* that William Randolph Hearst and Frank Munsey were buying up newspapers to make their power felt in the forthcoming presidential campaign. This was the power Bruce sought for the black press. Thus, the demise of the *Negro Daily Times* was a heavy blow to him.[25]

The few extant copies of Bruce's column in the daily, "The Passing Show," emphasized race pride and condemned white racism, particularly the odious practice of lynching. Forsaking his reliance on God to avenge the wrongs committed by whites, Bruce urged the lynching of white men who raped black women. He justified this by pointing out black males were brutally victimized by white mobs "for merely looking at white strumpets called 'beautiful' and 'innocent' [by white men]." These beastly attacks against defenseless black men led Bruce to describe the Caucasian as one of the "most immoral races." He accused them of leaving "a withering blight" wherever they have gone in Africa, Asia, and the Caribbean and of using their money "to cover up [their] filth and [to] hide [their] shame."[26]

It was this track record of racial misdeeds practiced by some whites that led Bruce to proclaim the following in October 1922: "I have never ... tried to feel or to think like a white man and I have never consciously sought to imitate a white man . . . and I never intend to." Instead, he attempted to emulate the lives of the humanist Frederick Douglass and the Pan-Africanist Martin R. Delany and Edward W. Blyden. Bruce would prefer to be one of these "able writers, clear thinkers and real men" above being "a good imitator of the greatest white man living or dead." His emulation of men as ideologically diverse as Douglass and Blyden reflected Bruce's ambivalence about his own status in the United States.

The dilemma he faced was shared by many others. Was he an American citizen denied his rights or an alien "African" resident in this country? Bruce wondered whether blacks could remain loyal in the face of lynching and discrimination. Could they sincerely sing "America the Beautiful" and "The Star Spangled Banner" and avoid being hypocrites and liars? Bruce was known during his final years as an outspoken foe of America's hypocrisy. Unlike integrationists, he saw little hope for African Americans to be truly integrated. While his writings reveal this aspect of his philosophy, it is not clear whether Bruce's critical opinion of his native land was irrevocable. Of course, he had forcefully declared his support for emigration in recent years; but some of his writings illustrate his ambivalence. Bruce hinted that blacks would identify America as their country if the nation saw fit to embrace them as full citizens. A nation committed to inclusion would have no hesitation in placing the images of men such as Douglass and Booker T. Washington on stamps or currency.[27] Further evidence to support this thesis occurred on November 19 when Bruce addressed a group of Virgin Islanders in Liberty Hall. They had become citizens after the United States purchased the islands from Denmark. Bruce advised them, "you must learn what are your rights as new citizens and then man fashion, demand them but you make your demands as one people." To accomplish this, he recommended that they unite their societies and organizations with their mainland counterparts.[28]

Bruce's suggestion that the blacks from the Virgin Islands seek their rights as American citizens raised many questions. If he believed that the Virgin Islanders were now part of a racist, Negrophobic society, as a Garveyite he should have expressed sympathy, even pity, for their fate. Instead, he provided advice expected more from the militant younger Bruce, who agitated for an end of racial discrimination and prejudice. For Bruce, the dilemma still existed. On one hand, he praised Garvey's cry for a home in Africa for Negroes that explicitly rejected American citizenship. Yet on the other hand, Bruce held out the possibility of a change that would lead to true racial integration. This latter point was underscored in a scene that amazed Bruce in 1923 while he was a patient in Manhattan's Eye, Ear, and Throat Hospital. Observing that blind and semiblind patients harbored no manifestation of racial prejudice, Bruce wrote that "Jews, Gentiles, Italians, Celt and Negroes here mingle together in social alliance and apparently forgot the difference of race."[29]

Perplexed, he could not help wonder if America would someday be a nation where color or race no longer mattered. Since Bruce formerly believed that white Americans would respect blacks if they knew and appreciated their many contributions to the development of the United States, he wrote about the nation's need for African Americans in a future war with Japan. In the first chapter of a proposed book, *The Call of a Nation,* Bruce described how, after the Japanese defeat of the American military, the president called upon 800,000 white and black volunteers to defend the nation against the "inferior race." Fear of Japanese occupation led the United States to put aside her race and color lines. Left unsaid in the proposal was Bruce's probable ending with the crisis being resolved in America's favor and African Americans gaining the complete freedom their sacrifices warranted.[30]

While these observations represented the America that Bruce longed to witness, he understood that America was a nation that never realized its ideals of equality and brotherhood. Unless the nation became color blind and recognized men for their characters instead of their skin color, Bruce was committed to working with Garvey, whose message was of self-reliance, race pride, and black solidarity. He believed that these were solutions superior to those of the integrationists and the socialists. If Bruce had lived longer, perhaps he would have come to a different evaluation. Were he and other persons of color American citizens with the right to militantly demand their inclusion, or should they have understood that no amount of agitation would alter their condition in the eyes of the nation's dominant group? Bruce's entire adult life, save the last few years, was devoted to the civil rights struggle. He had wanted to be recognized as an American, but events continued to show him that the struggle was futile. The fact that hundreds of thousands disagreed and opted to continue the fight for justice only added to Bruce's difficulty in reconciling his earlier advocacy of American inclusion with his support for the Garvey movement and its belief in an African destiny.

Garvey Must Go

The first half of 1923 was a lonely period for Bruce as a period of internal dissent, and rebellion threatened to seriously weaken if not destroy the UNIA. With the exception of Henrietta Vinton Davis, who traveled around the country and throughout the Caribbean shoring up support for Garvey, all of the members of the High Executive Council in the UNIA had resigned, and fifteen of twenty-one successfully sued for full salaries after Garvey attempted to reduce them.[31] Garveyism faced a major blow on January 15, 1923, when eight prominent race leaders petitioned U.S. Atty. Gen. Harry M. Daugherty to disband the UNIA and vigorously push the government's case against Marcus Garvey for mail fraud. The signers were Harry H. Pace, businessman; John E. Nail, a Harlem Realtor; Julia P. Coleman, president of the Hair Vim Chemical Company; Robert Abbott, publisher and editor of the *Chicago Defender;* Chandler Owen, coeditor of the *Messenger;* George V. Harris, editor of the *New York News;* William Pickens, NAACP field secretary; and Robert W. Bagnall, director of branches of the NAACP. Garvey had previously singled out all for vicious personal attacks, and his response to the publication of their letter was no less severe. He dismissed them as "liars and fabricators [and] wicked maligners" who were octoroons, quadroons, or, in the case of two, "black Negroes who had married octoroons," and, in the case of Owen, a person who wanted to marry a white woman until Garvey sounded the alarm. Joining Garvey in castigating the group was Bruce, who noted in early February that Garvey would survive the race traitors and would be organizing while his critics were forgotten or dead.[32] On February 24, Bruce wrote that he would continue to follow Garvey, who would never give up regardless of the attacks on "his manhood, his courage, his faith in his race, in himself, [and] in his bulldog tenacity." Swiping at those who sought to be middlemen between the race and the white power structure, Bruce dismissed the "need [for] colored wet nurses" since "the tail isn't going to wag the dog, the dog will do the wagging hereafter or something will burst."[33] Referring to these "wet nurses" as "colored" was Bruce's display of contempt for them. In his estimation, the term *colored* described middle-class persons whose desire for assimilation was an indication of their lack of race pride.

The complaints against Garvey from dissatisfied investors, his meeting with the Klan's leader, the charges that he was stealing funds, and the letter to the attorney general from Garvey's foes culminated in his indictment. Annoyed that his attorney was cooperating with the court (Judge Julian Mack wanted a speedy trial for personal reasons), Garvey acted as his own attorney and called many witnesses, including Henrietta Vinton Davis, a former member of the shipping corporation's board of directors. Garvey was infuriated by Davis's numerous responses of "I don't know" and "I don't remember" to many of his questions. Despite limited and questionable evidence, and the acquittals of his codefendants, Garvey was convicted in early June and sentenced to five years imprisonment, a fine of one thousand dollars, and payment for the cost of the trial. He spent three months in the Tombs prison in Manhattan before being released on bail. Bruce sought to lift up the spirits of the UNIA faithful on June 17 when they met in Harlem's Liberty Hall. Neither Garvey nor the organization can be crushed, he noted, for "like Mr. Rabbit and the tar baby, [Garvey] has another foot yet." Six days later, Garvey wrote from prison that District Attorney Maxwell Mattuck wanted him to be found guilty as a favor for the NAACP because a freed Garvey would use the force and power of the UNIA to destroy the civil rights organization.[34]

Justice for Garvey

Garvey's faithful supporters were angry that their leader was imprisoned. Bruce took note of this reservoir of anger. In his July 7 *Negro World* column, Bruce expressed concern that extreme rhetoric or physical display of anger would prove harmful and provide the government with an excuse to ruin Garvey and injure the UNIA. "Silence is golden," he reminded them, because Mattuck was spreading the rumor that armed men would attempt to release Garvey from his incarceration. "Let us do more thinking than talking. Vengeance is not justice. Justice is bound to prevail." One indication of Bruce's fear that the government would attempt to indict others in the UNIA was revealed in his letter to Florence. On July 1, Bruce wrote from Massachusetts to his wife warning her to watch herself in the Harlem UNIA office and not to leave money lying around. "*[D]on't trust anybody* to the extent of thinking they will not take advantage of you." Bruce's fear was justified; James Wormley Jones and other black federal agents had infiltrated Garvey's organization and had provided damaging information to their superiors.[35]

Garvey's supporters wanted him released from the Tombs on bail, which the prosecutor vehemently opposed. Bruce believed that Judge Julian Mack was biased, which is what he wrote on July 10 to George B. Christian Jr., the secretary to President Warren G. Harding. The gist of his letter was that Mack was a contributor to the NAACP and was, therefore, not an impartial judge. Bruce asked Christian to bring the matter to "the president whom we all want to see reelected." Continuing his argument that the government was prejudiced against Garvey, Bruce wrote in subsequent columns that Garvey's critics had predicted before the trial that the Jamaican would be sentenced to five years in prison. How did they know this, questioned Bruce, suggesting that Garvey's guilty verdict had been arranged months before the trial started. More telling, according to Bruce, was the threat made by John Amos, a government spy, to throw away his badge and club if Garvey was not "gotten."

This appeal to Harding became irrelevant with the president's untimely death by a stroke on August 2, 1923, while in San Francisco. Garvey proclaimed the dead president as "a true friend of the Negro race, as far as we can expect friendship from members of the opposite race who have not yet discovered their souls." However, Bruce was also able to write "Long live the president in the heart of his countrymen." Having witnessed for years the Republicans withdraw support for black Americans, Bruce urged African

Americans to make terms with the leaders of all parties and to "use his vote as a club to secure what belongs to him."[36]

On August 16, Bruce wrote to President Calvin Coolidge requesting his thoughts on the Negro's political and social position in America. He informed the president of his race's long association with the Republican Party, which they would continue to maintain provided Coolidge gave assurance that the party had their interest at heart. Such a positive statement, Bruce noted, would strengthen the confidence of the Negro "in you and your administration and increase your power in the nation at [this] psychological moment." Bruce requested that Coolidge make blacks feel that they were also American citizens "in fact, and that you are their president." Coolidge replied four days later that black migration to the North meant that the race problem was no longer a sectional issue. The president promised to give "earnest consideration" to the matter in order to assure that the condition of black Americans would change for the better. In the *Negro World,* the editor argued that Coolidge "could seize the opportunity to enshrine his name in the hearts of Negroes, or be but another instrument in placing Lincoln in even bolder relief."[37] Bruce's forthright letter and Coolidge's benign reply underlined the need for political activism. In 1924, the UNIA organized a Negro Political Union, which advised followers to vote "for principles, policies and faithful men who are friends of our race." The Negro Political Union was undoubtedly the brainchild of Bruce, and his influence was seen in the union's denunciation of unprincipled old-time black politicians who betrayed the race for a few dollars.[38]

Garvey was released on $15,000 bail in September 1923, which caused joyous enthusiasm from his supporters. An elated Garvey spoke at Liberty Hall on September 13. He told the faithful gathering that his conviction was not based on fraud, but rather because he advocated liberation of Africa and the worldwide empowerment of African people. Garvey added that he was convicted by wicked, malicious, and jealous enemies that misrepresented him to the government. Bruce lashed out at District Attorney Maxwell Mattuck, who argued that Garvey should be denied bail because his followers were alleged to have bombs or weapons to free him from the Tombs. Bruce considered Mattuck's behavior a "despicable piece of work for an attorney of reputation for honor and fair play." Bruce predicted vindication for Garvey, noting that "UNIA members have long memories and the patience to wait for the coming of the morning where justice shall have a hearing." Determined not to let Mattuck's charge dim the celebration, Bruce declared that the UNIA "should use all possible means to make this a red letter day ... because ... it is destined to play a very important role in the world's affairs." Shocking devout Christians, Bruce compared Garvey to Christ, as he "has endured much physical suffering for the freedom of his people."[39]

Defender of Garvey to the End

Bruce lashed out at those critics who called Garvey foolish. "If Garvey is a fool," Bruce asserted, "he is God's fool." Garvey was, to Bruce, the only one who could unite the African worldwide around the continent's redemption and advancement. He urged "American born Africans [to] catch the vision" of a glorious African nationhood and forget Du Bois's Pan-Africanist movement. It is significant that Bruce used the term *African* to describe those born in the United States; for years he had insisted that the Negro was an American and should be included in the nation. More alienated than ever, Bruce, in late 1923, derided the notion that blacks were true citizens. "If we are *true* citizens— disband all race centered organizations," he demanded. Instead, we are "beggars . . . a race without a country or a flag." This was his harshest denial of citizenship to date and a strong indicator that he had resolved his conflict over identity. Now he was proclaiming himself not an American seeking full inclusion but an African in exile. George A. Latimer challenged this declaration as mean-spirited. Bruce retorted that one could not be a citizen unless one enjoyed the rights of citizenship. To prove his point, he cited a popular ditty: "a nought's a nought; a figger's a figger. All for the white man. And nothing for the nigger."[40]

The notoriety of the Garvey trial convinced some that he was a naive visionary who foolishly thought that Europeans would abandon their resource-rich African holdings simply because the UNIA shouted "Africa for Africans at home and abroad." Still, the *AME Review,* organ of the AME Church, and one of Garvey's harshest critics, offered sympathy after his conviction. "Shall black men . . . cease to dream of reclaiming a part of Africa and administering a government of their own?" asked the *Review.* The publication answered its own question with a resounding "no," not as "long as race and color stand a bar to freedom and equality." In spite of this, the *Review* warned that other visionaries should avoid the path that led to Garvey's downfall. Garvey's conviction and high bail did not make him contrite. Agent Joseph G. Tucker informed his superiors that Garvey, at his speech on June 21, 1924, at Liberty Hall, stated that "the Negroes who think they can play the fool with the [UNIA] . . . as they played with the Black Star Line in 1921 . . . are playing the fool with hell." Garvey reportedly said also that "you will have a black Ku Klux Klan that will be worse than hell if you play the fool."[41]

Bruce informed Garvey's critics that the UNIA leader was not a fraud and that they lacked ammunition powerful enough to pierce his armor.[42] Others within the UNIA were not as steadfast, however. Resignations and defections proliferated as many became disgruntled with Garvey's leadership. For example, J. Raphiel Ralph Casimir, president of the UNIA division in Rouseau,

Dominica, resigned from his position. Amy Jacques Garvey wrote to Casimir on August 6, 1923, with news that her husband (who was in the Tombs) wanted to know why he resigned. She wrote, "I do hope you will take new courage, and in face of all opposition, fight on the cause of the [UNIA to] the uplift of Negroes and a free and redeemed Africa." Mrs. Garvey, worried about her husband's then incarceration, ended her letter by admonishing Casimir that "I, who have more to bear than you, am not discouraged. Why should you be?" Garvey scholar Tony Martin noted that Casimir resigned since the Dominica's UNIA mutual aid society paid the highest sickness and death benefits in the Caribbean and many beneficiaries did not contribute financially after recovering from illness. Casimir's resignation was all the more significant because it was he who, several years earlier, solicited Garvey for a UNIA charter that was issued in 1920.[43] In late November, Bruce wrote Casimir confidentially that "things are run in a rather upshod manner since Mr. Garvey's recent incarceration and it is hard to keep track of things I regret to say."[44] Nevertheless, Bruce was still creative enough to write a song to rally the membership to support Garvey. One typical stanza read as follows:

> We have cast our lot with Garvey
> And we're with him to the end.
> We have confidence in Garvey
> And him we will defend.[45]

Bruce's defense of Garvey was remarkable in light of his rapid declining health. In mid-February 1923, Timothy Thomas Fortune wrote Bruce and humored him with stories about his boil. He asked his friend to take care of himself long enough so that the two could "take an occasional swig while the bootleggers are able to place it where it can be got."[46] From April 24 to May 22 Bruce was hospitalized at Manhattan's Eye, Ear, and Throat Hospital for treatment for high blood pressure, diabetes, and double vision in his left eye. His tonsils were removed during his hospitalization.[47]

Bruce's health was poor during the period he was in the Boston area to shore up UNIA support for Garvey. On July 1, 1923, he wrote Florence that he was on a special diet to change the level of his blood sugar in preparation for a medical test. "I am going to help the doctors all I can to get well so I can come home again soon," he wrote. With loving attention, he cautioned Florence to be careful of cars and trolleys, for "if anything happened to you girl it would kill me." Despite his health concerns, Bruce enjoyed his cigars, and he asked Florence to bring ten five-cent cigars when she came to visit.[48] A relapse in the fall sent Bruce to New York's Presbyterian Hospital, where he remained from late September throughout October for the treatment of his eyes, diabetes, and other complications. He wrote Florence on October 24, concerned that she had left the hospital the previous day in a pouring rain. "I could hardly sleep thinking about you and how and when you got home." Bruce informed his wife that blood started to flow after he blew his nose. The next time, a clot of black blood came out; a passage had healed before the side of his nose had properly drained. A delighted patient wrote, "what a sense of relief it gave me and how good it made me feel. I am breathing all right and all the pain in my ear has left me."[49]

Bruce's improved health was a source of good news to his many friends. From Africa, Casely Hayford wrote that friends were praying that God would spare him "to complete the great task that you ... have taken up in the cause of our race uplift." Hayford was pleased that Bruce's improved health allowed him to become the special American representative of his new publication, the *Gold Coast Leader*.[50] Before accepting the assignment, Bruce wrote in the *Negro World*'s October 20, 1923, issue, "soon all Africa will be aroused and fully awakened as never before" due to the truth of Garvey's message of "Africa for Africans."[51]

Bruce's improved health proved to be fleeting. He was scheduled to enter the hospital again on November 24. Two days before his admission, Bruce confided to J. Raphiel Ralph Casimir that he hoped to be home in three or four weeks but would be unable to write regularly. Considerately, Bruce wrote Casimir, whom he believed deserved a reply, but he noted that "writing is more of a discipline with me than a pleasure."[52] Christmas holidays were a disappointment for Bruce, who was still in the hospital. He wrote Florence on January 1, 1924, "dear kiddo. You see I am coming back with my eyesight and [am] even writing clearer." Though New Year's Day began on an optimistic note, the future would be grim for Bruce during the following ten months. As his health rapidly deteriorated, he was in and out of hospitals.[53] He wrote to Casely Hayford. The envelope was addressed to Florence with a request to show it to Garvey for his approval before sending it to Hayford in Africa. Bruce suggested to Garvey that, if he agreed, he should cable to Hayford in Bruce's name the message that "Du Bois-*Crisis* on trip to Africa [is] Bent on mischief due to failure of his Pan African Congress. [He is] financed by Joel Spingarn[,] a Jew and other [white] interests inimical to African independence. Watch him. Letter follows. Make no committals." To Florence, he added, "I will tell Hayford what to do to break the force of Du Bois influence on the Gold Coast." Garvey shared Bruce's concern completely. His December 29 editorial in the *Negro World* warned that Du Bois was seeking to broker a deal between European imperialists and African mulattos to divide power among themselves at the expense of Negroes.[54]

Time was crucial if the UNIA expected to gain concessions before Du Bois arrived in Liberia, because it was believed that he wanted to get the U.S. government involved in establishing commercial relations with the African republic. Du Bois had sent a team of agricultural and industrial experts (precisely what the UNIA had ventured to do) to examine the investment and developmental possibilities. On February 1, a UNIA delegation consisting of Robert Lincoln Poston, Henrietta Vinton Davis, and J. Milton Lowe arrived in Liberia expecting to be the vanguard of African Americans who were coming "home." (Garvey had hoped to hold the UNIA's fourth annual convention in Liberia in August 1924.) The rivalry between Garvey and Du Bois was noted by the *Liberian News,* which deemed Du Bois's efforts in America as provincial. In contrast, Garvey's works were viewed as international, for his was "the voice crying in the wilderness." Both America and Europe looked with alarm upon Garvey's colonization scheme. France and England applied economic pressure on Liberia, forcing the small nation to inform the U.S. Department of State that it "opposed, both in principle and in fact, the policy of the [UNIA]." Eventually, however, Firestone Rubber Corporation acquired land previously promised to the UNIA. Soon, the African nation denied access to Garveyites unless they renounced Garvey, which few were willing to do.[55]

Despite Bruce's earlier intention to tell Hayford how to handle Du Bois, his declining health severely incapacitated him. In late February 1924, E. R. Mathews, business manager of the *Negro World,* wrote to Casimir, "Mr. Bruce is very ill and may not last much longer. He is now in the hospital."[56] A month later, William H. Weeks wrote from Cambridge, Massachusetts, to Florence imploring her not to give up hope, as Bruce had the "grit" to fight tenaciously for better health. A slight improvement in his condition encouraged Weeks, who wrote Florence on June 10, "I do trust Dad is improving as I am hoping to run down this summer for a few days."[57] Bruce was a proud man, and his feeble condition saddened his friends. One wrote to tell him to listen to Florence and his physician so that he soon would be "the sheik" again.[58]

We do not know what thoughts ran through his mind as Bruce lay in his sickbed. He, who had seen and done so much to elevate the black race, probably reflected on his life. In his papers were these undated words of reflection, which were probably written near the end of his life: "I stand at my age as on a mountain summit looking back on life's vicissitudes, ruminating on the success or foils of reminiscences."[59] If he had any regrets, perhaps one was that his frailties prevented him from visiting Africa. Near Christmas of 1922, Bruce noted in his *Negro World* column that if he were younger he would go to Africa and take with him mining engineers, carpenters, road builders, electricians, machinists, and other skilled individuals to develop the land of his ancestors. In his waning moments, Bruce probably thought about his impending passing; but death did not frighten him. In a journal entry on July 2, 1915, Bruce described a dream where he and a female friend were killed as a train collided with their horse and buggy. As his spirit was ascending toward Heaven, he glanced down at the horrified witnesses who turned away from seeing his mangled body. He felt neither pain nor fear, and he described Heaven as an idyllic place full of all nationalities at peace with each other. The paradise was blissful with its beautiful music. Bruce died at 3:15 P.M. on August 7, 1924, a victim of chronic myocarditis, senility, and general arteriosclerosis.[60]

Timothy Thomas Fortune eulogized his friend of a half century for his indefatigable support for the UNIA.[61] Casely Hayford wrote to J. Raphiel Ralph Casimir, "I have heard with pain the death of . . . Bruce. He was truly a great man . . . it is a terrible loss to our race."[62] One contributor to the *Negro World* asked, "why did he die who lived to serve our race? At one fell swoop death took the strength of ten when mighty Bruce laid down his trenchant pen."[63] In recognition of his pioneer historiography, Carter G. Woodson, editor of the *Journal of Negro History,* commented that the cause of historical inclusion of Negroes "lost a friend, and the world a great soul."[64] Despite the *Pittsburgh Courier*'s claim that Bruce was never an ardent Garveyite but only demanded fair play for the Jamaican, the UNIA knew that it had lost a true supporter. Bruce was honored with a church service followed by a tribute from the UNIA and a final salute from his Masonic brothers. Five thousand mourners solemnly listened to Beethoven's funeral march, a favorite of Bruce.[65] Garvey delivered a eulogy for his staunch defender. However, it was Arthur Schomburg who captured the essence of Bruce Grit. According to the bibliophile, Bruce would be remembered for his efforts to bring the Negro into contact with fellow blacks in West Africa and for encouraging people to recognize the contributions of Ethiopians and Egyptians to world civilization. Schomburg concluded his remarks with the observation that Bruce was one of the race's most erudite scholars despite barely possessing a grammar school education. "His career itself," noted Schomburg, "is a noble illustration of the possibility of a race whose cause he so manfully championed."[66]

The death of John Edward Bruce was not without controversy. Three weeks after his passing, the *Amsterdam News* in New York printed a letter from Olive Bruce Millar, his daughter, who informed the weekly that it had erred in listing Florence as his only survivor. An annoyed Mrs. Millar indicated that neither she nor Bruce's three grandchildren were informed of his death. This news is the more astounding, since Olive was unaware of her father's hospitalization from June 5 to his death on August 7.[67] Bruce's granddaughter Onaway (Onnie) Millar believes that Florence, Olive's senior by about twelve years, intensely disliked Olive and acted as a wedge between Bruce and his daughter. Still, Onnie remembers how, as a youngster of five or six, he would visit the family in their New Jersey home, which suggests that Bruce tried to be a loving family man.[68] The total absence of any correspondence in Bruce's voluminous collection between him and Olive adds credence to Onnie's claim that perhaps Florence destroyed any record of such correspondence before turning his papers over to Arthur Schomburg. Furthermore, according to the *Crusader* magazine, Bruce was viewed as "a model man, a *kind* father and husband" (emphasis added).[69]

The differences between Florence and Olive will never be known. Onnie Millar had no contact with Florence, and she does not recall her mother ever speaking about the reasons for the rift between the two women. Florence remained with the UNIA after the passing of her husband. Six months after his death, Florence admitted to a friend that it would take some time before she would able to "get over [her] husband's death." Garvey appreciated her work on behalf of the UNIA by knighting her Lady Bruce and awarding her title of Duchess of Uganda. By the early 1930s, the UNIA was barely functioning. Garvey was sent to federal prison in 1925, deported in 1927, and eventually exiled to London, where he remained until his death in 1940. The UNIA fractured into two rival organizations, and members defected to other self-help and black nationalist organizations. Like many others in the United States, Florence had to cope with the uncertainties of the Great Depression. Lameness caused by rheumatism and hardening of the arteries cost Florence her job in 1936. After being evicted, she sought assistance from Arthur Schomburg, who aided her in receiving home relief (welfare). Death claimed Florence Bruce on December 25, 1942, ironically twenty-seven days before the passing of Olive Bruce Millar on January 20, 1943.[70]

Epilogue

Arthur Schomburg noted in 1912 that his good friend, John Edward Bruce, was such a race man that he characterized him as one of those who "think and act and sleep and eat NEGRO."[1] Schomburg's praise was based on his intimate relationship with Bruce as a fellow bibliophile, colleague in the Negro Society for Historical Research and the American Negro Academy, and as a close friend who often shared cigars and liquor with Bruce in joyous times. Laudatory praise also came from others who admired and appreciated Bruce's efforts to defend the race from malicious racist accusations. Eric D. Waldron, a Harlem Renaissance literary figure and an associate editor of the *Negro World,* proclaimed in 1922 that Bruce was one of the twelve greatest living Negroes in the United States.[2] J. R. Ralph Casimir, who knew Bruce only as a correspondent, was so moved by his race devotion that he wrote a poem, "Bruce Grit." The first stanza was, "I love the man because he loves his kin and fights untiringly [for] freedom to win; He is true to his God and true to his race and defends his just cause with power and grace."[3]

Similar praise can be found in letters to the black press and to Bruce personally. Bruce is often mentioned in passing in books and articles as "militant," or "race conscious." His most militant statement was written in 1889 on the occasion of a lecture or a debate. He then concluded that the Mosaic law of "an eye for an eye, a tooth for a tooth" was applicable. Bruce exclaimed, "If they burn our houses, burn theirs; if they kill our wives and children, kill theirs; pursue them relentlessly, meet force with force everywhere it is offered. If they demand blood, exchange with them until they are satiated. By a vigorous adherence to this course the shedding of human blood by white men will soon become a thing of the past." While this view represents the popular image of Bruce held by his contemporaries, it is an inaccurate one. It is clearly an aberration of his true sentiments. More often, Bruce left revenge to the providence of God or cautioned against individuals striking against a superior force unless they had the support of the federal government. For example, in "The Hour of Prayer," written in 1899, Bruce intoned, "Heaven hear us and defend us." The 1921 burning at the stake of Henry Loury, a resident of Nordena,

Arkansas, elicited from Bruce the conservative view that "the day of doom for the white man is fast approaching" because God would make them pay for shedding Negro blood. He offered this same solution after whites erupted in a killing and burning rage in Tulsa, Oklahoma, in 1921 that destroyed that community's homes and businesses.

Although Bruce generally eschewed retaliatory violence, on rare occasions he resorted to a militancy that was similar to that expressed by Malcolm X before his departure from the Nation of Islam. On December 31, 1921, Bruce wrote that mob violence bred race hatred. He warned that unless the federal government acted to prevent violence against blacks, African Americans might retaliate. "When the worm turns the men who are standing in the stench will have to move," he declared. Again, this contradicts many of his earlier statements in support of providential intervention and makes him appear erratic.[4]

He was both a complex and contradictory personality. Bruce's race-first ideology was not always pure as concerns for financial security, political appointments, and allegiance to others placed him in compromising positions. At times, Bruce was quick to take a position that was at odds with his purported race-first ideology. An example was his blind support for Theodore Roosevelt when the president dismissed the men of the Twenty-fifth U.S. Colored Infantry after the Brownsville affray in 1906. The black press, clergy, and many politicians took the president to task for his rash and unwarranted action. While Bruce supported Roosevelt because he believed the man was fair and judicious in his rulings, he was clearly looking for a political reward from the administration. Bruce was not above confusing his own interests with those of the African American community.

Financial security was always a pressing concern for Bruce. In part, his attraction to Booker T. Washington was fueled by his need for a steady income. Nevertheless, unlike some radicals, he found much to admire in Washington. Initially, few in the African American community faulted Washington. They admired what he had accomplished at Tuskegee, and they generally agreed with his call for greater black ownership of land and businesses. The growing power of Washington, measured in large part by his close contacts with wealthy and influential whites, led critics to challenge his accommodationist views. Yet Bruce remained with Washington for the sake of needed funds when others deemed his accommodationism dangerous to the advancement of civil and political rights.

Bruce's views on Africa also shifted like sand in a storm. At first, Bruce, like millions of others, saw his destiny in America, not Africa. Bruce had fought consistently for the inclusion of African Americans in the American dream. He argued for decades that their unpaid labor during slavery and their sacrifices on the battlefields during all the nation's wars should have guaranteed their freedom. Progressive white men such as Charles Sumner, Roscoe Conkling, Thaddeus Stevens, Zachary Chandler, James S. Clarkson, and George F. Hoar had impressed Bruce with their devotion to equality for all. He admired these men while they were alive and lamented their loss after their demise. Disillusionment, however, set in, and during the last half decade of his life, Bruce bitterly condemned white America. Not only did he fault white politicians for lacking the moral courage of their nineteenth-century predecessors, but Bruce came to the conclusion that despite their battlefield sacrifices, African Americans would never be treated as less than aliens or interlopers unless they emigrated to Africa. This sentiment separated him from the vast majority of blacks, who opposed vigorously the dictum that America was not their home. They denied Bruce's assertion that the black race was reduced to "begging at the gate" or that they were a people "without a country or a flag." Near the end of his life, Bruce urged readers of the *Negro World* to "THINK BLACK, for every white man in this country is thinking white." It was this ideological base that fueled Bruce's desire to belong to a country that he could call his own. Prior to the period following the end of the First World War, Bruce had embraced moral suasion, protest politics, alliances with progressive whites, and militant pleas to white America to accept full integration of African Americans. However, in the twilight of his life, he gave up the belief that blacks could overcome in America. Shortly before his death, he strongly supported emigration as the only viable option for African Americans who wanted complete freedom and equality.[5]

All of his contradictory endeavors of behalf of his race were motivated by his sense of race pride and love of his people. While some of his solutions were debatable, it cannot be denied that Bruce left a lasting legacy. His pioneering work to make the study of the history and culture of African people, combined with the contributions of Arthur A. Schomburg, Joel A. Rogers, Carter G. Woodson, and other scholars, eventually led to the formation of Black Studies courses and departments throughout the nation and abroad. Bruce would be extremely proud to know that America not only decided to put images of prominent African Americans on stamps, but that there is a national holiday for an activist, Dr. Martin Luther King Jr., and that both major political parties routinely appoint African Americans to their cabinets and other government agencies. His voluminous collection of essays, opinion pieces, poetry, short stories, and news clippings became a major addition to the Schomburg Center for Research in Black Culture's collection. Finally, on a personal level, Bruce's activism influenced his daughter, Olive, who often brought her young children to demonstrations and marches during their formative years, leading to their lifetime involvement in the struggle against racial injustice.[6]

Notes

Preface

1. Charles A. Johnson, "John Edward Bruce," *Cleveland Gazette,* Feb. 21, 1891, 1. William A. Ferris, *The African Abroad,* 2 vols. (New Haven, Conn.: Tuttle, Morehouse & Taylor Press, 1913), 2:861. "John Edward Bruce," Daniel A. Murray Papers, reel 2. "The Bruce Collection," calendar of manuscripts in the Schomburg Collection of Negro Literature, pt. 1 (New York: Federal Writers Project Administration, 1942), 163.
2. Peter H. Gilbert, ed., *The Selected Writings of John Edward Bruce: Militant Black Journalist* (New York: Arno Press, 1971). Ralph L. Crowder has written essays on Bruce's thoughts and his relationships with leading Pan-Africanists. See, for example, "John Edward Bruce, Edward Wilmot Blyden, Alexander Crummell, J. Robert Love: Mentors, Patrons, and the Evolution of a Pan-African Network," *Afro-Americans in New York Life and History* 20 (July 1996): 59–92.
3. Bruce Grit, "Negro Journalism, Its Utility," *(Washington) Bee*, May 4, 1889, 4. Editorial, [no title], *Colored American,* Feb. 23, 1901, 8; Nov. 30, 1901, 8. George A. McBane, "A Noted Journalist," *Colored American,* Feb. 23, 1901, 1. Dennis S. Thompson to J. E. Bruce, May 6, 1901, Group B, Letters Received, MSS, Autographed Letters, MS 65, reel 1, Bruce Collection. Charles A. Johnson, "John Edward Bruce," *Cleveland Gazette,* Feb. 21, 1891, 1. "Carph," "sketch of J. E. Bruce," *Cleveland Gazette,* Sept. 12, 1891, 1.
4. John Bracey Jr., August Meier, and Elliot Rudwick, eds., *Black Nationalism in America* (Indianapolis: Bobbs-Merrill, 1970).
5. Bruce to Gen. [James S. Clarkson], Feb. 6, 1893, Group C, Letters Received, C 8, reel 1, Bruce Collection. [Tyler, Texas, lynching-fragment, n.d.], Group E, Bruce Fragment, reel 3, Bruce Collection. Bruce Grit, "Will Reap the Whirlwind," *Colored American*, Dec. 17, 1898, 2.
6. J. E. Bruce, [no title], *Negro Daily Times,* Feb. 21, 1921, in J. E. Bruce, clipping file, #000-746-1. J. E. Bruce, [no title], *Negro World,* Apr. 22, 1923, 6. J. E. Bruce, "King Tut Again," *Negro World,* Apr. 28, 1923, 4.
7. J. E. Bruce, "Past Glories," *Ledger,* Dec. 31, 1898. Bruce to Bishop Harris, *Star of Zion,* Dec. 15, 1889, Group E, misc., reel 4, Bruce Collection. For opposition to the term *Negro,* see *New York Sun,* May 16, 1897, 3; Gerald H. Gray to Daniel A. Murray, Apr. 6, 1910, Daniel A. Murray Papers, reel 1.

8. Olive Bruce Millar's 1943 death certificate stated that the approximately fifty-three-year-old woman was born about 1889 to Bruce and Alice Ayers. No marriage certificate could be located for the couple, although an Alice Ayers lived in Washington in 1883 (she is not listed for other years). There is no marriage certificate for the couple in the records of the District of Columbia, but a John E. and Lucy Bruce lived together in 1884 at 1404 South C Avenue, southeast Washington. The matter is further complicated when we consider that in September 1890, R. D. Ruffin informed Grace Dyson, principal of the Lovejoy School in Washington, that Bruce wanted to enroll his two children. Olive was not near school age, but family gossip indicates that Bruce had a son named Charles, whose mother and fate is unknown. This is the only reference in Bruce's voluminous personal papers that he had children. R. D. Ruffin to Grace Dyson, Sept. 22, 1890, in Group E, misc., 13-30, reel 3, Bruce Collection. *Boyd's Directory for District of Columbia,* 1884. Olive Bruce Millar's Certificate of Death #1963, Jan. 20, 1943, Bureau of Records, Dept. of Health, Borough of Manhattan., Birth Certificate for unnamed daughter of Lucy Bruce, #49295, July 22, 1888, District of Columbia Dept. of Health. Author's conversations with Onnie Millar, Oct. 22, 1998, and Feb. 19, 1999. My Dear Doctor [Alexander Crummell], Jan. 17, 1894, Group C, Letters Sent by Bruce, BL 4-62, reel 2, Bruce Collection. Crummell to Bruce, Jan. 17, 1894, Group C, Letters Received, C 14, reel 1, Bruce Collection.
9. Thomas L. Jones to Bruce, Apr. 1, 1895, Group B, Letters Received, MSS, Autographed Letters, MS 241, reel 1, Bruce Collection. *Washington Grit,* July 19, 1884, 2. Alexander Crummell to Bruce, Nov. 26, 1895, Letters from the Bruce Collection, reel 2, Bruce Collection. [Successful Marriages, n.d.], Group D, MSS, B 8-109, Bruce Collection. T. Thomas Fortune to Bruce, Dec. 8, 1897, Group F, Letters Received, F 3, reel 1, Bruce Collection. Emma Lou Thornbrough, *T. Thomas Fortune: Militant Journalist* (Chicago: Univ. of Chicago Press, 1972), 289, 294. "Bruce Gritisms," *Colored American,* Sept. 13, 1902, 10–11.

Chapter 1

1. John E. Bruce, "A Sketch of My Life," May 1, 1875, Group B, Letters Received, B 12, reel 1, Bruce Collection. U.S. Bureau of the Census, *Population Schedules of the Seventh Census of the United States. Schedule Two. Maryland Slave Schedules of 1850* (Washington: GPO, 1850), roll 301, 564, 655. U.S. Bureau of the Census, *Population Schedules of the Eighth Census . . . Schedule 1. Free Inhabitants in Fifth Election District in the County of Prince Georges State of Maryland, enumerated June 13, 1860.* (Washington: GPO, 1860), roll 478, 505. U.S. Bureau of the Census, *Population Schedule of the Eighth Census of the United States. Schedule Two. Slave Inhabitants in the Fifth Election District. Prince Georges County, Maryland* (Washington: GPO, 1860), roll 485, 3.
2. "The Last Meeting," n.d., Group C, MSS, Bruce Letters, BS 5-31, reel 2, Bruce Collection. Bruce Grit, "The Colonel's Narrative," *Crusader* 1 (Feb. 1919): 12, 27–28.
3. *Weekly Anglo-African,* Apr. 27, May 11, 1861. *Douglass Monthly,* vol. IV (May 1861): 451; (Sept. 1861), 516.
4. Bruce, "A Sketch of My Life," *Negro World,* May 12, 1923, 4. There is no evidence that Major Griffin petitioned Congress. U.S. Congress, House, *Report on*

Emancipated Slaves in the District of Columbia, Feb. 16, 1864. Vol. 9, 38th Cong., 1st sess., 1864, H. Doc. 42, 79 pages.
5. I. Garland Penn, *The Afro American Press and Its Editors* (Springfield, Mass.: Willey & Co., 1891), 344. "John Edward Bruce, Journalist," n.d., Daniel A. Murray Papers, reel 2.
6. Frances Ellen Watkins, "Our Greatest Want," *Anglo African Magazine* 1 (May 1859): 160.
7. William Hague and E. N. Kirk. *Address of Rev. Drs. Wm Hague and E. N. Kirk, of the Annual Meeting of the Educational Commission for Freedmen at the Old South Church, May 28, 1863* (Boston: David Clapp, printer 1863), 5, 16.
8. *Freedmen's Record* 1 (Jan. 1865): 3, 5, 6, 8. William J. Wilson to George Whipple, Oct. 25, 1865, #16515, District of Columbia, reel 2, American Missionary Association Papers.
9. *Freedmen's Record* 1 (Feb. 1865): 17–18; 1 (Oct. 1865): 162; 2 (Feb. 1866): 20–21. Herbert Aptheker, ed., *A Documentary History of the Negro People in the United States* (New York: Citadel Press, 1951), 1:509–10. *New York Times,* Dec. 15, 1866, 4.
10. Ferris, *The African Abroad,* 2:862. Penn, *The Afro American Press,* 344.
11. "Our Washington Letter," *Weekly Anglo-African,* Nov. 24, 1860, 2, 3. For Tanner, see William Seraile, *Fire in His Heart: Bishop Benjamin Tucker Tanner and the A.M.E. Church* (Knoxville: Univ. of Tenn. Press, 1998).
12. "Reminiscences of a Colored Journalist," n.d. in BS 5-16, reel 2, Bruce Collection.
13. "Martin R. Delaney," n.d. Group C, MSS, Bruce Letters, BS 5-11A, reel 2, Bruce Collection. "Major Martin R. Delaney," MSS, 9E-37, reel 2, Bruce Collection.
14. *Negro Daily Times,* Oct. 9, 1923. J. E. Bruce, clipping file.
15. "A Black Boy's Recollection of President Lincoln and J. Wilkes Booth," [1922?] in Group C, MSS, Bruce Letters, BS 5-24, reel 2, Bruce Collection. William Hanchett, *The Lincoln Murder Conspiracies* (Urbana: Univ. of Illinois Press, 1983), 48. "A Black Boy's Recollection of Some Great Men He Met," *Reformer,* Mar. 20, 1897 in Group E, misc., reel 4, Bruce Collection. "Martin R. Delaney."
16. "A Black Boy's Recollection of Some Great Men He Met."
17. *Negro Daily Times,* Dec. 24, 1922. J. E. Bruce, clipping file.
18. Howard K. Beale, *The Critical Years: A Study of Andrew Johnson and Reconstruction* (New York: Harcourt, Brace, 1930), 177. Leslie H. Fischel Jr., "Northern Prejudice and Negro Suffrage, 1865–1870," *Journal of Negro History* 39, no. 1 (Jan. 1954): 8. James McPherson, *The Struggle for Equality: Abolitionists and the Negro in the Civil War and Reconstruction* (Princeton: Princeton Univ. Press, 1964), 221.
19. Penn, *The Afro American Press,* 344. Rayford W. Logan, Michael R. Winston, Ernest Kaiser, eds., "John Edward Bruce," *The Dictionary of American Negro Biography* (New York: W. W. Norton & Co., 1982), 76–77. "Notable Colored Men and Women," [speech by J. E. Bruce, Apr. 26, 1915), in Group C, MSS, Bruce Letters, BS 5-15, reel 2, Bruce Collection. Bruce Grit's Column, *Negro World,* May 12, 1923, 4. Extant articles under the penname "Caleb Quotem" could not be found at the time of this writing.
20. Bruce, "A Sketch of My Life," Charles A. Johnson, "John Edward Bruce," *Cleveland Gazette,* Feb. 21, 1891, 1.
21. John E. Bruce, *Washington Colored Society* (Washington, 1877), 4, 6, 7, 10, 13–18, 20, 23–29. Bruce Grit, "The Yonkers News," *Colored American,* Feb. 14, 1903, 12.

22. Recommendation of C. Ridgely Waller to [Whom It May Concern], Dec. 29, 1877, in Group E, misc., 13–47, reel 3, Bruce Collection. Penn, *The Afro American Press*, 346.
23. [John E. Bruce], "Dare To Do Right," *St. Louis Tribune,* May 1878 in Group D, MSS, Bruce Poetry, B10-8, reel 3, Bruce Collection.
24. Untitled poem, written midnight, July 11, 1878, in Group D, MSS, Bruce Poetry, B 10-8, reel 3, Bruce Collection.
25. *Sunday Republic,* 1878 in Group D, MSS, Bruce Poetry, B 10-8, reel 3, Bruce Collection. *Washington Grit,* July 19, 1884, 2.
26. William V. Turner to J. E. Bruce, Aug. 23, 1878, in Group B, Letters Received, MSS, Autographed Letters, MS 177, reel 1, Bruce Collection.
27. "The Weekly Argus," in Group D, MSS, B8-126, reel 2, Bruce Collection. Penn, *The Afro American Press,* 346.
28. The quartet was composed of C. E. Howard, Theodore Ray, Richard J. Lee, and Bruce. "A Colored Campaign Club," *New York Times,* Sept. 24, 1880, 5. Bruce to J. A. Garfield, Sept. 24, 1880, reel 65, vol. 94, ser. 4, #005. Bruce to Garfield, Nov. 4, 1880, reel 66, vol. 95, ser. 4, #148. Bruce to Garfield, Mar. 17, 1881, reel 94, vol. 134, ser. 4, #260. James A. Garfield Papers.
29. "Edward W. Blyden, Alex. A. Crummell," in Group C, MSS, Bruce Letters, BS 5-21, reel 2, Bruce Collection.
30. Penn, *The Afro American Press,* 346. H. M. Shepard to Bruce, Sept. 3, 1881 in Group B, Letters Received, MSS, Autographed Letters, MS 137, reel 1, Bruce Collection.
31. "Negro Journalism," Oct. 19, 1881, in Group D, MSS, B7-83, reel 2, Bruce Collection.
32. J. E. Bruce to Mr. Hubbell, editor of the *Statesman,* June 16, 1914, in Group C, MSS, Bruce Letters, BS 5-26, reel 2, Bruce Collection. For Garnet's diplomatic career, see William Seraile, "The Brief Diplomatic Career of Henry Highland Garnet," *Phylon* 46 (spring 1985): 71–81.
33. A. T. Bissell to Bruce, Aug. 12, 1882, in Group B, Letters Received, MSS, Autographed Letters, MS 416, reel 1, Bruce Collection.
34. "Practical Questions," [1882] in Group D, MSS, B7-97, reel 2, Bruce Collection. Seraile, *Fire in His Heart,* 91, 115, 175.
35. *New York Globe,* Oct. 21, 1883, 1. "Reflections on the Decision in the Civil Right Cases," Nov. 1, 1883, [lecture by Bruce] in Group D, MSS, B6-47, reel 2, Bruce Collection. "Is This Our Country?" Nov. 7, 1888, in Group D, MSS, B7-99, reel 2, Bruce Collection. "Noted Race Women I Have Known and Met," Sept. 1, 1923, [lecture by Bruce] in Group C, MSS, Bruce Letters, BS 5-39, reel 2, Bruce Collection.
36. The paper was known as the *Grit* from its inaugural issue of December 21, 1883, until March 29, 1884, when it became known as the *Washington Grit.*

Chapter 2

1. "Public Men I Have Met," [1914], in Group C, Bruce Letters, BS 5-25, reel 2, Bruce Collection.
2. *Grit,* Dec. 21, 1883, 4; June 7, 1884, 2. *Washington Grit,* July 5, 1884, in Group E, misc., reel 4, Bruce Collection.
3. *New York Globe,* Feb. 9, 1884, 2. For the remarks of the *Kansan,* see *New York Globe,* Mar. 1, 1884, 2. For Fortune's remarks about Bruce's seedy dress, see the *Cleveland Gazette,* Oct. 12, 1889, 2. J. S. Clarkson to Bruce, Dec. 6, 1904, Group C, MSS, Bruce Letters, 4 A-3, reel 2, Bruce Collection.

4. *Grit*, Jan. 26, 1884, 4. *(Washington) Bee*, Jan. 5, 1884, 2, as quoted in Hal S. Chase, "Honey for Friends, Stings for Enemies: William Calvin Chase and the *Washington Bee,* 1882–1921" (Ph.D. diss., Univ. of Pennsylvania, 1973), 191.
5. Editorial, "The Arthur Boom," *Grit*, Feb. 9, 1884, 2.
6. Editorial, "Our Position and Our Politics," *Grit*, Mar. 1, 1884, 2. Editorial, "John A. Logan of Ill[inois]," *People's Advocate,* Mar. 29, 1884, 2.
7. *Grit*, Mar. 15, 1884, 2; May 3, 1884, 2; May 17, 1884, 2. Hanes Walton Jr., *Black Politics: A Theoretical and Structural Analysis* (Philadelphia: J. B. Lippincott Co., 1972), 90.
8. *Washington Grit,* Mar. 29, 1884, 2; Apr. 12, 1884, 2.
9. Ibid., May 3, 1884, 2; May 24, 1884, 2.
10. Ibid., May 3, 1884, 2; May 31, 1884, 2; July 5, 1884, 2; July 19, 1884, 2.
11. *Washington Grit,* July 12, 1884, 2.
12. Editorial, "The Nomination," *Washington Grit,* June 7, 1884, 2; June 14, 1884, 2.
13. James G. Blaine to Bruce, June 30, 1884, in Group B, Letters Received, B 2, reel 1, Bruce Collection.
14. Ibid., July 19, 1884, 2.
15. Ibid. *New York Globe,* Oct. 21, 1883, 1.
16. Editorial, "Our Leaders," *Washington Grit,* Aug. 2, 1884. See also June 21, 1884, 2; June 28, 1884, 2; and July 26, 1884, 2. B. F. Jones, chair Republican National Committee to Bruce, Aug. 22, 1884 in Group B, Letters Received, MSS, Autographed Letters, MS 417, reel 1, Bruce Collection.
17. To the Editor, Sept. 4, 1884, in Group C, Letters Sent by Bruce, BL 10, reel 2, Bruce Collection. *Washington Grit,* Sept. 6, 1884, 2; Sept. 20, 1884, 2.
18. Editorial, "The Kind of Republican We Are," *Washington Grit,* Sept. 27, 1884, 2.
19. *Washington Grit,* Oct. 18, 1884, 2.
20. Ibid., Sept. 6, 1884, 2; Oct. 11, 1884, 2. Bruce Grit, *New York Age,* Aug. 4, 1888, 1.
21. "The Democratic Return to Power: Its Effect?" *AME Church Review* 1 (July 1884): 213–50. For black views on Cleveland's victory, see "The Great Revolution," *New York Freeman,* Nov. 29, 1884, 1.
22. "Mr. Downing's Letter," *Cleveland Gazette,* Jan. 17, 1885, in John P. Green Papers, frame 1850, roll 6.
23. J. E. Bruce to the President [Grover Cleveland], Apr. 23, 1885, ser. 2, reel 11, Grover Cleveland Papers. Daniel Scott Lamont to J. E. Bruce, Apr. 23, 1885, ser. 4, reel 145, vol. 2, Grover Cleveland Papers.
24. [J. E. Bruce] to the editor [*Boston Traveller*], circa 1885 in Group C, Letters Sent by Bruce, BL 13, reel 2, Bruce Collection. M. E. Dodge to Bruce, Aug. 24, 1885, in Group B, Letters Received, MSS, Autographed Letters, MS 54, reel 1, Bruce Collection.
25. George F. Hoar to Bruce, Apr. 23, 1888, in Group H, Letters Received, H 14, reel 1, Bruce Collection.
26. Bruce Grit, "National Capitol Topics," *New York Age,* Apr. 28, 1888, 2.
27. Bruce Grit, "A Fraud," *New York Age,* May 12, 1888, 1.
28. Bruce Grit, "At The Nation's Capitol," *New York Age,* May 19, 1888, 1. *National Leader Supplement,* Washington, D.C., May 21, 1888, in Group D, MSS, B6-66, reel 2, Bruce Collection. Letter of Bruce in support of General Russell A. Alger, *National Leader Supplement,* May 21, 1888, in Group E, Bruce Fragments, no. 1, reel 3, Bruce Collection.

29. Bruce Grit, "At The National Capitol," *New York Age,* May 26, 1888, 1. Bruce to Magnus L. Robinson, Mar. 8, 1888, MSS, MG 253 in John E. Bruce Papers (additions).
30. T. Thomas Fortune to the *Sun,* May 21, 1888, in *New York Age,* June 2, 1888, 2. Bruce Grit, "Prejudice in the Church," *New York Age,* June 9, 1888, 1. T. Thomas Fortune, "The Parting of the Ways," *New York Age,* Dec. 15, 1888, 2. Editorial, "Where Is Your Proof?" *Cleveland Gazette,* Mar. 17, 1888, 2.
31. Wade Hampton, "What Negro Supremacy Means," *Forum* 5 (June 1888): 383.
32. Bruce Grit, "The Southern Conundrum," *New York Age,* June 2, 1888, 1. "Negro Votes of the North," *New York Age,* June 11, 1888, 1.
33. "Harrison and Morton," *New York Times,* June 26, 1888, 1. Editorial, "The Republican Platform," *New York Age,* June 30, 1888, 2. Bruce Grit, "The Negro Not an Issue," *New York Age,* July 14, 1888, 1. *Cleveland Gazette,* July 28, 1888, 2. T. McCants Stewart, "Opposed to Sideshows: Color Line in American Politics," *New York Age,* Aug. 1, 1888, 1.
34. Editorial, "Shame! Shame!" *Cleveland Gazette,* Sept. 1, 1888, 2.
35. Bruce Grit, "The President Making Campaign Thunder," *New York Age,* Sept. 1, 1888, 1.
36. Bruce Grit, "How the Workingman Is Controlled?" *New York Age,* Sept. 8, 1888, 1. "Ex-Rebels and Relatives in Office," *New York Age,* Oct. 6, 1888, 1. "Duty of Colored Voters," *New York Age,* Oct. 6, 1888, 1.
37. T. Thomas Fortune, "Fortune the Democrat," *Cleveland Gazette,* Oct. 27, 1888, 1.
38. Bruce Grit, "A Stroll in Philadelphia," *New York Age,* Nov. 10, 1888, 1.
39. Bruce Grit, "The Acts and the Apostates," *New York Age,* Nov. 10, 1888, 1. "The Negro in Politics: Colored Pastors in Harrison's Election," *New York Times,* Nov. 14, 1888, 1.
40. "They Say," *(Washington) Bee,* Jan. 26, 1889, 2. "New York Notes," *(Washington) Bee,* Mar. 9, 1889, 3. *New York Times,* Jan. 3, 1889, 2. *New York Age,* Jan. 12, 1889, 2. *Christian Recorder,* Jan. 31, 1889, 4.
41. Bruce Grit, "The Opinion in New York," *(Washington) Bee,* Feb. 2, 1889, 2.
42. Martha Bruce to My Dear Son, Feb. 7, 1889, in Group E, misc., reel 4, Bruce Collection.
43. Frederick Douglass to Magnus L. Robinson, Nov. 26, 1889, in *National Leader,* Jan. 19, 1889, 2. George F. Hoar to Bruce, Jan. 21, 1889, in Group H, Letters Received, H 8, reel 1, Bruce Collection. "Bruce Grit Interviews Rev. Dr. W. B. Derrick of New York," *(Washington) Bee,* Mar. 30, 1889, 2.
44. Editorial, "What the Colored People Need," *(Washington) Bee,* Mar. 23, 1889, 2. Bruce Grit, " Office Seekers," *Cleveland Gazette,* Mar. 30, 1889, 1.
45. Editorial, "The President and the Negro," *(Washington) Bee,* Apr. 13, 1889, 2.
46. *Cleveland Gazette,* Apr.? 1889 in Group E, misc., reel 4, Bruce Collection.
47. Bruce Grit, "How to Get Office," *Cleveland Gazette,* Apr. 6, 1889, 1.
48. Charles Stewart to Bruce, Apr. 9, 1889, in Group S, Letters Received, S 16, reel 1, Bruce Collection. E. M. Halford to Bruce in Group H, Letters Received, H 15, reel 1, Bruce Collection. Bruce Grit, "Chat and Chaff," *(Washington) Bee,* Apr. 13, 1889, 1.
49. Bruce Grit, "President Harrison as a Freemason," *(Washington) Bee,* Apr. 13, 1889, 1. Bruce Grit, "O'Hara After Office," *Cleveland Gazette,* May 4, 1889, 1. Editorial [no title], *Cleveland Gazette,* May 18, 1889, 2. J. E. Rankin to Frederick Douglass, [1889] John P. Davis Papers, reel 2.

50. Editorial, "The President," *(Washington) Bee,* May 11, 1889, 2.
51. Bruce Grit, "Scores Douglass," *Cleveland Gazette,* May 11, 1889, 1. Editorial, [no title] *Cleveland Gazette,* May 25, 1889, 2. J. E. Bruce, "Bruce versus Douglass," *Cleveland Gazette,* June 8, 1889, 1. Henry A. Spenser to Bruce, Mar. 22, 1910, Group B, Letters Received, MSS, Autographed Letters, typescript 274, reel 1, Bruce Collection. For Bruce's opposition to miscegenation, see Charles C. Dancy to Bruce, Jan. 30, 1899, Group B, Letters Received, reel 1, Bruce Collection. Bruce to Jesse S. Phillips, Mar. 23, 1910, Group C, Letters Sent by Bruce, BL 4-38, reel 2, Bruce Collection. Bruce Grit, "The Intermarrying of Races," *Colored American,* Jan. 11, 1902, 10. Bruce Grit, "Hot Shot," *Colored American,* June 28, 1902, 9. Bruce Grit, "Gotham Notes," *Colored American,* May 16, 1903, 6.
52. Editorial Notes, [circa 1889] in Group D, MSS, 9 E-2, reel 2, Bruce Collection.
53. W. E. Chandler to Bruce, May 20, 1889, in Group E, misc. articles, reel 3, Bruce Collection. Byron M. Cutcheon to Bruce, Mar. 11, 1890, in Group C, MSS, Bruce Letters, 4 A-37, reel 2, Bruce Collection. W. E Chandler to [J. M.] Townsend, Apr. 1, 1890, in Group C, MSS, Bruce Letters 4 A-14, reel 2, Bruce Collection. *(Washington) Bee,* May 18, 1889, 2. *(Washington) Bee,* June 29, 1889, 3.
54. "The President Is Alright," *Savannah Tribune,* May 25, 1889, 2.
55. Bruce Grit, "We Got the Best," *Cleveland Gazette,* June 1, 1889, 1. Editorial [no title], *Cleveland Gazette,* June 22, 1889, 2. Editorial [no title], *Cleveland Gazette,* July 6, 1889, 2.
56. Bruce Grit, "Up in Arms," *Cleveland Gazette,* July 13, 1889, 1.
57. "The Race's Doings," *Cleveland Gazette,* Aug. 24, 1889, 1. "Race's Doings," *Cleveland Gazette,* Oct. 5, 1889, 1. Editorial, "Harrison's Appointments," *Cleveland Gazette,* Oct. 19, 1889, 2. "Of Race Interest," *Cleveland Gazette,* Nov. 30, 1889, 1.
58. *(Washington) Bee,* Feb. 1, 1890, 1, 2.
59. Editorial, "The Recordership," *Cleveland Gazette,* Feb. 8, 1890, 2.
60. Bruce Grit, "Chandler Asks Aid," *Cleveland Gazette,* Mar. 1, 1890, 1. Editorial [no title], *Cleveland Gazette,* Mar. 8, 1890, 2.
61. *Cleveland Gazette,* Mar. 15, 1890, 1. [B. K.] Bruce to Frederick Douglass, Mar. 16, 1890, John P. Davis Papers, reel 2. Bruce Grit, "Mixed Schools," *Cleveland Gazette,* Apr. 26, 1890, 1.
62. "What I Saw and What I Heard," *(Washington) Bee,* May 3, 1890, 1. "For Shame," *Cleveland Gazette,* May 17, 1890, 1.
63. A check of the Washington's directories proved to be ambiguous. The 1876 directory listed a J. E. Bruce, messenger, residing at 411 K Street. There were two Charles Bruces, two Charles F. Bruces, and one Charles H. Bruce but no listing for a Charles E. Bruce. There was no listing for a John E. Bruce in 1877 (when presumably he was incarcerated) or 1878 (when he allegedly had been pardoned), but that name does appear in 1879 as a porter living at 912 Massachusetts Avenue, N. W., and the following year as an editor residing at 1305 12th Street, N. W. *(Washington) Bee,* May 17, 1890, 2. *New York Tribune,* Apr. 16, 1877, 1. *United States v Charles E. Bruce,* case 11, 291, box 45 16 E 3/14/12/2. Criminal Case files 1863–1934 RG 021 (Washington: National Archives and Records Center). *Boyd's Directory for the District of Columbia* (1876–1880). Bruce was arrested but not convicted on a petit larceny charge in 1880. Reports of Arrest in Records of Metropolitan Police, District of Columbia, RG 351.5, vol. 1, for year 1880. (Washington: National Archives and Records Center).

64. Bruce Grit, "Bruce Talks," *Cleveland Gazette,* May 31, 1890, 1.
65. Ibid.
66. Editorial, [no title] *Cleveland Gazette,* May 31, 1890, 2.
67. Editorial, "The Recorder's Answers," *Cleveland Gazette,* June 7, 1890, 2. J. E. Bruce, "Renews His Charges," *Cleveland Gazette,* June 14, 1890, 1. J. E. Bruce, "All White," *Cleveland Gazette,* June 21, 1890, 1. Editorial, "The Truth Will Out," *Cleveland Gazette,* June 21, 1890, 2.
68. Editorial, "Hold, Viper, You Bite a File," *(Washington) Bee,* July 5, 1890, 2. *(Washington) Bee,* Oct. 25, 1890, 2. *Cleveland Gazette,* Sept. 6, 1890, 1. *Cleveland Gazette,* Oct. 11, 1890, 1. *Cleveland Gazette,* Oct. 25, 1890, 1. Chase, "Honey for Friends," 39–40, 44. "On Tap," *Cleveland Globe* as reported in the *(Washington) Bee,* Oct. 11, 1890, 1.
69. The charge is not substantiated by any records. Editorial, "Hard Up," *(Washington) Bee,* June 2, 1894, 2. For Schayer's dismissal, see *(Washington) Bee,* Sept. 13, 1890, 2.
70. Bruce Grit, "Blair Bill Symposium," *Cleveland Gazette,* Mar. 15, 1890, 1. Bruce Grit, "The Race's Doings," *Cleveland Gazette,* May 3, 1890, 1. [Blair Educational Bill, 1890], in Group D, MSS, 9 E-44, reel 2, Bruce Collection.
71. [Force Bill, 1890], Group D, MSS, B 6-43, reel 2, Bruce Collection. Bruce Grit, "Opposed to It," *Cleveland Gazette,* Aug. 2, 1890, 1. J. E. Bruce, "Amend and Pass It," *Cleveland Gazette,* Aug. 23, 1890, 1. "Save the Party," *Cleveland Gazette,* Feb. 7, 1891, 1. [Force Bill, circa 1891], Group D, MSS, B 6-44, reel 2, Bruce Collection.
72. Frederick Douglass, "The True Problem," *Cleveland Gazette,* Nov. 15, 1890, 1.
73. "Townsend Talks," *Cleveland Gazette,* Feb. 15, 1890, 1. Editorial, "J. M. Townsend," *(Washington) Bee,* Dec. 1, 1890, 2. J. E. Bruce, "A Failure," *Cleveland Gazette,* Oct. 18, 1890, 1. J. E. Bruce, "Those Interviews," *Cleveland Gazette,* Dec. 20, 1890, 1. Editorial, "Apologists and Cringers," *Cleveland Gazette,* Dec. 13, 1890, 2. Bruce Grit, "Reciprocity," *Cleveland Gazette,* Feb. 28, 1891, 1. Bruce Grit, "We & Co.," *Cleveland Gazette,* June 20, 1891, 2. J. E. Bruce, "Bruce's Facts," *Cleveland Gazette,* July 11, 1891, 1. Bruce Grit, "Good Reasons," *Cleveland Gazette,* Aug. 15, 1891, 1. David A. Gerber, *Black Ohio and the Color Line,* 1860–1915 (Urbana: Univ. of Illinois Press, 1976), 331.
74. "The Race's Doings," *Cleveland Gazette,* Mar. 15, 1890, 1.
75. J. E. Bruce, "What Caused the Great Republican Waterloo of a Few Weeks Ago," *Cleveland Gazette,* Nov. 2, 1890, 1. *Cleveland Gazette,* Nov. 7, 1891, 2.
76. For a sketch of James S. Clarkson, see *(Washington) Bee,* Mar. 23, 1890, 1. "General Clarkson's Opinion," [Mar. 21, 1891 letter to Bruce], *Denver Statesman,* Sept. 25, 1903, in Group E, misc. articles, reel 3, Bruce Collection. Clarkson to Bruce, Mar. 21, 1891, in Group C, MSS, Bruce Letters, 4 A-61, reel 2, Bruce Collection. "People Talked About," circa 1916, Group D, MSS, 9 E-101, reel 2, Bruce Collection. Clarkson to Theodore Roosevelt, Nov. 15, 1901, Theodore Roosevelt Papers, reel 22, ser. 1.
77. George Chandler to Bruce, Aug. 3, 1891, MSS, Letters, 4 A-17, reel 2, Bruce Collection. A. B. Nettleton to Bruce, Aug. 22, 1891 in Group C, MSS, Bruce Letters, 4 A-10, reel 2, Bruce Collection. J. S. Clarkson to Bruce, Sept. 11, 1891 in Group C, MSS, Bruce Letters, 4 A-5, reel 2, Bruce Collection.
78. *Negro Daily Times,* Oct. 20, 1922 in J. E. Bruce, clipping file. Penn, *The Afro American Press and Its Editors,* 538. *Cleveland Gazette,* May 30, 1891, 3. [Letterhead] The

National Circulatory and Distributing Company [1890] in Group C, Letters Sent by Bruce, 4 BL-59, reel 2, Bruce Collection.
79. Richard L. Beard and Cyril E. Zoerner II, "Associated Negro Press: Its Founding, Ascendancy, and Demise," *Journalism Quarterly* 46 (spring 1969): 47–52.
80. J. S. Clarkson to Bruce, July 13, 1892, in Group C, MSS, Bruce Letters, 4 A-39, reel 2, Bruce Collection.
81. Mrs. John A. Logan to Bruce, Sept. 30, 1892, in Group C, MSS, Bruce Letters, 4 A-60, reel 2, Bruce Collection.
82. W. M. Ha[?], chairman, Speakers' Bureau, Republican National Committee to George A. Myers, Sept. 29, 1892, in George A. Myers Collection, frame 008, roll 1.
83. Editorial, "The Republicans Will Win," *Cleveland Gazette,* Oct. 22, 1892, 2.
84. Bruce to Benjamin Harrison, Oct. 25, 1892, Benjamin Harrison Papers, reel 85, ser. 2.
85. Editorial, "The Republican Defeat," *(Washington) Bee,* Nov. 12, 1892, 2. *New York Times,* Nov. 7, 1889, 1. Gerber, *Black Ohio and the Color Line,* 331.
86. [Tribute to Martha Bruce], Dec. 12, 1892, in J. E. Bruce, clipping file. [Dedication to Martha Bruce], Oct. 14, 1896, in Group D, MSS, D 10-4, reel 3, Bruce Collection. *Boyd's Directory for the District of Columbia, 1890–1892.*
87. Alexander Crummell to Bruce, Jan. 27, 1894, Group C, Letters Received, C 14, reel 1, Bruce Collection. James S. Clarkson to Bruce, Dec. 28, 1892, Group C, Letters Received, C 10, reel 1, ibid.
88. *Negro World,* May 12, 1923, 4.
89. Bruce to General [James S. Clarkson], Feb. 6, 1893, Group C, Letters Received, C 8, reel 1, Bruce Collection. [Tyler, Texas? lynching fragment, n.d.], Group E, Fragment, reel 3, Bruce Collection.
90. Bruce to Grover Cleveland, Mar. 25, 1893, Grover Cleveland Papers, ser. 2, reel 74.
91. J. K. Jones to Bruce, Apr. 12, 1893, Group C, Bruce Letters, 4 A-45, reel 2, Bruce Collection. Hoke Smith, Secretary [of the Interior] to Commissioner General Land Office, Dept. of the Interior, Washington, D.C., May 10, 1893, Group B, Letters Received, MSS, Autographed Letters, MS 418, reel 1, Bruce Collection.
92. My Dear Doctor [Alexander Crummell], Jan. 17, 1894, Group C, Letters Sent by Bruce, BL 4-62, reel 2, Bruce Collection.
93. The Irrespressible Conflict, Mar. 13, 1894 [draft of a speech?] Group D, MSS, B 7-104, reel 2, Bruce Collection.
94. [A Tribute to Fortune, circa 1894], T. Thomas Fortune Scrapbook. T. Thomas Fortune to Bruce, Mar. 23, 1893, Group F, Letters Received, F 2, reel 1, Bruce Collection.
95. Jere A. Brown to M. A. Hanna, Apr. 11, 1896, George A. Myers Collection, frames 338–339, roll 1.
96. S. R. Scottron to John P. Green, June 12, 1896, John P. Green Papers, frame 1151, roll 1.
97. Edward E. Cooper to John P. Green, July 20, 1896, John P. Green Papers, frame 0024, roll 2. Charles S. Olcott, *William McKinley* (Boston: Houghton Mifflin, 1916), 310.
98. M. A. Hanna to Daniel Murray, Aug. 6, 1896, Daniel A. Murray Papers, reel 1.
99. Edward W. Blyden to Bruce, Sept. 26, 1896, Group E, Bruce Scrapbook 1, reel 3, Bruce Collection.

100. Ernest Lyons to J. P. Green, Oct. 2, 1896, John P. Green Papers, frames 0094–0095, roll 2. Lyons to Green, Oct. 15, 1896, ibid., frame 0124, roll 2. Lyons to George A. Myers, George A. Myers Collection, frames 0112–0113, roll 1.
101. E. B. Cantine, President Albany County [N.Y.] Repub. Organization to Bruce, Oct. 26, 1896, Group B, Letters Received, MSS, Autographed Letters, typescript 201, reel 1, Bruce Collection.
102. *The Freeman,* Nov. 7, 1896, 4. *Congressional Quarterly's Guide to U.S. Elections,* 2d ed. (Washington: Congressional Quarterly, 1985), 344.
103. James S. Clarkson to B. T. Washington, Feb. 7, 1896, Harlan, *The Booker T. Washington Papers,* 14 vols. (Urbana: Univ. of Illinois Press, 1975–84), 4:110–14. Clarkson to Bruce, Nov. 25, 1896, Group B, Letters Received, MSS, Autographed Letters, typescript 131, reel 1, Bruce Collection.
104. Editorial, "What About the Colored Man," *Washington Post,* Nov. 7, 1896, 6. Editorial, "A Colored Minister," *(Washington) Bee,* July 4, 1896, 4. Blanche K. Bruce to B. T. Washington, Nov. 12, 1896; Jan. 25, 1897; Feb. 1, 1897; Feb. 4, 1897. Harlan, *The Booker T. Washington Papers,* 4:230, 258–59, 261. Louis R. Harlan, *Booker T. Washington: The Making of a Black Leader, 1856–1901* (New York: Oxford Univ. Press, 1972), 257. For a complete analysis of a black cabinet member, see William Seraile, "A Colored Man in the Cabinet: An Idea before Its Time," *Journal of the Afro-American Historical and Genealogical Society* 11 (spring and fall, 1990): 79–92.
105. Ralph W. Tyler to George A. Myers, Nov. 14, 1896, frames 585–87, roll 1; W. Arnett to Myers, Nov. 11, 1896, frame 574, roll 1; Samuel Thompson to Myers, Nov. 11, 1896, frames 578–80, roll 1, George A. Myers Collection
106. James S. Clarkson to Bruce, Nov. 25, 1896, Group B, Letters Received, MSS, Autographed Letters, typescript 131, reel 1, Bruce Collection. Clarkson to Bruce, Feb. 4, 1897, Group B, Letters Received, reel 1, Bruce Collection. John A. Porter to Bruce, Aug. 2, 1897, William McKinley Papers, ser. 2, reel 20, vol. 96:321.
107. F. J. Loudin to John P. Green, Apr. 11, 1897, John P. Green Papers, frames 0510–0519, roll 2.
108. Albert S. White to John P. Green, Jan. 23, 1897, John P. Green Papers, frame 0326, roll 2. "His Rule," *Cleveland World,* Apr. 25, 1897, John P. Green Papers, frame 1864, roll 6.
109. Will Green to Dear Parents, July 8, 1897, John P. Green Papers, frames 0669–0671, roll 2. M. A. Hanna to John P. Green (telegram), July 10, 1897, John P. Green Papers, frame 0672, roll 2.
110. B. K. Bruce to John P. Green, July 25, 189[?], John P. Green Papers, frames 0699–0700, roll 2. Charles W. Chesnutt to Green, Dec. 7, 1897, John P. Green Papers, frame 1098, roll 2. "Green's New Job," *Cleveland Plain Dealer,* Aug. 4, 1897, John P. Green Papers, frame 0726, roll 2.
111. *Colored American,* May 28, 1898, 4.
112. Ibid., Apr. 23, 1898, 1, 4. *Freeman,* May 7, 1898, as cited in Willard B. Gatewood, *"Smoked Yankees" and the Struggle for Empire: Letters from Negro Soldiers, 1898–1902* (Urbana: Univ. of Illinois Press, 1971), 4–6, 21. *Afro American Sentinel,* Apr. 16, 1898, 1.
113. George A. Myers to John P. Green, May 3, 1898, John P. Green Papers, frames 0207–0210, roll 3.

114. T. G. Steward, "The First Move in the War," *Independent* (Apr. 25, 1898): 535–36. Gatewood, *"Smoked Yankees,"* 21–23, 162.
115. F. J. Loudin to John P. Green, May 14, 1898, John P. Green Papers, frames 0225–0228, roll 3.
116. Bruce Grit, "Valor of Negro Soldier," *Colored American,* May 7, 1898, 1, 5.
117. Bruce Grit, "The Doom of the Spaniards," *Colored American,* May 14, 1898, 1.
118. Gatewood, *"Smoked Yankees,"* 8–11.
119. Ibid., 31–35, 82–83. "Bruce Grit Speaks," *Richmond Planet,* June 18, 1898, 1. Editorial, "The Post's Strictures," *Richmond Planet,* June 4, 1898, 2. Bruce Grit, "Hard Lines for the Post," *Colored American,* June 25, 1898, 1.
120. John P. Green to John M. Clark, June 20, 1898, John P. Green Papers, frame 0285, roll 3.
121. Alfred Brewington to John P. Green, Sept. 4, 1901, John P. Green Papers, frames 964–966, roll 3.
122. Bruce Grit, "Opposed to Color Line," *Colored American,* Apr. 2, 1899, 3. Gatewood, *"Smoked Yankees,"* 231–32.
123. W. E. B. Du Bois to B. T. Washington, Sept. 24, 1895, in Herbert Aptheker, *Correspondence of W. E. B. Du Bois,* 3 vols. (Amherst: Univ. of Massachusetts Press, 1973–78), 1:39. Bruce to Washington, Oct. 14, 1895, in Louis R. Harlan, ed., *The Booker T. Washington Papers,* 4:55–56. Editorial, "Apologizing for Wrongs," *(Washington) Bee,* Oct. 19, 1895, 4. Editorial, "Toadyism," *(Washington) Bee,* Nov. 2, 1895, 4.
124. Edward W. Blyden to Francis J. Grimke, Sept. 15, 1895 in Carter G. Woodson, ed., *The Works of Francis J. Grimke,* 4 vols. (Washington: Associated Publishers, 1942), 4:40–43. Blyden to B. T. Washington, Sept. 24, 1895, in Harlan, *The Booker T. Washington Papers,* 4:26–28.
125. For Crummell's views on higher education, see Harlan, *The Booker T. Washington Papers,* 4:255–56, 321–22. Crummell to Bruce, Nov. 4, 1895, Group C, Letters Received, C 15, reel 1, Bruce Collection.
126. Emmett J. Scott to B. T. Washington, July 16, 1898, Harlan, *The Booker T. Washington Papers,* 4:448. Bruce Grit, "Apostles of Industrialism," *Colored American,* July 6, 1898, 1, 2. [Undated draft], Group D, MS B 7-91, reel 2, Bruce Collection.
127. Bruce Grit, "Business Is the Key," *Denver Statesman,* June 24, 1899, Group E, misc., reel 4, Bruce Collection. Washington to Bruce, Apr. 21, 1896, Group W, Letters, W 4, reel 1, Bruce Collection. T. Thomas Fortune to Washington, Aug. 25, 29, 31, 1899; Sept. 7, 1899, Harlan, *The Booker T. Washington Papers,* 5:182–83, 185–86, 188, 193, 197; Edward E. Cooper to Washington, Sept. 8, 1899, 5: 199; Washington to Fortune, Sept. 16, 1899, 5:207.
128. *Cleveland Gazette,* Sept. 16, 1899, Group E, misc., reel 4, Bruce Collection. John E. Bruce, "Mr. Washington's Mission," *Colored American,* Sept. 23, 1899, 6. Washington to T. Thomas Fortune, Oct. 28, 1899, Harlan, *The Booker T. Washington Papers,* 5:249. Fortune to Washington, Nov. 1, 1899, *The Booker T. Washington Papers,* 5: 249 n. 2.
129. "A Distinguished Man," [1899], Group E, misc., reel 4, Bruce Collection. Charles Alexander, *One Hundred Distinguished Leaders* (Atlanta: Franklin Print Co., 1899), 57. Editorial, "Bouquet for 'Bruce Grit,'" *Colored American,* Sept. 2, 1899, 4. Edward E. Cooper to Bishop Alexander Walters, May 31, 1899, Group B, Letters Received, TS 317, reel 1, Bruce Collection.

130. Bruce Grit, "Will Reap the Whirlwind," *Colored American,* Dec. 17, 1898, 2.
131. Editorial, "Ex Governor Pinchback," *Colored American,* Dec. 17, 1898, 4. John C. Davey to Bruce, Dec. 27, 1898, Group B, Letters Received, MSS, Autographed Letters, MS 148, reel 1, Bruce Collection.
132. Thornbrough, *T. Thomas Fortune,* 181–84. Editorial, "As to Mass Meetings and Mr. Fortune," *Colored American,* Dec. 24, 1898, 4. Bruce Grit, "Facts for the Millions," *Colored American,* Jan. 21, 1899, 2. T. Thomas Fortune to B. T. Washington, Dec. 14, 1898, Harlan, *The Booker T. Washington Papers,* 4:530–31.
133. Mrs. J. M. Holland to B. T. Washington, [Dec. 21, 1898], Harlan, *The Booker T. Washington Papers,* 4: 543–44. For how Myers named Mark Hanna "uncle," see the *Guardian,* Mar. 12, 1904, 4. George A. Myers to John P. Green, Dec. 9, 1898, John P. Green Papers, frames 513–16, roll 3. Myers to Green, Dec. 20, 1898, John P. Green Papers, frames 533–36, roll 3. Myers to Green, Dec. 28, 1898, John P. Green Papers, frames 543–46, roll 3. Myers to Green, July 29, 1898, John P. Green Papers, frames 379–81, roll 3. Fortune to Washington, Dec. 14, 1898, Harlan, *The Booker T. Washington Papers,* 4:535. "Gentlemen from Georgia," *Savannah Tribune,* Dec. 24, 1898, 2, as quoted in *Colored American,* n.d.
134. John P. Green, *Facts Stranger than Fiction: Seventy Years of a Busy Life with Reminiscences of Many Great and Good Men and Women* (Cleveland: Rich Printing Co., 1920), 267–69.
135. Jere A. Brown to John P. Green, Jan. 21, 1899, John P. Green Papers, frames 597–98, roll 3.
136. Bruce Grit, "Dancy and Miller," *Star of Zion,* Jan. 12, 1899, Group E, misc., reel 4, Bruce Collection. Bruce Grit, "Caucasian Ties of Blood," *Colored American,* May 13, 1899, 7.
137. Bruce Grit, "What the Council Can Do," *Colored American,* Feb. 25, 1899, 5. Daniel Murray to Bruce, Mar. 1, 1899, Group M, MS 8, reel 1, Bruce Collection. "Disfranchising Negroes," *New York Evening Post,* Feb. 21, 1899, 4.
138. Bruce Grit, "Notes of the Inner Circle," *Colored American,* Apr. 8, 1899, 1.
139. [Untitled], Dec. 16, 1898, MSS, Letters, 4 A-40, reel 2, Bruce Collection. James S. Clarkson to Bruce, June 30, 1899, Group B, Letters Received, MSS, Autographed Letters, MS 353, reel 1, Bruce Collection. W. E. Chandler to Bruce, Dec. 20, 1899, Group C, MSS, Bruce Letters, 4 A-1, reel 2, Bruce Collection. James S. Clarkson to Bruce, Feb. 5, 1900, Group C, MSS, Bruce Letters, 4 A-44, reel 2, Bruce Collection.
140. Bruce Grit, "Bruce Grit on His Muscles," *Colored American,* Aug. 19, 1899, 3. "Two Presidents Compared," *Colored American,* May 27, 1899, 1, 4. "Arraignment of McKinley," *Colored American,* Aug. 5, 1899, 1, 4. "Bruce at Pilgrim's Rest," *Colored American,* Sept. 16, 1899, 1, 4. "Race First, Party Next," *Colored American,* Oct. 28, 1899, 6. "The Council Not Involved," *Colored American,* Nov. 11, 1899, 1, 5.

Chapter 3

1. Bruce Grit, "Mr. White As a Host," *Colored American,* Jan. 13, 1900, 2.
2. T. Thomas Fortune to B. T. Washington, Feb. 20, 1900, Harlan, *The Booker T. Washington Papers,* 5:444–45.
3. Joseph E. Ransdell to Washington, Feb. 9, 1900, Harlan, *The Booker T. Washington Papers,* 5:437–38. Ransdell to Washington, Mar. 10, 1900, Harlan, *The Booker*

T. *Washington Papers*, 6:420–21. For George H. White's views, see Aptheker, *A Documentary History of the Negro People in the United States*, 2:816–17. For Bruce's views, see *Colored American*, Feb. 25, 1899, 5; June 29, 1901, 4.
4. Bruce Grit, "Money for the Council," *Colored American*, Jan. 20, 1900, 1, 9.
5. Bruce Grit, "The Negro Not Inferior," *Colored American*, Feb. 24, 1900, 2.
6. Editorial, "We Americans Are a Funny People," *Colored American*, Apr. 21, 1900, 8. Bruce Grit, "A Southern Pastime," *Colored American*, Feb. 3, 1900, 1, 13. Bruce to Wu Ting Fan, May 26, 1900, Group B, Letters Received, B 16, reel 1, Bruce Collection. J. E. Bruce, *The Blood Red Record: A Review of the Horrible Lynchings and Burnings of Negroes by Civilized White Men in the United States* (Albany: Argus Co., 1900), 3, 5, 12, 13, 15, 23, 26–27. Bruce Grit, "Bruce on Business," *Colored American*, Mar. 16, 1901, 9.
7. *AME Church Review* (Oct. 1896): 235.
8. Frederic J. Loudin to Bruce, Apr. 29, 1900, in Martin Kilson and Adelaide Hill, *Apropos of Africa: Afro American Leaders and the Romance of Africa* (Garden City, N.Y.: Anchor Books, 1971), 141–45. "South Africa Widens Circle of Boer War Heroes to Honor Blacks," *New York Times*, Oct. 8, 1999, A7.
9. "The Political Horoscope," *Colored American*, June 23, 1900, 7.
10. *Colored American*, July 7, 1900, 8.
11. Bruce Grit, "Issues of the Hour," *Colored American*, July 7, 1900, 9. Bruce Grit, "Issues of the Hour," *Colored American*, July 28, 1900, 4. Bruce Grit, "The Big Convention," *Colored American*, June 30, 1900, 6. John Tweedy, *A History of Republican National Committees, 1856–1908* (Danbury, Conn., 1910), 324.
12. Editorial, "McKinley and Roosevelt," *Colored American*, June 23, 1900, 8.
13. Bruce Grit, "Vice Presidential Timber," *Colored American*, Mar. 10, 1900, 1, 3. Bruce Grit, "The Political Horoscope," *Colored American*, Apr. 14, 1900, 7.
14. Unidentified soldier to Bruce, June 12, 1899, Group B, Letters Received, MSS, Autographed Letters, MS 56, reel 1, Bruce Collection. Bruce Grit, "New York's Next Governor," *Colored American*, Oct. 22, 1898, 1.
15. Henry Y. Arnett to George A. Myers, Sept. 1, 1900, George A. Myers Collection, frames 0298–0300, roll 8. John E. Bruce, "A New Slavery," *Freeman*, Sept. 22, 1900, 4.
16. Bruce Grit, "Gotham Notes," *Colored American*, Aug. 4, 1900, 2.
17. Bruce Grit, "Bruce Grit's Melange," *Colored American*, Aug. 18, 1900, 2.
18. Ibid. J. E. Bruce, "The Impending Campaign," *Colored American*, Sept. 1, 1900, 2.
19. John E. Bruce, "Political Weekly Review," *Colored American*, Sept. 29, 1900, 5. Thornbrough, *T. Thomas Fortune*, 204–5.
20. For letters of dissatisfied soldiers, see Gatewood, *"Smoked Yankees,"* 247, 248, 252, 253, 257. Bruce Grit, "Russia's 'Black Byron,'" *Colored American*, July 8, 1899, 2. "Bruce at Pilgrim's Rest," *Colored American*, Sept. 16, 1899, 1, 4. Bruce Grit, "Issues of the Hour," *Colored American*, July 7, 1900, 9. Editorial, [no title], *Colored American*, Nov. 4, 1899, 4. Unidentified soldier to Bruce, June 22, 1899, Group B, Letters Received, reel 1, Bruce Collection.
21. Frank Moss, comp. *Story of the Riot* (New York: Citizens' Protective League, 1900), 1–79. Thornbrough, *T. Thomas Fortune*, 198–201. Bruce Grit, "The New York Race Riot," *Colored American*, Sept. 1, 1900, 7. John E. Bruce, "Politics in Greater New York City," *Freeman*, Sept. 8, 1900, 2. John E. Bruce, "Tammany and the Negro," *Colored American*, Sept. 8, 1900, 2. Bruce Grit, "The Negro in New York Politics," *Colored American*, Sept. 29, 1900, 3.

22. Benjamin W. Arnett to Charles Dick, July 8, 1900, George A. Myers Collection, frames 105–6, roll 4. C. F. Adams to Myers, July 18, 1900; July 22, 1900, George A. Myers Collection, frames 147, 169, roll 4.
23. Theophile T. Allain to Charles Dick, Aug. 8, 1900; Aug. 13, 1900, George A. Myers Collection, frames 0197, 0203, roll 8.
24. John P. Green to George A. Myers, Aug. 15, 1900, George A. Myers Collection, frames 0216–0218, roll 8.
25. "Press Association Notes," *Freeman,* Sept. 1, 1900, 4. Bruce Grit, "Facts for the Millions," *Colored American,* Jan. 21, 1899, 2.
26. Perry S. Heath to Bruce, Aug. 22, 1900, Group H, Letters Received, H 6, reel 1, Bruce Collection. Editorial, "The Hindsightedness of the National Committee," *Colored American,* Sept. 1, 1900, 8. "It Is Said," *Colored American,* Sept. 15, 1900, 13. George A. Myers to R. L. Hamilton, Sept. 26, 1900, George A. Myers Collection, frame 0354, roll 8.
27. Albert B. George, "The Colored Democrat Split," *Colored American,* Sept. 29, 1900, 10. For *Albany Spectator,* n.d., see *Colored American,* Mar. 3, 1900, 2.
28. "The Political Horoscope," *Colored American,* Oct. 6, 1900, 5.
29. Editorial, "Politics in New York," *Colored American,* Sept. 29, 1900, 8. C. F. Adams to My Dear Sir, Oct. 30, 1900, George A. Myers Collection, frame 0388, roll 8.
30. Jere A. Brown to Myers, Sept. 18, 1900, George A. Myers Collection, frames 0337–0339, roll 8. Adams to Myers, Nov. 17, 1900, frame 0425, roll 8. *Colored American,* Oct. 27, 1900, 8. Cyrus F. Adams to Myers, Nov. ? 1900, George A. Myers Collection, frame 397, roll 8.
31. John P. Green to Myers, Nov. 12, 1900, George A. Myers Collection, frames 0405–0408, roll 8.
32. George A. Myers to William McKinley, Nov. 15, 1900, George A. Myers Collection, frames 759–60, roll 3. Myers to John P. Green, Nov. ? 1900, George A. Myers Collection, frames 756–58, roll 3.
33. Grit, "Race First, Party Next," 2.
34. William T. Anderson to George A. Myers, Nov. 15, 1900, George A. Myers Collection, frame 0414, roll 4. Jere A. Brown to Myers, Nov. 26, 1900, George A. Myers Collection, frames 0442–0444, roll 4. Myers to John P. Green, Dec. 7, 1900, John P. Green Papers, frames 790–93, roll 3. Myers to Daniel A. Murray, Aug. 14, 1899, Daniel A. Murray Papers, reel 1.
35. G. F. Franklin to Bruce, Dec. 29, 1900, Group B, Letters Received, MSS, Autographed Letters, MS 342, reel 1, Bruce Collection. Editorial, [no title], *Colored American,* Mar. 16, 1901, 8; May 1, 1901, 8; July 20, 1901, 8.
36. John E. Bruce, "Hon. Theodore Roosevelt," *Colored American,* Apr. 27, 1901, 7. Editorial, [untitled], *Colored American,* Apr. 27, 1901, 8.
37. Alfred Brewington to John P. Green, Sept. 29, 1901, John P. Green Papers, frames 009–010, roll 3. For Parker, see *Colored American,* Sept. 14, 1901, 12.
38. Thornbrough, *T. Thomas Fortune,* 219–20.
39. James S. Clarkson to Theodore Roosevelt, Nov. 15, 1901, Theodore Roosevelt Papers, ser. 1, reel 22. George B. Cortelyou to Clarkson, Nov. 19, 1901, Theodore Roosevelt Papers, ser. 1, reel 327.
40. "Reward of the Faithful," *Colored American,* Mar. 1, 1902, 9.
41. Thornbrough, *T. Thomas Fortune,* 229–32.
42. Ibid., 232.

43. *Colored American,* July 5, 1902, 11. Bruce Grit, "Gotham's Notes," *Colored American,* July 26, 1902, 3. "John E. Bruce Appointed," *South African Spectator,* Aug. 23, 1902, Group E, misc., reel, 4, Bruce Collection.
44. Bruce Grit, "Time's Mutations," *Colored American,* Sept. 6, 1902, 2.
45. James S. Clarkson to Whitefield McKinlay, Oct. 13, 1902, Whitefield McKinlay Papers, reel 1. "The Political Horoscope," *Colored American,* Nov. 1, 1902, 2.
46. James S. Clarkson to Booker T. Washington, Oct. 16, 1902, Harlan, *The Booker T. Washington Papers,* 6:550–52. James S. Clarkson to William Loeb Jr., Oct. 20, 1902, Theodore Roosevelt Papers, reel 30. *New York Times,* Jan. 29, 1938, 15. "Plum for Anderson," *New York Age,* Mar. 9, 1905, 1; Mar. 30, 1905, 2.
47. Robert W. Taylor, "Disgraces the Race," *Colored American,* Jan. 11, 1902. Bruce Grit, "It Was a Boomerang," *Colored American,* Feb. 1, 1902, 1, 4.
48. Bruce Grit, "Gotham Notes," *Colored American,* Jan. 17, 1903, 11. *Denver Statesman,* Feb. 2, 1903, Group E, misc., reel 4, Bruce Collection.
49. Bruce Grit, "Hon. John C. Dancy," *Colored American,* Sept. 20, 1902, 5. Bruce Grit, "Gotham Notes," *Colored American,* Feb. 7, 1903, 2.
50. E. A. Johnson, "How to Help the South," *Colored American,* Sept. 27, 1902, 12.
51. Bruce Grit, "Gotham Notes," *Colored American,* Feb. 14, 1903, 2–3.
52. Bruce Grit, "Gotham Notes," *Colored American,* Mar. 21, 1903, 7, 9. J. E. Bruce, "The Negro and His Future," circa 1902, Group D, MS 9 E-71, reel 2, Bruce Collection.
53. *Brooklyn Daily Eagle,* Apr. 4, 1903, Group E, misc., reel 4, Bruce Collection.
54. "Grover Cleveland on Negro Problem," *New York Times,* Apr. 15, 1903, 20. [draft], Apr. 17, 1903, Group D, MSS, B 11-31, reel 3, Bruce Collection. Grit, "Bruce Grit's Melange," *Colored American,* Apr. 18, 1903, 2, 15. Grit, "Gotham Notes," *Colored American,* May 9, 1903, 6–7. J. E. Bruce to Editor, "Mr. Cleveland and the Negro," *New York Tribune,* May 11, 1903, 12. Harlan, *The Booker T. Washington Papers,* 7:113–18.
55. Bruce's diary entry for June 8, 1904, Group E., misc., reel 4, Bruce Collection. John E. Bruce, "Praises President's Letter," letter to the editor, *New York Tribune,* Dec. 5, 1902, 10. Bruce Grit, "The Impending Crisis," *Colored American,* Nov. 21, 1903, 9, 12. John E. Bruce, *Occasional Political Tracts,* nos. 1–2. [1904], Schomburg Center [microfilm].
56. Grit, "Gotham Notes," *Colored American,* Aug. 23, 1902, 11.
57. George A. Myers to John P. Green, July 5, 1904, John P. Green Papers, frames 0717–0722, roll 4.
58. B. T. Washington to Edwin Doak Mead, Oct. 24, 1904, Harlan, *The Booker T. Washington Papers,* 8:109–10. H. A. Williamson to the editor of *New York Sun,* Aug. 12, 1904, MSS, 52 (personal papers, correspondence) Henry A. Williamson Papers, reel 1.
59. Bruce's diary note, Dec. 17, 1904, Group E, misc., reel 4, Bruce Collection.
60. T. G. Steward to Adjutant General, Twenty-fifth Infantry, June 30, 1906; Col. R. W. Hoyt to Military Secretary, July 1, 1906, in vol. 6, S. Doc. #701, 61st Cong., 3d sess., Dec. 12, 1910, 1390–91.
61. *New York Times,* Aug. 21, 1906, 2. *New York Tribune,* Aug. 26, 1906, 4. For a full account, see John D. Weaver, *The Brownsville Raid* (New York: W. W. Norton, 1971).
62. *New York Times,* Nov. 25, 1906, pt. 3, magazine sect., 2. Theophilus G. Steward, "New Fort Brown Version," *New York Tribune,* Aug. 26, 1906, 4. Ann J. Lane, *The*

Brownsville Affair: National Crisis and the Black Reaction (Port Washington: Kennikat Press, 1971), 23. "Reprieve Granted Black Soldiers After Sixty-six Years," *Jet* 43 (Oct. 19, 1972): 20–21.
63. *New York Times,* Nov. 14, 1906, 3; Nov. 16, 1906, 1. Lewis N. Wynell, "Brownsville: The Reaction of the Negro Press," *Phylon* 33 (summer 1972): 156.
64. B. T. Washington to T. G. Steward, Nov. 10, 1906, Booker T. Washington Papers, reel 16, Library of Congress. Thornbrough, *T. Thomas Fortune*, 281–85. Washington to Theodore Roosevelt, Nov. 26, 1906, Harlan, *The Booker T. Washington Papers,* 9:147–48.
65. Washington to Roosevelt, Dec. 16, 1907, Harlan, *The Booker T. Washington Papers,* 9:422–423. Washington to Arthur I. Vorys, Dec. 25, 1907, Harlan, *The Booker T. Washington Papers,* 9:424.
66. Thornbrough, *T. Thomas Fortune*, 21. Editorial, *New York Age,* May 2, 1907. Ralph [Tyler] to George A. Myers, Sept. 3, 1907, George A. Myers Collection, frame 0252, roll 6.
67. *Boston Guardian*, Nov. 16, 1907, as quoted in Thornbrough, *T. Thomas Fortune*, 315–16. T. Thomas Fortune to editor, *Indianapolis Freeman,* Dec. 7, [1907], Harlan, *The Booker T. Washington Papers,* 9:417.
68. George A. Myers to John P. Green, Feb. 10, 1899, John P. Green Papers, frames 624–627, roll 3. Ralph W. Tyler to George A. Myers, Dec. 27, 1907, George A. Myers Collection, frames 0300–0304, roll 6. Tyler to Myers, Jan. 12, 1908, George A. Myers Collection, frames 0322–0324, roll 6.
69. "National Race Conference Called," *Guardian,* Jan. 4, 1908, 1. "Bishops of Three Churches Warn Republicans," *Guardian,* Feb. 22, 1908, 1, 4.
70. Tyler to Myers, Feb. 25, 1908, George A. Myers Collection, frames 0360–0363, roll 6.
71. Bruce to editor, *New York Tribune,* Apr. [25?] 1908, Group E, misc., reel 4, Bruce Collection. J. E. Bruce, "New York Notes," *Guardian,* Oct. 26, 1907, 2.
72. *Guardian,* Aug. 8, 1908, 3.
73. James S. Clarkson to Bruce, Aug. 12, 1907, Group C, MSS, Bruce Letters, 4 A-47, reel 1, Bruce Collection. Whitefield McKinlay to F. D. Patterson, Apr. 3, 1940, Daniel A. Murray Papers, reel 27.
74. Tyler to Myers, June 6, 1908, George A. Myers Collection, frames 0422-0425, roll 6. *New York Times,* June 19, 1908, 1.
75. Bruce [to the] editor, *(New York) World,* Aug 8, [1908], Group C, Letters Sent by Bruce, BL 16, reel 2, Bruce Collection.
76. Edward W. Blyden to Bruce, Aug. 19, 1905, Group B, Letters Received, B 5, reel 1, Bruce Collection.
77. Charles W. Anderson to B. T. Washington, Mar. 12, 1906, Harlan, *The Booker T. Washington Papers,* 8:547. For Turner's denial, see p. 542. Anderson to Washington, Oct. 21, 1907, Harlan, *The Booker T. Washington Papers,* 9:385.
78. J. E. Bruce, "Bryan and the Negro Vote," *New York Tribune,* Oct. 5, 1908, Group E, misc., reel 4, Bruce Collection.
79. Editorial, "Our Opportunity—Shall We Grasp It?" *Guardian,* Oct. 24, 1908, 4; see also p. 1.
80. Bruce to William H. Taft, Oct. 30, 1908, William H. Taft Papers, ser. 3, reel 99. Fred W. Carpenter to Bruce, Nov. 2, 1908, William H. Taft Papers, ser. 8, vol. 78, p. 102, reel 477.
81. Thomas C. Woodruff to Bruce, Nov. 7, 1908, Group W, Letters W 11, reel 1, Bruce Collection.

82. Aptheker, *A Documentary History of the Negro People in the United States*, 3:20–21. *New York Times*, Nov. 4, 1908, 1.
83. Aptheker, *A Documentary History of the Negro People in the United States*, 2:915.
84. Bruce to Daniel Murray, Mar. 24, 1910, Daniel A. Murray Papers, reel 1. "Gen. Jas. S. Clarkson," *Chicago Defender*, Apr. 30, 1910, 1.
85. Joseph C. Lundy to Bruce, Apr. 22, 1910, Group L, Letters Received, L 9, reel 1, Bruce Collection.
86. Robert Smalls to Whitefield McKinlay, Nov. 10, 1909, in Carter G. Woodson Papers, reel 2. Maritcha R. Lyons to Max Loeb, Aug. 15, 1918, Henry A. Williamson Papers, reel 1. [Speech draft], "The American White Man As Seen through the Eyes of an American Negro," Oct. 1909, Group E, Scrapbook 2, reel 3, Bruce Collection. Editorial notes, n.d., Group D, MSS, 9 E-21, reel 2, Bruce Collection.
87. [Speech draft], "Some Serious Phases of the Problems of Race," St. Marks Methodist Episcopal Church, NYC, Dec. 30, 1909, Group D, MSS, B 7-102, reel 2, Bruce Collection. "Disadvantages of Negro Citizenship," n.d., Group D, MSS, B 7-105, reel 2, Bruce Collection. Bruce Grit, "The Dawn of the Era of Disillusionment," circa 1910, Group D, MSS, 9 E-104, reel 2, Bruce Collection.
88. Bruce to Daniel Murray, Jan. 27, 1910, Murray Papers, reel 1.
89. Richard T. Greener to Daniel Murray, Dec. 6, 1910, Murray Papers, reel 1. Blyden to Edward W. Cooke, Mar. 7, 1910, Group B, Letters Received, B 7, reel 1, Bruce Collection. Hollis R. Lynch, *Edward Wilmot Blyden: Pan Negro Patriot* (London: Oxford Univ. Press, 1967), 138.
90. Cyrus Field Adams, *The Republican Party and the Afro American: A Book of Facts and Figures*, 3d ed. (New York: Republican National Committee, 1912), 7, 14. "Colonel and Taft Bury the Hatchet," *New York Times*, May 26, 1918, 1. "Roosevelt Grips the Hand of Taft," *New York Times*, May 27, 1918, 1.
91. Robert H. Terrell to George A. Myers, Aug. 10, 1912, George A. Myers Collection, frames 0151-0153, roll 7. "The Negro Question," Colonel [Theodore] Roosevelt's Statement at the National Progressive Convention, Coliseum, Chicago, Aug. 6, 1912, 1–15. Whitefield McKinlay to P. B. S. Pinchback, Aug. 16, 1912, Carter G. Woodson Papers, reel 2. George A. Myers to James F. Rhodes, Sept. 24, 1912, George A. Myers Collection, frames 0157–0160, roll 7. Myers to Rhodes, Oct. 15, 1912, George A. Myers Collection, frames 0164–0169, roll 7. "Gen. Jas. S. Clarkson," *Chicago Defender*, Apr. 30, 1910, 1.
92. "Presidential Vote Fell Off This Year," *New York Times*, Dec. 29, 1912, 13.
93. Charles Purvis to Francis J. Grimke, Nov. 16, 1912, McKinlay to Charles Purvis, May 1, 1913, Woodson, *The Works of Francis J. Grimke*, 4:128–29, 2:3.
94. Grimke to Woodrow Wilson, Nov. 20, 1912, Woodson, *The Works of Francis J. Grimke*, 4:129–30. Kathleen Long Wolgemuth, "Woodrow Wilson's Appointment Policy and the Negro," *Journal of Negro History* 24 (Nov. 1958): 458, 461–66. For Wilson's letters to Alexander Walters, see *Indianapolis Recorder*, Feb. 5, 1916, 1.
95. A. H. Underdon to Bruce [1912–1913], Group C, MSS, Bruce Letters, 4 A-50, reel 2, Bruce Collection.
96. Chase, "Honey for Friends, Stings for Enemies," 236. Ralph W. Tyler to George A. Myers, Apr. 16, 1913, George A. Myers Collection, frames 0250–0251, roll 7.
97. Francis J. Grimke to Woodrow Wilson, Sept. 5, 1913, Woodson, *The Works of Francis J. Grimke*, 4:133–34.

98. Wolgemuth, "Woodrow Wilson's Appointment Policy and the Negro," 462–63.
99. Robert H. Terrell to George A. Myers, Dec. 19, 1913, George A. Myers Collection, frames 0300–0301, roll 7. W. H. Clifford to Myers, Feb. 24, 1914, George A. Myers Collection, frame 0323, roll 7.
100. [White subjugation], May 7, 1913, Group D, MSS, 9 E-92, reel 2, Bruce Collection.
101. Bruce to Charles W. Anderson, June 17, 1916, Group C, Letters Sent by Bruce, reel 2, Bruce Collection. J. E. Bruce, "The Issues and the Negro," Nov. ? 1916, Group D, MSS, 9 E-4, reel 2, Bruce Collection. See election coverage, *New York Times,* Nov. 7, 1916, 3; Nov. 8, 1916, 6; Nov. 9, 1916, 6, 12; Nov. 11, 1916, 8; Nov. 14, 1916, 4; Nov. 15, 1916, 1; Nov. 18, 1916, 10; Nov. 20, 1916, 2. "Colored Office Holders Turned Out; Places Filled by White Democrats," *New York Age,* Oct. 26, 1916, 1. "Leading Colored Citizens Meet in New York City," *(Norfolk) Journal and Guide,* Oct. 21, 1916, 1. Aptheker, *The Correspondence of W. E. B. Du Bois,* 1:217–19.
102. J. E. Bruce, *The Awakening of Hezekiah Jones* (Hopkinsville, Ky.: P. H. Brown Pub., 1916), 1–62. "Bruce Grit's Column," circa 1924, Group D, MSS, B 11-16, reel 3, Bruce Collection.
103. [Black soldiers], circa 1914, Group E, Bruce Fragments, Bruce's MSS, reel 3, Bruce Collection.
104. Bruce Grit, "The Coming Climax," *Pioneer News* (Martinsburg, W.Va.), Feb. 27, 1915, Group E, misc., reel 4, Bruce Collection. W. E. Hawkins to Bruce, May 17, 1915, Group B, Letters Received, MS 224, reel 1, Bruce Collection. Casely Hayford to Bruce, Apr. 7, 1915, Group B, Letters Received, MSS, Autographed Letters, TS 321, reel 1, Bruce Collection.
105. To the editor [1915–17], Group E, misc., reel 4, ibid., "Getting by the Censor," [1914–18], Group D, MSS, 9 E-98, reel 2, Bruce Collection.
106. Arthur E. Barbeau and Florette Henri, *The Unknown Soldiers: Black American Troops in World War I* (Philadelphia: Temple Univ. Press, 1974), 12, 13, chaps. 3–8.
107. W. H. Crogman to Francis J. Grimke, Sept. 20, 1917, Woodson, *The Works of Francis J. Grimke,* 4:45 (see also Grimke's stray thoughts in 3:25–26, 45, 73–74).
108. Editorial, "Close Ranks," *Crisis* 16 (July 1918): 111. Editorial, "A Philosophy in Time of War," *Crisis* 16 (Aug. 1918): 164–65. W. E. B. Du Bois, "The African Roots of War," *Atlantic Monthly* 65 (May 1915): 707–14. Theophilus G. Steward to editor, *Crisis* 16 (Sept. 1918): 219.
109. Barbeau and Henri, *The Unknown Soldiers,* chaps. 3–8.
110. Bruce, "The Negro and the Coming of War," circa 1917, Group D, MSS, 9 E-134, reel 2, Bruce Collection.
111. Bruce Grit, "The Attitude of the American Negro towards the War," *African Times and Orient Review* 5 (Oct. 1917): 85. Bruce Grit, "The Negro Soldier," [1917–18], Group D, MSS, 9 E-35, reel 2, Bruce Collection. Gerald W. Patton, "War and Race: The Black Officer in the American Military, 1915–1925" (Ph.D. diss., Univ. of Iowa, 1978). John E. Bruce, *A Defence of the Colored Soldier Who Fought in the War of the Rebellion* (Yonkers: n.d.), 1–14.
112. Daniel Murray to Bruce, May 15, 1918, Group M, Letters Received, MS 9, reel 1, Bruce Collection. Maude Pearl La Van to Bruce, Apr. 28, 1918, Group B, TS 266, reel 1, Bruce Collection. Moses Da Rocha, "A Tribute for the Negro Soldier," *Crusader* 1 (July 1918): 14–15. Bruce and Franklin, Publishers to Dear Friend, n.d., Group D, MSS, B 8-127, reel 2, Bruce Collection. Remarks of Walter M. Chandler, Monday, June 3, 1918, inserted into *Congressional Record.* Chandler to

Bruce, May 29, 918, Group C, Letters Received, C 3, reel 1, Bruce Collection. Chandler to Bruce, May 31, 1918, Group C, Letters Received, C 4, Bruce Collection. Chandler to Bruce, June 5, 1918, Group C, Letters Received, C 5, Bruce Collection. See Bruce and Franklin ads in the *Crusader* 1 (Oct. 1918): 18. Bruce to Theodore Roosevelt, Feb. 27, 1918, Theodore Roosevelt Papers, ser. 1, reel 266; Bruce to Roosevelt, May 30, 1918, ibid., ser. 1, reel 278; Roosevelt to Bruce, June 3, 1918; ser. 3A, vol. 168, reel 404; Dear Sir [1918–19], Group C, Letters Sent by Bruce, 4 BL 58, reel 2, Bruce Collection.

113. [Incomplete synopsis of] *Somewhere in France—1918*, Group D, D 10-7, reel 3, Bruce Collection.

114. Ralph W. Tyler to George A. Myers, May 20, 1918, George A. Myers Collection, frame 0741, roll 7. Tyler to Myers, Jan. 26, 1919, George A. Myers Collection, frame 0755, roll 7.

115. Address of Welcome Given at a Reception Tendered to the Men Who Have Returned from the Battlefield by the Men's Progressive Club of the Fifteenth Street Presbyterian Church, Apr. 24, 1919, Francis J. Grimke Papers, box 40-6, folder 269, Moorland-Spingard Research Center. See also Woodson, *The Works of Francis J. Grimke* 1: 590–591. "Justice or Death Is the Watchword," *Afro American*, Apr. 4, 1919, 4. W. E. B. Du Bois, "We Return Fighting," *Crisis* 18 (May 1919): 14. Barbeau and Henri, *The Unknown Soldiers*, chap. 10.

116. Editorial, "'And Thou, Too, Brutus?'" *(Washington) Bee*, Mar. 29, 1919, 4. "Ralph Tyler Sues," *(Washington) Bee*, Mar. 29, 1919, 6. "Fine Record of Our Boys Blocked by Gross Discrimination," *Afro American*, Mar. 14, 1919, 1. [Challenge whites, draft of Bruce essay, 1918–19], Group D, MSS, B 7-98, reel 2, Bruce Collection. Editorial notes, [1918–19], Group D, MSS, 9 E-13, Bruce Collection. See also MSS, B 11-19, Bruce Collection. Bruce Grit, "The Great Illusion," *Crusader* 1 (Nov. 1918): 5. [Dream about the Pope], n.d., Group D, MSS, B 8-129, reel 2, Bruce Collection.

117. Bruce Grit, "The Call," Aug. 16, 1919, J. E. Bruce, clipping file, frame 000746-1. Editorial, "Nine Ex-Soldiers Lynched in 1919," *(Washington) Bee*, Jan. 31, 1920. Bruce Grit, "Grits," *Boston Chronicle*, Feb. 22, 1919, Group E, misc., reel 4, Bruce Collection.

118. House Resolution 5131, June 6, 1919, John E. Bruce Papers (additions), [Negro Soldier Monument], Bruce's speech at Liberty Hall, May 14, 1920, Group D, MSS, B 6-77, reel 2, Bruce Collection.

119. J. E. Bruce, "The Significance of Brotherhood," May 23, 1919, Group D, MSS, B 6-64, reel 2, Bruce Collection. For other drafts of the same speech, see "Worship Master and Brethren," ibid., B 6-73. For final version, see "The Significance of Brotherhood," May 23, 1919, Group E, misc., reel 4, Bruce Collection.

120. "Harding and the Black Voter," Aptheker, *A Documentary History of the Negro People in the United States*, 3:303. *Inaugural Addresses of the Presidents of the United States* (Washington: GPO, 1969), 207–14 Bruce to T. Roosevelt, Feb. 27, 1918, Roosevelt Papers, ser. 1, reel 266. Bruce Grit's Column, *Negro World*, Feb. 19, 1921, 5; Oct. 15, 1921, 7. J. E. Bruce, "Reconstruction—The Finale," *Negro World*, Dec. 17, 1921, 4.

121. J. E. Bruce, The Passing Show Column, *Negro World*, Nov. 17, 1923, 4. Bruce Grit's Column, *Negro World*, Aug. 25, 1923, 4. Bruce Grit's Column, *Negro World*, Nov. 11, 1922, 9.

Chapter 4

1. Aptheker, *A Documentary History of the Negro People,* 2:703–5.
2. Ibid., 679.
3. Albion W. Tourgee to Bruce, July 31, 1891 in Group T, Letters, T7, reel 1, Bruce Collection. Tourgee to Bruce, Nov. 17, 1891, in Group T, Letter, T8, reel 1, Bruce Collection.
4. J. E. Bruce, *Concentration of Energy* (Albany, 1899), 1–12. "Bruce Grit Doing Boston," *Colored American,* Dec. 2, 1899, 1, 8.
5. Bruce Grit, "The Hour of Prayer," *Colored American,* June 3, 1899, 4.
6. Bruce Grit, "New in Gotham," *Colored American,* Jan. 31, 1903, 1–4. Bruce Grit, "Slander," [1900?], Group D, MSS, B 11-18, reel 3, Bruce Collection.
7. [G.] A. W. Mebane, "The Passing Show," *Colored American,* Feb. 7, 1903, 1, 5. Ida D. Bailey, "Women for Hayes," *Colored American,* Feb. 7, 1903, 3.
8. Bruce Grit, "The Yonkers News," *Colored American,* Feb. 14, 1903, 12.
9. Bailey, "Women for Hayes," *Colored American,* Feb. 7, 1903, 3.
10. For Bishop Smith's remarks, see *Colored American,* Feb. 7, 1903, 9. Editorial, [untitled], *Colored American,* Feb. 7, 1903, 8.
11. Bruce Grit, "Gotham Notes," *Colored American,* Feb. 7, 1903, 2; Feb. 14, 1903, 2–3.
12. Bruce Grit, "Gotham Notes," *Colored American,* July 4, 1903, 3. Bruce Grit, "Gotham Notes," *Colored American,* July 11, 1903, 6. Editorial [untitled], *Colored American,* July 11, 1903, 8. J. E. Bruce, "Mr. Bruce Objects," *Colored American,* July 18, 1903, 5. Charles W. Anderson to B. T. Washington, July 6, 1903, Harlan, *The Booker T. Washington Papers,* 7:195.
13. "The Impending Conflict," *Denver Statesman,* July 6, 1903, Group E, misc., reel 4, Bruce Collection.
14. R. C. Black [Emmett J. Scott] to J. C. May [Wilford H. Smith], July 23, 1903; J. C. May [Wilford H. Smith] to R. C. Black [Emmett J. Scott], July 30, 1903; Harlan, *The Booker T. Washington Papers,* 7:219, 220.
15. Melvin Jack Chisum to Emmett Jay Scott, July 23, 1903; B. T. Washington to Scott, July 25, 1903; Charles W. Anderson to B. T. Washington, Feb. 17, 1904; Harlan, *The Booker T. Washington Papers,* 7:222–23, 224–25, 441–42.
16. B. T. Washington to Francis J. Garrison, Aug. 3, 1903, B. T. Washington to L. H. Latimer, Feb. 19, 1904, Booker T. Washington Papers, MG 182, box 1, Correspondence 1900–1904, Manuscript Division, Schomburg Center. See Harlan, *The Booker T. Washington Papers,* 7:229–54. Booker T. Washington to Whitefield McKinlay, Aug. 3, 1903, Harlan, *The Booker T. Washington Papers,* 7:252.
17. Aptheker, *A Documentary History of the Negro People in the United States,* 2:900–910.
18. Rev. Charles S. Morris to Bruce, Feb. 23, 1905, Group N (compiler thought his name was Norris) Letters Received, M 6, reel 1, Bruce Collection.
19. W. E. B. Du Bois to Bruce, Dec. 19, 1905, Group D, Letters Received, D 10, reel 1, Bruce Collection.
20. Editorial, "Misfortunes Sustained by the Race Despite Its Leadership," *New York Age,* Apr. 19, 1906, 2.
21. [J. E. Bruce], "New York News," *Guardian,* Aug. 25, 1906, 2.
22. Testimonial Dinner; Bruce to Arthur A. Schomburg, July 20, 1905, John E. Bruce Papers (additions). Committee on Testimonial to John E. Bruce, Group E, misc.,

reel 4, Bruce Collection. Edward W. Blyden to Bruce, Aug. 19, 1905, Group E. scrapbook, reel 3, Bruce Collection. Guarionex (Arthur A. Schomburg), "'Bruce Grit' Honored," *Guardian*, Oct. 7,1905, Group E, Bruce Scrapbook, reel 3, Bruce Collection. *Denver Statesman*, Oct. 13, 1905, Group E, misc., reel 4, Bruce Collection. Charles W. Anderson to B. T. Washington, Sept. 26, 1905, Harlan, *The Booker T. Washington Papers*, 8:375. *Boston Transcript*, Oct. 7, 1905 as cited in Elino Des Verney Sinnette, *Arthur A. Schomburg: Black Bibliophile and Collector* (Detroit: New York Public Library and Wayne State Univ. Press, 1989), 36–37. Charles W. Anderson to Bruce, Apr. 17, 1905, MG 253, John E. Bruce Papers (additions). For legal suits involving Anderson and Trotter, see Stephen R. Fox, *The Guardian of Boston: William Monroe Trotter* (New York: Atheneum, 1970), 94, 96, 123–25, 220. Bruce to editor of the *Guardian*, Apr. 17, 1905; Trotter to Bruce, Apr. 23, 1905; Bruce to Trotter, Apr. 24, 1905; Anderson to Bruce, Apr. 4, 17, 1905, John E. Bruce Papers (additions). For Bruce's credo on friendship see Bruce's diary entry, June 10, 1904, Group E, misc., reel 4, Bruce Collection.
23. [Bruce's Credo], Aug. 5, 1905, Group E, misc., reel 4, Bruce Collection.
24. For Crummell's views on higher education, see Harlan, *The Booker T. Washington Papers*, 4:255–56, 321–22.
25. Alfred A. Moss Jr., *The American Negro Academy: Voice of the Talented Tenth* (Baton Rouge: Louisiana State Univ. Press, 1981), 17–24, 26–30. William H. Crogman to Francis J. Grimke, Sept. 24, 1894, Woodson, *The Works of Francis J. Grimke*, 4:34.
26. Crummell to Bruce, Oct. 30, 1896; Dec. 5, 1896, reel 2, Bruce Collection.
27. Moss, *The American Negro Academy*, 3.
28. *New York Sun*, May 16, 1897, 3. C. H. J. Taylor to Bruce, Apr. 11, 1896, Group B, Letters Received, MS 434, reel 1, Bruce Collection. Bruce Grit, "The Race Question," n.d., Group E, misc., reel 4, Bruce Collection. For other criticisms of Henderson, see Joseph H. Ward, "A Pessimist Scored," *Freeman*, June 8, 1895, 4. Jas. E. Henderson, "Open Letter no. 8," *Freeman*, June 1, 1895, 1. For a fuller discussion of Fortune's thoughts on the color issue, see Moss, *The American Negro Academy*, 54–56. Gerald Hull Gray to Daniel Murray, Apr. 6, 1910, Daniel A. Murray Papers, reel 1. Bruce to Bishop Harris, *Star of Zion*, Dec. 15, 1889, Group E, misc., reel 4, Bruce Collection.
29. Alexander Crummell to Bruce, Sept. 27, 1897; Nov. 5, 1897; Dec. 9, 1897; Dec. 15, 1897, Letters from the Bruce Collection, reel 2, Bruce Collection.
30. T. Thomas Fortune to Bruce, Dec. 8, 1897, Group F, Letters Received, F 3, reel 1, Bruce Collection.
31. Bruce to Crummell, Nov. 6, 1897, Group C, Letters Sent by Bruce, BL 4-42, reel 2, Bruce Collection.
32. Crummell to Bruce, Jan. 21, 1898, Letters from the Bruce Collection, reel 2, Bruce Collection. J. Robert Love to Bruce, Dec. 29, 1893, John E. Bruce Papers (additions). Love to Bruce, July 4, 1894, Group L, Letters Received, L 5, reel 1, Bruce Collection. Love to Bruce, Mar. 5, 1899, Group L, Letters Received, L 7, reel 1, ibid. Crummell to Bruce, Apr. 7, 1894, Group C, Letters Received, C 13, reel 1, Bruce Collection. J. E. Bruce, "Past Glories," *Ledger*, Dec. 31, 1898, 1, as quoted in *Star of Zion*, n.d.
33. Bruce's diary entries, Dec. 26–30, 1919, Group E, Scrapbook 2, reel 3, Bruce Collection.

34. Moss, *The American Negro Academy,* 226. Bruce to Dear Frater (Arthur A. Schomburg), Mar. 14, 1914, Group C, Letters Sent by Bruce, BL 4-81, reel 2, Bruce Collection. Bruce to Schomburg, June 17, 1923, John E. Bruce Papers (additions), Schomburg to Bruce, Jan. 13, 1915, Group B, MS 22, Letters Received, MSS, Autographed Letters, reel 1, Bruce Collection. Schomburg to Bruce, July 14, 1916, Group B, MS 29, Bruce Collection. Schomburg to Bruce, n.d., Group B, MS 39, Bruce Collection.
35. Du Bois to Bruce, Sept. 27, 1911, Group B, Letters Received, MSS, Autographed Letters, TS 273, reel 1, Bruce Collection. Bruce to Alain L. Locke, Apr. 14, 1913, Box-Brop-Burk, Alain Leroy Locke Collection, Moorland-Spingard Collection, Howard Univ., as quoted in David L. Lewis, *W. E. B. Du Bois: Biography of a Race* (New York: Henry Holt and Co., 1993), 417. Bruce to Du Bois, Jan. 25, 1918, Du Bois Papers, reel 6.
36. Claude McKay, *The Negro Historical Society of New York* (New York: Federal Writers Program, Negroes of New York, 1939), reel 3, Schomburg Center. "The Negro Society for Historical Research," [1911], Group E, misc., 13-55, reel 3, Bruce Collection. George Shepperon, "Notes on Negro American Influences on the Emergence of African Nationalism," *Journal of African History* 1 (1960): 309. Duse Mohammed to Arthur Schomburg, Oct. 30, 1912, frame 00843, reel 4, Schomburg Papers. C. A. Franklin to Schomburg, Aug. 21, 1911, frame 00144, reel 3, Schomburg Papers. Mrs. J. E. Bruce, "Devotees of Dr. Crummell," *Colored American,* Dec. 4, 1899, 4. For a list of members, honorary members, corresponding members, see Kilson and Hill, *Apropos of Africa,* 203–5.
37. Schomburg to Bruce, Mar. 21, 1912, Group B, Letters Received, MSS, Autographed Letters, MS 334, reel 1, Bruce Collection.
38. Bruce Grit [1922?], Schomburg Papers, box 14, frame 00944, reel 10. Schomburg to Bruce, June 2, 1913, Group B, Letters Received, reel 1, Bruce Collection. Bruce Grit, "The Press Honored," *Colored American,* Mar. 3, 1900, 1, 9.
39. John W. Cromwell to Bruce, Feb. 3, 1912, Group B, Letters Received, MSS, Autographed Letters, MS 227, reel 1, Bruce Collection.
40. [The Negro Library Association], Robert T. Browne to Daniel Murray, Dec. 28, 1917, Daniel A. Murray Papers, reel 1. The officers were J. E. Bruce, historical section; Arthur A. Schomburg, research section; James Weldon Johnson, sociological section; Robert T. Browne, president.
41. Bruce to Carter G. Woodson, Sept. 15, 1917, Woodson Papers, reel 3. Schomburg to Bruce, Jan. 13, 1915, Group B, Letters Received, reel 1, Bruce Collection.
42. Bruce to Woodson, Jan. 17, Apr. 11, Apr. 30, July 31, Nov. 14, 1919, Woodson Papers, reel 3.
43. Bruce to Woodson, June 13, 30, July 1, 8, 15, 1921; Feb. 4, 8, Mar. 22, Oct.28, 1922; Jan. 1, 3, 1923; Woodson Papers, reel 3. "Annual Report of the Director," *Journal of Negro History* 8 (Oct. 1923): 466.
44. Bruce Grit's Column, *Negro World,* Nov. 11, 1922, 9. Arthur Schomburg, "Schomburg Tears Carter Woodson to Pieces for Historical Narrowness," *Negro World,* Nov. 4, 1922, Schomburg Papers, box 13, frame 0632, reel 10.
45. Bruce to Woodson, Jan. 14, 17, 1923, Woodson Papers, reel 3.
46. Bruce to Woodson, Jan. 17, 1923; Feb. 1, 1923; Mar. 4, 1923, Woodson Papers, reel 3.
47. [Think Black], circa 1913, Group D, MSS, B 6-63, B 6-64, reel 2, Bruce Collection.
48. *Yonkers Daily News,* Sept. 20, 1913, Group E, Scrapbook 2, reel 3, Bruce Collection.
49. [Intelligent Resistance], [1914], Group D, MSS, B 6-74, reel 2, Bruce Collection. For a full reading of the lecture, see Kilson and Hill, *Apropos of Africa,* 200–201.

50. Bruce to Schomburg, Sept. 7, 1913, John E. Bruce Papers (additions). Bruce Grit, "James Emman Kwegyir Aggrey," *African Times and Orient Review* 5 (Dec. 1917): 121–23.
51. Robert Hill, ed., *The Crusader* (New York: Garland Publishers Co., 1987). This is a facsimile of the original. See introduction, p. xx. *Crusader* 2 (Sept. 1919): 24.
52. Bruce Grit, "Acrostic," *Crusader* 1 (May 1919): 16. See also box 1, Book of Negro Poems and Songs, 1919, J. R. Ralph Casimir Collection, Schomburg Center.
53. D. E. Headley to Bruce, Sept. 12, 1919, Group B, MSS, Autographed Letters, MS 191, reel 1, Bruce Collection. Andrea Razafkeriefo, "John E. Bruce," *Crusader* 1 (Dec. 1918): 16.

Chapter 5

1. Jere A. Brown et al. to John P. Green, Mar. 11, 1897, John P. Green Papers, frames 0455–0456, roll 1. For criticism of George W. Williams's scholarship, see Bruce Grit, "The Negro in Literature," *Colored American,* June 4, 1898, 1. Robert H. Terrell to Bruce, Mar. 29, 1896, Group T, Letters Received, T 5, reel 1, Bruce Collection.
2. Alexander Crummell to Bruce, Dec. 5, 1896; Dec. 24, 1896; Letters Received, reel 2, Bruce Collection.
3. Crummell to Bruce, Nov. 5, 1897, Group C, Letters Received, C 18, reel 1, Bruce Collection. John E. Bruce to [Whom It May Concern], 1897[?], J. E. Bruce, clipping file. Bishop B. T. Tanner to Bruce, Aug. 189[?], Group T, Letters Received, T 1, reel 1, Bruce Collection. Tanner suggested that it be called the "Douglass Reader." Bruce to Crummell, Nov. 6, 1897, Group C, Letters Sent by Bruce, BL-42, reel 2, Bruce Collection. Charles Dudley Warner to Bruce, May 16, 1898, Group W, Letters Received, W 3, reel 1, Bruce Collection. [Reference to Moses Da Rocha, 1902], Group E, misc., 13-7, reel 3, Bruce Collection.
4. Crummell to Bruce, June 1, 1897; [June–Sept. 1897], July 4, 1897, Nov. 28, 1896, Letters Received, reel 2, Bruce Collection. Gregory U. Rigsby, *Alexander Crummell: Pioneer in Nineteenth Century Pan African Thought* (New York: Greenwood Press, 1987), 89–92.
5. Bruce to Crummell, Nov. 6, 1897, Group C, Letters Sent by Bruce, BL 4-42, reel 2, Bruce Collection.
6. Crummell to Bruce, Mar. 27, 1898; Apr. ? 1898, Letters Received, reel 2, Bruce Collection. Crummell to Bruce, Apr. [18]98, Group B, Letters Received, MSS, Autographed Letters, MS 17, reel 1, Bruce Collection.
7. Crummell to Bruce, Mar. 22, 1898, Group B, Letters Received, MSS, Autographed Letters, MS 16, reel 1, Bruce Collection. W. H. Council to Bruce, Nov. 16, 1898, Group B, Letters Received, MSS, Autographed Letters, MS 324, reel 1, Bruce Collection. W. H. Council to Bruce, Nov. 25, 1898, Group B, Letters Received, MSS, Autographed Letters, MS 340, reel 1, Bruce Collection.
8. Bruce Grit, "The Passing of Crummell," *Colored American,* Sept. 24, 1898, 1. "Bruce Grit's Shining Lance," *Colored American,* Apr. 9, 1898, 5. Rev. Henry L. Phillips, "In Memoriam of the Late Rev. Alex Crummell: An Address Delivered before the American Negro Historical Society of Philadelphia, 1898," 3, 7.
9. *Colored American,* June 18, 1898, 1, 5. For a biographical sketch of Davis, see William Seraile, "Henrietta Vinton Davis and the Garvey Movement," *Afro-*

Americans in New York Life and History 7 (July 1983): 7–24. "Rivals Uncle Tom's Cabin," *Ledger,* Dec. 24, 1898, 3, as cited in *Star of Zion,* n.d.
10. "Bruce Grit's Shining Lance," *Colored American,* Apr. 9, 1898, 1, 5.
11. For the editorial, "A Simple Problem in Arithmetic," see *Colored American,* June 25, 1898, 4 (for reprint of June 18 editorial). Bruce's letter is in the same issue, p. 4.
12. G. F. Franklin to Bruce, Dec. 29, 1900, Group B, Letters Received, MSS, Autographed Letters, MS 342, reel 1, Bruce Collection. Editorial, "The Twentieth Century Negro," *Freeman,* Nov. 7, 1896, 4.
13. "A Grand Talk," *Cleveland Gazette,* Mar. 28, 1901, 7.
14. William H. Thomas, *The American Negro* (New York: Macmillan Co., 1901), chap. 7. "Report on the Committee on Moral and Religion for July 1901," Carter G. Woodson Papers, reel 8.
15. James Hulme Canfield to B. T. Washington, Jan. 25, 1901, Harlan, *Booker T. Washington Papers,* 6:17–18.
16. F. J. Loudin to John P. Green, Apr. 14, 1901, John P. Green Papers, frames 817–22, roll 3.
17. Charles W. Chesnutt, "A Defense of His Race," *Critic* 38 (Apr. 1901): 350–51. Chesnutt to Bruce, May 6, 1901, Group C, Letters Received, C 7, reel 1, Bruce Collection.
18. C. T. Walker to Bruce, May 13, 1901, Group B, Letters Received, MSS, Autographed Letters, TS 250, reel 1, Bruce Collection.
19. John E. Bruce to Whitefield McKinlay, Apr. 17, 1901, Whitefield McKinlay Papers in Carter G. Woodson Papers, reel 1.
20. William Hayes Ward to B. T. Washington, Mar. 11, 1901, Harlan, *Booker T. Washington Papers,* 6:56. Bruce's comments are on p. 56, note 1.
21. John E. Bruce, "The Critic Revealed," *Colored American,* Apr. 13, 1901, 1, 9. John E. Bruce, "The Critic Revealed; or, The Deadly Peril," *Howard's American Magazine* 6 (Apr. 1901): 364–68.
22. Bruce Grit, "He Defames the Race," *Colored American,* Feb. 2, 1901, 2.
23. Bruce Grit, "Bruce in Business," *Colored American,* Mar. 16, 1901, 1, 9.
24. Bruce Grit, "The Color Line North," *Colored American,* Apr. 13, 1901, 1. Bruce Grit, "Mixed Schools," *Cleveland Gazette,* Apr. 26, 1890, 1–2.
25. Bruce Gritisms, "The Right to Strike," n.d., Group D, MSS, B 11-27, reel 3, Bruce Collection. Bruce Grit, "Lessons of the Strike," *Colored American,* May 25, 1901, 1, 4, 9. Editorial, "The Steel Strike," Bruce Collection, Aug. 17, 1901, 8. For Tanner's view, see Aptheker, *Documentary History of the Negro in the United States,* 2:650–51.
26. Bruce Grit, "Bruce Grit on the Strike Situation," *Colored American,* Oct. 18, 1902, 7. Editorial, "Labor Unions and the Negro," *Colored American,* Dec. 28, 1901, 8. Bruce Grit, "Anarchists," *Colored American,* Jan. 18, 1902, 3. Joseph H. Beall to Bruce, Feb. 22, 1908, Group B, Letters Received, MSS, Autographed Letters, TS 245, reel 1, Bruce Collection. [J. E. Bruce], "New York Notes," *Guardian,* Nov. 2, 1907, 2. J. E. Bruce, Address before the President and Members of The Yonkers Sunday Club, [1908?], Group D, MSS, BL 65, reel 2, Bruce Collection. Pauline E. Hopkins to Bruce, Apr. 6, 1906, Group H, Letters Received, H 13, reel 1, Bruce Collection. U.S. Bureau of the Census, *Thirteenth Census of the United States, Taken in 1910,* vol. 3, *pop. 1910* (Washington: GPO, 1913), 187, 213, 242. William Seraile, "Ben Fletcher, I.W.W. Organizer," *Pennsylvania History* 46 (July 1979): 213–32.
27. Bruce Grit, "The American Protective League," *Colored American,* Sept. 14, 1901, 4. For Bruce's views on industrial education, see "Industrial Education: Will It Solve the Negro Problem?" *Colored American Magazine* 7 (Jan. 1904): 13–21. John

E. Bruce, "The Necessity for Business Leagues," *Voice of the Negro* 1 (Aug. 1904): 338–39.
28. Bruce Grit, "What the Council Can Do," *Colored American,* Feb. 25, 1899, 5. Bruce Grit, "By the Sad Sea Waves," *Colored American,* July 20, 1901, 9. For Kipling's "White Man's Burden," see Willard B. Gatewood, *Black Americans and the White Man's Burden of Race, 1898–1903* (Urbana: Univ. of Illinois Press, 1975), 31–35.
29. Bruce Grit, "The White Man's Idea of Heaven," *Kingston Advocate* (Jamaica), Mar. 1900, Group E, misc., reel 4, Bruce Collection.
30. J. E. Bruce, *The Blood Red Record: A Review of the Horrible Lynchings and Burnings of Negroes by Civilized White Men in the United States* (Albany: Argus Co., 1900), 3, 5, 12, 13, 15, 23, 26–27.
31. For quotes on Wells, see Thornbrough, *T. Thomas Fortune,* 124–25. L. M. Hershaw to Bruce, July 12, 1894, Group H, Letters Received, reel 1, Bruce Collection.
32. Bruce Grit, "Bruce Grit's Melange," *Colored American,* Feb. 28, 1903, 1, 3 Benjamin T. Tanner, "Columbus' Discovery and the Negro: What?" *Independent* 44 (June 2, 1892): 753. Diary entry for Dec. 1, 1900, T. G. Steward Papers, Schomburg Center for Research in Black Culture, New York Public Library.
33. Rev. Dr. Majola Agbebi, Inaugural Sermon Delivered at the Celebration of the First Anniversary of the African Church, Lagos, Dec. 21, 1902 in Group E, misc., reel 4, Bruce Collection. Edward W. Blyden to Agbebi, Mar. 17, 1903, Bruce Collection. Bruce to Agbebi, Apr. 16, 1903, Bruce Collection. Bruce Grit, "The Impending Crisis," *Colored American,* Nov. 21, 1903, 12.
34. "The Yonkers Clippings," *Colored American,* Nov. 14, 1903, 15. Shepperson, "Notes on Negro Americans Influences on the Emergence of African Nationalism," 310. T. Lloyd Harrison to Bruce, Apr. 9, 1907, Group B, Letters Received, MS 167, reel 1, Bruce Collection. Bruce to Mrs [Adeola] Agbebi, Sept. 27, 1917, Group C, Letters Sent by Bruce, BL 4-67, reel 2, Bruce Collection.
35. John P. Jackson to Bruce, circa 1890s, Group J, reel 1, Bruce Collection. John E. Bruce, letter to the editor, *New York Tribune,* Aug. 21, 1903, 8.
36. John E. Bruce, letter to the editor, *New York Tribune,* Sept. 19, 1903, 9. [J. E. Bruce], "New York Notes," *Guardian,* July 27, 1907, 2. Aug. 10, 1907, 2. [J. E. Bruce], [speech on Negro achievers], To the Gentlemen of the [Yonkers] Sunday Club, circa 1907, Group D, MSS, B7-103, reel 2, Bruce Collection.
37. John E. Bruce, *Tracts for the People,* n.d. (tracts nos. 1, 3, 5, 7, 8, 9, 11, 15).
38. John E. Bruce, "The Black Sleuth," *McGirt's Magazine,* [1907–1909], Group E, misc., Bruce Magazine, Arts and Letters, reel 3, Bruce Collection. Moses Da Rocha to Bruce, Oct. 24, 1903, Bruce Collection. An earlier version appeared on an unknown date. See John C. Gruesser, ed., *The Black Sleuth* (Boston: Northeastern Univ. Press, 2002). Gruesser to author, June 24, 2002.
39. *Star of Zion,* Dec. 11, 1902, Group E, Bruce Collection. "Shreds and Patches," *Colored American,* Jan. 24, 1903, 12. "In The Gay World," *Colored American,* July 11, 1903, 10. See Bruce's diary entries for May 24, 27, 31, and June 2, 3, 1904, Group E, misc., reel 4, Bruce Collection.
40. Bruce's diary entries for May 22, June 6, 7, 1904, Group E, misc., reel 4, Bruce Collection.
41. Edward W. Blyden to Bruce, Mar. 7, 1910, Group B, Letters Received, B 8, reel 1, Bruce Collection. Joseph C. Lundy to Bruce, Apr. 22, 1910, Group L, Letters Received, L 9, reel 1, Bruce Collection. Hollis R. Lynch, *Edward Wilmot Blyden: Pan Negro Patriot* (London: Oxford Univ. Press, 1967), 245.

42. J. E. Robinson to Bruce, Mar. 22, 1912, Group B, Letters Received, Autograph MSS, TS 51, reel 1, Bruce Collection.
43. Ferris, *The African Abroad,* viii. Aptheker, *A Documentary History of the Negro in the United States,* 3:65–66.
44. Alice M. Dunbar to Bruce, Mar. 23, 1914, Group B, Letters Received, Autograph MSS, TS 52, reel 1, Bruce Collection.
45. Bruce to Daniel Murray, Mar. 24, 1910, Daniel A. Murray Papers, reel 1.
46. J. E. Bruce, *Short Biographical Sketches of Eminent Negro Men and Women in Europe and the United States* (Yonkers: Gazette Press, 1910), title page, preface.
47. A. J. Gary to Bruce, Mar. 14, 1910, Group C, Bruce Letters, 4 A-78, reel 2, Bruce Collection. Robert Smalls to Bruce, Apr. 7, 1910, Group S, Letters Received, S 8, reel 1, Bruce Collection. Alice M. Dunbar to Bruce, Mar. 23, 1914, Group B, Letters Received, Autograph MSS, TS 52, reel 1, Bruce Collection.
48. Bruce to Daniel Murray, Nov. 21, 1910, Daniel A. Murray Papers, reel 1. Bruce to editor, [*New York Age*], circa 1911–13, Group C, Letters Sent by Bruce, BL 1, reel 2, Bruce Collection.
49. Walter Everette Hawkins to Bruce, Mar. 10, 1910, Group B, Letters Received, MSS, Autographed Letters, MS 293, reel 1, Bruce Collection.
50. [The Significance of Brotherhood], Address Delivered by John Edward Bruce (Grit) before the Craftsmen's Club, Mar. 6, 1910, Masonic Temple, New York City, in Harry [Henry] A. Williamson Collection, folder 1, box 11, reel 5. John E. Bruce, "The Stronger Nations vs. the Weaker Nations," *Voice of the Negro* 2 (Apr. 1905): 256–57. [J. E. Bruce], "New York Notes," *Guardian,* Jan. 11, 1908, 2. *Africa and the Africans: Proceedings on the Occasion of a Banquet . . . August 15th, 1903, to Edward W. Blyden by West Africans in London* (London: C. M. Phillips, 1903), 14. [Bruce's notes], May 20, 1904; Dec. 17, 1904; June 5, 1905, Group E, misc., reel 4, Bruce Collection.
51. [J. E. Bruce], To the Relatives of Frances E. W. Harper, Mar. 17, 1911, John E. Bruce Papers (additions). J. E. Bruce, "Pioneer Race Man Honored," *Guardian,* Aug. 26, 1911, 2.
52. *African Times and Oriental Review* 1 (July 1912): 2.
53. Oswald Garrison Villard to Bruce, Aug. 3, 1912, Group B, Letters Received, Autographed MSS, Letters, TS 50, reel 1, Bruce Collection.
54. James S. Clarkson to Lafayette Young, Jan. 4, 1914, Group E, misc., 13-42, reel 3, Bruce Collection. Bruce's review of *Why Not Now* is in the *Denver Star,* May 30, 1914, Group E, misc., reel 3, Bruce Collection.
55. James S. Clarkson to Florence A. Bruce, Feb. [?], 1913, Group E, MS 3, Mrs. Bruce, reel 3, Bruce Collection.
56. J. R. Archer to Bruce, Nov. 26, 1913, Group E, A 3, reel 1, Bruce Collection. Archer to Bruce, Jan. 17, 1914, Group E, A 4, reel 1, Bruce Collection.
57. J[ames] Wilson to Bruce, Jan. 28, 1914, Group B, Letters Received, MSS, Autographed Letters, M 67, reel 1, Bruce Collection. Dr. York Russell to Bruce, Feb. 17, 1914, Group B, MS 348, reel 1, Bruce Collection.
58. Arthur A. Schomburg, *Racial Integrity: A Plea for the Establishment of a Chair of Negro History in Our Schools and Colleges, Read before the Teachers' Summer Class at Cheney Institute, July 1913, Occasional Paper No. 3.* (Yonkers: Negro Society for Historical Research), 1–19. The speech was dedicated to Bruce.
59. "Going through the Motions," [1915], Group D, MSS, 9 E-84, reel 2, Bruce Collection. John E. Bruce, 'Commercializing Race Prejudice,' *New York World,* Mar. 12, 1915, Group E, misc., reel 4, Bruce Collection.

60. *The Phalanx Hornet*, Feb. 7, 1915, Group D, MSS, B 8-118, reel 2, Bruce Collection. [Race solidarity], draft of speech to Phalanx Club, Nov. 21, 1915, Group D, MSS, B 6-67, reel 2, Bruce Collection.
61. *Washington Sun,* Apr. 9, 1915; *Star of Zion,* Nov. 9, 1916, J. E. Bruce, clipping file, frame 000746-1.
62. Philip H. Brown to Bruce, May 9, 1915, Group B, Letters Received, MSS, Autographed Letters, typescript 361, reel 1, Bruce Collection.
63. George W. Harris to Bruce, Apr. 21, 1915, ibid., typescript 307, reel 1, Bruce Collection.
64. *New York Times* to Bruce, June 29, 1915, Group B, Letters Received, MS 172, Bruce Collection. A. B. F. Perry to Bruce, Feb. 16, 1915, Group B, Letters Received, MSS, Autographed Letters, TS 302, reel 1, Bruce Collection. George W. Ellis to Bruce, Mar. 22, 1915, Group B, Letters Received, MSS, Autographed Letters, TS 303, reel 1, Bruce Collection.
65. Hubert [H. Harrison] to Bruce, Oct. 25, 1915, Group B, MS 42, Letters Received, MSS, Autographed Letters, reel 1, Bruce Collection. Schomburg to Bruce, Jan. 13, 1915, Group B, Letters Received, reel 1, Bruce Collection. [Speech of Bruce] to Ye Friends of Shakespeare, Group C, Letters Received, B 18, reel 1, Bruce Collection. Bruce to Ladies, n.d. Group C, Letters Sent by Bruce, BL 4-74, reel 2, Bruce Collection.
66. [Uncovering African History], lecture read by Bruce at St. Mark's Lyceum, Sept. 20, 1915, Group D, MSS, B 6-55, reel 2, Bruce Collection.
67. "Antonio Maceo Cuban Club," lecture read by Bruce at St. Mark's Lyceum, Dec. 7, 1915, Group D, MSS, B 6-59, reel 2, Bruce Collection. Bruce diary entries for Dec. 25, 1915, Jan. 1, 1916, Scrapbook 2, reel 3, Bruce Collection. Bruce diary entry for Feb. 22, 1916, Bruce Collection.
68. Emmett J. Scott to Bruce, Apr. 10, 1916, John E. Bruce Papers (additions). Melvin Jack Chisum to Emmett Jay Scott, Nov. 15, 1915, Harlan, *The Booker T. Washington Papers,* 13:446.
69. Henrietta Vinton Davis to Bruce, Apr. 30, 1916, Group B, Letters Received, MSS, Autographed Letters, MS 155, reel 1, Bruce Collection.
70. [Read Negro history], draft of essay written by Bruce, Feb. 25, 1916, Group E, Scrapbook 2, reel 3, Bruce Collection.
71. [Training Children], Bruce's draft to ladies, [1916?], Group C, Letters Sent by Bruce, BL 4-74, reel 2, Bruce Collection. Bruce Grit, "The Negro Woman," June 27, 1916, Group E, Scrapbook 2, reel 3, Bruce Collection. Bruce Fragment, n.d., Group E, reel 3, Bruce Collection. David Fulton, *A Plea for Social Justice for the Black Woman, Occasional Paper No. 2* (Yonkers: Negro Society for Historical Research), 1–11.
72. J. E. Bruce. "To Whom It May Concern," Aug. 2, 1916, Group C, Letters Sent by Bruce, B 14-83, reel 2, Bruce Collection.
73. Henrietta Vinton Davis to Bruce, Apr. 30, 1916, Group B, Letters Received, MS 155, reel 1 Bruce Collection. Bruce's diary entry, Jan. 1, 1917, Group E, Scrapbook, reel 3, Bruce Collection.
74. [Race Solidarity], Mar. 25, 1917, Group D, MSS, B 7-92, reel 2, Bruce Collection.
75. Bruce to Arthur Schomburg, July 11, 1917, John E. Bruce Papers (additions). J. E. Bruce, "The Negro Race," *New York Sun,* Jan. 16, 1918. Bruce, letter to the editor, *(Buffalo) Enterprise,* Mar. 18, 1919, J. E. Bruce, clipping file, frame 000746-1. J. A. Rogers to Arthur Schomburg, Jan. 12, 1919, Arthur Schomburg Papers, box 6, folder 44, frames 00459–00463.

76. Bruce's diary entry for Jan. 1, 1919, Group E, Scrapbook 2, reel 3, Bruce Collection.
77. Bruce's diary entries, Dec. 30, 1919, Bruce Collection. Jan. 1, 2, 1920, Group D, MSS, BL 137, reel 2, Bruce Collection.
78. J. E. Bruce, *The African Aeroplane,* circa 1918, Group D, MSS, F 10-19, reel 3, Bruce Collection.
79. Bruce Grit, "That Doctor," *(Omaha) Monitor,* Feb. 8, 1919, Group E, misc., reel 4, Bruce Collection.

Chapter 6

1. Edwin S. Redkey, *Black Exodus: Black Nationalist and Back-to-Africa Movements, 1890–1910* (New Haven: Yale Univ. Press, 1969), 1–23, 195–251.
2. "Edward W. Blyden, Alex. A. Crummell," in Group C, MSS, Bruce Letters, BS 5-21, reel 2, Bruce Collection.
3. Lynch, *Edward Wilmot Blyden,* 105.
4. Rufus. Perry to Bruce, Sept. 20, 1893, John E. Bruce Papers (additions). Seraile, *Fire in His Heart,* 104–6, 135, 153–54.
5. Alexander Crummell to Bruce, Nov. 16, 1893, Group B, Letters Received, MSS, Autographed Letters, MS 412, reel 1, Bruce Collection.
6. Edward W. Blyden to Bruce, Aug. 8, 1895, Group B, Letters Received, B 3, reel 1, Bruce Collection. Blyden to Bruce, Sept. 26, 1896, Group B, Letters Received, B 4, reel 1, Bruce Collection.
7. J. Robert Love to Bruce, July 30, 1897, Group B. Letters Received, MSS, Autographed Letters, MS 157, reel 1, Bruce Collection. Love to Bruce, May 1, 1896, Group B. Letters Received, MSS, Autographed Letters, MS 157, reel 1, Bruce Collection.
8. Bruce Grit, "A Dark Subject," *(Washington) Bee,* Apr. 20, 1889, 1. "Bruce Gritisms," circa 1902, Group D, MSS, B 11-26, reel 3, Bruce Collection.
9. To the editor of the *Planet,* circa 1900, Group C, Letters Sent by Bruce, BL 23, reel 2, Bruce Collection. Gilbert, *The Selected Writings of John Edward Bruce,* 61–62.
10. Lynch, *Edward Wilmot Blyden,* 191–98. For a further discussion, see Tunde Adeleke, *Unafrican Americans: Nineteenth-Century Black Nationalists and the Civilizing Missions* (Lexington: Univ. of Kentucky Press, 1998), 111–52.
11. Bruce Grit, "Fallen among Thieves," [19??], Group E, Bruce Fragments, no. 1, Bruce's MS, reel 3, Bruce Collection. See also Group D, MSS, 9 E-30, n.d., reel 2, Bruce Collection. Redkey, *Black Exodus,* 229–30.
12. Gilbert, *The Selected Writings of John Edward Bruce,* 61–62. John E. Bruce, *New York Age,* Dec. 5, 1903, Group E, misc., reel 3, Bruce Collection. Bishop Henry M. Turner, "The African Trip," *Colored American,* Feb. 21, 1903, 1, 5. John E. Bruce, "Negro Citizenship," *Indianapolis Freeman,* Dec. 27, 1902, Group E, misc., reel 4, Bruce Collection. Bruce Grit, "A Masterly Analysis of the American Negro Problem," *South African Spectator,* Jan. 31, 1903, Group E, Bruce Collection.
13. [Negro Confederation], circa 1915, Group D, MSS, B 11-5, reel 3, Bruce Collection. For Chief Sam, see Edwin S. Redkey, *Black Exodus,* 292–93. Alfred Sam to B. T. Washington, circa Feb. 1915, Harlan, *The Booker T. Washington Papers,* 13:246–47.
14. *New York Tribune,* July 8, 1881, 8. *Sixteenth Annual Report of the American Colonization Society,* Jan. 16–17, 1877, 14–17. [Untitled, n.d., Bruce was not the author,

as he had never visited Africa], Group C, Letters Sent by Bruce, BL 4-60, reel 2, Bruce Collection.
15. Bruce to Schomburg, Feb. 10, 1907, Arthur A. Schomburg Papers, frames 00746–00748, reel 1.
16. George W. Ellis to Bruce, Apr. 27, 1907, Group B, Letters Received, MSS, Autographed Letters, TS 196, reel 1, Bruce Collection.
17. Edward W. Blyden to Bruce, Apr. 2, 1908, Group B, Letters Received, B 6, reel 1, Bruce Collection. [Invitation for Reception, June 26, 1908], Group C, Letters Sent by Bruce, Bl 77, reel 2, Bruce Collection.
18. B. T. Washington to Ernest W. Lyons, May 12, 1908; Lyons to Washington, June 23, 1908; Washington to Elihu Root, June 16, 1908; Root to Washington, June 1, 1908; Harlan, *The Booker T. Washington Papers,* 9:535–36, 586, 578–79, 584.
19. Bruce to Schomburg, Oct. 31, 1908, Schomburg Papers, reel 1. Washington to Dossen, Mar. 16, 1910; Washington to Dossen, Mar. 17, 1910; Washington to Dossen, Apr. 19, 1910; Washington to editor of *Liberian Register,* Jan. 5, 1911; Harlan, *The Booker T. Washington Papers,* 10:278–79, 280–81, 321 n. 1, 531–32 (for Liberian Commission, see 10:xxii, 102).
20. Dossen to Bruce, Sept. 14, 1908, Group D, Letters Received, D 4, reel 1, Bruce Collection. Dossen to Bruce, Aug. 25, 1909, Group B, Letters Received, MSS, Autographed Letters, TS 60, reel 1, Bruce Collection.
21. Bruce Fragments, Feb. 21, 1912, Group E, MSS, reel 1, Bruce Collection. Gatewood, *"Smoked Yankees,"* 231–32, 234–35. Bruce Grit's Column, *Negro World,* Dec. 16, 1922, 4.
22. James J. Dossen to Bruce, Dec. 6, 1915, Group D, Letters Received, D 15, reel 1, Bruce Collection. [African Investment], Group D, MSS, 9 E-76, reel 2, Bruce Collection. Bruce to editor, *The [New York] Evening Sun,* [Sept. ? 1916], Group C, Letters Sent by Bruce, BL 20 reel 2, Bruce Collection. Lecture by M. J. Highes, Feb. [1917], Group E, misc., 13-2, reel 3, Bruce Collection. J. E. K. Agrey to Bruce, [May 15], 1918 (letter 1). Aggrey to Bruce, May 15, 1918, (letter 2), John E. Bruce Papers (additions). Aggrey to Schomburg, May 29, 1918, frames 00014–00015, reel 1, Schomburg Papers.
23. Bruce to Moses Da Rocha, July 28, 1920; Bruce to James J. Dossen, July 28, 1920; Bruce to Abayoni Cole, July 28, 1920, Group C, Letters Sent by Bruce, BL 4-52. Bruce Grit, "James Emman Kwegyir Aggrey," *African Times and Orient Review* 5 (Dec. 1917): 121–23.
24. *Star of Zion,* Mar. 27, 1919, Group E, misc., reel 4, Bruce Collection.

Chapter 7

1. Frederick Douglass [1900–1924], Group D, MSS, 9 E-22, reel 2, Bruce Collection. "In Memoriam," Dec. 31, 1916, Group E, Scrapbook 2, reel 3, Bruce Collection. [Draft of Untitled Speech on Frederick Douglass, n.d.], Group C, MSS, Letters, B 5-15, reel 2, Bruce Collection. Bruce Grit, "Frederick Douglass," *Crusader* 1 (Oct. 1918): 19. *Crusader* 1 (Nov. 1918): 8, 31–32.
2. Robert A. Hill, ed., *The Marcus Garvey and Universal Negro Improvement Association Papers,* 9 vols. (Berkeley: Univ. of California Press, 1983–95), 1:198–99.
3. [Bruce on Garvey], circa 1918–19, Group B, misc., 5-47, box 3, folder 9, Bruce Papers.

4. *The New Negro* for 1918 has not been located. Bruce's questions were reprinted in *Crusader* 5 (Dec. 1921): 31–32.
5. S. Newly for Col. Vernon George W. Kell to Lt. Col. H. A. Parkenham, Nov. 5, 1918, in Hill, *Marcus Garvey*, 1:314.
6. Col. John M. Dunn to Emmett J. Scott, Dec. 6, 1918. Scott to Military Intelligence Division, Attention Major Wrisley Brown, Dec. 11, 1918. H. A. Parkenham to Military Intelligence Division Section Four, Dec. 16, 1918. Hill, *Marcus Garvey*, 1:316–17, 323–24. Hill writes that there is no evidence of such letters between Bruce and Duse Mohammed; see 1:324.
7. Bruce to W. H. Loving, Jan. 13, 1919, Hill, *Marcus Garvey*, 1:349–50.
8. Bruce diary entry, Dec. 30, 1919, Group E, Scrapbook 2, reel 3, Bruce Collection. [Marcus Garvey], circa 1920, Group C, MSS, Bruce Letters, BS 5-14, reel 2, Bruce Collection.
9. *Crisis* 28 (May 1924): 8. *Messenger*, 1919–23. Fox, *The Guardian of Boston*, 251.
10. For Emanuel's poem, "Africa, Arise!," see "Collection of Rare Poems, *Indianapolis Recorder*, Sept. 9, 1916, 1. Seraile, "Henrietta Vinton Davis and the Garvey Movement," 7–24.
11. Bruce to editor, *Durham Reformer*, Aug. 7, 1914, Group E, misc., reel 4, Bruce Collection.
12. [Fool's Paradise], Bruce Grit's Column, circa 1920–24, Group D, MSS, B 11-1, reel 3, Bruce Collection.
13. [Self-Hatred], Bruce Grit's Column, n.d., Group D, MSS, B 11-14, reel 3, Bruce Collection. Tony Martin, *Race First: The Ideological and Organizational Struggle of Marcus Garvey and the Universal Negro Improvement Association* (Westport, Conn.: Greenwood Press, 1976), 164–67.
14. "The Oneness of the Darker Races," Group D, MSS, B 7-86, reel 2, Bruce Collection.
15. J. E. Bruce, "Present Tendencies (and Their Bearing on the Race Problem)," June 20, 1915, Group D, MSS, B 7-89, reel 2, Bruce Collection. Andrea Razafkeriefo, "John E. Bruce," *Crusader* 1 (Dec. 1918): 16.
16. "Can Garvey Win in Africa," *Afro American*, Sept. 10, 1920, 9.
17. "What the UNIA Offers the Negro Race," Commercial Intelligence, Bureau Liberia Bulletin, Jan. 22, 1920, 1:3, in Albert Porte Papers, Schomburg Center, roll 3.
18. Etta (Marie Duchatellier) to Bruce, Jan. 12, 1920, Group B, Letters Received, MSS, Autographed Letters, MS 189, reel 1, Bruce Collection.
19. George Wells Parker to [Bruce] one of the contributing editors of *The Negro World*, Mar. 30, 1920, in Hill, *Marcus Garvey*, 2:279.
20. Bruce's remarks, n.d., are in the editorial "The 'Star' of Newport News Under an Eclipse," *Negro World*, Oct. 25, 1919; Hill, *Marcus Garvey*, 2:106.
21. [Mr. Ajai], Bruce's MSS, Drama, D 10-1, n.d., reel 3, Bruce Collection.
22. Bruce to James J. Dossen, Apr. 3, 1920, Group C, Letters Sent by Bruce, BL 4-40, reel 2, Bruce Collection.
23. Announcement, Liberia's Natal Day Celebration, Group C, MSS, Bruce's Letters, 4 A-81, reel 2, Bruce Collection. [God Is on Africa's Side], Week of June 24, [19]20, Group D, MSS, 9 E-119, reel 2, Bruce Collection.
24. Bruce to Marcus Garvey, Aug. 17, 1920, Group C, Letters Sent by Bruce, BL 4-50, reel 2, Bruce Collection. [Incomplete letter], Bruce to Garvey, [Aug. 17, 1920], (two pages, p. 1 is missing), Bruce Fragment, Bruce MS, Group E, reel 3, Bruce Collection.
25. *Negro World*, Aug. 16, 1924, p. 6.

26. Hill, *Marcus Garvey*, 1: 278. Bruce Fragment, Bruce MS, Group E, reel 3, Bruce Collection.
27. R. H. Duff, "The Black Star Line," J. R. Ralph Casimir Papers, box 1, folder, Book of Poems and Songs, 1919.
28. E. M. E. Agbebi to Bruce, Feb. 20, 1920, Group B, Letters Received, MS 238, MSS, Autographed Letters, reel 1, Bruce Collection.
29. Akinbami Agbebi [Jr.] to Bruce, Apr. 8, 1920, Group B, Letters Received, MS 372, MSS, Autographed Letters, reel 1, Bruce Collection.
30. [Akinbami] Agbebi [Jr.] to Sir, May 15, 1920, Group B, Letters Received, TS 258, reel 1, Bruce Collection.
31. Akinbami [Agbebi Jr.] to Father [Bruce], May 18, 1920, Group B, Letters Received, MS 267, MSS, Autographed Letters, reel 1, Bruce Collection.
32. Adeotan Agbebi to Bruce, June 25, 1920, Group B, Letters Received, A 7, MSS, Autographed Letters, reel 1, Bruce Collection.
33. Akinbami Agbebi Jr. to President, Black Star Line, Aug. 4, 1920, Group B, Letters Received, MS 238, MSS, Autographed Letters, reel 1, Bruce Collection.
34. S. O[kagoo] Logemoh to Bruce, June 15, 1922, Hill, *Marcus Garvey*, 9:453.
35. Logemoh to Bruce, June 22, 1922, Group B, Letters Received, MS 43, MSS, Autographed Letters, reel 1, Bruce Collection. Logemoh to Bruce, June 24, 1922, Group B, Letters Received, MS 44, MSS, Autographed Letters, reel 1, Bruce Collection. Logemoh to Bruce, Jan. 15, 1923, Group B, Letters Received, MS 88, MSS, Autographed Letters, reel 1, Bruce Collection.
36. Logemoh to Bruce, Jan. 15, 1923, Bruce Collection. Cyril A. Crichlow, "A Simple Statement in Three Parts," *Crusader* 6 (Jan.–Feb. 1922): 23–24. Miss C. L. G[ooding], "Our Backward Brothers," *Liberian Patriot*, Aug. 27, 1921, 5–6, in Albert Porte Papers, roll 6.
37. A. S. Wynter Shackleford to Bruce, Aug. 5, 1921, *Negro World*, Sept. 10, 1921, in Hill, *Marcus Garvey*, 9:142. Bruce Grit, "African Fake Prince Exposed," *Negro World*, Feb. 26, 1921, 4.
38. Martin, *Race First*, 164–67. *New York Age*, Aug. 7, 1926, 3. *New York Times*, Aug. 2, 1926, 7.
39. T. McCants Stewart to Francis J. Grimke, Aug. 14, 1920; T. McCants Stewart, "Liberia, the Gem of West Africa"; Woodson, *The Works of Francis J. Grimke* 4:284, 362.
40. *Masonic Quarterly Review* 1 (June 1920), 7, Group E, misc., reel 4, Bruce Collection.
41. [Imitators of Whites], Bruce Grit's Column, week of July 20, 1920, Group D, MSS, B 11–20. reel 3, Bruce Collection.
42. "The White Man's Burden," circa 1920, Group D, MSS, 9 E-15, reel 2, Bruce Collection. "The Complacent Egotism of the White Man," circa 1920, Group D, MSS, 9 E-26, reel 2, Bruce Collection.
43. "The Potentiality of the Press," Aug. 1920, Group D, MSS, 9 E-116, reel 2, Bruce Collection.
44. [Negro Gullibility], Bruce Grit's Column, week of Aug. 28, 1920, Group D, MSS, B 11-13, reel 3, Bruce Collection. J. E. Bruce to editor, July 18, 1920, Group C, Letters Sent by Bruce, BL 9, reel 2, Bruce Collection.
45. Herbert Aptheker, ed., *The Correspondence of W. E. B. Du Bois*, 3 vols. (Amherst: Univ. of Massachusetts Press, 1973) 1:245–46. "Africa for Africans," *Afro American*, Aug. 6, 1920, 1.

46. Bruce to Du Bois, Mar. 3, 1921, Du Bois Papers, reel 9. Bruce to Du Bois, Jan. 25, 1918, Du Bois Papers, reel 6. Bruce Grit's Column, *Negro World,* Mar. 19, 1921, 5. "Garvey Upholds Ku Kluxism," *Crusader* 5 (Oct. 1921): 1243 (extract of *New York World* article of Sept. 9, 1921). Marcus Garvey, "Exposing the Game of Race Destruction among False Leaders," *Negro World,* Dec. 29, 1923, 1.
47. "Garvey Upholds Ku Kluxism," 1243–44.
48. Bruce Grit's Column, *Negro World,* Aug. 19, 1922, 4. Sept. 2, 1922, 7. *Liberian News* 6 (Nov. 1921) in Albert Porte Papers, roll 6.
49. "Back to Africa, a Militant Call," *AME Review* 37 (Oct. 1920): 88. "Marcus Garvey and His League of Nations," *AME Review* 37 (Jan. 1921): 165–66.
50. For Seligman's comments, see Hill, *Marcus Garvey,* 4:239–44. J. E. Bruce, "Mr. Seligman's Contribution," [1921], Group D, MSS, 9 E-40, reel 2, Bruce Collection.
51. Bruce to Arthur Schomburg, July 21, 1921, Schomburg Papers, frame 00754, reel 1. J. E. Bruce, *Negro World,* July 30, 1921, in Hill, *Marcus Garvey,* 3:559–60. *Negro World,* Aug. 24, 1920, in Martin, *Race First,* 34 n. 7. Bruce Grit's Column, *Negro World,* Aug. 21, 1921, 6.
52. *Negro World,* Apr. 2, 1921, in Hill, *Marcus Garvey,* 3:329.
53. John W. Cromwell to Bruce, July 5, 1921, Group B, Letters Received, MSS, Autographed Letters, MS 443, reel 1, Bruce Collection.
54. Bruce to the editor, July 18, 1921, (incomplete letter), Group C, Letters Sent by Bruce, BL 9, reel 2, Bruce Collection. Bruce Grit, 'Race First, Party Next,' *Colored American,* Oct. 28, 1899, 6.
55. Bruce to the editor, July 18, 1921, (incomplete letter), Group C, Letters Sent by Bruce, BL 9, reel 2, Bruce Collection.
56. E. D. Thompson to Bruce, Sept. 7, 1921, Group B, Letters Received, MSS, Autographed Letters, MS 242, reel 1, Bruce Collection. Bruce to Alfred Lefkow, Sept. 20, 1921, Group C, Letters Sent by Bruce, BL 4-39, reel 2, Bruce Collection. [Prayer], Group D, MSS, Bruce Poetry, P 10-5, Oct. 23, 1922, reel 3, Bruce Collection. L. Anwoke to *Negro World,* Sept. 24, 1921, in Hill, *Marcus Garvey,* 9:219.
57. Schomburg to Bruce, 192[?], Group B, Letters Received, MSS, Autographed Letters, MS 35, reel 1, Bruce Collection. Bruce to Flossie [Florence Bruce], July 1, 1922, Group C, Letters Sent by Bruce, 4 BL-34, reel 2, Bruce Collection. Bruce to Florence [Bruce], n. d., Group D, MSS, Bruce Poetry, BP 10-9, reel 3, John Edward Bruce Papers, Manuscripts, Archives and Rare Books Division, Schomburg Center for Research in Black Culture, New York Public Library, Astor, Lenox and Tilden Foundations. "A Love Song," 1919, MSS, 784-B, folder L-M, Sheet Music Collection, Harry T. Burleigh Collection.

Chapter 8

1. Hill, *Marcus Garvey,* 9:lxxiii, lxxiv, lxxv, lxxvii, lxxviii.
2. J. E. Bruce, [Editorial Notes], July 19, 1920[?], Group D, MSS, 9 E-31, reel 2, Bruce Collection. Margaret Robinson, "Garvey's Dangerous Incitements," *Crusader* 3 (Nov. 1920): 13.
3. Randall K. Burkett, *Black Redemption: Churchmen Speak for the Garvey Movement* (Philadelphia: Temple Univ. Press, 1978), 102–11, 117–20, 126–37. Burkett noted that at least 250 clergymen in the United States were Garvey supporters (see page 9).

Notes to Pages 183–89 **237**

4. J. E. Bruce, "The Reason Why," circa 1921, Group D, MSS, 9 E-56, reel 2, Bruce Collection. See also MSS, 9 E-57.
5. Bruce to the editor of *(New York) World,* Jan. 17, 1922, Group C, Letters Sent by Bruce, BL 4-27, reel 1, Bruce Collection.
6. Bruce to George C. Sherlock, Jan. 18, 1922, Group C, Letters Sent by Bruce, BL 4-57, reel 2, Bruce Collection.
7. J. E. Bruce's Notes. Lecture to Executive Secretaries, UNIA, Feb. 11, 1922, Group D, MSS, B 6-68, reel 2, Bruce Collection.
8. Bruce to J. R. Ralph Casimir, Feb. 16, 1922, J. Raphiel Ralph Casimir Papers, box 2, folder-scrapbook. *New York Times,* Nov. 9, 1921, 1.
9. Confidential Informant 800 to George F. Ruch, May 8, 1922, Hill, *Marcus Garvey,* 4:628–29.
10. Martin, *Race First,* 14.
11. Bruce, [draft of article], "The Problems That Face the Negro in America," May 28, 1922, Group D, MSS, B 7-94, reel 2, Bruce Collection.
12. J. E. Bruce, *The Making of a Race* (New York, 1922), 1-16, Group E, misc., reel 4, Bruce Collection. Editorial, "The Making of a Race," *Negro World,* July 29, 1922, 4.
13. Hill, *Marcus Garvey,* 9:xlix. Martin, *Race First,* 345–46.
14. Editorial, " The Ku Klux Klan: A Query," *Negro World,* Oct. 29, 1921, 4. Editorial, "Marcus Garvey and the K.K.K.," *Negro World,* July 29, 1922, 4. Bruce Grit's Column, *Negro World,* Apr. 23, 1921, 5. Aug. 12, 1922, 8. J. E. Bruce, Passing Show Column, *Negro World,* Nov. 10, 24, 1923, 4. Bruce [They Want to Kill Garvey], circa 1922, Group D, MSS, 9-46, reel 2, Bruce Collection. For rumors of assassination attempts on Garvey, see *Negro World,* Aug. 19, 1922.
15. Martin, *Race First,* 311–15.
16. Marcus Garvey to William Pickens, July 10, 1922; Pickens to Garvey, July 24, 1922, William Pickens Papers, box 7, reel 4.
17. Bruce to Florence [Bruce], June 21, 1922, Group C, Letters Sent by Bruce, BL 4-37, reel 2, Bruce Collection. Bruce to Florence, June 22, 1922, Group C, Letters Sent by Bruce, 4 MSL-28, reel 2, Bruce Collection. Bruce to Florence, June 2, 1922, Group C, Letters Sent by Bruce, reel 2, Bruce Collection.
18. John E. Bruce Papers (additions), July 1, 1922, Group C, Letters Sent by Bruce, 4 BL-34, reel 2, Bruce Collection.
19. Bruce to Florence Bruce, June 22, 1922, Group C. Letters Sent by Bruce, 4 MSL-28, reel 2, Bruce Collection.
20. Martin, *Race First,* 138–39.
21. J. E. K. Aggrey to Daddie Bruce, June 28, 1922, Group B, Letters Received, MSS, Autographed Letters, MS 63, reel 1, Bruce Collection.
22. R. E. Enright to Bruce, June 2, 1922, Group B, Letters Received, MSS, Autographed Letters, MS 346, reel 1, Bruce Collection. Marcus Garvey, "Awakened Africa Startles the World," *Negro World,* Apr. 14, 1923, 1.
23. Marcus Garvey to League of Nations, July 22, 1922, Hill, *Marcus Garvey,* 9:532–39.
24. "The Passing Show," *Negro Daily Times,* Oct. 19, 1922, J. E. Bruce, clipping file, 000746-1. Bruce Grit, "An Iridescent Dream," *Colored American,* Feb. 4, 1899, 1.
25. T. Thomas Fortune to Bruce, Feb. 14, 1923, Group C, MSS, Bruce Letters, 4 A-63, reel 2, Bruce Collection. Bruce Grit's Column, *Negro World,* June 30, 1923, 4.
26. "The Passing Show," *Negro Daily Times,* Oct. 17, 18, 23, 1922, J. E. Bruce, clipping file, 000746-1.

27. "The Passing Show," *Negro Daily Times,* Oct. 4, 1922, , J. E. Bruce, clipping file, 000746-1. Bruce Grit's Column, *Negro World,* June 10, 1922, 5. Bruce Grit, "Frederick Douglass," *Crusader* 1 (Oct. 1918): 19.
28. Speech of Bruce to Virgin Islanders, Nov. 19, 1922, Group D, MSS, B 6-71, reel 2, Bruce Collection.
29. Bruce Grit's Column, *Negro World,* June 2, 1923, 4.
30. J. E. Bruce, *The Call of a Nation,* n.d., Group D, MSS, F 10-5, reel 3, Bruce Collection.
31. Amy J. Garvey, comp., *Philosophy and Opinion of Marcus Garvey,* 2 vols. (London: Frank Cass & Co., 1967), 2: 283.
32. "The Passing Show," *Negro Daily Times,* Feb. 5, 1923, J. E. Bruce, clipping file, 000746-2. Garvey, *Philosophy and Opinion,* 2:293–308.
33. Bruce Grit's Column, *Negro World,* Feb. 24, 1923, 6.
34. Ibid., June 23, 1923, 4. Seraile, "Henrietta Vinton Davis and the Garvey Movement," 15. See also *Negro World,* June 16, 1923, 5. Marcus Garvey, "Gentlemen, Can You Let the Tiger Loose?"
35. *Negro World,* June 23, 1923, 1, 35; July 7, 1923, 4. Bruce to Florence [Bruce], July 1, 1923, Group C, Letters Sent by Bruce, BL 4-29, reel 2, Bruce Collection. "Garvey Indulges in Tilt with Judge," *New York Times,* June 6, 1923, 19. Theodore Kornweibel Jr., *"Seeing Red" Federal Campaigns Against Black Militancy, 1919–1925* (Bloomington: Indiana Univ. Press, 1998), chap. 6.
36. Bruce to George B. Christian, July 10, 1923, Hill, *Marcus Garvey,* 5:396–97. Bruce Grit's Column, *Negro World,* July 14, 1923, 4; July 28, 1923, 6; Aug. 11, 1923, 6; Aug. 25, 1923, 4. For Garvey, see *Negro World,* Aug. 11, 1923, 1.
37. The Aug. 16 letter from Bruce to Coolidge was printed in *Negro World,* Sept. 8, 1923, 2, 10. Coolidge to Bruce, Aug. 20, 1923, Group C, Letters Received, C 12, reel 1, Bruce Collection. "Coolidge and the Negro," *Negro World,* Sept. 8, 1923, 4.
38. *Negro World* printed full-page ads announcing the objectives of the Negro Political Union. See, for example, November 8, 1924.
39. [Bruce Grit's Column], circa, Sept.–Oct. 1923, box 3, folder 12, B 6-70, Bruce Collection. Bruce Grit's Column, *Negro World,* July 14, 1923, 4. Martin, *Race First,* 193–94. For Garvey's remarks, see *Negro World,* Sept. 22, 1923, 3.
40. *Negro World,* Oct. 27, 1923, 4. See also Bruce's column in *Negro World,* Sept. 22, 1923, 6, and Dec. 1, 1923, 4.
41. "The Golden Dream of Negro Nationality," *AME Review* 11 (July 1923): 44–45. Joseph G. Tucker, Special Report, June 28, 1924, in Henrietta Vinton Davis, FBI Files, Schomburg Center.
42. J. E. Bruce, "The Passing Show," *Negro World,* Nov. 24, 1923, 4.
43. Amy J. Garvey to J. R. Ralph Casimir, Aug. 6, 1923, box 1, Casimir Papers. For a fuller account of Casimir's activities, see Tony Martin, "A Pan Africanist in Dominica: J. R. Ralph Casimir and the Garvey Movement, 1919–1924," in John P. Henderson and Harry A Reed, eds., *Studies in the African Diaspora* (Dover, Mass.: Majority Press, 1989),124–44. J. R. Ralph Casimir, "Greetings from Dominica," *Crusader* 5 (Nov. 1921): 30–31.
44. Bruce to Casimir, Nov. 22, 1923, box 1, Casimir Papers.
45. Bruce-song, Group D, MSS, Bruce Poetry, P 10-14, reel 3, Bruce Collection.
46. Martin, *Race First,* 194–95. T. Thomas Fortune to Bruce, Feb. 14, 1923, Group C, MSS, Bruce Letters, 4 A-63, reel 2, Bruce Collection.
47. Bruce Grit's Column, *Negro World,* June 2, 1923, 4.

48. Bruce to Florence [Bruce], July 1, 1923, Group C, Letters Sent by Bruce, BL 4-29, reel 2, Bruce Collection.
49. Bruce to Casimir, *Negro World,* Oct. 6, 1923, 6. Bruce to Dear Florence, Oct. 24, 1923 Group C, Letters Sent by Bruce, BL 4- 35, reel 2, Bruce Collection.
50. Casely Hayford to Bruce, Nov. 24, 1923, Group H, Letters Received, H 5, reel 1, Bruce Collection.
51. *Negro World,* Oct. 20, 1923, 4.
52. Bruce to Casimir, Nov. 22, 1923, box 1, Casimir Papers.
53. Bruce to Dear Kiddo [Florence Bruce], Jan. 1, 1924, Group C, MSS, Bruce Letters, 4 A-36, reel 2, Bruce Collection.
54. Bruce to Casely Hayford, Jan. 2, 1924, Group C, MSS, Bruce Letters, BL 4-33, reel 2, Bruce Collection. Marcus Garvey, "Exposing the Game of Race Destruction among False Leaders," *Negro World,* Dec. 29., 1923, 1.
55. Martin, *Race First,* 136–37. *Liberian News* 9 (Feb. 1924): 3, in Albert Porte Papers, roll 6. *Negro World,* Sept. 6, 1924, 3, 10. *New York Times,* Aug. 27, 1924, 10; Aug. 28, 1924, 10, 16. "UNIA to Hold Conclave in Liberia," *New York Amsterdam News,* May 16, 1923, 8.
56. E. R. Mathews to Casimir, Feb. 24, 1924, box 1, Casimir Papers.
57. William H. Wilkes to Florence Bruce, Mar. 20, 1924, June 10, 1924, Group E, Mrs. Bruce (Florence), reel 3, Bruce Collection.
58. Enid L. to Bruce, circa 1924. John E. Bruce Papers (additions).
59. "Reminiscence," circa 1924, Group D, MSS, B 8-136, reel 2, Bruce Collection.
60. Bruce Grit's Column, Negro World, Dec. 16, 1922, 4. [Death], July 2, 1915, Group D, MSS, B 8- 110, reel 2, Bruce Collection. John E. Bruce's Death Certificate #26183, Aug. 7, 1924, Dept. of Health, State of New York.
61. T. Thomas Fortune, "Sir John Edward Bruce," *Negro World,* Aug. 16, 1924, 4.
62. Casely Hayford to Casimir, Jan. 10, 1925, Casely Hayford Correspondence Folder, box 1, Casimir Papers.
63. Tony Martin, ed., *African Fundamentalism: A Literary and Cultural Anthology of Garvey's Harlem Renaissance* (Dover, Mass.: Majority Press, 1990), 231–32.
64. *Journal of Negro History* 9 (Oct. 1924): 578.
65. *Pittsburgh Courier,* Aug. 16, 1924, Tuskegee, clipping file, reel 237.
66. For Schomburg's remarks and other resolutions, see *Negro World,* Aug. 16, 1924, 6; Aug. 30, 1924, 18.
67. Olive Bruce Millar to the editor, *New York Amsterdam News,* Aug. 29, 1924, J. E. Bruce, clipping file.
68. Author's interview with Onnie Millar, Jan. 5, 1998; Oct. 22, 1998.
69. "Men of Times," [John E. Bruce], *Crusader* 1 (Feb. 1919): 15.
70. F. A. Bruce to Miss Grant, Feb. 25, 1925, reel 3, Bruce Collection. F. A. Bruce to Arthur Schomburg, May 28, 1936, frames 000743–000745, reel 1, Schomburg Papers. Florence Bruce's Death Certificate #25990, Dec. 26, 1942 Dept. of Health, Borough of Manhattan.

Epilogue

1. Schomburg to Bruce, Jan. 1, 1912, in Sinnette, *Arthur A. Schomburg,* 216 n. 49. I could not find this comment in either Bruce's or Schomburg's papers.

2. Editorial, "The Twelve Greatest Negroes," *Negro World,* Aug. 26, 1922, 4.
3. J. R. Ralph Casimir, "Bruce Grit," *Negro World,* Oct. 6, 1923, 6.
4. [Untitled manuscript], Oct. 5, 1889, reel 2, Bruce Collection. Bruce Grit, "The Hour of Prayer," *The Colored American,* June 3, 1899, 4. Bruce Grit's Column, *Negro World,* Mar. 19, 1921, 5. Bruce Grit, "Tulsa: Field of Blood," *Negro World,* June 25, 1921, 5. Bruce Grit's Column, *Negro World,* Dec. 31, 1921, 4.
5. Bruce Grit's Column, *Negro World,* Apr. 23, 1921, 5. July 22, 1922, 6; Sept. 22, 1923, 6.
6. Interview with Onnie Millar, Oct. 22, 1998.

Bibliography

Books

Adams, Cyrus F. *The Republican Party and the Afro American: A Book of Facts and Figures.* 3d ed. New York: Republican National Committee, 1912.

Adeleke, Tunde. *Unafrican Americans: Nineteenth-Century Black Nationalists and the Civilizing Mission.* Lexington: Univ. of Kentucky Press, 1998.

Alexander, Charles. *One Hundred Distinguished Leaders.* Atlanta: Franklin Print Co., 1899.

Aptheker, Herbert A., ed. *A Documentary History of the Negro People in the United States.* Vols. 1–3. New York: Citadel Press, 1951–73.

———. *The Correspondence of W. E. B. Du Bois.* 3 vols. Amherst: Univ. of Massachusetts Press, 1973–78.

Bracey, John, August Meier, and Elliot Rudwick, eds. *Black Nationalism in America.* Indianapolis: Bobbs-Merrill, 1970.

Bruce, John E. *A Defense of the Colored Soldier Who Fought in the War of the Rebellion.* Yonkers, n.d.

———. *Concentration of Energy.* Albany, 1899.

———. *Short Biographical Sketches of Eminent Negro Men and Women in Europe and the United States.* Yonkers, 1900.

———. *The Awakening of Hezekiah Jones.* Hopkinsville, Ky.: P. H. Brown Pub., 1916.

———. *The Blood Red Record.* Albany: Argus Co., 1900.

———. *The Making of a Race.* New York, 1922.

———. *Washington Colored Society.* Washington, 1877.

Burkett, Randall K. *Black Redemption: Churchmen Speak for the Garvey Movement.* Philadelphia: Temple Univ. Press, 1978.

Ferris, William H. *The African Abroad.* 2 vols. New Haven, Conn.: Tuttle, Morehouse & Taylor Press, 1913.

Florette, Henri. *The Unknown Soldiers: Black American Troops in World War I.* Philadelphia: Temple Univ. Press, 1974.

Fox, Stephen R. *The Guardian of Boston: William Monroe Trotter.* New York: Atheneum, 1970.

Garvey, Amy J., comp. *The Philosophy and Opinions of Marcus Garvey.* 2 vols. London: Frank Cass & Co., 1967.

Gatewood, Willard B. *Black Americans and the White Man's Burden of Race, 1898–1903.* Urbana: Univ. of Illinois Press, 1975.

———. *"Smoked Yankees" and the Struggle for Empire: Letters from Negro Soldiers, 1898–1902.* Urbana: Univ. of Illinois Press, 1971.

Gerber, David A. *Black Ohio and the Color Line, 1860–1915.* Urbana: Univ. of Illinois Press, 1976.

Gilbert, Peter H., comp. and ed. *The Selected Writings of John Edward Bruce: Militant Black Journalist.* New York: Arno Press, 1971.

Green, John P. *Facts Stranger Than Fiction: Seventy Years of a Busy Life with Reminiscences of Many Great and Good Men and Women.* Cleveland: Rich Printing Co., 1920.

Harlan, John R. *Booker T. Washington: The Making of a Black Leader, 1856–1901.* New York: Oxford Univ. Press, 1972.

———. *The Booker T. Washington Papers.* 14 vols. Urbana: Univ. of Illinois Press, 1975–84.

Hatchett, William. *The Lincoln Murder Conspiracies.* Urbana: Univ. of Illinois Press, 1983.

Hill, Robert A., ed. *The Marcus Garvey and Universal Negro Improvement Association Papers.* 9 vols. Berkeley: Univ. of California Press, 1983–95.

Kilson, Martin, and Adelaide Hill, eds. *Apropos of Africa: Afro American Leaders and the Romance of Africa.* Garden City, N.Y. 1971.

Kornweibel, Theodore, Jr. *"Seeing Red": Federal Campaigns Against Black Militancy, 1919–1925.* Bloomington: Indiana Univ. Press, 1998.

Lane, Ann J. *The Brownsville Affair: National Crisis and the Black Reaction.* Port Washington: Kennikat Press, 1971.

Lewis, David L. *W. E. B. Du Bois: Biography of a Race.* Vol. 1. New York: Henry Holt and Co., 1993.

Logan, Rayford W., Michael R. Winston, Ernest Kaiser, eds. *The Dictionary of American Negro Biography.* New York: W. W. Norton & Co., 1982.

Lynch, Hollis R. *Edward Wilmot Blyden: Pan Negro Patriot.* London: Oxford Univ. Press, 1967.

Martin, Tony, ed. *African Fundamentalism: A Literary and Cultural Anthology of Garvey's Harlem Renaissance.* Dover, Mass.: Majority Press, 1990.

———. *Race First: The Ideological and Organizational Struggle of Marcus Garvey and the Universal Negro Improvement Association.* Westport, Conn.: Greenwood Press, 1976.

Moss, Alfred A. *The American Negro Academy: Voice of the Talented Tenth.* Baton Rouge: Louisiana State Univ. Press, 1981.

Moss, Frank, comp. *Story of the Riot.* New York: Citizens' Protective League, 1900.

Olcott, Charles J. *William McKinley.* Boston: Houghton Mifflin, 1916.

Penn, Garland I. *The Afro American Press and Its Editors.* Springfield, Mass.: Willey & Co., 1891.

Redkey, Edwin S. *Black Exodus: Black Nationalism and Back-to-Africa Movements, 1890–1910.* New Haven: Yale Univ. Press, 1969.

Rigsby, Gregory U. *Alexander Crummell: Pioneer in Nineteenth Century Pan African Thought.* New York: Greenwood Press, 1987.

Seraile, William. *Fire in His Heart: Bishop Benjamin Tucker Tanner and the A.M.E. Church.* Knoxville: Univ. of Tenn. Press, 1998.

Sinnette, Elinor Des Verney. *Arthur A. Schomburg: Black Bibliophile and Collector.* Detroit: New York Public Library and Wayne State Univ. Press, 1989.

Thomas, William H. *The American Negro.* New York: Macmillan Co., 1901.

Thornbrough, Emma Lou. *T. Thomas Fortune: Militant Journalist.* Chicago: Univ. of Chicago Press, 1972.

Tweedy, John. *A History of Republican National Committees, 1856–1908.* Danbury, Conn., 1910.

Walton, Hanes, Jr. *Black Politics: A Theoretical and Structural Analysis.* Philadelphia: J. B. Lippincott Co., 1972.

Weaver, John D. *The Brownsville Raid.* New York: W. W. Norton, 1971.

Woodson, Carter G., ed. *The Works of Francis J. Grimke.* 4 vols. Washington: Associated Publishers, 1942.

Articles

Beard, Richard L., and Cyril E. Zoerner. "Associated Negro Press: Its Founding, Ascendancy, and Demise." *Journalism Quarterly* 46 (spring 1969): 47–52.

Bruce, John E. "Frederick Douglass." *Crusader* 1 (Oct. 1918): 19.

———. "The Critic Revealed; or, the Deadly Peril." *Howard's American Magazine* 6 (Apr. 1901): 364–68.

———. "The Necessity for Business Leagues." *Voice of the Negro* 1 (Aug. 1904): 338–39.

———. "The Stronger Nations vs. the Weaker Nations." *Voice of the Negro* 2 (Apr. 1905): 256–57.

Crichlow, Cyril A. "A Simple Statement in Three Parts." *Crusader* 6 (Jan.–Feb. 1922): 23–24.

Crowder, Ralph L. "John Edward Bruce, Edward Wilmot Blyden, Alexander Crummell, and J. Robert Love: Mentors, Patrons, and the Evolution of a Pan-African Network." *Afro-Americans in New York Life and History* 20 (July 1996): 59–91.

Da Rocha, Moses. "A Tribute for the Negro Soldier." *Crusader* 1 (July 1918): 14–15.

"The Democratic Return to Power: Its Effects?" *AME Church Review* 1 (July 1884): 213–50.

Du Bois, W. E. B. "The African Roots of War." *Atlantic Monthly* 45 (May 1915): 707–14.

"The Golden Dream of Negro Nationality." *AME Review* 11 (July 1923): 44–45.

Hampton, Wade. "What Negro Supremacy Means." *Forum* 5 (June 1888): 383.

"Industrial Education: Will It Solve the Negro Problem?" *Colored American Magazine* 7 (Jan. 1904): 13–21.

Martin, Tony. "A Pan Africanist in Dominica: J. R. Ralph Casimir and the Garvey Movement, 1919–1923." In *Studies in the African Diaspora,* ed. John P. Henderson and Harry A. Reed. Dover, Mass., 1989.

"Reprieve Granted Black Soldiers after Sixty-six Years." *Jet* 43 (Oct. 19, 1972): 20–21.

Seraile, William. "A Colored Man in the Cabinet: An Idea Before Its Time." *Journal of the Afro American Historical and Genealogical Society* 2 (spring and fall 1990): 79–92.

———. "Henrietta Vinton Davis and the Garvey Movement." *Afro Americans in New York Life and History* 7 (July 1983): 7–24.

———. "The Brief Diplomatic Career of Henry Highland Garnet." *Phylon* 46 (spring 1985): 71–81.

Shepperson, George. "Notes on Negro American Influences on the Emergence of African Nationalism." *Journal of African History* 1 (1960): 299–312.

Steward, T. G. "The First Move in the War." *Independent* (Apr. 25, 1898): 535–36.

Thornbrough, Emma Lou. "Booker T. Washington As Seen by His White Contemporaries." *Journal of Negro History* 53 (Apr. 1968): 161–81.

Watkins, Frances Ellen. "The Greatest Want." *Anglo African Magazine* 1 (May 1859): 160.

Wolgemuth, Kathleen L. "Woodrow Wilson's Appointment Policy and the Negro." *Journal of Negro History* 24 (Nov. 1958): 458–66.

Wynell, Lewis N. "Brownsville: The Reaction of the Negro Press." *Phylon* 33 (summer 1972): 153–60.

Directory

Boyd's Directory for the District of Columbia, 1876–1893. Washington, D.C.: R. L. Polk & Co.

Dissertations

Chase, Hal S. "Honey for Friends, Stings for Enemies: William Calvin Chase and the *(Washington) Bee,* 1882–1921." Univ. of Pennsylvania, 1973.

Pattan, Gerald W. "War and Race: The Black Officer in the American Military, 1915–1925." Univ. of Iowa, 1978.

Manuscript Collections

American Missionary Association. Papers. Schomburg Center for Research in Black Culture, New York Public Library.

Bruce, John E. Papers (additions). Schomburg Center for Research in Black Culture, New York Public Library.

Bruce, John E. Clipping file. John E. Bruce Collection, Schomburg Center for Research in Black Culture, New York Public Library.

Burleigh, Harry T. Collection. Schomburg Center for Research in Black Culture, New York Public Library.

Casimir, J. R. Ralph. Papers. Schomburg Center for Research in Black Culture, New York Public Library.

Cleveland, Grover. Papers. Library of Congress, Washington, D.C. Microfilm copy, Columbia Univ. Library, New York.

Davis, John P. Papers. Schomburg Center for Research in Black Culture, New York Public Library.

Du Bois, W. E. B. Papers. Schomburg Center for Research in Black Culture, New York Public Library.

Fortune, T. Thomas. Scrapbook. Schomburg Center for Research in Black Culture, New York Public Library.

Garfield, James A. Papers. Library of Congress, Washington, D.C. Microfilm copy, Columbia Univ. Library, New York.

Green, John P. Papers. Western Reserve Historical Society, Cleveland. Microfilm copy, Schomburg Center for Research in Black Culture, New York Public Library.

Harrison, Benjamin. Papers. Library of Congress, Washington, D.C. Microfilm copy, Columbia Univ. Library, New York.

McKinlay, Whitefield. Papers. Schomburg Center for Research in Black Culture, New York Public Library.

McKinley, William. Papers. Library of Congress, Washington, D.C. Microfilm copy, Columbia Univ. Library, New York.

Murray, Daniel A. Papers. State Historical Society of Wisconsin. Microfilm copy, Schomburg Center for Research in Black Culture, New York Public Library.

Myers, George A. Collection. Ohio Historical Society, Columbus. Microfilm copy, Schomburg Center for Research in Black Culture, New York Public Library.

Pickens, William. Papers. Schomburg Center for Research in Black Culture, New York Public Library.

Porte, Albert. Papers. Schomburg Center for Research in Black Culture, New York Public Library.

Roosevelt, Theodore. Papers. Library of Congress, Washington, D.C. Microfilm copy, Columbia Univ. Library, New York.

Schomburg, Arthur A. Papers. Schomburg Center for Research in Black Culture, New York Public Library.

Taft, William H. Papers. Library of Congress, Washington, D.C. Microfilm copy, Columbia Univ. Library, New York.

Washington, Booker T. Papers. Library of Congress, Washington, D.C., and Schomburg Center for Research in Black Culture, New York Public Library.

Williamson, Henry A. Papers. Schomburg Center for Research in Black Culture, New York Public Library.

Woodson, Carter G. Papers. Schomburg Center for Research in Black Culture, New York Public Library.

Birth and Death Certificates

Bruce, Florence. Death Certificate #25990, Dec. 25, 1942. Dept. of Health. Borough of Manhattan.

Bruce, John E. Death Certificate #26183, Aug. 7, 1924. Dept. of Health. State of New York.

Bruce, [Olive]. Birth Certificate #49295, July 22, 1888. Dept. of Health. District of Columbia.

Millar, Olive Bruce. Death Certificate #1963, Jan. 20, 1943. Dept of Health. Borough of Manhattan.

Archival and Government Records

Bruce, John Edward. Bruce Collection. Calendar of manuscripts in the Schomburg Collection of Negro Literature, pt. 1, 1942. New York Public Library.

Davis, Henrietta Vinton. Federal Bureau of Investigation File. Schomburg Center for Research in Black Culture, New York Public Library.

Metropolitan Police, Washington, D.C. Reports of arrests for 1880. Record Group 351.5 National Archives, Washington, D.C.

U.S. Bureau of the Census. *Population Schedules of the Seventh Census of the United States. Schedule Two: Maryland Slave Schedules of 1850.* Washington, D.C., 1850

U.S. Bureau of the Census, *Population Schedules of the Eighth Census of the United States. Schedule One: Free Inhabitants in Fifth Election District in the County of Prince Georges State of Maryland, enumerated June 13, 1860.* Washington, D.C., 1860.

U.S. Bureau of the Census. *Population Schedules of the Eighth Census of the United States. Schedule Two: Slave Inhabitants in the Fifth Election District. Prince Georges County, Maryland.* Washington, D.C., 1860.

U.S. Bureau of the Census. *Thirteenth Census of the United States, Taken in the Year 1910.* Vol. 111. Washington, D.C., 1913.

U.S. Congress. House. *Report on Emancipated Slaves in the District of Columbia, Feb. 16, 1864.* Vol. 9, 38th Cong., 1st sess., 1864, H. Doc. 42.

United States v Charles E. Bruce. Case 11, 291, Box 45. Criminal case file 1863–1934. Record Group 021. National Archives, Washington, D.C.

Newspapers

African Times and Orient Review (London)
(Baltimore) Ledger
(Boston) Guardian
Boston Traveller
(Charlotte, N.C.) Star of Zion
Chicago Defender
Cleveland Gazette
Cleveland Herald
Denver Statesman
(Indianapolis) Freeman
Kingston Advocate (Jamaica)
New York Age
New York Evening Post
New York Globe
(New York) Negro Daily Times
(New York) Negro World
New York Times
New York Tribune
New York World
(Norfolk) Journal and Guide
(Omaha) Afro American Sentinel
(Philadelphia) Christian Recorder
Pittsburgh Courier
(Richmond) Planet
Savannah Tribune
South African Spectator
St. Louis Tribune
(Washington) Bee
Washington Grit
(Washington) People's Advocate
(Washington) Sunday Republic
Yonkers Daily News
(Yonkers) Statesman

Addresses

Bruce, John E. Address before the President and Members of the Yonkers Sunday Club, [1908?] Yonkers, N.Y.

Bruce, John E. "The Blot on the Escutcheon: An Address Delivered before the Afro-American League," Apr. 4, 1890, Washington, D.C.

Bruce, John E. "The Significance of Brotherhood. An Address Delivered by John E. Bruce before the Craftsmen's Club," Mar. 6, 1910, New York.

Hague, William, and E. N. Kirk. *Address of Rev. Drs. Wm Hague and E. N. Kirk. Annual Meeting of the Educational Commission for Freedmen at the Old South Church, May 28, 1863.* Boston: David Clapp, printer 1863.

Inaugural Addresses of the Presidents of the United States, 1789–1969, Washington, D.C., 1969.

Phillips, Henry L. "In Memoriam of the Late Rev. Alex Crummell. An Address Delivered before the American Negro Historical Society of Philadelphia," 1898.

Schomburg, Arthur A. "Racial Integrity: A Plea for the Establishment of a Chair of Negro History in Our Schools and Colleges," Occasional Paper No. 3, July 1913, Negro Society for Historical Research, New York.

Index

Abbott, Lyman, 79, 148
Abbott, Robert, 192
Adams, Cyrus F., 70, 71, 72, 88–89
Africa: African American emigration to, 152, 153; African American investment in, 157, 174–75; belittled by African Americans, 134; Bruce's desire to visit, 14, 171; Butler Bill and, 153; contribution to world history, x, 134; Du Bois visit to, 197; European colonization of, 156; European presence in, 156; redemption of, 170; true home of the Negro, 179, 180; UNIA and, 198
African Abroad, The (Ferris), 139
African Americans: allegiance to Republican party, 64, 79–80; anti-lynching concerns of, 44, 65–66, 97, 98; books about, 123, 127–29; citizenship rights denied to, 87; defection to Democratic party, 43–44, 65–66, 97, 98; economic condition of, 127–28; education of, 5–6, 39–40; labor unions and, 130–31; lynching of, 44–45, 65–66, 133, 201; morals of, 127–29; patriotism of, 94; racism and, 87; Republican party patronage and, 31–38, 47–49, 72–73, 76; Theodore Roosevelt's presidential policies and, 68, 81, 85; as soldiers, 52–53, 80–81, 94–96
African Blood Brotherhood, 178, 186
African Times and Orient Review, 142, 146
Afro-American Council, 59, 64, 66; Bruce as financial secretary of, 101; Bruce's effort to undermine, 105–6; dissolution of, 108; Hayes' incident and, 105; infiltrated by B. T. Washington's spies, 102, 105–6; stop Taft movement and, 83; Alexander Walters and, 56, 82, 101; weakness of, 103
Afro-American League: agenda of, 101; and Bruce, 100; criticism of, 101; dissolution of, 101; failure to confront Republican party, 101; founded by Timothy Thomas Fortune, 100; leadership of, 101; membership of, 101
Afro-American News Syndicate, 47

Afro-American Steamship and Mercantile Co., 153
Agebi, Adeotan, 174
Agebi, Akinbami, Jr., 173
Agebi, E. M. E., 173
Agebi, Mojola, 116, 135, 173
Aggrey, James E. K., 120; criticizes Garvey, 188; Phelps-Stokes Fund and, 162, 187; relationship with Bruce, 187; scholarship of, 162; solicits Bruce and Schomburg for investment scheme, 161–62
Alexander, Charles, 58
Alger, Russell B., 28
Ali, Duse Mohammed, 93, 142, 165–66, 187
Allain, Theophile T., 70, 71
Allison, William B., 47
AME Review, 130, 179, 195
American Colonization Society (ACS), 14, 152–53
American Negro, The (Thomas), 127–29
American Negro Academy (ANA): agenda of, 110; and Bruce, 110–12; and Alexander Crummell, 110; and color issue, 112–13; criticism of leadership, 113–14; demise of, 111; membership of, 111, 226n.36; origins of, 110; and Arthur Schomburg, 114
American Protective League, 132
Amos, John, 193
Anderson, Charles W., 71, 72, 76, 84, 91, 105, 106, 109, 187
Anderson, J. C., 164
Anderson, William T., 72
Antrobus, Reginald, 138
Arabic Bible in the Soudan, The (Blyden), 138
Archer, J. R., 143
"Argus." *See* Bruce, John Edward
Arnett, Benjamin W., 31, 47, 48, 60, 70, 71, 72–73
Arnett, Henry Y., 68
Arthur, Chester A., 14, 16, 22, 24
Associated Correspondents of Race Newspapers, 42–43

249

Index

Associated Negro Press, 43
Association for the Study of Negro Life and History (ASNLH), 117
Avery, W. B., 23
Awakening of Hezekiah Jones, The (Bruce), 92
Ayers, Alice, xi
Azor, The, 152

Bagnall, Robert W., 192
Bailey, Ida D., 104, 105
Baldwin, William H., Jr., 79
Barclay, Arthur, 159
Barnett, Claude A., 43
Bee, The, 20, 36, 54
Benton, Thomas H., 8
Bethesda Literary Society, 17
Birth of A Nation, The (Griffith), 143, 144
Bishop, Florence. *See* Bruce, Florence
Bissell, A. T., 16
Black, R. C. *See* Scott, Emmett J.
Black and White: Land, Labor and Politics in the South (Fortune), 28
Black Nationalism in America (Bracey, Meier and Rudwick), ix
"Black Sleuth, The" (Bruce), 137
Black Star Shipping Line: Africans as agents of, 173–74; Africans encouraged by Bruce to invest in, 172–73; Bruce and financial problems of, 175; insolvency of, 175, 182
Blaine, James G., 22, 24–25, 26, 28
Blair, Henry W., 38–39
Blair Educational Bill, 1890, 39
Blood Red Record, The (Bruce), 133
Blyden, Edward W., viii, 14, 123, 135, 136, 151, 163, 167; on American race relations, 47; on benefits of British imperialism, 156; calls for third political party, 47; correspondence with Bruce, 156, 158; death of, 138; declining health of, 138; on limited emigration to Africa, 153; as mentor to Bruce, 84, 190; on mulattoes, 149, 153; on Negro's destiny in Africa, 155; urges Negroes to eschew politics, 88, 103; pension of, 138; solicits Bruce as American agent, 138; on B. T. Washington, 47, 55
Booth, John Wilkes, 7, 30
Brady, R. T., 118
Braithwaite, E. J., 150
Brewington, Alfred, 52, 74
Briggs, Cyril V., 121, 178, 186
Brown, Emma, 5
Brown, Jere A., 46, 60, 71–72
Brown, J. P., 161–62
Brown, Philip H., 144
Brown, R. H., 135

Brown, Wrisley, 165
Browne, Robert T., 117, 176
Browning, Robert, 18
Brownsville Affray, 80–81
Bruce, Blanche Kelso: criticized by J. E. Bruce, 25, 32, 40; as Recorder of Deeds, 36–38; seeks political appointment, 49
Bruce, Charles, 211n.63
Bruce, Charles E., 37, 211n.63
Bruce, Charles F., 211n.63
Bruce, Charles H., 211n.63
Bruce, Florence, xi–xii, 181, 187, 193, 196, 199–200
Bruce, John E., 2, 31, 37; absence of father, 2; accuse Du Bois of being tool of white economic interest, 197; accuse Matthew Mattuck of unfair play in Garvey trial, 193; addressed Virgin Islanders on citizenship rights, 190; admiration for Chinese and Japanese, 120, 141, 150–51; advised by Joseph C. Lundy to form political party, 187; and African citizenship, 47; African interpretation of Christianity supported by, 135; African investment schemes and, 159–62; on Africa's contribution to world history, 122, 134, 137; Afrocentric views of, 119, 123; Afro-American Council and, 64; Afro-American League and, 101; and Afro American News Syndicate, 47; agrees with Blyden that temporary European control of Africa is necessary, 156; and James E. K. Aggrey, 120, 161-62, 188; alleged criminal activities of, 37, 211n.63; on alliance with "good whites," 78; and ambivalence about his status as an "American," 191; on America as a white man's country, 195; and American Colonization Society, 14–15; and American Negro Academy, 110–13; and American Protective League, 132; on anarchists, 130, 131; ancient African civilizations praised by, 122; and anti-lynching movement, 65–66, 133; and Associated Correspondent of Race Newspapers, 42–43; on Association for Study of Negro Life and History, 117–19; attacks James E. Henderson, 111–12; author of UNIA prayer, 172; autobiographical sketch of, 2, 11; as bibliophile, x, 16; birth of, 2; black editors' praise of, 58, 71, 74, 144; on black press's role in American society, 15–16; on black press's role in 1900 presidential election, 71; and Black Republican Glee Club, 13; on black theater, 126; blind support for Theodore Roosevelt, Blyden's American publication effort assisted by, 119, 138; books by, 95, 139–40, 187; breaks with anticolonizationists in 1900, 155; breaks with Monroe

Trotter, 109; on Brownsville Affray, 83; calls on Black America to raise funds to support Liberian education, 162; calls for civil rights for African Americans, 17, 87; calls for lynching of white rapists, 189; calls for Negro brotherhood, 16, 98, 141; calls for unions to organize black and white workers, 131; calls on UNIA members to stick with Garvey, 183, 193; calls for whites to study Negro history, 65; chided by E. M. E. Agebi, 173; childhood under slavery, 2, 4; classify American Negroes as "Africans," 195; on color line, 113–14, 122, 148–49; compares blacks to Jews, ix, 16, 45, 58, 184; compares Garvey to Jesus Christ, 194; compares McKinley to Ulysses Grant, 63; condemns New York's 1900 police riot, 70; considered by *Negro World* to be one of world's greatest living Negroes, 201; contempt for Grover Cleveland, 31, 79; contrasts America with ancient Africa, 136; co-organizer of Associated Correspondents of Race newspapers, 42–43; correspondence with Akinbami Agebi Jr., 173; correspondence with Edward Blyden, 138, 156, 158; correspondence with J. Ralphiel R. Casimir, 183–84, 197; correspondence with Alexander Crummell, 124–25, 156; correspondence with S. Okagoo Logemoh, 174; correspondence with J. Robert Love, 111–12, 156; correspondence with Pan-Africanists, 111–12, 156, 197; and criticism of Lyman Abbott, 148; and criticism of Chester A. Arthur, 24; and criticism of back-to-Africa movements, 155; and criticism of *The Birth of A Nation*, 143; and criticism of black Democrats, 24, 68, 77, 85; and criticism of black leadership, 34–36, 103–4, 192; and criticism of black press for lack of substance, 177, 189; and criticism of books on black history, 123; and criticism of B. K. Bruce, 36–38; and criticism of William Calvin Chase, 36–38; and criticism of Grover Cleveland, 45; and criticism of Democratic party, 68, 69; and criticism of Frederick Douglass, 34, 163; and criticism of W. E. B. Du Bois, 177–78, 179, 195, 197; and criticism of T. T. Fortune, 60; and criticism of John G. Gordon, 179; and criticism of the *Guardian,* 76; and criticism of Warren G. Harding, 98–99; and criticism of McKinley's policies, 61–62; and criticism of Schomburg's leadership of American Negro Academy, 114; and criticism of Herbert Seligman's attack on Garvey, 179; and criticism of Thomas's *The American Negro,* 128–29; and criticism of Monroe Trotter, 76; and criticism of Henry M. Turner's African schemes, 156; and criticism of J. Milton Turner, 29; and criticism of whites, 8, 75, 120, 129, 144, 176, 189–90; and criticism of white labor unions, 130–31; and criticism of white press for ignorance about Negroes, 143, 176, 177; and criticism of whites who attended B. T. Washington fundraiser, 79; criticism of writing style in *The Crisis,* 115; criticized by Ida Bailey and others, 104; criticized by Timothy T. Fortune, 56–57; and Henrietta V. Davis, 126; daughter unaware of death of, 199; death of, 199; death of Harding commented on by, 193; death of mother, 44; death premonition of, 198–99; declares that blacks are a race without a country, 195; declines Du Bois's offer to attend Pan-African Congress, 178; declines presidency of UNIA American sector, 171; declines to represent UNIA in Africa, 171; defends John C. Dancy, 77; defends Garvey, 172–79, 183, 185, 187, 192; demands retraction from Monroe Trotter, 109; and Democratic party, 18, 69; denies existence of color line in UNIA, 179–80; denies that Negroes are citizens, 87, 180, 197; denied patronage, 33, 49, 73, 84, 85; denounces white supremacy, 17, 78, 122; departs Washington for Albany, 45; desire to visit Africa, 14, 171; on Charles Dickens, 7; discrimination and, 129, 131; dismissed from position in Dept. of Interior, 45; on Frederick Douglass, 25, 41, 163; Du Bois and, 86, 108; earliest encounter with Pan-Africanism, 18; early journalistic career of, 10–13; economic difficulties of, 14–15; as editor, vii; education of, 5–6; elected member of Republican party's executive committee, 50; on emigration to Africa, 46, 60, 176; encouraged by Edovardo Rodriguez to promote emigration to Cuba, 160; encourages investment in Africa, 159–61, 173–74; encourages investment in Black Star Shipping Line, 172–73; Enquiring Club and, 18; Equal Rights League, 101; escapes from slavery, 4; establishes National Housing Cleaning Bureau, 43; eulogized, 199; on Europe's role in African Development, 156; express interest in publishing his letters and newspaper articles, 124, 125; fails to receive appointment from Taft, 85; family history of, 2; fair play committee and, 188; as father figure, 121, 145, 161, 188; fear of losing government position, 84; feud with W. B. Avery, 23; feud with William Calvin Chase, 36–38;

Bruce, John E. (*cont.*)
fictional writings of, 92; financial problems of, 45; and Timothy Thomas Fortune, 46, 56–57; on freemasonry, 141; friendship with Charles Anderson, 109; funeral of, 199; Hamitic League and, 121; and Hubert Harrison, 145, 171, 186; Hayes' Incident and, 105; health condition of, 138, 148, 171, 180–81, 187; hopes to vote for Roosevelt in 1920, 98; as a hustler, 14; illness of mother, 44; on importance of Negro history, 122–23; induction into the Knighthood of the Sublime Order of the Nile, 181; initial opposition to Garvey, 164–66; initial support for Lodge Bill, 39; insist that Negroes are American citizens, 46; on intelligence as a weapon, ix, 58, 61, 77, 78, 87, 201; inventions of, 148; invited to visit Africa, 159; on Jews as role model, 87, 103, 148; joins Hakluyt Society, 139; joins forces with Monroe Trotter, 108; joins UNIA, 167; on labor barons, 130–31; on labor strife, 130–31; Liberia's Humane Order of African Redemption conferred upon, 159; as a lothario, xi, 13; and Loyal order of the Sons of Africa, 119–20; lukewarm support for candidacy of Charles Evans Hughes, 91; on lynching, 44–45; on Antonio Maceo, 146; and *Making of a Race,* 184; marriages of, xi–xii, 49, 181; masons called upon to erect temple by, 141; meets governor of Massachusetts, 129, 187; mentors younger writers, 140, 144, 145; on mob violence, 60–61; on morality of whites, 60–61, 129, 131; most militant statement of, 201; on mother, 44; on mulattoes, 149; and National Association for Advancement of Colored People, 115; and National Capital News Syndicate, 43; and National Negro Memorial Commission, 97; negative views of whites and, 60–61, 131; and *Negro Daily Times,* 189; and Negro Political Union, 194; and Negro Society for Historical Research, 115–16; on Negroes destiny in Africa, 155, 160, 180, 202; on Negroes destiny in America, 168, 180, 202; and Niagara Movement, 108–9; newspapers' account of death of, 199–200; noms de plume of, vii, 11, 19; nonfiction writing of, 95; offers to have Sable Choristers sing at White House, 26; opinion of American Christians, 45; opinion of John Wilkes Booth, 7; opinion of heaven, 133; opinion of Abraham Lincoln, 7; opposition to anarchy, 102; opposition to William J. Bryan, 70, 72; opposition to "Greenland's Icy Mountain," 172; opposition to National Negro Business League, 132; pan-Africanist views of, 155, 162; as pioneer historian, 123, 198; and Phalanx Club, 144; and *Phalanx Hornet,* 144; place in history, 203; plans to write a history book for children, 123; plays by, 95, 126, 146, 168; poem in honor of, 201; poetry of, 12–13; praise for J. R. Archer's election to chief magistrate of a London borough, 143; praise for W. E. B. Du Bois, 86, 115, 177; praise for Ulysses S. Grant, 63; praise of *Superman to Man,* 149; praise for B. T. Washington, 54, 57; praise for Timothy C. Woodruff, 67; praised by contemporaries, vii, 121, 144–45, 198; prayers of, 12, 102, 201–2; predicts race war, 97; professional memberships of, 101, 166; on proper racial nomenclature, 111, 113; proposed New York State "miscegenation" bill and, 34; protest of *The Birth of a Nation* and, 143; on providential intervention, ix, 45, 61, 102, 189, 201–2; questioned Archibald Grimke's leadership of American Negro Academy, 113; race first ideology questioned, 83, 84, 202; race pride and, 53, 98, 102, 135, 147; race solidarity and, 78, 98, 102, 109–10, 127, 129, 169; racial discrimination experienced by, 129, 131; on racial harmony, 104, 191; on A. Philip Randolph, 167; reaction to Garvey's meeting with the Klan, 185–86; recommends that Liberian teachers teach Negro history, 162; recruits for UNIA, 170; refuses to support anti-Roosevelt coalition, 84; refuses to ghost write for B. T. Washington, 86; refuses to imitate whites, 122, 136; rejects Lodge Bill, 40; relationship with black activists, 28, 46, 77, 84; relationship with Florence Bruce, 181, 187, 196–97; relationship with daughter, xi, 200–201; relationship with T. T. Fortune, 28, 46; religious faith of, 11–12, 134, 138, 146, 150; and Republican Party, 18, 23, 29, 41, 43, 67, 75, 84; on retaliatory violence, ix, 45, 58, 77, 78, 97, 201–2; ridicules idea of Negro confederation, 157; Joel A. Rogers attacked by, 148–49; on Roman Catholic Church, 22, 28, 39; satirical writings of, 11, 125, 132–33; seeks to entertain President Garfield, 13–14; seeks funds for newspaper campaign work, 25; seeks political appointment for self, 49; seeks solution to disfranchisement, 88; self-description of, 109; on self-hating Negroes, 130, 168, 176; severs ties with Afro-American Council, 106; short stories of, 150–51; and sixtieth birthday, 146; on socialism, 167; speeches of, 98, 102, 120, 131, 132, 141; on status of blacks in America, 129, 190; on striking white workers, 130–31; supports Russell A. Alger's presidential

Index **253**

interest, 28; supports black writers, 144–45; supports James G. Blaine's candidacy, 25; supports the Crumpacker Bill, 64–65; supports the *Journal of Negro History,* 117–19; supports John A. Logan's candidacy, 22, 24; supports William McKinley's candidacy in 1896 and 1900, 28, 69; supports Theodore Roosevelt's bid for president, 73, 79; supports Roosevelt and Taft over Brownsville Affray, 83; supports William H. Taft's presidential bid, 83–85; supports United States involvement in wars, 50–53; testimonial dinner for, 109; on thinking black, 145, 169, 203; and Albion W. Tourgee, 101; on union membership, 131; urges blacks to build own hotels, 129; urges blacks to desert Republican Party, 63; urges blacks not to beg for political rights, 72; urges blacks to "root hog or die," 99; urges blacks to shun white unions, 130; urges calm after Garvey's conviction, 183; urges Harding to provide appointment for Mary Church Terrell, 98; urges Republican party to use Negro newspapers in 1900 campaign, 71; urged by Oswald G. Villard to write governor of Virginia to stay death penalty of Virginia Christian, 142; as vice-president of Afro-American Press Association, 71; view that Negroes are not American citizens rejected by George A. Latimer, 195; views on Roosevelt's character, 73; views on World War I, 92–95; and the Virginia Theological Seminary and College Alumni, 143; vows to support Democrat James C. Matthews, 63; warns *Negro World* readers to avoid a fake African prince, 175; writes "The Black Sleuth," a detective novel, 137; and B. T. Washington memorial, 146; on women activists, 147; writes for Booker T. Washington, 56; writing skills praised by others, viii, 58, 72, 142, 144–45; writing style of, viii, 144; and Carter G. Woodson, 117–19; and Ye Sons of Shakespeare, 145; and Yonkers labor strike, 131; youth of, 7–8
Bruce, Martha, 2, 4, 27, 42, 44
Bruce, Olive, xi, 203
Bruce, Robert, 2
Bryan, William Jennings, 47, 48, 68, 70, 71, 72, 83, 85
Buchanan, James, 83
Burkett, Randall, 182
Burleigh, H. F., 129, 181
Butler, Matthew, 153

Calder, William M., 184
Call of a Nation, The (Bruce), 191

Canfield, James H., 127
Capers, John G., 74
Carnegie, Andrew, 79, 160
"Carph." *See* Tyler, Ralph W.
Carson, Perry H., 23–24
Carter, Harriet, 5
Casimir, J. R. Ralph, 183–84, 195–96, 198, 201
Castro, Fidel, 53
Chafin, Eugene W., 85
Chandler, George W., 27, 42
Chandler, William E., 34, 35, 62
Chandler, Zachary, 203
Chase, William C., 20–21, 22, 32, 33; appointment for, 38, 72; black press criticism of, 38; calls for a Negro in the cabinet, 48; criticizes J. E. Bruce, 35, 37; criticizes B. T. Washington, 54; criticizes Woodrow Wilson, 90; supports President Harrison, 32, 34; on B. T. Washington's payroll, 57
Cheatham, Henry P., 49, 59, 60, 73, 104
Chesnutt, Charles W., 50, 128
Children of the Sun, The (Parker), 121
Chisum, Melvin J., 106
Christian, George B., Jr., 193
Christian, Virginia, 142
Civil Rights Act, 1875, 10
Civil War, U.S., 1, 3–4
Clark, John M., 52
Clark, Peter H., 29
Clarke, Edward Y., 185
Clarke, R. Johnson, 179
Clarkson, James Sullivan, 41, 84, 114, 137, 167, 203; on black leadership, 87; and Bruce's 1913 birthday party, 142; on Bruce's writing skills, 142; considers Roosevelt Negro's best friend, 75; correspondence with Florence Bruce, 142; correspondence with John E. Bruce, 44, 49, 83; influences Roosevelt's political policy, 75–76; predicts defeat for Republicans in 1892, 40; president of New York–New Jersey Bridge Company, 74; propose appointment of Negro to McKinley's cabinet, 48; provides position for Bruce, 75; racial equality views of, 127, 142; relationship with Bruce, 42, 43, 49, 142; scolds Bruce over Hayes' Incident, 105; supports potential presidential candidacy of George B. Cortelyou, 83; sympathy for plight of Negroes, 42; and Underground Railroad, 42; urges blacks to divide vote in 1912, 89; urges Roosevelt to find solution to race problem, 74
Cleveland, Grover, 29, 30, 45, 66, 79; black reactions to his first presidency, 20, 24, 26; Bruce's views of, 30, 79; election defeat of, 30; election victories of, 26, 44

Cleveland Gazette, 28, 29, 30, 31, 33, 36, 37, 38, 69, 71, 127
Clifford, J. R., 68
Clifford, W. H., 90
Clinton, George W., 57
Cole, Abayoni, 162
Coleman, Julia P., 192
Colored American, The, 57, 64, 65, 67, 69–70, 72, 73, 74, 75, 104, 105, 107, 130
"Concentration of Energy" (Bruce), 102
Conkling, Roscoe, 16, 203
Conway, Agnes, xi
Cooke, Edward W. 88,
Coolidge, Calvin, 98, 193
Cooper, Edward E., 57, 58, 64, 107, 127
Cooper, John H., 131
Coppin, Levi P., 111
Coppinger, William, 14, 153
Cortelyou, George B., 83
Council, William H., 125
Cowan, Mr., 158
Cox, Channing H., 187
Cox, Minnie, 77
Crogman, William H., 94, 110
Cromwell, John W., 20–22, 113, 116–17, 140
Crouse, L. L., 10
Crum, William D., 75, 104
Crummell, Alexander, viii, xi, 45, 55, 151, 163, 167; black politicians criticized by, 125; on color line, 110, 149; death of, 115, 125; T. T. Fortune called liar by, 112; as founder of American Negro Academy, 110; opposition to R. T. Greener joining American Negro Academy, 112–13; and Pan-Africanism, 113; on proper racial terms, 111; relationship with Bruce, 55, 103, 123–24; relationship with Sidney Crummell, 124, 125; views on mothers as saints, 44; views on mulattoes, 149, 154
Crumpacker, Edgar D., 64
Crumpacker Bill, 64
Crusader, The, 150
Cuba, 50, 52, 53, 60, 72, 160
Cuffee, Paul, 152
Curran, Henry H., 184
Cushite, The (Perry), 154
Cutcheon, Byron M., 35
Czolgosz, Leon, 74

Daily Morning Chronicle, 8
Daily Negro Times, 189
Dancy, John C., 59, 77
Da Rocha, Moses, 124, 137, 162
Daugherty, Harry M., 192
Davey, John C., 58

Davis, Alex G., 43
Davis, Henrietta V., 126, 146, 148, 168, 187, 191, 198
Deas, E. A., 74
Debs, Eugene, 85
Defense of the Colored Soldiers who Fought in the War of the Rebellion, A (Bruce), 95
Delany, Martin, 7, 123, 128, 151, 154, 190
Democratic Party: criticized by black leaders, 23, 24, 30, 68, 70, 71; election of Cleveland, 26, 44; fear of Negro domination, 23, 29; political patronage for blacks and, 26; support of white supremacy, 24; and Woodrow Wilson, 89–91; wooing of black voters by, 23, 68, 70
Deniyi, Madorikan D., 175
Dent, F. L., 8
Derrick, William B., 32
Dewey, George, 50
Dick, Charles, 49, 70
Dickens, Charles, 7
Disraeli, Benjamin, 129, 184
Dix, John A., 86
Dixon, Thomas, 90
Dodge, M. E., 27
Dorsey, William H., 7
Dossen, James S., 158–59, 160, 162, 171
Douglass, Charles A., 126
Douglass, Frederick, 3, 30, 32, 40, 43, 50, 151, 190; criticized by Bruce, 25, 41; controversy over marriage to Helen Pitts, 34; memorialized by Bruce, 163; political appointment for, 35–36; on political patronage, 33–34; supports Lodge Bill, 40
Douglass, Lewis, 50
Douglass Monthly, 3
Dove, Elmer, 60
Downing, George T., 23, 26, 28
Dreyfus Affair, 65
Du Bois, Felix, 184
Du Bois, W. E. B., 57, 86–87, 111, 164, 166; accused by Bruce and Garvey of seeking racial amalgamation, 178; attacked for support of World War I, 94; criticized by Bruce, 178; criticized by Garvey, 177–78; criticized by *Liberian News,* 198; criticizes U.S. post World War I racial policy, 96; criticizes B. T. Washington, 76–77; defended by Cyril V. Briggs, 178; invites Bruce to attend Pan-African Congress, 178; and Niagara Movement, 108; praise B. T. Washington's 1895 speech, 54; praised by Bruce, 86, 115; rebukes Wilson's racial policy, 91; requests Bruce's help in obtaining *Crisis'* subscribers, 115; seeks Bruce's assistance in Niagara Movement, 108; supports U.S. entry into

World War I, 94; works with Bruce on Fair Play Committee, 188
Duchatellier, Etta M., 170
Dumas, Alexander, 139
Dunbar, Alice M., 139, 140
Dunbar, Charles B., 158
Dunbar, Paul L., 111, 123, 139, 147
Dunn, John M., 165
Dyer, L. C., 97
Dyson, Grace, 206n.8

Edge, Walter, 97
Educational Commission for Freedmen, 5. *See* New England Freedmen's Aid Society
Election, federal supervision of, 39–40
Elliott, Robert, 124
Ellis, George W., 145, 158
Emerson, Ralph W., 18
Emigration: Blyden's views on, 153, 155; Bruce's views on, 155; Chief Alfred Sam and, 157; failure of schemes for, 157
Emmanuel, Charles A., 168
Enright, Richard E., 188
Equal Rights League, 101
Evangelical religious bodies, 5

Falkner, Roland P., 159
Fan, Wu Ting, 66
Ferris, William H., 111, 139, 184, 185
Field, David D., 9
Fletcher, Benjamin H., 131
Foraker, Joseph B., 82, 83
Forbes, George W., 107, 179
Fortune, Timothy Thomas, xii, 2, 17, 20–21, 28, 29, 67, 72, 163; as advisor to B. T. Washington, 58; and Afro-American League, 100, 101; and Afro American News Syndicate, 47; assigned to Republican National Committee, 71; blamed for New York City riot, 70; as chair of Citizens Protective League, 70; calls for Afro-American bank, 100; criticizes black nationalists, 108, 112; criticizes Bruce, 56, 57; criticizes McKinley's racial policies, 58, 60, 69; criticizes Republican party, 46; criticizes Roosevelt's discharge of black soldiers, 80–81; criticizes Roosevelt's southern policy, 75, 81; defends B. T. Washington's leadership, 108; dismissed as editor of *New York Age,* 81; as editor of *Negro Daily Times,* 189; faults Crummell's marriage to a mulatto, 112; joins Trotter in criticizing Roosevelt and Taft, 81; on race nomenclature, 111; relationship with Bruce, 28, 189, 196; retracts anti-McKinley view, 69
Franklin, Charles A., 136
Franklin, G. F., 73, 127
Franklin, T. J., 158
From Superman to Man (Rogers), 149
Fulton, D. B., 120

Garfield, James A., 13–14
Garnet, Henry H., 8, 16, 123, 154, 157
Garrison, Francis J., 107
Garrison, William L., 107
Garvey, Amy J., 196
Garvey, Marcus, 100; accused of fleecing investors, 179; acting Imperial Wizard of Klan meets with, 185; on Africa for Africans, 188; African support for, 179; *AME Review* on, 179, 195; arrives in New York in 1916, 164; assassination attempt on, 186; blames New York Republicans for his legal troubles, 184; British military interest in, 165; considered fraud by U.S. War Department, 165; considered hustler by Duse Mohammed Ali, 165; considers Klan to be invisible Government, 185; conviction of, 192; criticized by Cyril V. Briggs, 178; criticized by Bruce, 164–66; criticized by Herbert J. Seligman, 179; criticizes Du Bois's racial leadership, 177; Henrietta V. Davis and, 192; defended by Bruce, 172, 178–79, 185, 187, 192; denies that UNIA practices color line, 179; dismiss Du Bois's Pan-Africanist viewpoint, 178; dismissed by Emmett J. Scott, 165; eight Negroes calls for arrest of, 191–92; exiled to Jamaica, 200; on Harding's death, 193; holds Bruce in high regard, 164; incarcerated in the Tombs, 192; indicted for mail fraud, 175, 183, 185, 192; investigated by U.S. military intelligence, 165–66; and Liberia, 160; meets prominent black New Yorkers, 164; mulatto class criticized by, 168, 192; opposed by black clergy, 182; and William Pickens, 186–87; released on bail, 194; responds to black critics, 192; on self-determination, 188; sentenced to federal prison, 192; shares Bruce's views on race pride, 168; spies and, 193, 195; sued by former UNIA officers, 191; supported by black clergy, 182; warns of a black Ku Klux Klan, 195; and B. T. Washington, 164
Garvey Must Go Campaign, 191–92
Gary, A. J., 140
Ghana. *See* Gold Coast
Gibson, Garretson, W., 158
Gilbert, Peter, viii
Gold Coast, 120, 138, 161, 182
Gold Coast Aborigine Society, 161
Goodall, James L., 129
Grandison, C. N., 39

Grant, Ulysses S., 5, 8, 99
Granville, E. G., 120
Green, John P., 26, 46, 47, 49–50, 51, 52, 59, 60, 71, 72, 74, 80, 82, 128
Green, L. D., 45
Green, Will, 45
Greener, Richard T., 47, 48, 88, 112–13
Griffin, Thomas H., 2, 4
Grimke, Archibald, 107
Grimke, Francis J., 55, 89, 90, 94, 110, 113, 176
Grit, The, 19. *See* Bruce, John E.
Grit, Bruce. *See also* Bruce, John E.

Hague, William, 5
Haiti, 155
Haklyut Society, 139
Halford, E. M., 33
Hamitic League of the World, 150, 170
Hampton, Wade, 210n.31
Hanna, Mark (Marcus), 47, 49, 59, 62, 70
Harding, Warren G., 98, 193
Harper, Francis E. W., 141–42, 147. *See also* Watkins, Francis E.
Harris, Arthur, 70
Harris, George V., 192
Harris, George W., 144
Harris, Mrs. Arthur, 70
Harrison, Benjamin, 29, 30, 31–38, 44
Harrison, Carrie Scott, 44
Harrison, Hubert, 145, 171, 186
Hawkins, Walter E., 93, 140–41
Hayes, Benjamin F., 17, 21, 37
Hayes, James H.: criticized in black press, 105; elites and, 104; supported by Ida Bailey, 104; supported by Bruce, 105
Hayford, Casely, 93, 119, 197, 198
Hayne, J. E., 31
Headley, D. E., 121
Hearst, William R., 189
Heath, Perry, 4
Henderson, James E., 111–12
Henry, Cyril, 170
Hershaw, Lafayette M., 133
Hewin, J. Thomas, 97
Highes, M. J., 161
Hill, James, 67
Hill, Robert A., 166
History of Abyssinia (Ludolph), 184
History of the Negro Race in America, The (Williams), 123, 143
Hoar, George F., 27, 32, 40, 203
Hobart, Garret, 47
Holland, Mrs. J. M., 59
Hood, Tom, 138
Hopkins, Albert J., 612
Hopkins, Pauline E., 131

Horsa, The, 153
Houston, Robert C., 33
Howard, C. E., 208n.28
Howard, James H. W., 97
Hughes, Charles Evans, 91
Hyland, John F., 184

Impending Conflict, The, 106
Industrial Workers of the World, 131

Jackson, John P., 136
Jackson, W. A., 30
Jamaica, 111, 155
Johnson, Andrew, 8
Johnson, Charles, viii
Johnson, E. A., 78, 123
Johnson, Henry, 36, 37
Johnson, James W., 117
Jones, Alfred L., 138
Jones, B. F., 209n.16
Jones, Hezekiah, 92
Jones, James K., 45
Jones, James W., 193
Jones, Thomas L., xi
Journal of Negro History, 117; Bruce's support of, 117–19; financial condition of, 118

Kell, George W., 165
Kellogg, William P., 44
King, C. D. B., 161, 171, 176
Kipling, Rudyard, 132
Kirk, E. N., 5
Ku Klux Klan, 185–86

Lacy, S. S., 15
Langston, John M., 32, 48
Latimer, George A., 195
Latimer, Lewis H., 107
Lee, Benjamin F., 111
Lee, Ferdinand D., 97
Lee, Richard, 208n.28
Lewis, William H., 89, 90
Liberia: border conflict of, 152, 159, 160; Bruce's views on, 160, 162, 180; color line in, 153; denies entry to UNIA members, 198; and Du Bois, 197–98; emigration to, 153; European economic pressure on, 160; honors Bruce with medal, 159; seeks loan, 158–59; seeks support of African Americans, 159–60; solicits investors, 159; UNIA delegation to, 171; United States protectorate over, 159; and B. T. Washington, 159
Liberian Joint Stock Steamship Company, 128
Liberty Hall, 192, 194
Lincoln, Abraham, 4, 7–8, 86
Locke, Alain, 115, 116

Lockwood, Belva, 6
Lodge, Henry C., 39, 159
Lodge Bill, 39–40
Logan, John A., 22, 24
Logan, Mrs. John, 43
Logan, Rayford, 103
Logemoh, S. O., 174–75
Longfellow, Henry W., 18
Loudin, F. J., 49, 50, 66, 128
Loury, Henry, 201
Love, J. Robert, 111–12, 154–55
Loving, W. H., 166
Lowe, J. Milton, 198
Loyal Order of the Sons of Africa, 119–20
Ludolph, Hiob, 184
Lundy, Joseph C., 87, 138
Lynch, John R., 25, 30, 32, 35, 36, 40, 43, 47
Lyons, Ernest W., 47, 159
Lyons, Judson W., 59, 60, 73
Lyons, Maritcha R., 87

Mack, Julian, 192, 193
Making of a Race, The (Bruce), 184
Martin, Charles D., 116, 120
Martin, Harry, 120
Martin, Tony, 196
Masons, 98, 141, 161
Masterpieces of Negro Eloquence (Dunbar), 139
Matthews, James C., 63, 64
Matthews, Victoria E., 18
Mattuck, Matthew, 193
May, J. C. *See* Smith, Wilford H.
McBane, George, 104
McCallum, T. S., 185
McGirt's Magazine, 137
McGuire, George, 182
McKelwaly, St. Clair, 79
McKinlay, Whitefield, 75, 83, 89, 107, 128
McKinley, William, 16, 28, 43, 46, 47, 49, 50, 52, 63, 79; assassination of, 74; black appointments of, 49; black criticism of, 53, 58–59, 66, 68, 69; black press and, 47; and J. E. Bruce, 16, 28, 61–62, 69; election victories of, 47, 48
McPherson, Edward, 16
McPherson, James, 9
Mead, Edwin D., 80
Messenger, The, 93, 186, 192
Millar, Onaway (Onnie), xi, 199–200
Miller, Kelly, 111
Mitchell, John, Jr., 52
Mohammed, Duse, 165. *See* Ali, Duse Mohammed
Moore, Fred, 81
Morgan, J. P., 130
Morgan, John T., 65

Morris, Charles S., 108
Morton, Levi P., 29, 47
Moskowitz, Henry, 86
Munsey, Frank, 189
Murphy, Edgar G., 79
Murray, Daniel, 47, 61, 64, 86, 88, 89, 117, 139, 140
Murtagh, William J., 37
Myers, George, 43, 46, 48, 50, 52, 59, 68, 70, 71, 72, 80, 81, 82, 83, 89, 90, 96
Mystery Solved: The Negro A Beast, The (Carroll), 128

Nail, John E., 192
Nassay, Adolph, 161
National Afro-American Association, 105
National Association for the Advancement of Colored People (NAACP), 86, 115
National Capital News Syndicate, 43
National House Cleaning Bureau, 43
National Independent Civil and Political League of America, 83
National Negro American Political League, 83
National Negro Business League, 85, 132
National Negro Memorial Commission, 97
National Negro Suffrage League, 104
Negro. *See* African American
Negro Daily Times, 171, 189
Negro Factories Corporation, 173
Negro in the American Revolution, The (Williams) 123
Negro Library Association, 117
Negro Political Union, 194
Negro Society for Historical Research, 201; founded by Bruce, 115; members of, 116; officers of, 116; purpose of, 115–16
Negro World: banned by European colonial African governments, 182; Bruce's writings in, 171; and Garvey Movement, 194
Nelson, R. M. R., 42, 160
Nettleton, A. B., 42
New England Freedmen's Aid Society, 5
New York News, 144
New York Times, 144
New York Tribune, 85, 136
Niagara Movement, 108–9
Nigeria, 120, 138, 182
Noble, John W., 43
North American Review, The, 138

Okukenu, Majola, 137
One Hundred Distinguished Leaders (Alexander), 58
Otley, Charles N., 13
"Our Greatest Want" (Watkins), 5
"Our Old Kentucky Home" (Bruce), 126

Overton, Mary, 86
Owen, Chandler, 93, 186

Pace, Harry H., 192
Parkenham, H. A., 165
Parker, Alton B., 79
Parker, George W., 121, 170
Parker, James B., 74
Parks, William S. 164
Patterson, A. E., 90
Patterson, Busie, 4, 8
Patterson, F. D., 83
Payn, Louis T., 49
Peabody, George F., 79
Pelham, Robert A., 114
People's Advocate, The, 20, 22, 23, 41, 117
Perkins, Francis W., 5
Perry, Andrew B. F., 145
Perry, Rufus P., 123, 154
Phalanx Club, The, 144
Phalanx Hornet, The, 144
Pickens, William, 167, 185, 186, 187, 192
Pinchback, P. B. S., 30, 58, 89
Pinkwood, Lucy. *See* Bruce, Lucy
Pioneer Press, The, 68
Pitts, Helen, 34
Pittsburgh Courier, 199
Platt, Thomas C., 76
Pledger, William A., 33, 67, 70
Politics In The South (Fortune), 28
Porter, John A., 49
Poston, Albert L., 198
Presidential campaigns: 1884, 22, 24, 26; 1888, 27–31; 1892, 43–44; 1896, 46–47; 1900, 67–72; 1904, 79–80; 1908, 82–85; 1912, 88–89; 1916, 91; 1920, 98
Price, John C., 101
Progressive American, 10
Purvis, Charles, 89

Quay, Matthew S., 47

Racial nomenclature, x, 103, 111
Racial riots, 97
Rainey, Joseph H., 26
Randolph, A. Philip, 93, 166, 167, 186
Rankin, J. R., 33
Ray, Theodore, 208n.28
Razafkeriefo, Andrae, 121, 169
Reconstruction, 8–10, 23
Reed, Thomas, 47
Republican party: black criticism of, 23, 73; and the black press, 73; Bruce and criticism of, 67; Bruce and patronage policy of, 33, 49, 73; lily white policy of, 67, 74; loses black support over Brownsville Affray, 80–81. *See also*
Harrison, Benjamin; McKinley, William; Roosevelt, Theodore; Taft, William H.
Republicans, Radical, 8
Richardson, R. B., 136
Roane, Henry, 37
Robinson, Magnus L., 28
Rockefeller, John D., 49, 130, 160
Rodriquez, Edovardo, 160
Rogers, Joel A., 148–49, 203
Roosevelt, Theodore, 202; advised blacks to be patient, 75; advised by James S. Clarkson to solve race problem, 74; appoints William D. Crum, 75; assumes presidency upon McKinley's death, 74; and black voters, 74, 89; character praised by Bruce, 67–68, 73; condemned by black radicals, 68, 79, 85, 88, 89; criticized for discharging black soldiers, 80–81; death of, 98; elected president, 80; feud with Taft, 88; inconsistent civil rights record of, 77; keeps Minnie M. Cox on payroll, 77; praised by black press, 73; praised by Bruce for taking on southern Bourbons, 77; receives copy of Bruce's *A Tribute for the Negro Soldier,* 95; relies on B. T. Washington for advice on racial matters, 74; replaces lily white Republicans with gold Democrats, 74–75; selected as McKinley's running mate, 67; supported by Bruce over Brownsville, 83; unfairly discharges black troops in Brownsville, 80–81
Root, Elihu, 83, 159
Ruch, George F., 184
Ruffin, R. D., 206n.8
Russell, York, 143

Sale, George, 159
Sam, Alfred, 157
Savannah Tribune, 35
Sawyer, Philatatus, 27
Scarborough, William S., 140
Schomburg, Arthur, 135, 140, 143, 150, 159, 201; and African investment, 161–62; friendship with Bruce, 114, 198; leadership criticized, 114; and Loyal Order of the Sons of Africa, 120; and Negro Society for Historical Research, 115–16; as pioneer historian, 203; on Carter G. Woodson's scholarship, 117–18
School History of the Negro Race in America (Johnson), 123
Scott, Dred, 147
Scott, Emmett J., 56, 106, 146, 159, 165
Scott, William H., 46
Scottron, Samuel R., 46
Selected Writings of John Edward Bruce (Gilbert), viii
Seligman, Herbert J., 179

Shackleford, A. S. W., 175
Shakespeare, William, 18
Shepard, H. M., 15
Sherwood, Isaac, 97
Short Biographical Sketches of Eminent Negro Men and Women in the United States and Europe (Bruce), 139, 140
"Significance of Brotherhood, The" (Bruce), 98, 141, 230n50
Simmons, William J., 185
Sketch of My Life (Bruce), 11
Slaughter, Henry P., 116
Smalls, Robert, 27, 30, 33, 87, 140
Smith, Charles S., 105
Smith, Henry C., 28, 35, 71
Smith, Hoke, 45
Smith, Wilford H., 106
Smythe, John H., 47, 111, 157
Souls of Black Folk (Du Bois), 77
Sprague, Rosetta Douglass, 136
St. Mark Lyceum, 145
Star of Zion, 138, 144
Stevens, Thaddeus, 8, 99, 203
Stevenson, Adlai E., 68
Steward, Theophilus G., 80, 111, 134
Stewart, George W., 24
Stewart, T. M., 29, 111, 175–76
Still, William, 26
Stimson, Henry L., 85
Sumner, Charles, 8, 10, 26, 99, 203
Sunday Item, The, 15
Surratt, Mary E., 7
Symmons, T. T., 42

Taft, William H.: alienates black activists in 1908, 81, 82, 85, 160; blacks dismayed at prospect of second presidency, 88; carries out order to discharge black soldiers at Brownsville, 81; feud with Roosevelt gives Wilson victory in 1912, 89; ineffective in combating race problem, 88; makes up with Roosevelt, 88; praised by Cyrus F. Adams before 1912 election, 88–89; supported by Bruce in 1908 election, 86
Talley, Truman H., 179
Tanner, Benjamin T., 7, 17, 31, 50, 111, 123, 130, 154
Taylor, Charles H. J., 29, 111
Taylor, Robert W., 76
Terrell, Mary C., 98, 147
Terrell, Robert H., 47, 89, 90, 97, 111, 123
Thomas, Edward M., 7
Thomas, William H., 127–29
Thompson, E. D., 180–81
Thompson, Richard W., 144
Thorpe, Robert J., 70

Thurman, Allen G., 30
Tilden, Samuel, 21
Tillman, Benjamin, 68, 70
Timbuctoo: The Mysterious (Dubois), 184
Tourgee, Albion W., 101
Townsend, James M., 35, 40–41
Tribute for the Negro Soldier, A (Bruce), 95
Trotter, James M., 37
Trotter, William M., 106, 163, 167; arrested after leading riot against B. T. Washington, 107; criticism of B. T. Washington, 76; criticizes Bruce, 109; and the *Guardian,* 76; informs Bruce that Charles W. Anderson is a spy, 109; lambasted by Bruce, 109; urged by Fortune to attack Roosevelt and Taft, 81, 82
Tucker, Joseph G., 195
Turner, Henry M., 57, 153, 155, 156, 179
Turner, J. Milton, 29
Turner, Nat, 147
Turner, William, v, 13
Tyler, Ralph W., viii, 48, 81, 82,90. 96, 114

Underdon, A. H., 89
Universal Negro Improvement Association (UNIA), 97, 99, 100; African representatives and, 173–74; and Black Star Shipping Line, 172–73; Bruce's defense of, 180; defection of members, 182, 191, 195–96; demise of, 200; internal conflict in, 199, 200; and Negro Political Union, 194; sends delegation to Liberia, 171, 198; spies in, 193. *See also* Bruce, John E.; Garvey, Marcus; *Negro World*

Van Wyck, Robert A., 70
Villard, Oswald G., 79, 142
Vorys, Arthur, 81

Waldron, Eric, 201
Walker, C. T., 128
Waller, C. Ridgely, 11
Walling, William E., 86
Walters, Alexander, 56, 57, 64, 82, 89, 101, 162
Walters, Leila, 162
War: Civil War, U.S., 3–4; Spanish-American: black criticism of American imperialism, 50; black press and, 52; black soldiers in, 52–53; Bruce support for, 50–52; call for recruitment of black officers, 52–53; World War I: Africa as prize of, 94; black disagreement over fighting in, 93–94; black heroes of, 95; black troops in French combat units, 94; Bruce and, 92, 94, 95; Du Bois and, 94; returning soldiers and racial conflict, 96. *See also* Bruce, J. E., and Du Bois, W. E. B.
Warner, Charles D., 124

Washington, Booker T., 2, 58, 104, 106, 111, 131, 157, 163; accommodationist policy of, 167, 202; advised by Fortune to avoid support for Crumpacker Bill, 64; advises Roosevelt on racial matters, 74; allegedly picked Taft as Roosevelt's successor, 83; Atlanta Compromise speech of, 54–55; on Boston riot, 107; and John E. Bruce, 54, 56; criticized by black activists, 74, 87, 107; declining influence of, 86; denies interest in cabinet position, 48; express fear over a possible Parker victory in 1904 presidential race, 80; express private doubts over Taft's 1904 presidential expectations, 81; Harvard honorary degree conferred upon, 47; Liberia's Knight of the National Order of African Redemption awarded to, 159; and loans for Liberia, 158–59; reacts negatively to Thomas's *The American Negro*, 128; relationship with Timothy T. Fortune, 81, 108; supports Roosevelt over dismissal of black soldiers, 81

Washington Colored Society (Bruce), 11
Washington Grit, The. See Grit, The
Washington Post, The, 37, 48
Washington Sun, The, 144
Watkins, Francis E., 5. *See* Harper, Frances E.
Weekly Anglo African, 3
Weekly News, The, 144
Weeks, William W., 150, 187
Wells, Ida B. *See* Wells-Barnett, Ida
Wells-Barnett, Ida, 133, 147, 164
Wheatley, Phyllis, 155
White, George H., 59, 64, 65, 73

Wibecan, George, 105
Wilkens, Beriah, 48
Williams, George W., 123, 143
Williamson, Henry A., 80
Wilson, J. T., 52
Wilson, James, 143
Wilson, William J., 5
Wilson, Woodrow: appeal to dissatisfied black Taft supporters, 89; appoints A. E. Patterson, 90; appoints white man to Haitian consular position, 90; attacked by Francis Grimke, 89; *The Birth of A Nation* praised by, 144; black patronage and, 90–91; denounced by black activists, 90–91; dismisses black officeholders, 90; initially supported by prominent black leaders, 89; Negro appointment protested by Thomas Dixon, 90; reelected to second term, 91; on self-determination, 97; wins presidency in 1912, 89
Witherspoon, B. F., 31
Wood, George, 7
Wood, Samuel R., 161
Woodruff, Timothy L., 67
Woodruff, Thomas C., 85
Woodson, Carter G., 117–19, 203
Woodward, C. Vann, 9
Wright, Richard R., Jr., 110, 164

X, Malcolm, 202

Ye Sons of Shakespeare, 145
Young, Charles, 98
Young, Lafayette, 142

Bruce Grit was designed and typeset on a Macintosh computer system using QuarkXPress software. The body text is set in 10.5/13.5 Granjon and display type is set in Franklin Gothic. This book was designed by Cheryl Carrington, typeset by Kimberly Scarbrough, and manufactured by Thomson-Shore, Inc.

www.ingramcontent.com/pod-product-compliance
Lightning Source LLC
Chambersburg PA
CBHW030309080526
44584CB00012B/499